Sources of World Societies

VOLUME 1: TO 1600

SECOND EDITION

Walter D. Ward

UNIVERSITY OF ALABAMA AT BIRMINGHAM

Denis Gainty

GEORGIA STATE UNIVERSITY

BEDFORD/ST. MARTIN'S   BOSTON ◆ NEW YORK

For Bedford/St. Martin's

Publisher for History: Mary V. Dougherty
Executive Editor for History: Traci M. Crowell
Director of Development for History: Jane Knetzger
Developmental Editor: Lynn Sternberger
Production Supervisor: Dennis J. Conroy
Senior Executive Marketing Manager: Jenna Bookin Barry
Project Management: Books By Design, Inc.
Permissions Manager: Kalina K. Ingham
Cover Designer: Billy Boardman
Cover Art: *Portrait of a Woman*, from Fayum, 1st–4th century (encaustic wax on wood)
   by Roman Period Egyptian (c. 30 BC–AD 337)
Composition: Books By Design, Inc.
Printing and Binding: Haddon Craftsmen, Inc., an RR Donnelley & Sons Company

President: Joan E. Feinberg
Editorial Director: Denise B. Wydra
Director of Marketing: Karen R. Soeltz
Director of Production: Susan W. Brown
Associate Director, Editorial Production: Elise S. Kaiser
Manager, Publishing Services: Andrea Cava

Library of Congress Control Number: 2011935105

Manufactured in the United States of America.

7 6 5 4
i h g f

For information, write: Bedford/St. Martin's, 75 Arlington Street, Boston, MA 02116
(617-399-4000)

ISBN: 978-0-312-56970-9

Acknowledgments

Acknowledgments and copyrights are continued at the back of the book on pages 369–374, which constitute an extension of the copyright page.

The primary sources comprising *Sources of World Societies* span pre-history to the present, capturing the voices of individuals within the context of their times and ways of life, while enriching the cross-cultural fabric of history as a whole. Now with visual sources and 50 percent more documents, *Sources* draws from the records of rulers and subjects alike, men and women, philosophers, revolutionaries, economists, laborers, and artists, among others, to present a textured view of the past. With a parallel chapter structure and documents hand-picked to extend the textbook, this reader is designed to complement *A History of World Societies*, Ninth Edition. *Sources of World Societies* animates the past for students, providing resonant accounts of the people and events that changed the face of world history, from myths of creation to accounts of hardship and conflict, from a local to a global scale.

With input from the textbook authors, as well as from current instructors of the world history survey course, we have compiled these documents with one goal foremost in mind: to make history's most compelling voices accessible to students, from the most well-known thinkers and documentarians of their times to the galvanized or introspective commoner. While students have access to formative documents of each era, lesser-heard voices reveal life as the great majority of people lived it. In Chapter 30, for example, popular folk song lyrics, a speech before a National Socialist association, letters to the editor debating abortion in Russia, and the Nuremberg Laws illustrate the social effects of the Depression, the radicalization of fascist movements, and the social and political developments that helped fuel the Second World War from multiple citizen and government perspectives. Students can juxtapose President Truman's press release on the bombing of Hiroshima with the firsthand account of a Japanese survivor of the atomic bomb drop.

We have stepped back from drawing conclusions and instead provide just enough background to enable students' own analysis of the sources at hand. Chapter-opening paragraphs briefly review the major events of the time and place the documents that follow within the framework of the corresponding textbook chapter. A concise headnote for each document provides context about the author and the circumstances surrounding the document's creation, while gloss notes supply clarification to aid comprehension of unfamiliar terms and references. Each document is followed by Reading and Discussion Questions that spur student analysis of the material, while chapter-concluding Comparative Questions encourage students to contemplate the relationships among the sources within and, when called for, between the chapters. All of the questions in *Sources* aim to form a dynamic connection for students that bridges the events of the past with their own evolving understandings of power and its abuses, of the ripple effects of human agency, and of the material conditions of life. The excerpts range in length to allow for a variety of class assignments.

NEW TO THIS EDITION

The second edition of *Sources* offers new pedagogical tools and provides instructors with greater flexibility in the development of their syllabi. Now expanded to an average of six sources per chapter with over half new sources overall, this edition offers a greater variety of topics to explore and further illuminates the themes of the textbook.

Each chapter now features two or three "Viewpoints" selections that allow students to compare and contrast differing accounts of one topic or event. In Chapter 7, for example, students can debate the origin and practice of Buddhism in China after analyzing a sixth-century image of a preaching Buddha, studying Zhu Seng Du's biographical defense of Buddhism, and reading Emperor Wuzong's ninth-century edict suppressing the religion. In Chapter 19, a "Viewpoints" feature on the African slave trade juxtaposes free British citizen Anna Maria Falconbridge's account of her voyage aboard a ship transporting slaves with Olaudah Equiano's controversial tale of his own enslavement and eventual freedom.

The addition of visual documents gives students the opportunity to practice the analysis of art and photographs. Volume 1 includes images ranging from a Neolithic burial to the high art of ancient Greece, from Islamic and African architecture to a Song Dynasty landscape painting. Volume 2 pairs an excerpt from the Islamic tale *The Conference of the Birds* with an original illustration of the story and presents photographs documenting people and their conditions of life in an increasingly global world, such as early twentieth-century Jews in Munich and the present-day residents of Venezuelan slums.

Acknowledgments

Thanks to the instructors whose insightful comments and thorough reviews of the first edition helped shape the second edition: Cynthia Bisson, Belmont University; David Bovee, Fort Hays State University; Rick Gianni, Westwood College; Nicole Howard, Eastern Oregon University; Robert Kunath, Illinois College; Elaine MacKinnon, University of West Georgia; Erik Maiershofer, Pacific Christian College; Larry Marvin, Berry College; Anne Parrella, Tidewater Community College; Chris Rasmussen, Fairleigh Dickinson University; Kenneth Straus, North Shore Community College; Teresa Thomas, Fitchburg State College; and Amos Tubb, Centre College.

Thanks to Lynn Sternberger for her tireless encouragement, her warm support, and her good ideas, all of which made this experience a real pleasure; to Jan Fitter for her insightful comments and prudent edits; and to Jane Knetzger and Laura Arcari for their guidance throughout. Andrea Cava of Bedford/St. Martin's and Nancy Benjamin of Books By Design produced this book with remarkable finesse. Thanks also for the support of the wonderful student assistants in the Department of History at Georgia State University, whose help made this book possible. Thanks to John van Sant, Brian Steele, Forrest Sweeney, Brandon Wicks, and Yorke Rowan for loaning materials and making suggestions about source selections; and to Melissa Anderson, Agatha Anderson, and Nico Ward for their love and support.

CONTENTS

16 The Acceleration of Global Contact

INTRODUCTION: ANALYZING PRIMARY SOURCES

Historians credit the ancient Greek writer Herodotus (fifth century B.C.E.) with inventing the study of history, which today is defined as the rational study of the past of the human species. Although many peoples kept records prior to the Greeks, only a few groups attempted to interpret the past and form a cohesive narrative for understanding their place in the world. For example, the ancient Hebrews recorded events from their past, and their works still survive in the form of the Hebrew Bible and the Old Testament of the Christians. The Hebrews, however, believed that their history was dictated by divine providence and that it was affected by the will of their God. Herodotus, and many later Greek and Roman writers, excluded the divine and supernatural from their histories and sought the causes of events in the actions of humans.

The Greek word *historia*, the origin of our word *history*, was used in the sense of "inquiry" and indicated an active seeking of information. Historians, therefore, practice an inquiry about the past. They ask questions about the past to produce an interpretation of events. In doing so, they look for change and continuity; they want to determine cause and effect. Historians also seek to make history relevant to today's society, which means that our understanding of the past changes as our culture transforms. Not only does history itself change as we perceive it, but historians are not always in agreement. One historian's inquiry into the past may very well lead him or her to draw a different conclusion than another historian. To determine cause and effect, and to shape those dynamics into a fuller picture, historians must carefully examine the available sources, which provide the evidence for their interpretations.

HISTORY AND PREHISTORY

Historians are most accustomed to working with written and visual documents. For more modern periods, recorded documents abound: newspapers, archives, magazines, law codes, merchant records, novels, religious works, and almost everything else that is written, not to mention photographs and films. The farther back one looks, the less written material remains. For example, very few records exist of the day-to-day running of the Roman or Han Empires compared to the more plentiful records of the early modern British Empire. To compensate for missing written records, but also to provide more material for analysis, historians often examine artifacts from the period they are studying. From early Egypt, for example, scholars investigate pharaohs' tombs, mummies, paintings, and royal architecture, in addition to everyday artifacts like plates and drinking cups. Religious sculpture and images can be of vital use for historians seeking to understand belief systems, just as coins can indicate chronological periods and state propaganda.

Historians are traditionally so indebted to written evidence for developing historical narratives that they designate any place and period that lacks writing as "prehistoric." This just means that because of the lack of a written record it is virtually impossible to understand specific events and their causes in these societies. Writing began around 3000 B.C.E. in Mesopotamia and Egypt, and later elsewhere. The earliest writing in China is thought to have been developed sometime before 1200 B.C.E., while in Mesoamerica, it first appeared around 900 B.C.E. Thus, prehistory extends longer in some places than in others. The fact that writing did not exist in these places does not mean people were not keeping oral records of their past or of how they understood the world. For historians, working with oral histories can be problematic because of the possibility that they have changed over time, but they remain one of the few ways, along with artifacts, of understanding the past and exploring the beliefs of prehistoric societies.

PRIMARY AND SECONDARY SOURCES

Documents and artifacts used by historians can be divided into two categories: primary sources and secondary sources. Primary sources are those sources that are captured as close to the events they record as possible. In today's world, primary sources could be diaries, home movies, census records, or other items that tell how life was at the time a document or artifact was created. Secondary sources, in contrast, use primary sources to build a particular narrative. These include textbooks, documentaries, and most works of scholarship. In other words, secondary sources are histories. They attempt to make sense of the past, often by examining the order of events and the cause and effect of human actions.

To take a simple example from modern life: in a traffic accident, the eyewitness statements would be primary sources, but the police officer's report, which is an interpretation of several eyewitness accounts, would be a secondary source. The officer attempts to determine how the accident occurred by analyzing the eyewitness accounts. The officer's report is a history of the accident.

The older the source, the more difficult it is to differentiate between primary and secondary sources. Many secondary sources can also be considered primary sources about their own time. For example, in his first book on the history of Rome, Livy (59 B.C.E.–17 C.E.) described events that he believed took place over seven hundred years prior to his lifetime. Livy's history could therefore be considered a secondary source: He clearly used accounts by other Roman writers and oral histories to compose his narrative of the history of Rome. However, we can also think of Livy's work as a primary source because the author reflects what Romans of his day thought about their past, and in many ways his work reveals more about Livy's own time than about the Roman past.

DOING HISTORY: CONTEXT AND INTERPRETATION

Just because a document was written close in time to the event or person it describes, that alone does not make it trustworthy. Everyone sees the world through his or her own lens of life experiences. A wealthy elite may have a very different idea about manual labor than a woman who has worked her entire life. Members of social groups constructed around occupation, wealth, gender, ethnicity, religion, or any combination of characteristics might view other people and their beliefs with suspicion, tolerance, or maybe curiosity. Frequently, people are not conscious of the agendas or biases that inform their assumptions about what they perceive and influence the way they record and interpret events.

To return to our traffic accident, for example, each eyewitness has a different viewpoint. The drivers who were involved in the accident might remember things differently than someone who was not involved. The drivers even have an incentive to describe the accident in a way that minimizes their responsibility. The officer who listens to these accounts must therefore critically examine the statements and the intentions of the witnesses to determine what most likely happened.

To study history properly, you need to learn how to interpret primary sources. To interpret any primary source, it is necessary to ask the following five questions about it:

- Who wrote the document or created the artifact?
- Where and when was it made?
- What kind of document or artifact is it?
- Why was it written or created?
- What was the audience for the source?

The point of asking these questions is simple: you need to determine whether the source is trustworthy and what the source's bias might be. For example, an outsider's writings about a culture will surely be much different from the writings of a member of that culture. With the answers to the basic questions in mind, you can address the deeper questions: What does this source tell us about the events, the society, or the individuals involved? Each of the sources in this book is followed by a set of questions that asks you to delve deeply.

To understand the documents in this book, it will be important to understand the context of the source. In literature, this would be called "the setting." To begin to understand the complexities of each document, you need to know something about the culture and society of the time; these will not be explained by the source. Therefore, pay close attention to the headnotes that introduce each of the documents; they will often highlight issues that might affect your interpretation of the source. The headnotes explain the specific historical context of the sources and give you a brief introduction to the life of the author. Your other course work and your textbook will provide the broader historical context for the period.

The sources in this book have been selected to allow you, the student, to accomplish two goals. First, these documents provide tangible examples of human life and expression in world history. Second, they give you a way to practice being a historian. By reading and analyzing these documents and artifacts, you will learn what a historian does, and along the way you will develop critical reading skills.

To help you understand how this analysis works, we will begin by looking at a document and an artifact from the period covered in Chapter 16 of the textbook, "The Acceleration of Global Contact, 1450–1600." These sources are presented in the format used throughout this book. Let's begin with the following document.

CAH OF TAHNAB

Petition to the Viceroy of Mexico

1605

Columbus arrived at the Yucatan Peninsula in modern Mexico in 1502 and encountered a native people who spoke a dialect of the Mayan language. By 1562, smallpox had ravaged the indigenous Maya population, and Spanish

---

Matthew Restall, *Maya Conquistador* (Boston: Beacon Press, 1998), 173–175.

forces easily conquered the area. In addition to imposing Christianity, the Spanish quickly set up institutions to exploit the remaining natives, often requiring tribute in the form of both goods and unpaid labor. The following petition from the cah, *a self-governing village of indigenous Maya in Tahnab, was an attempt to lessen the villagers' burden. Written by the village council, it is addressed to the Spanish viceroy (governor) of Mexico.*

For the Viceroy, who is in the great *cah* of Mexico. I who am don Alonso Puc, the governor, along with Simón Piste and Francisco Antonio Canul, the *alcaldes*,[1] Juan Ucan, Gonzalo Poot, Gaspar Ku and Pedro Dzul, the *regidores*,[2] we the *cabildo*[3] have assembled ourselves in the name of God Almighty and also in the name of our redeemer, Jesus Christ. We now lower our heads before you, kneeling in great adoration in your presence, in honor of God, beneath your feet and your hands, you our great lord the king [i.e. the Viceroy], supreme ruler, in order that you hear our statement of petition, so that you will hear, our lord, what it is that we recount and explain in our said petition. O lord, we reside here in the heart of the road to the *cah* of San Francisco Campeche. O lord, here is the poverty that is upon us, that we are going through. Here at the heart of the road, O lord, day and night, we carry burdens, take horses, carry letters, and also take turns in serving in the guest house and at the well. Here at the road's heart, O lord, it is really many leagues to the *cah* of Campeche. Our porters, letter carriers, and horse takers go ten leagues as far as our *cah*, day and night. Nor are our people very great in number. The tribute that we give, O lord, is sixty cotton blankets. The tally of our tribute adds up to sixty, O lord, because they add us, the *alcaldes*, and all the widows too. That is why we are relating our miseries for you to hear, O lord. Here is our misery. When the lord governor marshall came he gave us very many forced labor rotations, seventeen of them, though our labor rotations had been abolished by our lord the *oidor*[4] Doctor Palacio because of the excessive misery we experience here on the road. Our misery is also known by our lords the past governors, and our lords the padres also know it, O lord. Every day there are not enough of us to do so much work, and being few, neither can we manage our fields nor sustain our children. In particular we are unable to manage the tribute burden that is upon us. Within each year we give

---

[1] *alcaldes*: Members of the Maya nobility.
[2] *regidores*: Village councilors.
[3] *cabildo*: The village council.
[4] *oidor*: A judge and member of the high court in Mexico City.

a tribute of two *mantas*, two measures of maize, one turkey and one hen. This is what we give, O lord, and we really cannot manage it, because of the great work load that we have. Thus our people run away into the forest. The number of our people who have fled, O lord, who have left their homes, is fifty, because we are burdened with so much work. O lord, this is why we humbly place ourselves before you, our great lord ruler, the King, in honor of our redeemer Jesus Christ, we kiss your feet and hands, we the worst of your children. We want there to be an end to the labor obligations under which we serve, with which we are burdened. Because our fathers, many of them principal men, along with our porters, letter-carriers and horse-takers, serve day and night. We want to look after you, our lord, and greatly wish that you will be compassionate and turn your attention to us. We have neither fathers nor mothers. We are really poor here in our *cah* in the heart of the road, O lord; nobody helps us. Three times we have carried our petition before you, our lord the *señor* governor, but you did not hear our words, O lord. Nor do we have any money in order that we may petition before you; our *cah* is poor. Here, O lord, is the reason why our people flee, because it is known that in the forest, through the use [sale] of beeswax, one is given money on credit by our lord Francisco de Magaña. It really is the governor's money that is given to people. This is our petition in your presence, lord, our great ruler, the king, made here in the *cah* of Tahnab, today the ninth day of the month of July in the year 1605. Truly we give our names at the end.

> Don Alonso Puc, governor; Pedro Ku, notary; Francisco Antonio Canul, *alcalde*; Simón Piste, *alcalde*; Juan Ucan, Gonzalo Poot, *regidoresob*; Gaspar Ku, *regidor*.

READING AND DISCUSSION QUESTIONS

1. What is the power relationship between the Spanish and the Maya?
2. How does the *cah* attempt to reduce the level of the villagers' tribute?
3. How did the Spanish treat the conquered Maya?

Before answering the specific Reading and Discussion Questions, begin your analysis by revisiting the basic questions listed earlier. Who wrote the document? Where and when was it made? What kind of document is it? Why was it written? What was the audience for the source? After answering these questions, you can proceed to the Reading and Discussion

Questions, which help reveal what the source tells us about the place, time, and people.

After reading this document, we understand that the petition was written by the village council of the *cah* of Tahnab. The headnote makes clear that it was written about forty years after the Spanish conquest. The petition asks for a reduction in the amount of labor that the Maya people have to perform for the Spanish rulers, and it was addressed to the senior member of the Spanish administration in Mexico.

1. What is the power relationship between the Spanish and the Maya?

The *cah* is undoubtedly the inferior in this relationship, and the petitioners feel obligated to employ flattery, as shown by the way they address the viceroy as "great lord" and "supreme ruler." They humble themselves before the viceroy, stating that they kiss his feet and hands and calling themselves the worst of his children. They lower their heads and kneel "in great adoration" before him.

The reason for the supplications is not clear from the document itself, and this is where historical background and a close reading of the headnote are helpful. The headnote introduces the document by stating that it had been a generation since the Spanish conquered these people, which explains the power dynamic at play here. In the document, the petitioners mention that the *cah* has repeatedly requested similar benefits from the viceroy, but its requests have gone unheeded. This happened even though a Spanish governmental official, the *oidor* Doctor Palacio, had previously abolished the labor requirement of the village. Therefore, we can assume that in the established administrative structure, the viceroy has supreme power and the *cah* is unable to stand up for itself, even with the occasional support of other Spanish officials.

2. How does the *cah* attempt to reduce the level of the villagers' tribute?

The petitioners attempt to obtain redress for the *cah*'s concerns through a few methods. The first is the expression of subservience to the viceroy. They also present evidence of the *cah*'s poverty and oppression. They claim to be unable to provide the assessed tribute because of the time they spend laboring on behalf of the Spanish. Because of the forced labor and their inability to pay the tribute, many of the *cah*'s people have run away, making it even harder for the remaining villagers to pay their due. Third, the petitioners stress the *cah*'s Christian faith, opening the document by invoking "God Almighty" and "our Redeemer, Jesus Christ." This reflects one of the most lasting policies of Spanish occupation: the forced conversion of the native inhabitants to Christianity. By proclaiming their faith, the councilors emphasize the *cah*'s obedience to the Spanish and the common ground between the Spanish and the Maya people.

3.   How did the Spanish treat the conquered Maya?

Through this document, we can also examine how the Spanish treated the conquered people. As we read here, the Spanish imposed both tribute on the sixty people of the village (two cotton blankets, two measures of maize, one turkey, and one hen) and forced labor. The petition states that this tribute is excessive and has damaged the village, but we have no way of knowing if this is true. On the other hand, this document indicates that some Spanish officials have attempted to protect the villagers. The *oidor* Doctor Palacio abolished the requirement of forced labor. The *cah* seems to be able to use the Spanish legal system fairly well, and the councilors demonstrate that they know how to present an argument to the viceroy. So this document tells us how conquered peoples were subjugated, but it also indicates that the relationship between the authorities and conquered peoples was one based on negotiation, showing that the natives did have an ability to try to better their lives within the Spanish system, if only with limited success.

Now we move on to a visual source: an image from an anonymous woodcutter, probably from Augsburg, Germany.

The Peoples of the Islands Recently Discovered

1505

Following Columbus's first expedition to islands in the Caribbean, he and later explorers reached additional New World lands, such as Brazil, where the Portuguese explorer Pedro Álvares Cabral (ca. 1467–1520) arrived in 1500. These new lands came to be known as America because of the writings of Amerigo Vespucci (1454–1512), who published a series of descriptions of the European explorations. The following woodcut image, carved in 1505 by an unknown artist in Germany, was based on the description of Brazilian natives found in Vespucci's works. From this model, thousands of cheap paper copies of the image were printed, allowing Europeans of all social classes to possess a copy.

Sye figuc anzaigt vns das volck vnd insel vns gefunden ist durch den christenlichen künig zu Portigal oder von seinen vnterthonen. Die leüt sind also nacket hübsch braun wolgestalt von leib ir heübter bäls armen schäm fäß steen vnd mann ain wenig mit federn bedeckt. Auch haben die mann in iern angesichten vnd brust vil edel gestain. Es hat auch nyemants nichts sunder sind alle ding gemain. Vnnd die mann habendt weyber welche in gefallen es sey mütter schwester oder freündin haben fy kain vntterscheyd. Sy streyten auch mit einander. Sy essen auch ainander selbs die erschlagen werden vnd henckten das selbig flaisch in den rauch. Sy werden alt hundert vnd fünffzig iar. Vnd haben kain regiment.

The New York Library/Art Resource, N.Y.

READING AND DISCUSSION QUESTIONS

1. How are the natives depicted in this image?
2. What might Europeans have thought about the natives in this image?

Once again, you should first address the five guiding questions. Who created the artifact? Where and when was it made? What kind of artifact is it? Why was it created? What was the audience for the source? The image was made by a woodcutter in Germany, and it was used as a model for many printed copies, but the name of the artist is unknown. It was carved in 1505, only five years after Cabral reached Brazil, and was created for a European audience to publicize the encounter with the natives of Brazil.

1. How are the natives depicted in this image?

Looking at the entire image, we see that the artist has depicted a group of about ten people. The men and women wear a bare minimum of clothing.

Both sexes wear loincloths, anklets, necklaces, and headbands made of feathers, leaving the women's breasts exposed. One woman is nursing a completely naked baby, while two almost naked children stand nearby. Under the canopy of branches lashed together, a couple engages in an amorous scene in public. The impression is that the people in the newly discovered islands lack European ideas of sexual modesty. No Europeans would engage in such behavior in the open, nor would they wear such scanty clothing.

If we examine the woodcut a little closer, we see that most of the male figures are armed with bows. A torso is hanging from a tree and looks like it is roasting on a fire. In the top-left corner of the woodcut, it appears that a figure is eating a severed arm. There is a definite suggestion that the people depicted in this drawing are warlike cannibals.

2.   What might Europeans have thought about the natives in this image?

When interpreting the impact of this woodcut, or any of the artifacts in this book, you will have to rely on what you know about the period and culture based on the other documents in the chapter, your class work, and the textbook. In this woodcut, it is very clear that the people depicted are alien to Europeans. They lack clothing, perform intimate acts in public, and eat human flesh. Depending on how you interpret this image, you may think that the Europeans would view the islanders as savages because of their practice of cannibalism. Or perhaps the Europeans would see the islanders as innocent because they are not shamed by love, nudity, or breastfeeding. Maybe the Europeans would see them as fresh minds ready to accept Christianity, as indicated by the crosses on the European ship in the background. All of these interpretations involve some knowledge of European culture at the time, and all are valid based on what we know.

While reading the documents and examining the images and artifacts in this source reader, you will find that most sources can invite different interpretations. Differing interpretations can be considered valid until more extensive study of the relevant period and place suggests otherwise. In fact, new and different interpretations of primary source material constitute one of the ways that new historical discoveries are made. Newly found sources and new interpretations of older ones keep the study of history relevant and moving forward. If you use the five questions given here as a guide for analysis, you will produce revealing interpretations of the sources in this book. Good luck!

The Earliest Human Societies

to 2500 B.C.E.

Humans must have communicated their thoughts, desires, anxieties, and stories for thousands of years prior to the invention of writing, and the primary sources in this first chapter represent the period before the extensive use of written records. The chapter therefore presents other kinds of historical data: four creation stories and two prehistoric images. Three of the creation stories originate with tribal societies that retained their traditional lifestyles until confronted by European imperialism in the eighteenth and nineteenth centuries. Such stories might have been told and passed down among prehistoric hunter and gatherer populations to explain how the world originated and the place of humans in the universe. The final creation story comes from one of the earliest Greek authors and considerably predates the three stories collected in modern times. Two examples of prehistoric images are provided — a cave painting and a burial site with a grave good — as scholars also rely upon nonwritten human records, such as art, architecture, everyday items, and graves and their contents, to learn about the past.

VIEWPOINTS

Origins of the World

DOCUMENT 1-1

ABORIGINES OF AUSTRALIA
Yhi Brings Life to the World
ca. 1965

The Aborigines were the original settlers of Australia, having arrived there around 50,000 years ago. Archaeology suggests that Aboriginal society adapted through many climatic changes, and by the time of contact with Europeans, Aborigines lived a seminomadic lifestyle and obtained food by a combination of agriculture and hunting. One of their most important religious beliefs is known as Dreamtime, the time when the world was created. As recounted in this story, all living things exist in Dreamtime before life, and all return to Dreamtime after death. After European contact in the eighteenth century, Aboriginal societies almost disappeared because of disease, marginalization, and forced assimilation.

In the beginning the world lay quiet, in utter darkness. There was no vegetation, no living or moving thing on the bare bones of the mountains. No wind blew across the peaks. There was no sound to break the silence.

The world was not dead. It was asleep, waiting for the soft touch of life and light. Undead things lay asleep in icy caverns in the mountains. Somewhere in the immensity of space Yhi stirred in her sleep, waiting for the whisper of Baiame, the Great Spirit, to come to her.

Then the whisper came, the whisper that woke the world. Sleep fell away from the goddess like a garment falling to her feet. Her eyes opened and the darkness was dispelled by their shining. There were coruscations [glimmers] of light in her body. The endless night fled. The Nullarbor Plain[1] was bathed in a radiance that revealed its sterile wastes.

A. W. Reed, *Aboriginal Stories of Australia* (Sydney: Reed Books, 1980), 11, 12, 14.

[1] **Nullarbor Plain:** An arid plain along the southern coast of Australia that is famous for its lack of trees.

Yhi floated down to earth and began a pilgrimage that took her far to the west, to the east, to north, and south. Where her feet rested on the ground, there the earth leaped in ecstasy. Grass, shrubs, trees, and flowers sprang from it, lifting themselves towards the radiant source of light. Yhi's tracks crossed and recrossed until the whole earth was clothed with vegetation.

Her first joyous task completed, Yhi, the sun goddess, rested on the Nullarbor Plain, looked around her, and knew that the Great Spirit was pleased with the result of her labour.

"The work of creation is well begun," Baiame said, "but it has only begun. The world is full of beauty, but it needs dancing life to fulfil its destiny. Take your light into the caverns of earth and see what will happen."

Yhi rose and made her way into the gloomy spaces beneath the surface. There were no seeds there to spring to life at her touch. Harsh shadows lurked behind the light. Evil spirits shouted, "No, no, no," until the caverns vibrated with voices that boomed and echoed in the darkness. The shadows softened. Twinkling points of light sparkled in an opal mist. Dim forms stirred restlessly.

"Sleep, sleep, sleep," the evil spirits wailed, but the shapes had been waiting for the caressing warmth of the sun goddess. Filmy wings opened, bodies raised themselves on long legs, metallic colours began to glow. Soon Yhi was surrounded by myriads of insects, creeping, flying, swarming from every dark corner. She retreated slowly. They followed her out into the world, into the sunshine, into the embrace of the waiting grass and leaves and flowers. The evil chanting died away and was lost in a confusion of vain echoes. There was work for the insects to do in the world, and time for play, and time to adore the goddess.

"Caves in the mountains, the eternal ice," whispered Baiame. Yhi sped up the hill slopes, gilding their tops, shining on the snow. She disappeared into the caverns, chilled by the black ice that hung from the roofs and walls, ice that lay hard and unyielding, frozen lakes in ice-bound darkness.

Light is a hard thing, and a gentle thing. It can be fierce and relentless, it can be penetrating, it can be warm and soothing. Icicles dripped clear water. Death came to life in the water. There came a moving film over the ice. It grew deeper. Blocks of ice floated to the surface, diminished, lost their identity in the rejoicing of unimprisoned water. Vague shapes wavered and swam to the top — shapes which resolved themselves into fish, snakes, reptiles. The lake overflowed, leaped through the doorways of caves, rushed down the mountain sides, gave water to the thirsty plants, and sought the distant sea. From the river the reptiles scrambled ashore to find a new home in grass and rocks, while fish played in the leaping waters and were glad.

"There are yet more caves in the mountains," whispered Baiame.

There was a feeling of expectancy. Yhi entered the caves again, but found no stubborn blocks of ice to test her strength. She went into cave after cave and was met by a torrent of life, of feather and fur and naked skin. Birds and animals gathered round her, singing in their own voices, racing down the slopes, choosing homes for themselves, drinking in a new world of light, colour, sound, and movement.

"It is good. My world is alive," Baiame said.

Yhi took his hand and called in a golden voice to all the things she had brought to life.

"This is the land of Baiame. It is yours for ever, to enjoy. Baiame is the Great Spirit. He will guard you and listen to your requests. I have nearly finished my work, so you must listen to my words.

"I shall send you the seasons of summer and winter — summer with warmth which ripens fruit ready for eating, winter for sleeping while the cold winds sweep through the world and blow away the refuse of summer. These are changes that I shall send you. There are other changes that will happen to you, the creatures of my love.

"Soon I shall leave you and live far above in the sky. When you die your bodies will remain here, but your spirits will come to live with me."

She rose from the earth and dwindled to a ball of light in the sky, and sank slowly behind the western hills. All living things sorrowed, and their hearts were filled with fear, for with the departure of Yhi darkness rushed back into the world.

Long hours passed, and sorrow was soothed by sleep. Suddenly there was a twittering of birds, for the wakeful ones had seen a glimmer of light in the east. It grew stronger and more birds joined in until there came a full-throated chorus as Yhi appeared in splendour and flooded the plains with her morning light.

One by one the birds and animals woke up, as they have done every morning since that first dawn. After the first shock of darkness they knew that day would succeed night, that there would always be a new sunrise and sunset, giving hours of daylight for work and play, and night for sleeping.

The river spirit and the lake spirit grieve most of all when Yhi sinks to rest. They long for her warmth and light. They mount up into the sky, striving with all their might to reach the sun goddess. Yhi smiles on them and they dissolve into drops of water which fall back upon the earth as rain and dew, freshening the grass and the flowers and bringing new life.

One last deed remained to be done, because the dark hours of night were frightening for some of the creatures. Yhi sent the Morning Star to herald her coming each day. Then, feeling sorry for the star in her loneliness, she gave her Bahloo, the Moon, for her husband. A sigh of satisfaction arose from the earth when the white moon sailed majestically across the sky, giving birth to myriads of stars, making a new glory in the heavens.

READING AND DISCUSSION QUESTIONS

1. According to this creation myth, where did living creatures come from? In what order were living things created?
2. What is the role of light and water in this creation story?
3. How does this story explain the changing of the seasons?

DOCUMENT 1-2

KONO OF WEST AFRICA
On the Origin of Death
ca. 2001

This story about the origin of death originated with the Kono people of western Africa. The history of the Kono people is largely unknown, as they only appear in historical records in the seventeenth century, when they immigrated into modern Guinea. Large numbers moved into modern Sierra Leone during the British rule of West Africa. Their society is divided into clans, like other neighboring tribes. Today, most Kono practice subsistence agriculture, but it is thought they remained hunters and gatherers until the last century.

In the beginning, before anything was created, there was only darkness. But there also lived Sa (Death), with his wife and daughter. Sa was very magical and could conjure weird things as he pleased.

Buchi Offodile, *The Orphan Girl and Other Stories: West African Folk Tales*, retold by Buchi Offodile (New York/Northampton, Mass.: Interlink Books, 2001), 104–106.

One day Sa decided to create a sea of mud. Soon after, Alatangana (God) visited him, saying, "What a dirty place you have made here. How can you live in such a place? You have no light. You have no plants. You could drown in the mud."

But Sa told Alatangana that he did what he could and had no way of making his creation better. So Alatangana helped Sa to make the world look better. He made the mud stronger, so that it could be stepped upon. But the mud alone had no life. So he created the stars, the plants and trees, and all kinds of animals.

Then said Sa, "That is indeed remarkable. Now the world is greener and filled with life. I like the improvements. You and I should be great friends."

Sa became friendly with Alatangana. He entertained him and they talked and ate. The two visited each other regularly and their friendship grew. Over time, Alatangana, who was a bachelor, asked Sa for the hand of his daughter in marriage. But Sa was reluctant to part with his only daughter. He made all sorts of excuses why Alatangana should not marry his daughter. But Alatangana and the girl were very much in love. Finally, since Sa would not give his consent to the marriage, Alatangana secretly married the girl.

Alatangana and the girl were very happy together. They had fourteen children — seven boys and seven girls. Four of the boys and four of the girls were of the same race, but the other three boys and three girls were different.

The parents were surprised that their children looked so different. Furthermore, they spoke different languages among themselves. Their parents didn't understand them. Alatangana was annoyed with this and went to ask Sa why this was the case.

"Why is it that my children with your daughter are different?" Alatangana asked Sa. "They speak in different languages that we cannot understand. Is this of your making?"

"Yes," replied Sa. "It is of my making that they are different and speak different languages. That is your punishment for taking my only daughter without my consent and without any dowry. You shall never understand what they say."

"You have to remove your curse on my children," said Alatangana.

"Sorry," replied Sa. "It is too late. But, because they are also my children, I will give them gifts to help them live a happy life. To some of them I have given paper and ink and wisdom. They will be able to put down what they think so they can help their brothers, sisters, and children. To others, I have also given wisdom, strength, and tools they need to help their brothers, sisters, and children. Go then and have them paired up, a boy of a kind to a girl of the same kind and disperse them to populate the world."

Alatangana was happy that Sa was patient enough to talk with him, given how he had eloped with his daughter. So he accepted what Sa said. He immediately set for his home, paired up his children and dispersed them to all parts of the world. They procreated and gave rise to the different peoples and races of the world.

But the world was still living in darkness. So Alatangana sent the Rooster to Sa. "When you get there, ask him what we should do for the stars are not enough and the world is still very much in darkness."

When Sa saw Alatangana's messenger, he remembered his daughter again. He was angry all over. But for the love of his daughter, his anger subsided.

"You have come on a very long journey," Sa told the Rooster. "Get some rest while I think of what Alatangana should do about the darkness."

When the Rooster had rested, Sa sent him back to Alatangana saying, "When you get back, you should face the east and sing this song, 'Koko ro Oko o!' On hearing you, the King of the Stars shall wake up so that the day will come and the people can go about their business in full light."

The Rooster was very happy that he had the power to wake up the King of the Stars. He thanked Sa and hurried back to Alatangana with the message. When he rested from his long trip, he faced the east and sang his song, "Koko ro Oko o!" Directly, there was a faintness of light in the sky. A few moments later, the Rooster sang his song again, "Koko ro Oko o," and there was something that looked like an outstretched hand, then the King of the Stars, the Sun, woke up. Thus the first day was born.

The Sun was answering the call of the Rooster. He traveled across the sky answering the Rooster as he called all day. When the Rooster became tired and quit calling him, the Sun went back to sleep on the other side of the earth and darkness came again. Directly, the stars and the moon came to help people see when the Sun went to bed.

Then one day Sa called on Alatangana.

"In spite of what you have done by taking my only daughter away from me, I have given you light. But you have not given me anything for my kindness. Not even a dowry for my daughter. In return for all my deeds, you owe me a service."

"You are right, Sa," said Alatangana. "I owe you what you shall ask."

"All right," replied Sa. "Since you have taken my daughter without as much as a dowry, I have no more children. In return, you must give me one of my grandchildren, any time I call for one. Whenever I want one of them, I will call the one by the sound of my calabash.[2] The one will hear the rattle of my calabash in his dream. When he does, he must come running and answer to my call."

In keeping with his promise, Alatangana had no choice but to let his children go and answer Sa, whenever he called. Thus even today, Alatangana's children still answer the call of Sa. All because Alatangana didn't pay a dowry when he married Sa's daughter.

READING AND DISCUSSION QUESTIONS

1. What kind of relationship did Sa (Death) have with Alatangana (God)?

2. How did the Kono people explain human death, and what does this say about their social values?

3. What was the role of Sa (Death) in bringing light into the world?

DOCUMENT 1-3

YUCHI TRIBE OF NORTH AMERICA
In the Beginning
ca. 1929

When Spanish explorer Hernando de Soto came upon the Yuchi, the tribe had been living in eastern Tennessee since at least the sixteenth century. De Soto described several settlements in the region that consisted of small, fortified villages dominated by constructed mounds, which may have functioned

---

Maria Leach, *The Beginning: Creation Myths Around the World* (New York: Funk & Wagnalls, 1956), 88–89. Story based on the myth in the W. O. Toggle Collection in the Bureau of American Ethnology, John R. Swanton, *Myths and Tales of the Southeastern Indians* (Washington, D.C.: U.S. Government Printing Office, 1929).

[2] **calabash**: A bottle gourd, sometimes used as a musical instrument.

as tombs for elite members of society. The Yuchi language is unrelated to any other known language and currently has fewer than a dozen speakers. After European encroachment on their territory, the Yuchi first moved south into Georgia and Florida before being forced into Oklahoma by the U.S. government in the early 1800s. There, they related this story to their Creek Indian neighbors about how they came to be.

In the beginning there was only water. And Someone said, "Who will make the land?"

"I will make the land," said Crawfish. And he dived down to the bottom of that great sea and stirred up the mud with his eight legs and his tail. And he took the mud in his fingers and made a little pile.

The owners of the mud down there said, "Who is stirring up the mud?" And they watched to see. But Crawfish kept stirring up the mud with his tail so that they could not see.

Every day Crawfish dived into the deep water and got a little more mud and put it on the pile. Day by day he piled it up. At last one day as he piled the mud on top of the pile, his hands came out of the water into the air! At last the land appeared above the water.

It was very soft, for it was mud.

Someone said, "Who will stretch out the land? Who will make it hard? Who will make it dry?"

Buzzard stretched out the earth and dried it. He spread his long wings and stretched it. He sailed over the earth; he spread it wide and dried it. Then, tiring, he had to flap his wings and this made the mountains and valleys.

Someone said, "Who will make the light?"

Star said, "I will make light." But it was not enough.

It was said, "Who will make more light?"

"I will make light," said Moon. But it was still night.

Someone said, "More light."

Sun said, "I will make light. I am the mother."

So Sun moved over into the east, and all at once a great beautiful light spread over the world. And then as Sun moved from east to west, a drop of her blood fell and sank into the earth. From this blood and this earth came forth the first people, the Yuchi Indians. They called themselves *Tsohaya,* People of the Sun, and every man who took this name had a picture of the sun on his door.

READING AND DISCUSSION QUESTIONS

1. According to the Yuchi, what was the role of animals in the creation of the world?
2. Where did the Yuchi believe they came from? What did they feel was their place in the world? What was their relationship to the Sun?

DOCUMENT 1-4

HESIOD

From Theogony

ca. 700 B.C.E.

Hesiod was one of the earliest Greek authors, along with Homer (see Document 5-1). His most famous work, The Works and Days, *describes contemporary Greek society and recounts how his brother unlawfully took his family's inheritance. The creation story included here appears in his other major work,* Theogony, *which means "the birth of the gods." Theogony describes a war between the Titans and the Olympian gods. While the story is told in Greek, and is elaborated on by later Greek authors, earlier versions have been discovered from the Near East.*

    First of all there came Chaos,
      and after him came
Gaia[3] of the broad breast,
      to be the unshakable foundation
of all the immortals who keep the crests
      of snowy Olympos,[4]
and Tartaros[5] the foggy in the pit
      of the wide-wayed earth,

Richard Lattimore, trans., *Hesiod* (Ann Arbor: University of Michigan Press, 1959), 130–131.

[3] **Gaia**: The Earth.
[4] **Olympos**: In Greek mythology, the mountain where the gods lived.
[5] **Tartaros**: The prison beneath the Underworld.

and Eros, who is love, handsomest among all
    the immortals,
who breaks the limbs' strength,
    who in all gods, in all human beings
overpowers the intelligence in the breast,
    and all their shrewd planning.
From Chaos was born Erebos, the dark,
    and black Night,
and from Night again Aither and Hemera,
    the day, were begotten,
for she lay in love with Erebos
    and conceived and bore these two.
But Gaia's first born was one
    who matched her every dimension,
Ouranos, the starry sky,
    to cover her all over,
to be an unshakable standing-place
    for the blessed immortals.
Then she brought forth the tall Hills,
    those wild haunts that are beloved
by the goddess Nymphs who live on the hills
    and in their forests.
Without any sweet act of love
    she produced the barren
sea, Pontos, seething in his fury of waves,
    and after this
she lay with Ouranos, and bore him
    deep-swirling Okeanos
the ocean-stream; and Koios, Krios,
    Hyperion, Iapetos,
and Theia too and Rheia, and Themis,
    and Mnemosyne,
Phoibe of the wreath of gold,
    and Tethys the lovely.[6]
After these her youngest-born
    was devious-devising Kronos,
most terrible of her children;
    and he hated his strong father.

---

[6] **Koios . . . Tethys the lovely**: Those named were all Titans who were overthrown by
the Olympian gods.

READING AND DISCUSSION QUESTIONS

1. According to Hesiod, where does the world come from?
2. How does Hesiod describe the gods? Do they appear to share more traits with humans or more traits with the natural world?

DOCUMENT 1-5

Double Burial from Mantua, Italy

ca. 6000–5000 B.C.E.

When studying the period before written documents, scholars have to turn to other methods of discovering the past, such as archaeology. Occasionally, modern construction uncovers archaeological remains, like the burial shown here from Mantua, Italy. The teeth of these individuals are only slightly worn, suggesting that they died relatively young. Their grave included several flint stone tools (one lying on the individual on the right). Near this burial site were a number of other burials, all of single individuals, and a small Neolithic village.

Felice Calabro/AP.

READING AND DISCUSSION QUESTIONS

1. What can this burial tell us about the relationships among humans at this time? Why might the individuals have been buried in such an intimate fashion?

2. How can we use grave goods, such as the flint tool seen here, but also pottery and jewelry, to understand more about human life in the past? What if an individual is buried without grave goods? What might grave goods indicate about the formation of social hierarchies?

3. Why might these individuals have been buried with useful items?

DOCUMENT 1-6

Cave Painting from Southern Algeria

ca. 12,000–4000 B.C.E.

Even though writing was not invented until the late fourth millennium B.C.E., humans had been expressing themselves for thousands of years through artwork. Archaeologists think the earliest surviving paintings in caves date to 30,000 years before the present, but body art may have been practiced even earlier. This cave painting was discovered in Southwestern Algeria, which is currently an extremely arid region of the Sahara desert. Cave paintings such as this one suggest that the region was much wetter in the past, as they show flora and fauna that could not survive in the region today.

Robert Estall Photo Agency/Alamy.

READING AND DISCUSSION QUESTIONS

1. Describe the differences between the central figure, a musican with a flute, and the surrounding warriors. Which figure or figures appear more natural? What could account for the different styles of these figures?

2. What can the objects that the figures are holding tell us about early human culture?

COMPARATIVE QUESTIONS

1. How do the four creation stories account for the creation of light? What about the creation of living creatures?

2. Do these creation myths share similar themes? If so, what specifically is similar? What is different?

3. What do the creation stories tell us that the images do not? What different information do the images provide compared to the creation myths?

CHAPTER 2

The Rise of the State in Southwest Asia and the Nile Valley

3200–500 B.C.E.

With the development of agriculture and animal husbandry in the Neolithic period (ca. 7000–3000 B.C.E.), humans began to construct more complex societies that required systems of organization and communication. Around 3000 B.C.E., the Sumerians in Mesopotamia invented writing for administrative purposes. Early writing was cumbersome and limited to a select group of scribes, but as writing became less complex, more people learned to read and write. Although literacy was still restricted to the priests and elite members of society, this larger audience prompted the recording of cultural, political, and religious documents such as myths, laws, scriptures, imperial propaganda, poems, and personal letters. Ancient Egyptians developed writing soon after the Sumerians, possibly after seeing how it was used in Mesopotamia. All successive civilizations in the Near East, such as the Hebrews, Assyrians, and Phoenicians, followed with written forms of their own languages.

DOCUMENT 2-1

From The Epic of Gilgamesh

ca. 2700–2500 B.C.E.

The exact composition date of The Epic of Gilgamesh *is unknown, but the legendary king Gilgamesh probably ruled the city of Uruk around 2700* B.C.E. *While the core of the poem had been written by 2000* B.C.E., *each*

The Epic of Gilgamesh, 3d ed., trans. N. K. Sanders, Penguin Classics (Baltimore: Penguin, 1972). Copyright © N. K. Sanders, 1960, 1964, 1972.

successive culture in Mesopotamia added to or altered elements of the story to incorporate their own myths. The epic recounts the friendship of Gilgamesh and the warrior Enkidu and their various adventures in Mesopotamia and the Near East. A fire in the seventh century B.C.E. *destroyed the library of Nineveh in ancient Assyria, but clay tablets bearing the standard text of the Epic survived and they were later excavated from the library's ruins.*

As Enkidu slept alone in his sickness, in bitterness of spirit he poured out his heart to his friend. "It was I who cut down the cedar,[1] I who leveled the forest, I who slew Humbaba[2] and now see what has become of me. Listen, my friend, this is the dream I dreamed last night. The heavens roared, and earth rumbled back an answer; between them stood I before an awful being, the somber-faced manbird; he had directed on me his purpose. His was a vampire face, his foot was a lion's foot, his hand was an eagle's talon. He fell on me and his claws were in my hair, he held me fast and I was smothered; then he transformed me so that my arms became wings covered with feathers. He turned his stare towards me, and he led me away to the palace of Irkalla, the Queen of Darkness [Goddess of the underworld], to the house from which none who enters ever returns, down the road from which there is no coming back.

"There is the house whose people sit in darkness; dust is their food and clay their meat. They are clothed like birds with wings for covering, they see no light, they sit in darkness. I entered the house of dust and I saw the kings of the earth, their crowns put away forever; rulers and princes, all those who once wore kingly crowns and ruled the world in the days of old. They who had stood in the place of the gods like Anu [King of the gods] and Enlil,[3] stood now like servants to fetch baked meats in the house of dust, to carry cooked meat and cold water from the waterskin. In the house of dust which I entered were high priests and acolytes, priests of the incantation and of ecstasy; there were servers of the temple, and there was Etana, that king of Kish[4] whom the eagle carried to Heaven in the days of old. There was Ereshkigal the Queen of the Underworld; and Belit-Sheri

---

[1] **cedar**: He refers to a journey to Lebanon during which Gilgamesh and Enkidu cut down the cedar forest that Humbaba was appointed to guard.

[2] **Humbaba**: A giant from Lebanon whom Gilgamesh and Enkidu killed.

[3] **Enlil**: God of the sky who guided human affairs.

[4] **Kish**: A Sumerian city. Etana wanted to obtain a magical plant from heaven that would allow him to father a son.

squatted in front of her, she who is recorder of the gods and keeps the book of death. She held a tablet from which she read. She raised her head, she saw me and spoke: 'Who has brought this one here?' Then I awoke like a man drained of blood who wanders alone in a waste of rushes; like one whom the bailiff has seized and his heart pounds with terror."

[After Enkidu dies Gilgamesh realizes that fame is no substitute for life. Facing his own imminent death, he begins a desperate search for immortality. He travels to the end of the Earth where he meets Siduri, a female tavern keeper, who offers the following advice:]

"Gilgamesh, where are you hurrying to? You will never find that life for which you are looking. When the gods created man they allotted to him death, but life they retained in their own keeping. As for you, Gilgamesh, fill your belly with good things; day and night, night and day, dance and be merry, feast and rejoice. Let your clothes be fresh, bathe yourself in water, cherish the little child that holds your hand, and make your wife happy in your embrace; for this too is the lot of man."

[Gilgamesh refuses to be deterred. After many harrowing experiences he finally reaches Utnapishtim, a former mortal whom the gods had sent to eternal paradise, and addresses him.]

"Oh, father Utnapishtim, you who have entered the assembly of the gods, I wish to question you concerning the living and the dead, how shall I find the life for which I am searching?"

Utnapishtim said, "There is no permanence. Do we build a house to stand forever, do we seal a contract to hold for all time? Do brothers divide an inheritance to keep forever, does the flood-time of rivers endure? It is only the nymph of the dragon-fly who sheds her larva and sees the sun in his glory. From the days of old there is no permanence. The sleeping and the dead, how alike they are, they are like a painted death. What is there between the master and the servant when both have fulfilled their doom? When the Anunnaki [gods], the judges, come together, and Mammetun, the mother of destinies, together they decree the fates of men. Life and death they allot but the day of death they do not disclose."

Then Gilgamesh said to Utnapishtim the Faraway, "I look at you now, Utnapishtim, and your appearance is no different from mine; there is nothing strange in your features. I thought I should find you like a hero prepared for battle, but you lie here taking your ease on your back. Tell me truly, how was it that you came to enter the company of the gods and to possess everlasting life?" Utnapishtim said to Gilgamesh, "I will reveal to you a mystery, I will tell you a secret of the gods."

"You know the city Shurrupak [a Sumerian city] it stands on the banks of Euphrates? That city grew old and the gods that were in it were old. There was Anu, lord of the firmament, their father, and warrior Enlil their counselor, Ninurta the helper, and Ennugi watcher over canals; and with them also was Ea [God of water]. In those days the world teemed, the people multiplied, the world bellowed like a wild bull, and the great god was aroused by the clamor. Enlil heard the clamor and he said to the gods in council, 'The uproar of mankind is intolerable and sleep is no longer possible by reason of the babel.' So the gods agreed to exterminate mankind. Enlil did this, but Ea because of his oath [to protect mankind] warned me in a dream. He whispered their words to my house of reeds, 'Reed-house, reed-house! Wall, O wall, hearken reed-house, wall reflect; O man of Shurrupak, son of Ubara-Tutu; tear down your house and build a boat, abandon possessions and look for life, despise worldly goods and save your soul alive. Tear down your house, I say, and build a boat. . . . Then take up into the boat the seed of all living creatures.'

"When I had understood I said to my lord, 'Behold, what you have commanded I will honor and perform, but how shall I answer the people, the city, the elders?' Then Ea opened his mouth and said to me, his servant, 'Tell them this: I have learnt that Enlil is wrathful against me, I dare no longer walk in his land nor live in his city; I will go down to the Gulf to dwell with Ea my lord. But on you he will rain down abundance, rare fish and shy wildfowl, a rich harvest-tide. In the evening the rider of the storm will bring you wheat in torrents.' . . .

"On the seventh day the boat was complete. . . .

"I loaded into her all that I had of gold and of living things, my family, my kin, the beast of the field both wild and tame, and all the craftsmen. I sent them on board. . . . The time was fulfilled, the evening came, the rider of the storm sent down the rain. I looked out at the weather and it was terrible, so I too boarded the boat and battened her down. . . .

"For six days and six nights the winds blew, torrent and tempest and flood overwhelmed the world, tempest and flood raged together like warring hosts. When the seventh day dawned the storm from the south subsided, the sea grew calm, the flood was stilled; I looked at the face of the world and there was silence, all mankind was turned to clay. The surface of the sea stretched as flat as a roof-top; I opened a hatch and the light fell on my face. Then I bowed low, I sat down and I wept, the tears streamed down my face, for on every side was the waste of water. I looked for land in vain, but fourteen leagues distant there appeared a mountain, and there the boat grounded; on the mountain of Nisir the boat held fast, she held fast and did not budge. . . . When the seventh day dawned I loosed a dove and let her go. She flew away, but finding no resting-place she returned. Then I loosed a swallow, and she flew away but finding no resting-place she returned. I loosed a raven, she saw that the waters had retreated, she ate, she flew around, she cawed, and she did not come back. Then I threw everything open to the four winds, I made a sacrifice and poured out a libation [liquid offering] on the mountain top. Seven and again seven cauldrons I set up on their stands, I heaped up wood and cane and cedar and myrtle. When the gods smelled the sweet savor, they gathered like flies over the sacrifice.[5] Then, at last, Ishtar [Goddess of love and war] also came, she lifted her necklace with the jewels of Heaven [rainbow] that once Anu had made to please her. 'O you gods here present, by the lapis lazuli[6] round my neck I shall remember these days as I remember the jewels of my throat; these last days I shall not forget. Let all the gods gather round the sacrifice, except Enlil. He shall not approach this offering, for without reflection he brought the flood; he consigned my people to destruction.'

"When Enlil had come, when he saw the boat, he was wrath and swelled with anger at the gods, the host of Heaven, 'Has any of these mortals escaped? Not one was to have survived the destruction.' Then the god of the wells and canals Ninurta opened his mouth and said to the warrior Enlil, 'Who is there of the gods that can devise without Ea? It is Ea alone who knows all things.' Then Ea opened his mouth and spoke to warrior Enlil, 'Wisest of gods, hero Enlil, how could you so senselessly bring down the flood?' . . . It was not that I revealed the secret of the gods; the wise man learned it in a dream. Now take your counsel what shall be done with him.

"Then Enlil went up into the boat, he took me by the hand and my wife and made us enter the boat and kneel down on either side, he standing between us. He touched our foreheads to bless us saying, 'In time past Utnapishtim was a mortal man; henceforth he and his wife shall live in the distance at the mouth of the rivers.' Thus it was that the gods took me and placed me here to live in the distance, at the mouth of the rivers."

---

[5] **like flies over the sacrifice**: The gods were thought to consume the smoke of incense and animal offerings.
[6] **lapis lazuli**: A gemstone with a deep blue color often used in Egyptian jewelry.

Utnapishtim said, "As for you, Gilgamesh, who will assemble the gods for your sake, so that you may find that life for which you are searching?"

[After telling his story, Utnapishtim challenges Gilgamesh to resist sleep for six days and seven nights. When Gilgamesh fails the test, Utnapishtim points out how preposterous it is to search for immortality when one cannot even resist sleep. Out of kindness, Utnapishtim does tell Gilgamesh where he can find a submarine plant that will at least rejuvenate him. Consequently, the hero dives to the bottom of the sea and plucks it. However, humanity is to be denied even the blessing of forestalling old age and decrepitude, because the plant is stolen from Gilgamesh by a serpent. His mission a failure, Gilgamesh returns to Uruk.]

The destiny was fulfilled which the father of the gods, Enlil of the mountain, had decreed for Gilgamesh: "In nether-earth the darkness will show him a light: of mankind, all that are known, none will leave a monument for generations to come to compare with his. The heroes, the wise men, like the new moon have their waxing and waning. Men will say, 'Who has ever ruled with might and with power like him?' As in the dark month, the month of shadows, so without him there is no light. O Gilgamesh, this was the meaning of your dream. You were given the kingship, such was your destiny, everlasting life was not your destiny. Because of this do not be sad at heart, do not be grieved or oppressed; he has given you power to bind and to loose, to be the darkness and the light of mankind. He has given unexampled supremacy over the people, victory in battle from which no fugitive returns, in forays and assaults from which there is no going back. But do not abuse this power, deal justly with your servants in the palace, deal justly before the face of the Sun." . . .

Gilgamesh, the son of Ninsun, lies in the tomb. At the place of offerings he weighed the bread-offering, at the place of libation he poured out the wine. In those days the lord Gilgamesh departed, the son of Ninsun, the king, peerless, without an equal among men, who did not neglect Enlil his master. O Gilgamesh, lord of Kullab [in Uruk], great is thy praise.

READING AND DISCUSSION QUESTIONS

1. How does this passage describe the afterlife?

2. How are the gods characterized in this passage? What is the gods' attitude toward mortals?

3. Would you describe *The Epic of Gilgamesh* as pessimistic or optimistic? Why?

HAMMURABI

Hammurabi's Code: Laws on Society and Family Life

ca. 1800 B.C.E.

Among Hammurabi of Babylon's many accomplishments were the unification of Mesopotamia under Babylonian rule, the establishment of the supremacy of the Babylonian god Marduk, and the composition of a law code. Although Hammurabi's code is not the first known law code, it is the earliest one to survive largely intact. The code deals with the family, commercial activities, and agricultural life, providing valuable insight into Babylonian society. The following selections are typical of the laws in the code and exemplify the brutal nature of Babylonian justice, often characterized by the phrase "an eye for an eye."

THE PROLOGUE

When lofty Anum, king of the Anunnaki,[7]
(and) Enlil, lord of heaven and earth,
the determiner of the destinies of the land,
determined for Marduk, the first-born of Enki,[8]
the Enlil functions over all mankind,
he made him great among the Igigi,[9]
called Babylon by its exalted name,
made it supreme in the world,
established for him in its midst an enduring kingship,
whose foundations are as firm as heaven and earth —
at that time Anum and Enlil named me
to promote the welfare of the people,
me, Hammurabi, the devout, god-fearing prince,

James B. Pritchard, ed., *Ancient Near Eastern Texts Relating to the Old Testament*, 3d ed. with supplement (Princeton, N.J.: Princeton University Press, 1969), 170–175.

[7] **Anunnaki**: Divine servants of Anu.
[8] **Enki**: God of the Earth and springs, father of Marduk.
[9] **Igigi**: Divine servants of Enlil.

to cause justice to prevail in the land,
to destroy the wicked and the evil,
that the strong might not oppress the weak,
to rise like the sun over the black-headed (people),
and to light up the land. . . .

CODE OF LAWS

128. If a seignior[10] acquired a wife, but did not draw up the contracts for her, that woman is no wife.

129. If the wife of a seignior has been caught while lying with another man, they shall bind them and throw them into the water. If the husband of the woman wishes to spare his wife, then the king in turn may spare his subject.

130. If a seignior bound the (betrothed) wife of a(nother) seignior, who had had no intercourse with a male and was still living in her father's house, and he has lain in her bosom and they have caught him, that seignior shall be put to death, while that woman shall go free.

131. If a seignior's wife was accused by her husband, but she was not caught while lying with another man, she shall make affirmation by god and return to her house.

132. If the finger was pointed at the wife of a seignior because of another man, but she has not been caught while lying with the other man, she shall throw herself into the river for the sake of her husband.

133. If a seignior was taken captive, but there was sufficient to live on in his house, his wife [shall not leave her house, but she shall take care of her person by not] entering [the house of another].

133a. If that woman did not take care of her person, but has entered the house of another, they shall prove it against that woman and throw her into the water.

134. If the seignior was taken captive and there was not sufficient to live on in his house, his wife may enter the house of another, with that woman incurring no blame at all.

135. If, when a seignior was taken captive and there was not sufficient to live on in his house, his wife has then entered the house of another before his (return) and has borne children, (and) later her husband has returned and has reached his city, that woman shall return to her first husband, while the children shall go with their father.

---

[10] **seignior**: This is a free man (not a slave) and could include members of the upper class.

136. If when a seignior deserted his city and then ran away, his wife has entered the house of another after his (departure), if that seignior has returned and wishes to take back his wife, the wife of the fugitive shall not return to her husband because he scorned his city and ran away.

137. If a seignior has made up his mind to divorce a lay priestess, who bore him children, or a heirodule[11] who provided him with children, they shall return her dowry to that woman and also give her half of the field, orchard and goods in order that she may rear her children; after she has brought up her children, from whatever was given to her children they shall give her a portion corresponding to (that of) an individual heir in order that the man of her choice may marry her.

138. If a seignior wishes to divorce his wife who did not bear him children, he shall give her money to the full amount of her marriage-price and he shall also make good to her the dowry which she brought from her father's house and then he may divorce her.

139. If there was no marriage-price, he shall give her one mina[12] of silver as the divorce-settlement.

140. If he is a peasant, he shall give her one-third mina of silver.

141. If a seignior's wife, who was living in the house of the seignior, has made up her mind to leave in order that she may engage in business, thus neglecting her house (and) humiliating her husband, they shall prove it against her; and if her husband has then decided on her divorce, he may divorce her, with nothing to be given her as her divorce-settlement upon her departure. If her husband has not decided on her divorce, her husband may marry another woman, with the former woman living in the house of her husband like a maidservant.

142. If a woman so hated her husband that she has declared, "You may not have me," her record shall be investigated at her city council, and if she was careful and was not at fault, even though her husband has been going out and disparaging her greatly, that woman, without incurring any blame at all, may take her dowry and go off to her father's house.

143. If she was not careful, but was a gadabout, thus neglecting her house (and) humiliating her husband, they shall throw that woman into the water.

144. When a seignior married a hierodule and that hierodule gave a female slave to her husband and she has then produced children, if

---

[11] **hierodule**: A female slave of the temple.

[12] **mina**: A weight equal to just over one pound.

that seignior has made up his mind to marry a lay priestess, they may not allow that seignior, since he may not marry the lay priestess.

145. If a seignior married a hierodule and she did not provide him with children and he has made up his mind to marry a lay priestess, that seignior may marry the lay priestess, thus bringing her into his house, (but) with that lay priestess ranking in no way with the hierodule.

146. When a seignior married a hierodule and she gave a female slave to her husband and she has then borne children, if later that female slave has claimed equality with her mistress because she bore children, her mistress may not sell her; she may mark her with the slave-mark and count her among the slaves.

147. If she did not bear children, her mistress may sell her.

148. When a seignior married a woman and a fever has then seized her, if he has made up his mind to marry another, he may marry (her), without divorcing his wife whom the fever seized; she shall live in the house which he built and he shall continue to support her as long as she lives.

149. If that woman has refused to live in her husband's house, he shall make good her dowry to her which she brought from her father's house and then she may leave.

150. If a seignior, upon presenting a field, orchard, house, or goods to his wife, left a sealed document with her, her children may not enter a claim against her after (the death of) her husband, since the mother may give her inheritance to that son of hers whom she likes, (but) she may not give (it) to an outsider. . . .

153. If a seignior's wife has brought about the death of her husband because of another man, they shall impale that woman on stakes.

154. If a seignior has had intercourse with his daughter, they shall make that seignior leave the city.

155. If a seignior chose a bride for his son and his son had intercourse with her, but later he himself has lain in her bosom and they have caught him, they shall bind that seignior and throw him into the water.

156. If a seignior chose a bride for his son and his son did not have intercourse with her, but he himself has lain in her bosom, he shall pay to her one-half mina of silver and he shall also make good to her whatever she brought from her father's house in order that the man of her choice may marry her.

157. If a seignior has lain in the bosom of his mother after (the death of) his father, they shall burn both of them. . . .

195. If a son has struck his father, they shall cut off his hand.

196. If a seignior has destroyed the eye of a member of the aristocracy, they shall destroy his eye.
197. If he has broken a(nother) seignior's bone, they shall break his bone.
198. If he has destroyed the eye of a commoner or broken the bone of a commoner, he shall pay one mina of silver.
199. If he has destroyed the eye of a seignior's slave or broken the bone of a seignior's slave, he shall pay one-half his value.
200. If a seignior has knocked out a tooth of a seignior of his own rank, they shall knock out his tooth.
201. If he has knocked out a commoner's tooth, he shall pay one-third mina of silver.
202. If a seignior has struck the cheek of a seignior who is superior to him, he shall be beaten sixty (times) with an oxtail whip in the assembly.
203. If a member of the aristocracy has struck the cheek of a(nother) member of the aristocracy who is of the same rank as himself, he shall pay one mina of silver.
204. If a commoner has struck the cheek of a(nother) commoner, he shall pay ten shekels [coins] of silver.
205. If a seignior's slave has struck the cheek of a member of the aristocracy, they shall cut off his ear.
206. If a seignior has struck a(nother) seignior in a brawl and has inflicted an injury on him, that seignior shall swear, "I did not strike him deliberately"; and he shall also pay for the physician.
207. If he has died because of his blow, he shall swear (as before), and if it was a member of the aristocracy, he shall pay one-half mina of silver.
208. If it was a member of the commonalty, he shall pay one-third mina of silver.
209. If a seignior struck a(nother) seignior's daughter and has caused her to have a miscarriage, he shall pay ten shekels of silver for her fetus.
210. If that woman has died, they shall put his daughter to death.
211. If by a blow he has caused a commoner's daughter to have a miscarriage, he shall pay five shekels of silver.
212. If that woman has died, he shall pay one-half mina of silver.
213. If he struck a seignior's female slave and has caused her to have a miscarriage, he shall pay two shekels of silver.
214. If that female slave has died, he shall pay one-third mina of silver.
215. If a physician performed a major operation on a freeman with a bronze lancet and has saved the freeman's life, or he opened up the eye-socket of a freeman with a bronze lancet and has saved the freeman's eye, he shall receive ten shekels of silver.

216. If it was a commoner, he shall receive five shekels of silver.

217. If it was a freeman's slave, the owner of the slave shall give two shekels of silver to the physician.

218. If a physician performed a major operation on a freeman with a bronze lancet and has caused the freeman's death, or he opened up the eye-socket of a freeman and has destroyed the freeman's eye, they shall cut off his hand.

219. If a physician performed a major operation on a commoner's slave with a bronze lancet and has caused his death, he shall make good slave for slave.

220. If he opened up [the slave's] eye-socket with a bronze lancet and has destroyed his eye, he shall pay half his value in silver.

READING AND DISCUSSION QUESTIONS

1. Why did Hammurabi produce this law code? Where does he claim his authority and kingship comes from?

2. What different social classes does this passage define? How does justice differ for these various classes?

3. In what ways do these selections attempt to regulate the family and relationships? What practices are banned?

DOCUMENT 2-3

NEBMARE-NAKHT

Advice to Ambitious Young Egyptians from a Royal Scribe

ca. 1350–1200 B.C.E.

The Egyptians used the fiber of a plant from the Nile to make sheets of papyrus, on which they recorded both important religious and official texts and personal letters. Egypt's dry climate prevented the disintegration of papyri and preserved a great deal of information about everyday life. The following

---

Miriam Lichtheim, trans. and ed., *Ancient Egyptian Literature*, Vol. 3: *The Late Period* (Berkeley: University of California Press, 1973), 3:168–172.

*passage was originally written to encourage a young scribe to continue work-
ing at his profession. The surviving examples of this text are likely exercises
copied by students, as they contain frequent spelling and grammatical mistakes. The errors might indicate the difficulty of the training, and why the
young scribe in this passage was ignoring his studies.*

1. TITLE

[Beginning of the instruction in letter writing made by the royal scribe and
chief overseer of the cattle of Amen-Re, King of Gods, Nebmare-nakht] for
his apprentice, the scribe Wenemdiamun.

2. PRAISE OF THE SCRIBE'S PROFESSION

[The royal scribe] and chief overseer of the cattle of Amen-[Re, King of
Gods, Nebmare-nakht speaks to the scribe Wenemdiamun]. [Apply yourself
to this] noble profession. "Follower of Thoth" [God of wisdom] is the good
name of him who exercises it. —. He makes friends with those greater than
he. Joyful —. Write with your hand, read with your mouth. Act according
to my words. —, my heart is not disgusted. —. — to my instructing you.
You will find it useful. — [with bread and] beer. You will be advanced by
your superiors. You will be sent on a mission —. Love writing, shun dancing; then you become a worthy official. Do not long for the marsh ticket.
Turn your back on throw stick and chase. By day write with your fingers;
recite by night. Befriend the scroll, the palette. It pleases more than wine.
Writing for him who knows it is better than all other professions. It pleases
more than bread and beer, more than clothing and ointment. It is worth
more than an inheritance in Egypt, than a tomb in the west.

3. ADVICE TO THE UNWILLING PUPIL

Young fellow, how conceited you are! You do not listen when I speak. Your
heart is denser than a great obelisk, a hundred cubits[13] high, ten cubits
thick. When it is finished and ready for loading, many work gangs draw it.
It hears the words of men; it is loaded on a barge. Departing from Yebu [in
Upper Egypt] it is conveyed, until it comes to rest on its place in Thebes
[the capital of Egypt].

   So also a cow is bought this year, and it plows the following year. It
learns to listen to the herdsman; it only lacks words. Horses brought from
the field, they forget their mothers. Yoked they go up and down on all his

---

[13] **a hundred cubits**: A cubit was a unit of measurement equal to the length of a
forearm.

majesty's errands. They become like those that bore them, that stand in the stable. They do their utmost for fear of a beating.

But though I beat you with every kind of stick, you do not listen. If I knew another way of doing it, I would do it for you, that you might listen. You are a person fit for writing, though you have not yet known a woman. Your heart discerns, your fingers are skilled, your mouth is apt for reciting.

Writing is more enjoyable than enjoying a basket of — and beans; more enjoyable than a mother's giving birth, when her heart knows no distaste. She is constant in nursing her son; her breast is in his mouth every day. Happy is the heart (of) him who writes; he is young each day. . . .

5. ALL OCCUPATIONS ARE BAD EXCEPT THAT OF THE SCRIBE

See for yourself with your own eye. The occupations lie before you.

The washerman's day is going up, going down. All his limbs are weak, (from) whitening his neighbors' clothes every day, from washing their linen.

The maker of pots is smeared with soil, like one whose relations have died. His hands, his feet are full of clay; he is like one who lives in the bog.

The cobbler mingles with vats. His odor is penetrating. His hands are red with madder, like one who is smeared with blood. He looks behind him for the kite, like one whose flesh is exposed.

The watchman prepares garlands and polishes vasestands. He spends a night of toil just as one on whom the sun shines.

The merchants travel downstream and upstream. They are as busy as can be, carrying goods from one town to another. They supply him who has wants. But the tax collectors carry off the gold, that most precious of metals.

The ships' crews from every house (of commerce), they receive their loads. They depart from Egypt for Syria, and each man's god is with him. (But) not one of them says: "We shall see Egypt again!"

The carpenter who is in the shipyard carries the timber and stacks it. If he gives today the output of yesterday, woe to his limbs! The shipwright stands behind him to tell him evil things.

His outworker who is in the fields, his is the toughest of all the jobs. He spends the day loaded with his tools, tied to his tool-box. When he returns home at night, he is loaded with the tool-box and the timbers, his drinking mug, and his whetstones.

The scribe, he alone, records the output of all of them. Take note of it!

6. THE MISFORTUNES OF THE PEASANT

Let me also expound to you the situation of the peasant, that other tough occupation. [Comes] the inundation and soaks him —, he attends to his equipment. By day he cuts his farming tools; by night he twists rope. Even his midday hour he spends on farm labor. He equips himself to go to the field as if he were a warrior. The dried field lies before him; he goes out to get his team. When he has been after the herdsman for many days, he gets his team and comes back with it. He makes for it a place in the field. Comes dawn, he goes to make a start and does not find it in its place. He spends three days searching for it; he finds it in the bog. He finds no hides on them; the jackals have chewed them. He comes out, his garment in his hand, to beg for himself a team.

When he reaches his field he finds (it) [broken up]. He spends time cultivating, and the snake is after him. It finishes off the seed as it is cast to the ground. He does not see a green blade. He does three plowings with borrowed grain. His wife has gone down to the merchants and found nothing for [barter.] Now the scribe lands on the shore. He surveys the harvests. Attendants are behind him with staffs, Nubians with clubs. One says (to him): "Give grain." "There is none." He is beaten savagely. He is bound, thrown in the well, submerged head down. His wife is bound in his presence. His children are in fetters. His neighbors abandon them and flee. When it's over, there's no grain.

If you have any sense, be a scribe. If you have learned about the peasant, you will not be able to be one. Take note of it! . . .

8. THE SCRIBE DOES NOT SUFFER LIKE THE SOLDIER

Furthermore. Look, I instruct you to make you sound; to make you hold the palette freely. To make you become one whom the king trusts; to make you gain entrance to treasury and granary. To make you receive the shipload at the gate of the granary. To make you issue the offerings on feast days. You are dressed in fine clothes; you own horses. Your boat is on the river; you are supplied with attendants. You stride about inspecting. A mansion is built in your town. You have a powerful office, given you by the king. Male and female slaves are about you. Those who are in the fields grasp your hand, on plots that you have made. Look, I make you into a staff of life! Put the writings in your heart, and you will be protected from all kinds of toil. You will become a worthy official.

Do you not recall the (fate of) the unskilled man? His name is not known. He is ever burdened (like an ass carrying) in front of the scribe who knows what he is about.

Come, (let me tell) you the woes of the soldier, and how many are his superiors: the general, the troop commander, the officer who leads, the standard-bearer, the lieutenant, the scribe, the commander of fifty, and the garrison-captain. They go in and out in the halls of the palace, saying: "Get laborers!" He is awakened at any hour. One is after him as (after) a donkey. He toils until the Aten [sun] sets in his darkness of night. He is hungry, his belly hurts; he is dead while yet alive. When he receives the grain-ration, having been released from duty, it is not good for grinding.

He is called up for Syria.[14] He may not rest. There are no clothes, no sandals. The weapons of war are assembled at the fortress of Sile. His march is uphill through mountains. He drinks water every third day; it is smelly and tastes of salt. His body is ravaged by illness. The enemy comes, surrounds him with missiles, and life recedes from him. He is told: "Quick, forward, valiant soldier! Win for yourself a good name!" He does not know what he is about. His body is weak, his legs fail him. When victory is won, the captives are handed over to his majesty, to be taken to Egypt. The foreign woman faints on the march; she hangs herself (on) the soldier's neck. His knapsack drops, another grabs it while he is burdened with the woman. His wife and children are in their village; he dies and does not reach it. If he comes out alive, he is worn out from marching. Be he at large, be he detained, the soldier suffers. If he leaps and joins the deserters, all his people are imprisoned. He dies on the edge of the desert, and there is none to perpetuate his name. He suffers in death as in life. A big sack is brought for him; he does not know his resting place.

Be a scribe, and be spared from soldiering! You call and one says: "Here I am." You are safe from torments. Every man seeks to raise himself up. Take note of it!

READING AND DISCUSSION QUESTIONS

1. What were the benefits of being a scribe?
2. According to the passage, why were other occupations worse than being a scribe? What does this imply about the social status of laborers, craftsmen, peasants, and scribes?
3. Describe the problems with military life. What would motivate someone to become a soldier?

---

[14] **Syria**: During the New Kingdom (1570–1075 B.C.E.), Egyptian power extended into the Near East.

4. Although the passage implies that being a scribe was better than other occupations, the teacher still had to encourage his pupil. Why might the life of a scribe be unattractive?

DOCUMENT 2-4

Hymn to the Nile

ca. 1350–1100 B.C.E.

Ancient Egypt, unlike Mesopotamia, shared a unified political structure, religious beliefs, and culture for most of its history. Around 3100 B.C.E., King Narmer-Menes unified the two separate kingdoms of Egypt: Lower Egypt, the delta land where the Nile emptied into the Mediterranean, and Upper Egypt, a narrow strip of land that the Nile watered as it ran north through the desert. The economy of the ancient Egyptians depended entirely on the success of crops and trade along the river, and the Egyptians worshipped the river as a god. As this hymn extols the river's virtues, it becomes a catalogue of daily life in Egypt.

WORSHIP OF THE NILE

Hail to thee, O Nile, that issues from the earth and comes to keep Egypt alive! Hidden in his form of appearance, a darkness by day, to whom minstrels have sung. He that waters the meadows which Re created, in order to keep every kid alive. He that makes to drink the desert and the place distant from water: that is his dew coming down (from) heaven. The beloved of Geb [God of the earth], the one who controls Nepri [God of grain], and the one who makes the craftsmanship of Ptah[15] to flourish.

The lord of fishes, he who makes the marsh-birds to go upstream. There are no birds which come down because of the hot winds. He who makes barley and brings emmer [wheat] into being, that he may make the temples festive. If he is sluggish, . . . the nostrils are stopped up, and everybody is poor. If there be (thus) a cutting down in the food-offerings of the

---

James B. Pritchard, ed., *Ancient Near Eastern Texts Relating to the Old Testament*, 3d ed. with supplement (Princeton, N.J.: Princeton University Press, 1969), 372–373.

[15] **Ptah:** God of creation who was associated with inundated fields.

gods, then a million men perish among mortals, covetousness is practiced, the entire land is in a fury, and great and small are on the execution-block. (But) people are different when he approaches. Khnum[16] constructed him. When he rises, then the land is in jubilation, then every belly is in joy, every backbone takes on laughter, and every tooth is exposed.

The bringer of food, rich in provisions, creator of all good, lord of majesty, sweet of fragrance. What is in him is satisfaction. He who brings grass into being for the cattle and (thus) gives . . . sacrifice to every god, whether he be in the underworld, heaven, or earth, him who is under his authority. He who takes in possession the Two Lands [Upper and Lower Egypt], fills the magazines,[17] makes the granaries wide, and gives things (to) the poor.

He who makes every beloved tree to grow, without lack of them. He who brings a ship into being by his strength, without hewing in stone. The enduring image with the White Crown.[18] He cannot be seen; (he has) no taxes; he has no levies; no one can read of the mystery; no one knows the place where he is; he cannot be found by the power of writing. (He has) no shrines; he has no portion. He has no service of (his) desire. (But) generations of thy children jubilate for thee, and men give thee greeting as a king, stable of laws, coming forth (at) his season and filling Upper and Lower Egypt. . . . (Whenever) water is drunk, every eye is in him, who gives an excess of his good.

He who was sorrowful is come forth gay. . . . Vomiting forth and making the field to drink. Anointing the whole land. Making one man rich and laying another, (but) there is no coming to trial with him, who makes satisfaction without being thwarted, for whom no boundaries are made.

A maker of light when issuing from darkness, a fat for his cattle. His limits are all that is created. There is no district which can live without him. Men are clothed . . . with flax from his meadows, for (he) made Hedjhotep [Goddess of weaving] for his service. (He) made anointing with his unguents, being the associate of Ptah in his nature, bringing into being all service in him, all writings and divine words, his responsibility in Lower Egypt.

Entering into the underworld and coming forth above, loving to come forth as a mystery. If thou art (too) heavy (to rise), the people are few, and one begs for the water of the year. (Then) the rich man looks like him who is worried, and every man is seen (to be) carrying his weapons. This is no companion backing up a companion. There are no garments for clothing;

---

[16] **Khnum**: God who was both the source of the Nile and creator of human bodies.
[17] **magazines**: Stores for military equipment.
[18] **White Crown**: The symbol of Upper Egypt worn by the pharaohs.

there are no ornaments for the children of nobles. There is no listening at night, that one may answer with coolness. There is no anointing for anybody.

He who establishes truth in the heart of men, for it is said: "Deceit comes after poverty." If one compares thee with the great green sea, which does not . . . control the Grain-God, whom all the gods praise, there are no birds coming down from his desert. His hand does not beat with gold, with making ingots of silver. No one can eat genuine lapis lazuli. (But) barley is foremost and lasting.

Men began to sing to thee with the harp, and men sing to thee with the hand. The generations of thy children jubilate for thee. Men equip messengers for thee, who come (back) bearing treasures (to) ornament this land. He who makes a ship to prosper before mankind; he who sustains hearts in pregnant women; he who loves a multitude of all (kinds of) his cattle.

When thou risest in the city of the ruler, then men are satisfied with the goodly produce of the meadows. . . . Oh for the little lotus-blossoms, everything that pours forth upon earth, all (kinds of) herbs in the hands of children! They have (even) forgotten how to eat. Good things are strewn about the houses. The land comes down frolicking.

When the Nile floods, offering is made to thee, oxen are sacrificed to thee, great oblations[19] are made to thee, birds are fattened for thee, lions are hunted for thee in the desert, fire is provided for thee. And offering is made to every (other) god, as is done for the Nile, with prime incense, oxen, cattle, birds, and flame. The Nile has made his cavern in Thebes, and his name is no (longer) known in the underworld. Not a god will come forth in his form, if the plan is ignored.

O all men who uphold the Ennead,[20] . . . fear ye the majesty which his son, the All-Lord, has made, (by) making verdant the two banks. So it is "Verdant art thou!" So it is "Verdant art thou!" So it is "O Nile, verdant art thou, who makest man and cattle to live!"

It has come to a good and successful end.

READING AND DISCUSSION QUESTIONS

1. In what ways did ancient Egyptians worship and describe the Nile?

2. What does the Nile provide for Egypt? What harm can the Nile cause?

1) as a great ancient God from the underworld who provides all that is needed, he is a mystery who all adore.

[19] **oblations**: Offerings.
[20] **Ennead**: A group of nine deities.

2) barley, water, grass. He can flood the town.

3. Why did the gods honor the Nile? How does this affect your concep-
    tion of the Egyptian deities?

4. What details about daily life in Egypt can you find in this passage?

Book of Exodus: Moses Leads the Hebrews from Egypt

ca. 950–450 B.C.E.

*The book of Exodus, the second book of the Hebrew Torah and the Christian
Old Testament, recounts the escape of the Hebrew people (Israelites) from captivity in Egypt and their forty-year journey through the desert to the "promised
land," modern-day Israel and Palestine. Although Moses, who led the Hebrew
people, is traditionally thought to have written the Torah, modern scholars
argue that the work was composed over many centuries. The following passage
recounts the climactic events of the Exodus, when the Hebrew people fled
Egypt and later when Moses received the Covenant from God. It establishes
monotheism, the worship of only one God, as a tenet of the Hebrew religion.*

[14:5–16]

When the king of Egypt was told that the people had fled, the mind of
Pharaoh and his servants was changed toward the people, and they said,
"What is this we have done, that we have let Israel go from serving us?" So
he made ready his chariot and took his army with him, and took six hundred picked chariots and all the other chariots of Egypt with officers over
all of them. And the Lord hardened the heart of Pharaoh king of Egypt
and he pursued the people of Israel as they went forth defiantly. The Egyptians pursued them, all Pharaoh's horses and chariots and his horsemen
and his army, and overtook them encamped at the sea, by Pi-ha-hi'roth, in
front of Ba'al-ze'phon.

When Pharaoh drew near, the people of Israel lifted up their eyes,
and behold, the Egyptians were marching after them; and they were in

---

Exodus 14:5–16, 21–31; 19:16–25; 20:1–26; 21:1–36, from the *New Revised Standard
Version of the Bible.*

great fear. And the people of Israel cried out to the Lord; and they said to
Moses, "Is it because there are no graves in Egypt that you have taken us
away to die in the wilderness? What have you done to us, in bringing us
out of Egypt? Is not this what we said to you in Egypt, 'Let us alone and let
us serve the Egyptians'? For it would have been better for us to serve the
Egyptians than to die in the wilderness." And Moses said to the people,
"Fear not, stand firm, and see the salvation of the Lord, which he will work
for you today; for the Egyptians whom you see today, you shall never see
again. The Lord will fight for you, and you have only to be still."

The Lord said to Moses, "Why do you cry to me? Tell the people of
Israel to go forward. Lift up your rod, and stretch out your hand over the
sea and divide it, that the people of Israel may go on dry ground through
the sea." . . .

[14:21–31]

Then Moses stretched out his hand over the sea; and the Lord drove the
sea back by a strong east wind all night, and made the sea dry land, and the
waters were divided. And the people of Israel went into the midst of the sea
on dry ground, the waters being a wall to them on their right hand and on
their left. The Egyptians pursued, and went in after them into the midst
of the sea, all Pharaoh's horses, his chariots, and his horsemen. And in the
morning watch the Lord in the pillar of fire and of cloud looked down
upon the host of the Egyptians, and discomfited the host of the Egyptians,
clogging their chariot wheels so that they drove heavily; and the Egyptians
said, "Let us flee from before Israel; for the Lord fights for them against
the Egyptians."

Then the Lord said to Moses, "Stretch out your hand over the sea,
that the water may come back upon the Egyptians, upon their chariots,
and upon their horsemen." So Moses stretched forth his hand over the
sea, and the sea returned to its wonted flow when the morning appeared;
and the Egyptians fled into it, and the Lord routed the Egyptians in the
midst of the sea. The waters returned and covered the chariots and the
horsemen and all the host of Pharaoh that had followed them into the sea;
not so much as one of them remained. But the people of Israel walked on
dry ground through the sea, the waters being a wall to them on their right
hand and on their left.

Thus the Lord saved Israel that day from the hand of the Egyptians;
and Israel saw the Egyptians dead upon the seashore. And Israel saw the
great work which the Lord did against the Egyptians, and the people feared
the Lord; and they believed in the Lord and in his servant Moses. . . .

[19:16–25]

On the morning of the third day there were thunders and lightnings, and a thick cloud upon the mountain, and a very loud trumpet blast, so that all the people who were in the camp trembled. Then Moses brought the people out of the camp to meet God; and they took their stand at the foot of the mountain. And Mount Sinai was wrapped in smoke, because the Lord descended upon it in fire; and the smoke of it went up like the smoke of a kiln, and the whole mountain quaked greatly. And as the sound of the trumpet grew louder and louder, Moses spoke, and God answered him in thunder.

And the Lord came down upon Mount Sinai, to the top of the mountain; and the Lord called Moses to the top of the mountain, and Moses went up. And the Lord said to Moses, "Go down and warn the people, lest they break through to the Lord to gaze and many of them perish. And also let the priests who come near to the Lord consecrate themselves, lest the Lord break out upon them."

And Moses said to the Lord, "The people cannot come up to Mount Sinai; for thou thyself didst charge us, saying, 'Set bounds about the mountain, and consecrate it.'"

And the Lord said to him, "Go down, and come up bringing Aaron with you; but do not let the priests and the people break through to come up to the Lord, lest he break out against them." So Moses went down to the people and told them.

[20:1–26]

And God spoke all these words, saying,

"I am the Lord your God, who brought you out of the land of Egypt, out of the house of bondage.

"You shall have no other gods before me.

"You shall not make for yourself a graven image, or any likeness of anything that is in heaven above, or that is in the earth beneath, or that is in the water under the earth; you shall not bow down to them or serve them; for I the Lord your God am a jealous God, visiting the iniquity of the fathers upon the children to the third and the fourth generation of those who hate me, but showing steadfast love to thousands of those who love me and keep my commandments.

"You shall not take the name of the Lord your God in vain; for the Lord will not hold him guiltless who takes his name in vain.

"Remember the sabbath day, to keep it holy. Six days you shall labor, and do all your work; but the seventh day is a sabbath to the Lord your God; in it you shall not do any work, you, or your son, or your daughter, your manservant, or your maidservant, or your cattle, or the sojourner who is within your gates; for in six days the Lord made heaven and earth, the sea, and all that is in them, and rested the seventh day; therefore the Lord blessed the sabbath day and hallowed it.

"Honor your father and your mother, that your days may be long in the land which the Lord your God gives you.

"You shall not kill.

"You shall not commit adultery.

"You shall not steal.

"You shall not bear false witness against your neighbor.

"You shall not covet your neighbor's house; you shall not covet your neighbor's wife, or his manservant, or his maidservant, or his ox, or his ass, or anything that is your neighbor's."

Now when all the people perceived the thunderings and the lightnings and the sound of the trumpet and the mountain smoking, the people were afraid and trembled; and they stood afar off, and said to Moses, "You speak to us, and we will hear; but let not God speak to us, lest we die." And Moses said to the people, "Do not fear; for God has come to prove you, and that the fear of him may be before your eyes, that you may not sin." And the people stood afar off, while Moses drew near to the thick darkness where God was.

And the Lord said to Moses, "Thus you shall say to the people of Israel: 'You have seen for yourselves that I have talked with you from heaven. You shall not make gods of silver to be with me, nor shall you make for yourselves gods of gold. An altar of earth you shall make for me and sacrifice on it your burnt offerings and your peace offerings, your sheep and your oxen; in every place where I cause my name to be remembered I will come to you and bless you. And if you make me an altar of stone, you shall not build it of hewn stones; for if you wield your tool upon it you profane it. And you shall not go up by steps to my altar, that your nakedness be not exposed on it.'"

[21:1–36]

"Now these are the ordinances which you shall set before them. When you buy a Hebrew slave, he shall serve six years, and in the seventh he shall go out free, for nothing. If he comes in single, he shall go out single; if he comes in married, then his wife shall go out with him. If his master gives him a wife and she bears him sons or daughters, the wife and her children shall be her master's and he shall go out alone. But if the slave plainly says, 'I love my master, my wife, and my children; I will not go out free,' then his master shall bring him to God, and he shall bring him to the door or the doorpost; and his master shall bore his ear through with an awl; and he shall serve him for life.

"When a man sells his daughter as a slave, she shall not go out as the male slaves do. If she does not please her master, who has designated her for himself, then he shall let her be redeemed; he shall have no right to sell her to a foreign people, since he has dealt faithlessly with her. If he designates her for his son, he shall deal with her as with a daughter. If he takes another wife to himself, he shall not diminish her food, her clothing, or her marital rights. And if he does not do these three things for her, she shall go out for nothing, without payment of money.

"Whoever strikes a man so that he dies shall be put to death. But if he did not lie in wait for him, but God let him fall into his hand, then I will appoint for you a place to which he may flee. But if a man willfully attacks another to kill him treacherously, you shall take him from my altar, that he may die.

"Whoever strikes his father or his mother shall be put to death.

"Whoever steals a man, whether he sells him or is found in possession of him, shall be put to death.

"Whoever curses his father or his mother shall be put to death.

"When men quarrel and one strikes the other with a stone or with his fist and the man does not die but keeps his bed, then if the man rises again and walks abroad with his staff, he that struck him shall be clear; only he shall pay for the loss of his time, and shall have him thoroughly healed.

"When a man strikes his slave, male or female, with a rod and the slave dies under his hand, he shall be punished. But if the slave survives a day or two, he is not to be punished; for the slave is his money.

"When men strive together, and hurt a woman with child, so that there is a miscarriage, and yet no harm follows, the one who hurt her shall be fined, according as the woman's husband shall lay upon him; and he shall pay as the judges determine. If any harm follows, then you shall give life for life, eye for eye, tooth for tooth, hand for hand, foot for foot, burn for burn, wound for wound, stripe for stripe.

"When a man strikes the eye of his slave, male or female, and destroys it, he shall let the slave go free for the eye's sake. If he knocks out the tooth of his slave, male or female, he shall let the slave go free for the tooth's sake.

"When an ox gores a man or a woman to death, the ox shall be stoned, and its flesh shall not be eaten; but the owner of the ox shall be clear. But if the ox has been accustomed to gore in the past, and its owner has been warned but has not kept it in, and it kills a man or a woman, the ox shall be stoned, and its owner also shall be put to death. If a ransom is laid on him, then he shall give for the redemption of his life whatever is laid upon him. If it gores a man's son or daughter, he shall be dealt with according to this same rule. If the ox gores a slave, male or female, the owner shall give to their master thirty shekels of silver, and the ox shall be stoned.

"When a man leaves a pit open, or when a man digs a pit and does not cover it, and an ox or an ass falls into it, the owner of the pit shall make it good; he shall give money to its owner, and the dead beast shall be his.

"When one man's ox hurts another's, so that it dies, then they shall sell the live ox and divide the price of it; and the dead beast also they shall divide. Or if it is known that the ox has been accustomed to gore in the past, and its owner has not kept it in, he shall pay ox for ox, and the dead beast shall be his.

READING AND DISCUSSION QUESTIONS

1. What role does the Hebrew God play for his people? How does Moses act as an intermediary between God and the people?

2. How should the followers of the Hebrew God live their lives in a way that is acceptable to him? What actions are specifically prohibited?

3. What do these passages reveal about Hebrew society? What, if any, evidence of different social classes can you find?

VIEWPOINTS

Propaganda in the Ancient Near East

DOCUMENT 2-6

ASHUR-NASIR-PAL II

An Assyrian Emperor's Résumé

ca. 875 B.C.E.

Ashur-Nasir-Pal II (r. 883–859 B.C.E.) was responsible for expanding the emerging Neo-Assyrian Empire west from northern Mesopotamia to the Mediterranean. His account of the expansion describes excessively bloody

D. D. Luckenbill, ed., *Ancient Records of Assyria and Babylonia* (Chicago: University of Chicago Press, 1926), 1:151–154.

and violent conquests and the use of terror as a common tactic to control conquered regions. Ashur-Nasir-Pal II most likely began the Assyrian habit of deporting people from their homelands and spreading them throughout the empire in order to prevent rebellions. The following selection is an official account of Ashur-Nasir-Pal II's campaigns in Mesopotamia.

YEAR 4: A THIRD CAMPAIGN AGAINST ZAMUA

In the eponymy of Limutti-adur,[21] while I was staying in Nineveh, men brought me word that Ameka and Arashtua [Mesopotamian cities] had withheld the tribute and forced labor due unto Assur,[22] my lord. At the word of Assur, the great lord, my lord, and of Nergal [God of war and the sun], my leader, on the first day of the month of *Simanu*[23] I ordered a call to arms for the third time against the land of Zamua. I did not wait for my chariots and hosts; I departed from the city of Kakzi, the Lower Zab I crossed. I entered the pass of Babite, I crossed the Radanu, drawing nearer every day to the foot of Mount Simaki. Cattle, sheep and wine, the tribute of the land of Dagara, I received. The — chariots and picked cavalry (men) I took with me, and all the night, until the dawn, I marched from (along) the foot of the mountain of Simaki. I crossed the Turnat, and with all haste to the city of Ammali, the stronghold of Arashtua, I drew near. With battle and assault I stormed the city, I took (it). 800 of their fighting men I struck down with the sword, with their corpses I filled the streets of their city, with their blood I dyed their houses. Many men I captured alive with my hand, and I carried off great spoil from them; the city I destroyed, I devastated, I burned with fire.

The city of Hudun and twenty cities of its neighborhood I captured; I slew the inhabitants thereof, their spoil, their cattle, and their sheep I carried off; their cities I destroyed, I devastated, I burned with fire; their young men and their maidens I burned in the flames. The city of Kisirtu, their stronghold, ruled by Sabini, together with ten cities of its neighborhood, I captured, I slew their inhabitants, their spoil I carried away. The cities of the Bareans, which were ruled by Kirtiara, and those of the men of Dera and of Bunisa, as far as the pass of Hashmar, I destroyed, I devastated, I burned with fire, I turned them into mounds and ruins. I departed from

---

[21] **eponymy of Limutti-adur**: In the Assyrian calendar, the names of an elected official called "limmu" were used to name the year. The name Limutti-adur does not survive in any of the Assyrian lists, but this year probably corresponds to 879 B.C.E.

[22] **Assur**: Chief god of the Assyrians.

[23] *Simanu*: May or June in the modern calendar.

the cities of Arashtua, I entered the pass between the steep mountains of Lara and Bidirgi, which for the passage of chariots and hosts was not suited to Zamri, the royal city of Ameka of the land of Zamua, I drew near.

Ameka became afraid before my mighty weapons and my fierce battle array, and occupied a steep mountain. The goods of his palace and his chariot I carried away; from the city of Zamri I departed. I crossed the Lalle and marched to Mount Etini, a difficult region, which was not suited for the passage of chariots and armies, and unto which none among the kings, my fathers, had come nigh. The king, together with his armies, climbed up into Mount Etini. His goods and his possessions, many copper utensils, a copper wild-ox, vessels of copper, bowls of copper, cups of copper, the wealth of his palace, his heaped-up treasures, I carried out of the mountain, returned to my camp and spent the night. With the help of Assur and Shamash [God of justice], the gods, my helpers, I departed from that camp, and I set out after him. I crossed the Edir River and in the midst of the mighty mountains of Su and Elaniu I slew multitudes of them. His goods and his possessions, a copper wild-ox, vessels of copper, bowls of copper, dishes of copper; many copper utensils, tables which were overlaid with gold, their cattle and their flocks, their possessions, their heavy spoil, from the foot of Mount Elaniu I carried off. I took his horse from him. Ameka, to save his life, climbed up into Mount Sabua.

The cities of Zamru, Arasitku, Ammaru, Parsindu, Iritu, and Suritu, his strongholds, together with 150 cities which lay round about, I destroyed, I devastated, I burned with fire, into mounds and ruin heaps I turned them. While I was staying before the city of Parsindi, I placed in reserve the cavalry and pioneers.[24] Fifty of Ameka's warriors I slew in the field, I cut off their heads and bound them to the tree trunks within his palace court. Twenty men I captured alive and I immured them in the wall of his palace. From the city of Zamri I took with me the cavalry and pioneers, and marched against the cities of Ata, of Arzizu, unto which none among the kings my fathers had come nigh. The cities of Arzizu and Arsindu, his strongholds, together with ten cities which lay round about on the steep mountain of Nispi, I captured. I slew the inhabitants thereof; the cities I destroyed, I devastated, I burned with fire, and returned to my camp.

At that time I received copper, *tabbili* of copper, and rings of copper, and many *shariate* from the land of Sipirmena who(se inhabitants) speak like women.

---

[24] **pioneers**: Soldiers trained in siege warfare.

From the city of Zamri I departed and into the difficult mountain of Lara, which was not suited for the passage of chariots and armies, with hatchets of iron I cut and with axes of bronze I hewed (a way), and I brought over the chariots and troops and came down to the city of Tukulti-Assur-asbat, which the men of the land of Lullu call Arakdi. All the kings of the land of Zamua were affrighted before the fury of my arms and the terror of my dominion, and embraced my feet. Tribute and tax, — silver, gold, lead, copper, vessels of copper, garments of brightly colored wool, horses, cattle, sheep, and wine I laid upon them (in greater measure) than before and used their forced laborers in the city of Calah. While I was staying in the land of Zamua, the men of the cities Huduni, Hartishi, Hubushkia and Gilzani were overwhelmed with the terrifying splendors of Assur, my lord, and they brought me tribute and tax, — silver, gold, horses, garments of brightly colored wool, cattle, flocks, and wine. The people, such as had fled from before my arms, climbed up into the mountains. I pursued them. Between the mountains of Aziru and Simaki they had settled themselves, and had made the city of Mesu their stronghold. Mount Aziru I destroyed, I devastated, and from the midst of Mount Simaki as far as the river Turnat I strewed their corpses. 500 of their warriors I slew and carried off their heavy spoil, the cities I burned with fire.

At that time, in the land of Zamua, the city of Atlila, which for the scepter of the king of Karduniash they had seized, had decayed and had become a mound and ruin heap. Assur-Nasir-Pal restored it. I surrounded it with a wall, and I erected therein a palace for my royal dwelling, I adorned it and made it glorious and greater than it was before. Grain and straw from the whole land I heaped up within it, and I called its name Der-Assur.

READING AND DISCUSSION QUESTIONS

1. How does Ashur-Nasir-Pal II describe his victories? What aspects of the story might he have exaggerated to make them seem more impressive?

2. Why would Ashur-Nasir-Pal II want to publicize his conquests? What does this say about him as a leader?

DOCUMENT 2-7

An Audience with the "King of Kings"

ca. 470 B.C.E.

Assyrian rule over the Near East eventually crumbled when various sub-ject peoples, angry over Assyrian use of terrorism, revolted. After a period of competing empires, the Persian ruler Cyrus conquered much of the Near East, and his successors added Egypt and other territories. Ruling with a more tolerant attitude, the Persians allowed the ancient Israelites to return home from Babylon and allowed other peoples to practice their ancestral customs. In return, the Persian rulers asked for obedience and tribute. This image, from the imperial palace at the Persian capital of Persepolis, depicts the delivery of incense as tribute to King Darius I. His son Xerxes and other court attendants stand behind the seated ruler.

National Museum of Iran, Tehran, Iran/The Bridgeman Art Library International.

READING AND DISCUSSION QUESTIONS

1. Examine the figure to the right of Darius. What kind of gesture is he making? What does this imply about the relationship between Darius and the attendant?

2. How is Darius depicted? What makes him stand out from the rest of the figures?

3. What role are the attendants playing in this image?

4. How would the delivery of tribute and an audience with the king help hold the Persian Empire together?

COMPARATIVE QUESTIONS

1. How are the laws in Hammurabi's code similar to or different from those in the Hebrew book of Exodus?

2. The passages in this chapter illustrate various ways in which humans relate to their gods. How do the Sumerian, Egyptian, and Hebrew peoples differ in this respect?

3. How does the life of a soldier described by Nebmare-nakht compare to the account of war by Ashur-Nasir-Pal II?

4. What differences can you discern between the everyday life and religious beliefs of Mesopotamians and those of Egyptians? What might account for those differences?

5. How do the depictions of kings differ in Hammurabi's code, Ashur-Nasir-Pal II's résumé, and an audience with the "King of Kings"?

CHAPTER 3

The Foundation of Indian Society

to 300 C.E.

The earliest society in South Asia was the Harappan civilization (ca. 2500–2000 B.C.E.) based in the Indus River Valley. They left written records, but their script remains undeciphered. With the Harappans' decline, a group who called themselves Aryans came to dominate North India. Around 1500 B.C.E., the Aryans began to compose oral poetry in Sanskrit, an Indo-European language closely related to ancient Persian and Hittite. According to the *Rigveda*, the earliest record of this sacred poetry, the Aryan religion initially focused on ritual sacrifices conducted by the priestly caste (Brahmans), who sought material benefits. Later religious movements in India, such as Buddhism, instead sought to fill spiritual needs and ignored the Aryans' strict caste system. In reaction to Buddhism, the Brahmans rejected ritual sacrifices and helped spread the worship of gods, such as Krishna, to all levels of society.

DOCUMENT 3-1

From Rigveda

ca. 600 B.C.E.

The Rigveda *is the oldest and most important Aryan scripture. Originally composed and transmitted in oral form between 1500 and 1000 B.C.E., it was only written down in Sanskrit around 800–500 B.C.E. because the Brahmans had long resisted losing control of the text to the lower castes. The* Rigveda *contains many different types of texts, such as hymns to gods, creation*

The Rig Veda, trans. Wendy Doniger O'Flaherty (New York: Penguin Books, 1981), 160–162.

47

*stories, and instructions for religious rituals. The following passage describes
the myth of the sacrifice of Purusha, which created the world.*

To Purusha

A thousand heads had Purusha,[1] a thousand eyes, a thousand feet.
> He covered earth on every side, and spread ten fingers' breadth beyond.
> This Purusha is all that yet has been and all that is to be;
> The lord of immortality which waxes greater still by food.
> So mighty is his greatness; yea, greater than this is Purusha.
> All creatures are one-fourth of him, three-fourths eternal life in heaven.
> With three-fourths Purusha went up: one-fourth of him again was here.
> Thence he strode out to every side over what eats not and what eats.
> From him Viraj [masculinity] was born; again Purusha from Viraj was
born.
> As soon as he was born he spread eastward and westward o'er the earth.
> When gods prepared the sacrifice with Purusha as their offering,
> Its oil was spring, the holy gift was autumn; summer was the wood.
> They balmed as victim on the grass Purusha born in earliest time.
> With him the deities and all Sadhyas [lesser gods] and Rishis [sages]
sacrificed.
> From that great general sacrifice the dripping fat was gathered up.[2]
> He formed the creatures of the air, and animals both wild and tame.
> From that great general sacrifice Richas and Samahymns [elements of
the *Rigveda*] were born:
> Therefrom the meters[3] were produced, the Yajus had its birth from it.
> From it were horses born, from it all creatures with two rows of teeth:
> From it were generated cows, from it the goats and sheep were born.
> When they divided Purusha how many portions did they make?
> What do they call his mouth, his arms? What do they call his thighs
and feet?
> The Brahmin [priest caste] was his mouth, of both his arms was the
Rajanya [warrior caste] made.

---

[1] **Purusha:** The cosmic being who is both the sacrifice and the one performing the
sacrifice.

[2] **From that great general sacrifice . . . up:** Vedic rituals involved the cooking of
animal flesh.

[3] **the meters:** The *Sama Veda*, another sacred text of the Aryans.

His thighs became the Vaisya [merchant and artisan caste, including herders and farmers], from his feet the Sudra [laborer caste] was produced.

The Moon was gendered from his mind, and from his eye the Sun had birth;

Indra and Agni [God of sacrifice and fire] from his mouth were born, and Vayu [the wind] from his breath.

Forth from his navel came mid-air; the sky was fashioned from his head;

Earth from his feet, and from his ear the regions. Thus they formed the worlds.

Seven fencing-logs had he, thrice seven layers of fuel were prepared [for a sacrifice],

When the gods, offering sacrifice, bound, as their victim, Purusha.

Gods, sacrificing, sacrificed the victim: these were the earliest holy ordinances.

The mighty ones attained the height of heaven, there where the Sadhyas, gods of old, are dwelling.

READING AND DISCUSSION QUESTIONS

1. According to this passage, how was the world created?
2. How does the division of Purusha's body give justification for the social statuses of the castes in India?

VIEWPOINTS
What Is Ultimate Reality?

DOCUMENT 3-2

THE BUDDHA
The Buddha Obtains Enlightenment
ca. 530–29 B.C.E.

The Buddha was born into a kshatriya *(warrior caste) family near the Hima-*
laya mountains around 563 B.C.E. *At the age of twenty-nine, he had four*
visions that made him question the value of his sheltered and comfortable
life. He envisioned an old man, a sick person, a dead person, and a monk.
Following in the path of the monk, he experimented with extreme forms
of asceticism before developing the "Middle Path." Through meditation he
obtained Enlightenment, or the freedom from reincarnation and desire that
results from understanding the reality of life, which the Buddha taught was
based on suffering. He spent the rest of his life promoting his ideas through-
out the Ganges Valley.

The following passage includes two selections from the "Pali Canon."
Theravada Buddhists believe that the "Pali Canon" contains the words of
the Buddha, but the current text was not written down until 29 B.C.E., *after*
having circulated orally for five centuries.

And the Future Buddha, thinking, "I will carry austerity to the uttermost,"
tried various plans, such living on one sesamum seed or on one grain of
rice a day, and even ceased taking nourishment altogether, and moreover
rebuffed the gods when they came and attempted to infuse nourishment
through the pores of his skin. By this lack of nourishment his body became
emaciated to the last degree, and lost its golden color, and became black,
and his thirty-two physical characteristics as a great being became obscured.
Now, one day, as he was deep in a trance of suppressed breathing, he was

Henry C. Warrant, ed. and trans., *Buddhism in Translation* (Cambridge, Mass.: Har-
vard University Press, 1909), 70–81.

attacked by violent pains, and fell senseless to the ground, at one end of his walking-place. . . .

Now the six years which the Great Being thus spent in austerities were like time spent in endeavoring to tie the air into knots. And coming to the decision, "These austerities are not the way to enlightenment," he went begging through villages and market-towns for ordinary material food, and lived upon it. And his thirty-two physical characteristics as a great being again appeared, and the color of his body became like unto gold. . . .

Then the Great Being, saying to himself, "This is the immovable spot on which all The Buddhas have planted themselves! This is the place for destroying passion's net!" took hold of his handful of grass by one end, and shook it out there. And straightway the blades of grass formed themselves into a seat fourteen cubits long, of such symmetry of shape as not even the most skilful painter or carver could have design.

Then the Future Buddha turned his back to the trunk of the Bo-tree and faced the east. And making the mighty resolution, "Let my skin, and sinews, and bones become dry, and welcome! and let all the flesh and blood in my body dry up! but never from this seat will I stir, until I have attained the supreme and absolute wisdom!" he sat himself down cross-legged in an unconquerable position, from which not even the descent of a hundred thunder-bolts at once could have dislodged him.

At this point the god Māra,[4] exclaiming, "Prince Siddhattha is desirous of passing beyond my control, but I will never allow it!" went and announced the news to his army, and sounding the Māra war-cry, drew out for battle. Now Māra's army extended in front of him for twelve leagues, and to the right and to the left for twelve leagues, and in the rear as far as to the confines of the world, and it was nine leagues high. And when it shouted, it made an earthquake-like roaring and rumbling over a space of a thousand leagues. And the god Māra, mounting his elephant, which was a hundred and fifty leagues high, and had the name "Girded-with-mountains," caused a thousand arms to appear on his body, and with these he grasped a variety of weapons. Also in the remainder of that army, no two persons carried the same weapon; and diverse also in their appearances and countenances, the host swept on like a flood to overwhelm the Great Being.

. . . [Buddha is attacked many times by the armies of Māra, but he resists them.]

---

[4] **Māra**: Here, ignorance of the true nature of reality is represented as a demon.

And the followers of Māra fled away in all directions. No two went the same way, but leaving their head-ornaments and their cloaks behind, they fled straight before them.

Then the hosts of the gods, when they saw the army of Māra flee, cried out, "Māra is defeated! Prince Siddhattha has conquered! Let us go celebrate the victory!" And the snakes egging on the snakes, the birds the birds, the deities the deities, and the Brahma-angels the Brahma-angels, they came with perfumes, garlands, and other offerings in their hands to the Great Being on the throne of wisdom. And as they came —

274. "The victory now hath this illustrious Buddha won!
     The Wicked One, the Slayer, hath defeated been!"
     Thus round the throne of wisdom shouted joyously
     The bands of snakes their songs of victory for the Sage; . . .

When thus he had attained to omniscience, and was the centre of such unparalleled glory and homage, and so many prodigies were happening about him, he breathed forth that solemn utterance which has never been omitted by any of The Buddhas: —

278. "Through birth and rebirth's endless round,
     Seeking in vain, I hastened on,
     To find who framed this edifice.
     What misery! — birth incessantly!

279. "O builder! I've discovered thee!
     This fabric thou shalt ne'er rebuild!
     Thy rafters all are broken now,
     And pointed roof demolished lies!
     This mind has demolition reached,
     And seen the last of all desire!"

At that time The Buddha, The Blessed One, was dwelling at Uruvelā at the foot of the Bo-tree on the banks of the river Nerañjarā, having just attained the Buddhaship. Then The Blessed One sat cross-legged for seven days together at the foot of the Bo-tree experiencing the bliss of emancipation.

Then The Blessed One, during the first watch of the night, thought over Dependent Origination both forward and back: —

On ignorance depends karma;
On karma depends consciousness;
On consciousness depend name and form;
On name and form depend the six organs of sense;
On the six organs of sense depends contact;
On contact depends sensation;
On sensation depends desire;
On desire depends attachment;
On attachment depends existence;
On existence depends birth;
On birth depend old age and death, sorrow, lamentation, misery,
    grief, and despair.

Thus does this entire aggregation of misery arise. But on the complete
fading out and cessation of ignorance ceases karma; on the cessation of
karma ceases consciousness; on the cessation of consciousness cease name
and form; on the cessation of name and form cease the six organs of sense;
on the cessation of the six organs of sense ceases contact; on the cessation
of contact ceases sensation; on the cessation of sensation ceases desire; on
the cessation of desire ceases attachment; on the cessation of attachment
ceases existence; on the cessation of existence ceases birth; on the cessation of birth cease old age and death, sorrow, lamentation, misery, grief,
and despair. Thus does this entire aggregation of misery cease.

READING AND DISCUSSION QUESTIONS

1. How does the Buddha begin his quest for Enlightenment? Is he
   successful?
2. What does the Buddha try in his second attempt? What opposes him?
3. In this passage, Māra (Ignorance) is personified. Why is this the case?
4. What knowledge does Enlightenment bring? How is Enlightenment
   described?

DOCUMENT 3-3

From the Upanishads: *On the Nature of the Soul*

ca. 450 B.C.E.

The development of Buddhism, which stressed spiritual, rather than material, concerns, led to reform within the priestly caste in India. Although the Vedas were still revered, the Vedic sacrifices and rituals became less important than a metaphysical understanding of the world and humankind's place within it. This movement is represented in the texts called the Upanishads, *which are considered the end of the Vedas* (vedanta). *Composed by many different writers with many different philosophical viewpoints, the* Upanishads *stress that each individual soul* (atman) *is a part of the spiritual substance of the universe* (Brahman).

THE NEED FOR A COMPETENT TEACHER OF THE SOUL

7. He who by many is not obtainable even to hear of,
   He whom many, even when hearing, know not —
   Wonderful is the declarer, proficient the obtainer of Him!
   Wonderful the knower, proficiently taught!

8. Not, when proclaimed by an inferior man, is He
   To be well understood, [though] being manifoldly considered.
   Unless declared by another, there is no going thither;
   For He is inconceivably more subtile than what is of subtile measure.

9. Not by reasoning is this thought to be attained.
   Proclaimed by another, indeed, it is for easy understanding, dearest
     friend! —
   This which thou hast attained! Ah, thou art of true steadfastness!
   May there be for us a questioner the like of thee, O Naciketas!

STEADFAST RENUNCIATION AND SELF-MEDITATION REQUIRED

Naciketas:[5]

10. I know that what is known as treasure is something inconstant.
    For truly, that which is steadfast is not obtained by those who are
      unsteadfast.

Robert Ernest Hume, *The Thirteen Principal Upanishads* (London: Oxford University Press, 1921), 347–352.

[5] **Naciketas**: The seeker of knowledge.

Therefore the Naciketas-fire has been built up by me,
And with means which are inconstant I have obtained that which is
    constant.

Death:

11. The obtainment of desire, the foundation of the world,
The endlessness of will, the safe shore of fearlessness,
The greatness of praise, the wide extent, the foundation (having seen),
Thou, O Naciketas, a wise one, hast with steadfastness let [these] go!

12. Him who is hard to see, entered into the hidden,
Set in the secret place [of the heart], dwelling in the depth, primeval —
By considering him as God, through the Yoga-study of what pertains
    to self,
The wise man leaves joy and sorrow behind.

THE ABSOLUTELY UNQUALIFIED SOUL

13. When a mortal has heard this and fully comprehended,
Has torn off what is concerned with the right, and has taken Him as
    the subtile,
Then he rejoices, for indeed he has obtained what is to be rejoiced in.
I regard Naciketas a dwelling open [for Ātman].

14. Apart from the right and apart from the unright,
Apart from both what has been done and what has not been done
    here,
Apart from what has been and what is to be —
What thou seest as that, speak that!

[Naciketas being unable to mention that absolutely unqualified object,
Death continues to explain:]

THE MYSTIC SYLLABLE "OM" AS AN AID

15. The word which all the Vedas rehearse,
And which all austerities proclaim,
Desiring which men live the life of religious studentship —
That word to thee I briefly declare.
That is *Om*!

16. That syllable, truly, indeed, is Brahma!
That syllable indeed is the supreme!
Knowing that syllable, truly, indeed,
Whatever one desires is his!

17. That is the best support.
    That is the supreme support.
    Knowing that support,
    One becomes happy in the Brahma-world.

THE ETERNAL INDESTRUCTIBLE SOUL

18. The wise one [i.e., the soul, the self] is not born, nor dies.
    This one has not come from anywhere, has not become anyone.
    Unborn, constant, eternal, primeval, this one
    Is not slain when the body is slain.

19. If the slayer think to slay,
    If the slain think himself slain,
    Both these understand not.
    This one slays not, nor is slain. . . .

[FROM THE THIRD VALLI]
PARABLE OF THE INDIVIDUAL SOUL IN A CHARIOT

3. Know thou the soul as riding in a chariot,
   The body as the chariot.
   Know thou the intellect as the chariot-driver,
   And the mind as the reins.

4. The senses, they say, are the horses;
   The objects of sense, what they range over.
   The self combined with senses and mind
   Wise men call "the enjoyer."

5. He who has not understanding,
   Whose mind is not constantly held firm —
   His senses are uncontrolled,
   Like the vicious horses of a chariot-driver.

6. He, however, who has understanding,
   Whose mind is constantly held firm —
   His senses are under control,
   Like the good horses of a chariot driver.

INTELLIGENT CONTROL OF THE SOUL'S CHARIOT NEEDED
TO ARRIVE BEYOND TRANSMIGRATION

7. He, however, who has not understanding,
   Who is unmindful and ever impure,

Reaches not the goal,
But goes on to transmigration.[6]

8. He, however, who has understanding,
Who is mindful and ever pure,
Reaches the goal
From which he is born no more.

9. He, however, who has the understanding of a chariot-driver,
A man who reins in his mind —
He reaches the end of his journey,
That highest place of Vishnu.[7]

READING AND DISCUSSION QUESTIONS

1. According to the text, why does a student need a teacher to understand the *Upanishads*? How should one go about seeking the nature of the soul? What ways of seeking ultimate reality are discouraged by this text?

2. What is the nature of the soul? What is the body?

3. How are the soul and body like a chariot?

4. What is the consequence of not obtaining knowledge of the soul and the universe? What happens to a person who dies knowing about the soul?

DOCUMENT 3-4

From the Mahabharata: *Selections from the* Bhagavad Gita

500 B.C.E.–500 C.E.

The following passage comes from the Mahabharata, *one of the most famous epics of Indian literature. Because the* Upanishads *(see Document 3-3) stressed knowledge and the use of a teacher, many people were unable to*

Juan Mascaró, trans., *The Bhagavad Gita* (London: Penguin Books, 1962), 9–11, 22–24.

[6] **transmigration**: In Hinduism, the soul is thought to live in many bodies through many cycles of reincarnation.
[7] **Vishnu**: This normally refers to the Hindu god of restoration, but here has a more metaphorical connotation of heavenly understanding.

participate. Over several hundred years, a different path, based on devotion (bhakti) to the gods, appeared. The Bhagavad Gita *is the most famous passage from the* Mahabharata. *In this excerpt, Arjuna is about to lead his troops in battle against his own relatives. At first he refuses to fight, but the god Krishna urges him to do his duty and later explains the nature of the soul and the path of devotion.*

ARJUNA

4   I owe veneration to Bhishma and Drona. Shall I kill with my arrows my grandfather's brother, great Bhishma? Shall my arrows in battle slay Drona, my teacher?

5   Shall I kill my own masters who, though greedy of my kingdom, are yet my sacred teachers? I would rather eat in this life the food of a beggar than eat royal food tasting of their blood.

6   And we know not whether their victory or ours be better for us. The sons of my uncle and king, Dhrita-rashtra, are here before us: after their death, should we wish to live?

7   In the dark night of my soul I feel desolation. In my self-pity I see not the way of righteousness. I am thy disciple, come to thee in supplication: be a light unto me on the path of my duty.

8   For neither the kingdom of the earth, nor the kingdom of the gods in heaven, could give me peace from the fire of sorrow which thus burns my life.

SANJAYA

9   When Arjuna the great warrior had thus unburdened his heart, "I will not fight, Krishna," he said, and then fell silent.

10   Krishna smiled and spoke to Arjuna — there between the two armies the voice of God spoke these words:

KRISHNA

11   Thy tears are for those beyond tears; and are thy words words of wisdom? The wise grieve not for those who live; and they grieve not for those who die — for life and death shall pass away.

12   Because we all have been for all time: I, and thou, and those kings of men. And we shall be for all time, we all for ever and ever.

13   As the Spirit of our mortal body wanders on in childhood, and youth and old age, the Spirit wanders on to a new body: of this the sage has no doubts.

14 From the world of the senses, Arjuna, comes heat and comes cold, and pleasure and pain. They come and they go: they are transient. Arise above them, strong soul.

15 The man whom these cannot move, whose soul is one, beyond pleasure and pain, is worthy of life in Eternity.

16 The unreal never is: the Real never is not. This truth indeed has been seen by those who can see the true.

17 Interwoven in his creation, the Spirit is beyond destruction. No one can bring to an end the Spirit which is everlasting.

18 For beyond time he dwells in these bodies, though these bodies have an end in their time; but he remains immeasurable, immortal. Therefore, great warrior, carry on thy fight.

19 If any man thinks he slays, and if another thinks he is slain, neither knows the ways of truth. The Eternal in man cannot kill: the Eternal in man cannot die.

20 He is never born, and he never dies. He is in Eternity: he is for evermore. Never-born and eternal, beyond times gone or to come, he does not die when the body dies.

21 When a man knows him as never-born, everlasting, never-changing, beyond all destruction, how can that man kill a man, or cause another to kill?

22 As a man leaves an old garment and puts on one that is new, the Spirit leaves his mortal body and then puts on one that is new.

23 Weapons cannot hurt the Spirit and fire can never burn him. Untouched is he by drenching waters, untouched is he by parching winds.

24 Beyond the power of sword and fire, beyond the power of waters and winds, the Spirit is everlasting, omnipresent, never-changing, never-moving, ever One.

25 Invisible is he to mortal eyes, beyond thought and beyond change. Know that he is, and cease from sorrow.

26 But if he were born again and again, and again and again he were to die, even then, victorious man, cease thou from sorrow. . . .

KRISHNA

3 Today I am revealing to thee this Yoga eternal, this secret supreme: because of thy love for me, and because I am thy friend. . . .

5 I have been born many times, Arjuna, and many times hast thou been born. But I remember my past lives, and thou hast forgotten thine.

6   Although I am unborn, everlasting, and I am the Lord of all, I come to my realm of nature and through my wondrous power I am born.

7   When righteousness is weak and faints and unrighteousness exults in pride, then my Spirit arises on earth.

8   For the salvation of those who are good, for the destruction of evil in men, for the fulfilment of the kingdom of righteousness, I come to this world in the ages that pass.

9   He who knows my birth as God and who knows my sacrifice, when he leaves his mortal body, goes no more from death to death, for he in truth comes to me.

10   How many have come to me, trusting in me, filled with my Spirit, in peace from passions and fears and anger, made pure by the fire of wisdom!

11   In any way that men love me, in that same way they find my love: for many are the paths of men, but they all in the end come to me.

12   Those who lust for early power offer sacrifice to the gods of the earth; for soon in this world of men success and power come from work.

13   The four orders of men arose from me, in justice to their natures and their works. Know that this work was mine, though I am beyond work, in Eternity.

14   In the bonds of works I am free, because in them I am free from desires. The man who can see this truth, in his work he finds his freedom.

15   This was known by men of old times, and thus in their work they found liberation. Do thou therefore thy work in life in the spirit that their work was done.

16   What is work? What is beyond work? Even some seers see this not aright. I will teach thee the truth of pure work, and this truth shall make thee free.

17   Know therefore what is work, and also know what is wrong work. And know also of a work that is silence: mysterious is the path of work.

18   The man who in his work finds silence, and who sees that silence is work, this man in truth sees the Light and in all his works finds peace.

19   He whose undertakings are free from anxious desire and fanciful thought, whose work is made pure in the fire of wisdom: he is called wise by those who see.

20   In whatever work he does such a man in truth has peace: he expects nothing, he relies on nothing, and ever has fullness of joy.

21   He has no vain hopes, he is the master of his soul, he surrenders all he has, only his body works: he is free from sin.

22 He is glad with whatever God gives him, and he has risen beyond the two contraries here below; he is without jealousy, and in success or in failure he is one: his works bind him not.

23 He has attained liberation: he is free from all bonds, his mind has found peace in wisdom, and his work is a holy sacrifice. The work of such a man is pure.

24 Who in all his work sees God, he in truth goes unto God: God is his worship, God is his offering, offered by God in the fire of God.

READING AND DISCUSSION QUESTIONS

1. Why does Arjuna refuse to fight? What does Krishna tell him about the nature of duty, the world, and the soul?

2. Why is the body compared to clothes?

3. Who is Krishna? What comforts does the path of devotion to Krishna offer?

DOCUMENT 3-5

From The Laws of Manu

ca. 100 B.C.E.–200 C.E.

The Laws of Manu *were likely compiled by more than one person and later edited and expanded by others. In Indian mythology Manu was the sole survivor of a flood, much like Utnapishtim from* The Epic of Gilgamesh *(Document 2-1). In many ways,* The Laws of Manu *are less a legal code than an instruction manual, explaining how different social classes by birth (varna) and occupation (jati) should fulfill their duty (dharma). Ascribing the laws to Manu suggests that they were given divine sanction and had universal meaning.*

B. Guehler, trans., *The Laws of Manu*, in F. Max Mueller, ed., *The Sacred Books of the East*, 50 vols. (Oxford: Clarendon Press, 1879–1910), 25:24, 69, 84–85, 195–197, 260–326, 329–330, 343–344, 370–371, 402–404, 413–416, 420, 423.

VARNA[8]

The Brahmin, the Kshatriya, and the Vaisya castes are the twice-born ones,[9] but the fourth, the Sudra, has one birth only; there is no fifth caste.[10] . . .

To Brahmins he [Brahman, the creator god] assigned teaching and studying the Vedas, sacrificing for their own benefit and for others, giving and accepting of alms.

The Kshatriya he commanded to protect the people, to bestow gifts, to offer sacrifices, to study the Vedas, and to abstain from attaching himself to sensual pleasures;

The Vaisya to tend cattle, to bestow gifts, to offer sacrifices, to study the Vedas, to trade, to lend money, and to cultivate land.

One occupation only the lord prescribed to the Sudra, to serve meekly . . . these other three castes.

JATIS[11]

From a male Sudra are born an Ayogava, a Kshattri, and a Kandala, the lowest of men, by Vaisya, Kshatriya, and Brahmin females respectively, sons who owe their origin to a confusion of the castes.[12] . . .

Killing fish to Nishadas; carpenters' work to the Ayogava; to Medas, Andhras, Kunkus, and Madgus, the slaughter of wild animals. . . .

But the dwellings of Kandalas . . . shall be outside the village. . . .

Their dress shall be the garments of the dead, they shall eat their food from broken dishes, black iron shall be their ornaments, and they must always wander from place to place.

A man who fulfills a religious duty, shall not seek intercourse with them; their [Kandala] transactions shall be among themselves, and their marriages with their equals. . . .

At night they shall not walk about in villages and in towns.

---

[8] varna: The technical term for the castes, originally meaning "color." Some scholars believe that the caste system was originally based on skin color, with the lighter-skinned Aryans supplanting the darker-skinned Dasas.

[9] the twice-born ones: Those castes whose members could read the Vedas. They participated in a ceremony known as Upanayana in which they learned about the nature of the universe and so became born again.

[10] fifth caste: The untouchables would later rank below the Sudra.

[11] jatis: Occupations or subcastes.

[12] sons . . . confusion of the castes: These jatis were occupied by children whose parents belonged to different castes; the child of a male Sudra and female Brahmin occupied the lowest jati.

By day they may go about for the purpose of their work, distinguished by marks at the king's command, and they shall carry out the corpses of persons who have no relatives; that is a settled rule.

By the king's order they shall always execute the criminals, in accordance with the law, and they shall take for themselves the clothes, the beds, and the ornaments of such criminals.

DHARMA[13]

A king who knows the sacred law must inquire into the laws of castes [jatis], of districts, of guilds, and of families, and settle the peculiar law of each. . . .

Among the several occupations the most commendable are teaching the Vedas for a Brahmin, protecting the people for a Kshatriya, and trade for a Vaisya.

But a Brahmin, unable to subsist by his peculiar occupations just mentioned, may live according to the law applicable to Kshatriyas; for the latter is next to him in rank. . . .

A man of low caste [varna] who through covetousness lives by the occupations of a higher one, the king shall deprive of his property and banish.

It is better to discharge one's own duty incompletely than to perform completely that of another; for he who lives according to the law of another caste is instantly excluded from his own.

A Vaisya who is unable to subsist by his own duties, may even maintain himself by a Sudra's mode of life, avoiding however acts forbidden to him, and he should give it up, when he is able to do so. . . .

Abstention from injuring creatures, veracity, abstention from unlawfully appropriating the goods of others, purity, and control of the organs,[14] Manu has declared to be the summary of the law for the four castes.

THE NATURE OF WOMEN

It is the nature of women to seduce men in this world; for that reason the wise are never unguarded in the company of females. . . .

For women no rite is performed with sacred texts, thus the law is settled; women who are destitute of strength and destitute of the knowledge of Vedic texts are as impure as falsehood itself; that is a fixed rule.

---

[13] **dharma:** The duties of each caste.

[14] **control of the organs:** Especially sexual organs.

HONORING WOMEN

Where women are honored, there the gods are pleased; but where they are not honored, no sacred rite yields rewards.

Where the female relations live in grief, the family soon wholly perishes; but that family where they are not unhappy ever prospers.

FEMALE PROPERTY RIGHTS

A wife, a son, and a slave, these three are declared to have no property; the wealth which they earn is acquired for him to whom they belong. . . .

What was given before the nuptial fire, what was given on the bridal procession, what was given in token of love, and what was received from her brother, mother, or father, that is called the six-fold property of a woman.

Such property, as well as a gift subsequent and what was given to her by her affectionate husband, shall go to her offspring, even if she dies in the lifetime of her husband. . . .

But when the mother has died, all the uterine [biological] brothers and the uterine sisters shall equally divide the mother's estate.

A WOMAN'S DEPENDENCE

In childhood a female must be subject to her father, in youth to her husband, when her lord is dead to her sons; a woman must never be independent.

She must not seek to separate herself from her father, husband, or sons; by leaving them she would make both her own and her husband's families contemptible. . . .

Him to whom her father may give her, or her brother with the father's permission, she shall obey as long as he lives, and when he is dead, she must not insult his memory.

BETROTHAL

No father who knows the law must take even the smallest gratuity for his daughter; for a man who, through avarice, takes a gratuity, is a seller of his offspring. . . .

Three years let a damsel wait, though she be marriageable,[15] but after that time let her choose for herself a bridegroom of equal caste and rank. If, being not given in marriage, she herself seeks a husband, she incurs no guilt, nor does he whom she weds.

---

[15] **marriageable**: Girls were often married beginning at age 12.

Marriage and Its Duties

To be mothers were women created, and to be fathers men; religious rites, therefore, are ordained in the Vedas to be performed by the husband together with the wife. . . .

No sacrifice, no vow, no fast must be performed by women apart from their husbands; if a wife obeys her husband, she will for that reason alone be exalted in heaven. . . .

By violating her duty towards her husband, a wife is disgraced in this world, after death she enters the womb of a jackal, and is tormented by diseases as punishment for her sin. . . .

Let the husband employ his wife in the collection and expenditure of his wealth, in keeping everything clean, in the fulfillment of religious duties, in the preparation of his food, and in looking after the household utensils. . . .

Drinking spirituous liquor, associating with wicked people, separation from the husband, rambling abroad, sleeping at unreasonable hours, and dwelling in other men's houses, are the six causes of the ruin of women. . . .

Offspring, religious rites, faithful service, highest conjugal happiness and heavenly bliss for the ancestors and oneself, depend on one's wife alone. . . .

"Let mutual fidelity continue until death" . . . may be considered as the summary of the highest law for husband and wife.

Let man and woman, united in marriage, constantly exert themselves, that they may not be disunited and may not violate their mutual fidelity.

Divorce

For one year let a husband bear with a wife who hates him; but after a year let him deprive her of her property and cease to cohabit with her. . . .

But she who shows aversion towards a mad or outcaste[16] husband, a eunuch,[17] one destitute of manly strength, or one afflicted with such diseases as punish crimes,[18] shall neither be cast off nor be deprived of her property. . . .

A barren wife may be superseded [replaced] in the eighth year, she whose children all die in the tenth, she who bears only daughters in the eleventh, but she who is quarrelsome without delay.

---

[16] **outcaste**: Someone literally removed from their caste.

[17] **eunuch**: A castrated male. Here, eunuch may mean an impotent man.

[18] **such diseases as punish crimes**: Illness caused by evil karmic actions.

But a sick wife who is kind to her husband and virtuous in her conduct, may be superseded only with her own consent and must never be disgraced.

READING AND DISCUSSION QUESTIONS

1. Describe the social structure advocated in this passage. What is expected from the various levels of society?
2. What are the status and role of women in Indian society?

DOCUMENT 3-6

ASHOKA
From Thirteenth Rock Edict
256 B.C.E.

Ashoka was the third king of the Mauryan dynasty of India. Having embarked on a series of conquests culminating at the battle of Kalinga, Ashoka converted to Buddhism. He began reforming the rule of his empire and, to publicize his actions, he set up fifty-foot-tall rock pillars in at least thirty locations. These pillars were rediscovered and translated in the early nineteenth century. They seem to reflect the speaking style of Ashoka himself and are not written in a highly polished style. In the following edict, Ashoka describes the reasons for his conversion to Buddhism.

When the king, Beloved of the Gods and of Gracious Mien, had been consecrated eight years Kalinga was conquered, 150,000 people were deported, 100,000 were killed, and many times that number died. But after the conquest of Kalinga, the Beloved of the Gods began to follow Righteousness (Dharma), to love Righteousness, and to give instruction in Righteousness. Now the Beloved of the Gods regrets the conquest of

Wm. Theodore de Bary, Stephen N. Hay, Royal Weiler, and Andrew Yarrow, eds., *Sources of Indian Tradition* (New York: Columbia University Press, 1958), 146–147.

Kalinga, for when an independent country is conquered people are killed, they die, or are deported, and that the Beloved of the Gods finds very painful and grievous. And this he finds even more grievous — that all the inhabitants — brāhmans, ascetics, and other sectarians, and householders who are obedient to superiors, parents, and elders, who treat friends, acquaintances, companions, relatives, slaves, and servants with respect, and are firm in their faith — all suffer violence, murder, and separation from their loved ones. Even those who are fortunate enough not to have lost those near and dear to them are afflicted at the misfortunes of friends, acquaintances, companions, and relatives. The participation of all men in common suffering is grievous to the Beloved of the Gods. Moreover there is no land, except that of the Greeks,[19] where groups of brāhmans and ascetics are not found, or where men are not members of one sect or another. So now, even if the number of those killed and captured in the conquest of Kalinga had been a hundred or a thousand times less, it would be grievous to the Beloved of the Gods. The Beloved of the Gods will forgive as far as he can, and he even conciliates the forest tribes of his dominions; but he warns them that there is power even in the remorse of the Beloved of the Gods, and he tells them to reform, lest they be killed.

For all beings the Beloved of the Gods desires security, self-control, calm of mind, and gentleness. The Beloved of the Gods considers that the greatest victory is the victory of Righteousness; and this he has won here (in India) and even five hundred leagues beyond his frontiers in the realm of the Greek king Antiochus, and beyond Antiochus among the four kings Ptolemy, Antigonus, Magas, and Alexander.[20] Even where the envoys of the Beloved of the Gods have not been sent hear of the way in which he follows and teaches Righteousness, and they too follow it and will follow it. Thus he achieves a universal conquest, and conquest always gives a feeling of pleasure; yet it is but a slight pleasure, for the Beloved of the Gods only looks on that which concerns the next life as of great importance.

I have had this inscription of Righteousness engraved that all my sons and grandsons may not seek to gain new victories, that in whatever victories they may gain they may prefer forgiveness and light punishment, that

---

[19] **Greeks**: Areas conquered by Alexander but by this time split up into many different realms, known as the Hellenistic kingdoms.

[20] **Antiochus . . . Alexander**: Antiochus was the king of Seleucid Asia, which shared a border with Ashoka in central Asia; Ptolemy was king of Hellenistic Egypt; Antigonus of Hellenistic Macedon; Magas of Cyrene (modern-day Libya); and Alexander of the island of Epirus on the west coast of Greece.

they may consider the only [valid] victory the victory of Righteousness, which is of value both in this world and the next, and that all their pleasure may be in Righteousness.

READING AND DISCUSSION QUESTIONS

1. Why did Ashoka convert to Buddhism? What does this edict reveal about the view of war among Buddhists?

2. According to Ashoka, what is a Buddhist conquest? How should a Buddhist king rule?

3. How does Ashoka understand Buddhism? Does he seem to have a deep knowledge of Buddhist theology? Does he mention the Four Noble Truths?

DOCUMENT 3-7

Naga Relief from the Ajanta Caves

ca. 200 B.C.E. – 400 C.E.

When Hindus converted to Buddhism, they brought many of their previously held beliefs with them. This was only natural since Buddha himself adapted and incorporated Hindu ideas into his teachings. This image reflects the complex mingling of religious ideas from this period. A statue of the Buddha lies in a niche next to a representation of a Naga, or snake, a deity popular amongst Hindus of the region. These sculptures were discovered inside an incredibly extensive cave complex that once served as shrines for Buddhist worshipers. Buddhists seem to have adopted the idea of using a cave as a shrine from similar, earlier Hindu cave temples.

Vanni/Art Resource, N.Y.

READING AND DISCUSSION QUESTIONS

1. Describe the position of these figures in relation to one another. How are the divine figures integrated into the shrine decoration?

2. Describe how the figures are depicted. What might this reveal about Indian ideals of beauty and sensuality in this period?

3. How does this cave decoration show the mingling of Buddhist and Hindu ideas?

COMPARATIVE QUESTIONS

1. How is inequality in Indian society justified? Use evidence from the *Rigveda* and *The Laws of Manu* to justify your answer.

2. How do the later movements of Hinduism (represented in the *Upanishads* and the *Baghavad Gita*) represent a reaction to Buddhism? What similar ideas do these forms of religion share? What are some of the differences between Buddhism and Hinduism?

3. Compare Ashoka's edict in this chapter with Hammurabi's code and Ashur-Nasir-Pal II's résumé in Chapter 2. Are there more similarities or more differences between Indian styles of rule and those in Mesopotamia?

4. What are the differences between ancient Indian religion and the religions practiced in the ancient Near East? (See Chapter 2.)

CHAPTER 4

China's Classical Age

to 221 B.C.E.

The Shang Dynasty (ca. 1500–1050 B.C.E.) was the first Chinese dynasty to leave behind evidence of its culture, including written texts and bronze weapons. Following its collapse, China shifted between periods of unified empire and civil war, which often ushered in new dynasties. The Zhou Dynasty (ca. 1050–256 B.C.E.) helped establish this pattern by ascribing the fall of the Shang to the "Mandate of Heaven," which argued that dynasties lose Heaven's blessing when they become corrupt and can be overthrown. After a long period of rule, even the Zhou Dynasty lost control of China, leading to a period of civil war known as the Warring States Period (403–221 B.C.E.). The political chaos of this time inspired a series of important political philosophies, such as Confucianism, Daoism, and Legalism, on which later Chinese culture would be built.

DOCUMENT 4-1

Shang Oracle Bones

ca. 1200–1050 B.C.E.

At the turn of the twentieth century, Chinese peasants were discovering "dragon bones" near ancient sites. The peasants crushed and drank these "bones" until scholars realized that the bones were inscribed with the earliest form of Chinese writing. They were not the bones of dragons, but rather tortoise shells or shoulder blade bones of bulls that had been heated until they cracked. By cracking the bones, officials in the Shang court attempted to divine the will of the ancestors (and occasionally the high god Di). Years of excavation at the ceremonial center at Anyang have revealed more than

Patricia Buckley Ebrey, ed., *Chinese Civilization and Society: A Sourcebook*, 2d ed., trans. David N. Keightley (New York: Free Press, 1993), 4–5.

one hundred thousand examples, only a few of which are printed below. In addition to including a question for the ancestors, the bones often reveal their divined response, and a record of the actual result.

MILITARY CAMPAIGNS

[A] Divined: "It should be Zhi Guo whom the king joins to attack the Bafang, [for if he does] Di will [confer assistance] on us."

[B] "It should not be Zhi Guo whom the king joins to attack the Bafang [for if he does] Di may not [confer assistance] on us."

METEOROLOGICAL PHENOMENA

[A] [Preface:] Crack-making on *bingshen* [day 33], Que divined: [Charge:] "On the coming *yisi* [day 42], [we] will perform the *you*-ritual to Xia Yi [the twelfth king]." [Prognostication:] The king read the cracks and said: "When [we] perform the *you*-ritual there will be occasion for calamities; there may be thunder." [Verification:] On *yisi* [day 42], [we] performed the *you*-ritual. At dawn it rained; at the beheading sacrifice it stopped raining; when the beheading sacrifice was all done, it likewise rained; when [we] displayed [the victims] and split them open, it suddenly cleared.

[B] [Verification:] In the night of *yisi* [day 42] there was thunder in the west.

AGRICULTURE

[A] [Preface:] Crack-making on [*bing-*]*chen* [day 53], Que divined: [Charge:] "We will receive millet harvest."

[B] [Preface:] Crack-making on *bingchen* [day 53], Que divined: [Charge:] "We may not receive millet harvest." (Postface:) Fourth moon.

[C] [Prognostication:] The king read the cracks and said: "Auspicious. We will receive this harvest."

SICKNESS

Divined: "There is a sick tooth; it is not Father Yi [the twentieth king, Wu Ding's father] who is harming [it]."

CHILDBIRTH

[A] [Preface:] Crack-making on *jiashen* [day 21], Que divined: [Charge:] "Lady Hao [a consort of Wu Ding] will give birth and it will be good." [Prognostication:] The king read the cracks and said: "If it be on a *ding*[1] day that she give birth, it will be good. If it be on a *geng*[2] day that she give birth, it will be prolonged auspiciousness." [Verification:] [After] thirty-one days, on *jiayin* [day 51], she gave birth. It was not good. It was a girl.

[B] [Preface:] Crack-making on *jiashen* [day 21], Que divined: [Charge:] "Lady Hao will give birth and it may not be good." [Verification:] [After] thirty-one days, on *jiayin* [day 51], she gave birth. It really was not good. It was a girl.

DISASTER, DISTRESS, OR TROUBLE

[A] Crack-making on *jiashen* [day 21], Zheng divined: "This rain will be disastrous for us."

[B] Divined: "This rain will not be disastrous for us."

DREAMS

[A] Crack-making on *jichou* [day 26], Que divined: "The king's dream was due to Ancestor Yi."

[B] Divined: "The king's dream was not due to Ancestor Yi."

SETTLEMENT BUILDING

[A] Crack-making on *renzi* [day 49], Zheng divined: "If we build a settlement, Di will not obstruct [but] approve." Third moon. . . .

DIVINE ASSISTANCE OR APPROVAL

[A] Crack-making on *xinchou* [day 38], Que divined: "Di approves the king."

[B] Divined: "Di does not approve the king."

REQUESTS TO ANCESTRAL OR NATURE POWERS

Crack-making on *xinhai* [day 48], Gu divined: "In praying for harvest to Yue [a mountain spirit], [we] make a burnt offering of three small penned sheep [and] split open three cattle." Second moon.

THE NIGHT OR THE DAY

[A] Crack-making on *renshen* [day 9], Shi divined: "This night there will be no disasters."

[B] Divined: "This night it will not rain." Ninth moon.

---

[1] **ding**: The day of the week when sacrifices were usually made.

[2] **geng**: The seventh day of the Shang ten-day week.

Hunting Expeditions and Excursions

On *renzi* [day 49] the king made cracks and divined: "[We] hunt at Zhi; going and coming back there will be no harm." [Prognostication:] The king read the cracks and said: "Prolonged auspiciousness." [Verification:] This was used. [We] caught forty-one foxes, eight *mi*-deer, one rhinoceros.

The Ten-Day Week

[A] On *guichou* [day 50], the king made cracks and divined: "In the [next] ten days, there will be no disasters." [Prognostication:] The king read the cracks and said: "Auspicious."

[B] On *guihai* [day 60], the king made cracks and divined: "In the [next] ten days, there will be no disasters." [Prognostication:] The king read the cracks and said: "Auspicious."

READING AND DISCUSSION QUESTIONS

1. What do these bones reveal about the relationship between the Shang rulers and their ancestors?

2. What are some of the topics that the Shang rulers asked about? What might this reveal about their interests?

3. How might you use these kinds of documents to understand Shang history?

DOCUMENT 4-2

From Book of Documents

ca. 900–100 B.C.E.

The Book of Documents *is one of the five texts traditionally ascribed to Confucius (551–479 B.C.E.) and studied as the basis of Confucianism. It was compiled in its original form by 300 B.C.E.; however, it had to be*

James Legge, trans., *The Sacred Books of China: The Texts of Confucianism*, in F. Max Mueller, ed., *The Sacred Books of the East*, 50 vols. (Oxford: Clarendon Press, 1879–1910), 3:92–95.

reconstructed by Chinese scholars after the Qin Dynasty (221–206 B.C.E.) attempted to destroy all Confucian texts. The Book of Documents *claims to draw from the most ancient periods of Chinese history, but many of the texts are forgeries or fakes. The following advice given to the heir of Zheng Tang, the first Shang king, by Zheng Tang's chief minister supposedly dates to the early Shang Dynasty (1500–1050 B.C.E.), but its references to the Mandate of Heaven suggest it was written during the Zhou period (1050–256 B.C.E.) to provide a precedent for revolt against the Shang Dynasty.*

In the twelfth month of the first year . . . Yi Yin sacrificed to the former king [Zheng Tang], and presented the heir-king reverently before the shrine of his grandfather. All the princes from the domain of the nobles and the royal domain were present; all the officers also, each continuing to discharge his particular duties, were there to receive the orders of the chief minister. Yi Yin then clearly described the complete virtue of the Meritorious Ancestor [Zheng Tang] for the instruction of the young king.

He said, "Oh! of old the former kings of Xia[3] cultivated earnestly their virtue, and then there were no calamities from Heaven.[4] The spirits of the hills and rivers likewise were all in tranquility; and the birds and beasts, the fishes and tortoises, all enjoyed their existence according to their nature. But their descendant did not follow their example, and great Heaven sent down calamities, employing the agency of our ruler [Zheng Tang] who was in possession of its favoring appointment. The attack on Xia may be traced to the orgies in Ming Tiao [where Jie, the last Xia ruler, was defeated]. . . . Our king of Shang brilliantly displayed his sagely prowess; for oppression he substituted his generous gentleness; and the millions of the people gave him their hearts. Now your Majesty is entering on the inheritance of his virtue; — all depends on how you commence your reign. To set up love, it is for you to love your relations; to set up respect, it is for you to respect your elders. The commencement is in the family and the state. . . .

"Oh! the former king began with careful attention to the bonds that hold men together. He listened to expostulation, and did not seek to resist it; he conformed to the wisdom of the ancients; occupying the highest position, he displayed intelligence; occupying an inferior position, he

---

[3] **Xia**: Traditionally defined as the first dynasty in China.

[4] **no calamities from Heaven**: This seems to refer to the later concept of the Mandate of Heaven developed by the Zhou Dynasty and used to justify the overthrow of the Shang.

displayed his loyalty; he allowed the good qualities of the men whom he employed and did not seek that they should have every talent. . . .

"He extensively sought out wise men, who should be helpful to you, his descendant and heir. He laid down the punishments for officers, and warned those who were in authority, saying, 'If you dare to have constant dancing in your palaces, and drunken singing in your chambers, — that is called the fashion of sorcerers; if you dare to set your hearts on wealth and women, and abandon yourselves to wandering about or to the chase, — that is called the fashion of extravagance; if you dare to despise sage words, to resist the loyal and upright, to put far from you the aged and virtuous, and to seek the company of . . . youths, — that is called the fashion of disorder. Now if a high noble or officer be addicted to one of these three fashions with their ten evil ways, his family will surely come to ruin; if the prince of a country be so addicted, his state will surely come to ruin. The minister who does not try to correct such vices in the sovereign shall be punished with branding.' . . .

"Oh! do you, who now succeed to the throne, revere these warnings in your person. Think of them! — sacred counsels of vast importance, admirable words forcibly set forth! The ways of Heaven are not invariable: — on the good-doer it sends down all blessings, and on the evil-doer it sends down all miseries. Do you but be virtuous, be it in small things or in large, and the myriad regions will have cause for rejoicing. If you not be virtuous, be it in large things or in small, it will bring the ruin of your ancestral temple."

READING AND DISCUSSION QUESTIONS

1. What Shang religious rituals does this passage describe?
2. How does Yi Yin tell his son how he should rule? What are the qualities of a good ruler?
3. What actions are considered evil according to Zheng Tang? What are the consequences of living an evil life?
4. How does this text justify the Shang rebellion against the Xia Dynasty?

VIEWPOINTS
How Society Should Function

CONFUCIUS
From Analects
ca. 500 B.C.E.–50 C.E.

Like the Book of Documents, *the* Analects *were ordered burned by Qin Shihuangdi (First Emperor). The surviving text, therefore, was compiled and edited more than three hundred years after the death of Confucius. Confucius did not write down the* Analects; *rather, the sayings in the* Analects *were recorded after his death by his students. The actual text contains hundreds of sayings, completely out of context, and is traditionally read with later commentaries to aid in understanding. The readings in this passage are representative of the topics contained in the* Analects *and are presented without commentaries.*

[BOOK I]

V. The Master said, "To rule a country of a thousand chariots, there must be reverent attention to business, and sincerity; economy in expenditure, and love for the people; and the employment of them at the proper seasons."

VI. The Master said, "A youth, when at home, should be filial, and, abroad, respectful to his elders. He should be earnest and truthful. He should overflow in love to all, and cultivate the friendship of the good. When he has time and opportunity, after the performance of these things, he should employ them in polite studies."

VII. Tsze-hea said, "If a man withdraws his mind from the love of beauty, and applies it as sincerely to the love of the virtuous; if, in serving his parents, he can exert his utmost strength; if, in serving his prince, he can devote his life; if, in his intercourse with his friends, his words are

James Legge, ed., *The Life and Teachings of Confucius* (London: N. Trübner & Co., 1872), 118, 122–123, 125–126, 134–137.

sincere: — although men say that he has not learned, I will certainly say that he has." . . .

[Book II]

III. 1. The Master said, "If the people be led by laws, and uniformity sought to be given them by punishments, they will try to avoid *the punishment*, but have no sense of shame.

2. "If they be led by virtue, and uniformity sought to be given them by the rules of propriety, they will have the sense of shame, and moreover will become good.". . .

V. 1. Măng E asked what filial piety was. The Master said, "It is not being disobedient."

2. *Soon after*, as Fan Ch'e was driving him, the Master told him, saying, "Măng-sun asked me what filial piety was, and I answered him — 'Not being disobedient.'"

3. Fan Ch'e said, "What did you mean?" The Master replied, "That parents, when alive, should be served according to propriety; that when dead, they should be buried according to propriety; and that they should be sacrificed to according to propriety."

VI. Măng Woo asked what filial piety was. The Master said, "Parents are anxious lest their children should be sick."

VII. Tsze-yew asked what filial piety was. The Master said, "The filial piety of now-a-days means the support of one's parents. But dogs and horses likewise are able to do something in the way of support; — without reverence, what is there to distinguish the one support given from the other?"

VIII. Tsze-hea asked what filial piety was. The Master said, "The difficulty is with the countenance. If, when *their elders* have any *troublesome* affairs, the young take the toil of them, and if, when *the young* have wine and food, they set them before their elders, is THIS to be considered filial piety?". . .

XIX. The Duke Gae asked, saying, "What should be done in order to secure the submission of the people?" Confucius replied, "Advance the upright and set aside the crooked, then the people will submit. Advance the crooked and set aside the upright, then the people will not submit."

XX. Ke K'ang asked how to cause the people to reverence *their ruler*, to be faithful to him, and to urge themselves to virtue. The Master said, "Let him preside over them with gravity; — then they will reverence him. Let him be filial and kind to all; — then they will be faithful to him. Let him advance the good and teach the incompetent; — then they will eagerly seek to be virtuous." . . .

[BOOK IV]

II. The Master said, "Those who are without virtue cannot abide long either in a condition of poverty and hardship, or in a condition of enjoyment. The virtuous rest in virtue; the wise desire virtue."

III. The Master said, "It is only the truly virtuous man who can love, or who can hate, others."

IV. The Master said, "If the will be set on virtue, there will be no practice of wickedness."

V. 1. The Master said, "Riches and honours are what men desire. If it cannot be obtained in the proper way, they should not be held. Poverty and meanness are what men dislike. If it cannot be obtained in the proper way, they should not be avoided.

2. "If a superior man abandon virtue, how can he fulfil the requirements of that name?

3. "The superior man does not, even for the space of a single meal, act contrary to virtue. In moments of haste, he cleaves to it. In seasons of danger, he cleaves to it."

VI. 1. The Master said, "I have not seen a person who loved virtue, or one who hated what was not virtuous. He who loved virtue would esteem nothing above it. He who hated what is not virtuous, would practise virtue in such a way that he would not allow anything that is not virtuous to approach his person.

2. "Is any one able for one day to apply his strength to virtue? I have not seen the case in which his strength would be insufficient.

3. "Should there possibly be any such case, I have not seen it."

VII. The Master said, "The faults of men are characteristic of the class to which they belong. By observing a man's faults, it may be known that he is virtuous." . . .

X. The Master said, "The superior man, in the world, does not set his mind either for anything, or against anything; what is right he will follow."

XI. The Master said, "The superior man thinks of virtue; the small man thinks of comfort. The superior man thinks of the sanctions of law; the small man thinks of favours *which he may receive*."

XII. The Master said, "He who acts with a constant view to his own advantage will be much murmured against."

XIII. The Master said, "Is *a prince* able to govern his kingdom with the complaisance proper to the rules of propriety, what difficulty will he have? If he cannot govern it with that complaisance, what has he to do with the rules of propriety?" . . .

XVI. The Master said, "The mind of the superior man is conversant with righteousness; the mind of the mean man is conversant with gain."

XVII. The Master said, "When we see men of worth, we should think of equalling them; when we see men of contrary character, we should turn inwards and examine ourselves."

READING AND DISCUSSION QUESTIONS

1.   How, according to the *Analects*, should a son interact with his parents? What is filial piety?
2.   How should a ruler govern his people?
3.   What are the duties of a gentleman? What is virtue?

DOCUMENT 4-4

LAOZI

From Dao De Jing:
Administering the Empire

ca. 500–400 B.C.E.

According to tradition, the Dao De Jing (The Book of the Way) *was written by the sage Laozi, an official of the Zhou court. It was eventually adopted as the basis of the Chinese philosophy of Daoism, which teaches that action should be spontaneous, not purposeful, and that the universe works through the dual forces of yin and yang. The text of the* Dao De Jing *contains many short passages: some are speculative, some philosophical, and some, such as those printed here, give advice to the rulers of China. As you read this document, think about how different Laozi's advice is compared to that offered by Confucius (Document 4-3).*

Lao-Tzu, *Tao Te Ching*, trans. D. C. Lau (London: Penguin Books, 1963).

LXII

The way is the refuge for the myriad creatures.
It is that by which the good man protects,
And that by which the bad is protected.
Beautiful words when offered will win high rank in return;
Beautiful deeds can raise a man above others.
Even if a man is not good, why should he be abandoned?
Hence when the emperor is set up and the three ducal ministers
    [highest-ranking advisers] are appointed, he who makes a present of
    the way without stirring from his seat is preferable to one who offers
    presents of jade disks followed by a team of four horses. Why was this
    way valued of old? Was it not said that by means of it one got what
    one wanted and escaped the consequences when one transgressed?
Therefore it is valued by the empire.

LXIII

Do that which consists in taking no action; pursue that which is not
    meddlesome; savor that which has no flavor.
Make the small big and few many; do good to him who has done you an
    injury.
Lay plans for the accomplishment of the difficult before it becomes
    difficult; make something big by starting with it when small.
Difficult things in the world must needs have their beginnings in the
    easy; big things must needs have their beginnings in the small.
Therefore it is because the sage never attempts to be great that he
    succeeds in becoming great.
One who makes promises rashly rarely keeps good faith; one who is in
    the habit of considering things easy meets with frequent difficulties.
Therefore even the sage treats some things as difficult. That is why in the
    end no difficulties can get the better of him.

LXIV

It is easy to maintain a situation while it is still secure;
It is easy to deal with a situation before symptoms develop;
It is easy to break a thing when it is yet brittle;
It is easy to dissolve a thing when it is yet minute.
Deal with a thing while it is still nothing;
Keep a thing in order before disorder sets in.
A tree that can fill the span of a man's arms
Grows from a downy tip;
A terrace nine storeys high

Rises from hodfuls of earth;
A journey of a thousand miles
Starts from beneath one's feet.
Whoever does anything to it will ruin it; whoever lays hold of it will lose it.
Therefore the sage, because he does nothing never ruins anything; and,
    because he does not lay hold of anything, loses nothing.
In their enterprises the people
Always ruin them when on the verge of success.
Be as careful at the end as at the beginning
And there will be no ruined enterprises.
Therefore the sage desires not to desire
And does not value goods which are hard to come by;
Learns to be without learning
And makes good the mistakes of the multitude
In order to help the myriad creatures to be natural and to refrain from
    daring to act.

LXV

Of old those excelled in the pursuit of the way did not use it to enlighten
    the people but to hoodwink them. The reason why the people are
    difficult to govern is that they are too clever.
Hence to rule a state by cleverness
Will be to the detriment of the state;
Not to rule a state by cleverness
Will be a boon to the state.
These two are models.
Always to know the models
Is known as mysterious virtue.
Mysterious virtue is profound and far-reaching,
But when things turn back it turns back with them.
Only then is complete conformity [to the way] realized.

READING AND DISCUSSION QUESTIONS

1. What advice does Laozi give to the rulers of China? Is this advice
   practical? Could an empire be run using Laozi's suggestions?
2. What role do opposites play in these verses?
3. Do these passages depict humans as good or evil? How do they depict
   government?

DOCUMENT 4-5

HAN FEI
The Five Vermin
ca. 250–25 B.C.E.

Han Fei (ca. 280–233 B.C.E.) is the best-known proponent of the Chinese philosophy called Legalism, created by combining elements of Confucianism, Daoism, and Han Fei's own ideas. Han Fei studied under a Confucian master, Xunzi, and wrote a commentary on the Dao De Jing *(Document 4-4). He served as a minister of the Qin Dynasty until a rival forced him to commit suicide. Legalism is renowned for its emphasis on harsh punishments and penalties for petty crimes. In Legalism, power should be concentrated in the hands of the ruler.*

Past and present have different customs; new and old adopt different measures. To try to use the ways of a generous and lenient government to rule the people of a critical age is like trying to drive a runaway horse without using reins or whip. This is the misfortune that ignorance invites.

Now the Confucians and the Mohists[5] all praise the ancient kings for their universal love of the world, saying that they looked after the people as parents look after a beloved child. And how do they prove this contention? They say, "Whenever the minister of justice administered some punishment, the ruler would purposely cancel all musical performances; and whenever the ruler learned that the death sentence had been passed on someone, he would shed tears." For this reason they praise the ancient kings.

Now if ruler and subject must become like father and son before there can be order, then we must suppose that there is no such thing as an unruly father or son. Among human affections none takes priority over the love of parents for their children. But though all parents may show love for their children, the children are not always well behaved. . . . And if such love cannot prevent children from becoming unruly, then how can it bring the people to order? . . .

Wm. Theodore de Bary, ed., *Sources of East Asian Tradition*. Volume 1: *Premodern Asia* (New York: Columbia University Press, 2008), 112–114.

[5] **Mohists:** A fourth school of thought in China that advocated moral values and rejected violence.

Now here is a young man of bad character. His parents rail at him, but he does not reform; the neighbors scold, but he is unmoved; his teachers instruct him, but he refuses to change his ways. Thus, although three fine influences are brought to bear on him — the love of his parents, the efforts of the neighbors, the wisdom of his teachers — yet he remains unmoved and refuses to change so much as a hair on his shin. But let the district magistrate send out the government soldiers to enforce the law and search for evildoers, and then he is filled with terror, reforms his conduct, and changes his ways. . . .

The best rewards are those that are generous and predictable, so that the people may profit by them. The best penalties are those that are severe and inescapable, so that the people will fear them. The best laws are those that are uniform and inflexible, so that the people can understand them. . . .

Hardly ten men of true integrity and good faith can be found today, and yet the offices of the state number in the hundreds. If they must be filled by men of integrity and good faith, then there will never be enough men to go around; and if the offices are left unfilled, then those whose business it is to govern will dwindle in numbers while disorderly men increase. Therefore the way of the enlightened ruler is to unify the laws instead of seeking for wise men, to lay down firm policies instead of longing for men of good faith. Hence his laws never fail him, and there is no felony or deceit among his officials. . . .

Farming requires a lot of hard work, but people will do it because they say, "This way we can get rich." War is a dangerous undertaking, but people will take part in it because they say, "This way we can become eminent." Now if men who devote themselves to literature or study the art of persuasive speaking are able to get the fruits of wealth without the hard work of the farmer and can gain the advantages of eminence without the danger of battle, then who will not take up such pursuits? . . .

Therefore, in the state of an enlightened ruler there are no books written on bamboo slips; law supplies the only instruction. There are no sermons on the former kings; the officials serve as the only teachers. There are no fierce feuds of private swordsmen; cutting off the heads of the enemy is the only deed of valor. Hence, when the people of such a state make a speech, they say nothing that is in contradiction to the law; when they act, it is in some way that will bring useful results; and when they do brave deeds, they do them in the army. Therefore, in times of peace the state is rich, and in times of trouble its armies are strong. . . .

These are the customs of a disordered state: Its scholars praise the ways of the former kings and imitate their humaneness and rightness, put on a fair appearance and speak in elegant phrases, thus casting doubt upon the laws of the time and causing the ruler to be of two minds. Its speechmakers propound false schemes and borrow influence from abroad, furthering their private interests and forgetting the welfare of the state's altars of the soil and grain. Its swordsmen gather bands of followers about them and perform deeds of honor, making a fine name for themselves and violating the prohibitions of the five government bureaus. Those of its people who are worried about military service flock to the gates of private individuals and pour out their wealth in bribes to influential men who will plead for them, in this way escaping the hardship of battle. Its merchants and artisans spend their time making articles of no practical use and gathering stores of luxury goods, accumulating riches, waiting for the best time to sell, and exploiting the farmers.

These five groups are the vermin of the state. If the rulers do not wipe out such vermin, and in their place encourage men of integrity and public spirit, then they should not be surprised, when they look about the area within the four seas, to see states perish and ruling houses wane and die.

READING AND DISCUSSION QUESTIONS

1. According to Han Fei, how should a ruler exercise power?
2. What kind of laws does Han Fei advocate? Why?
3. Why does Han Fei consider education to be a problem for China? What should be done to scholars?

DOCUMENT 4-6

Anecdotes from the Warring States Period

ca. 206–1 B.C.E.

When the Zhou Dynasty took control over China (ca. 1050 B.C.E.), they appointed officials to govern outlying lands. Over time, the officials passed the positions to their sons, who asserted more independence from the Zhou government. In 771 B.C.E., one of these officials revolted and killed the emperor. Although the Zhou defeated this uprising, they lost control of China by 500 B.C.E. Many states battled for supremacy, resulting in the Warring States Period (403–221 B.C.E.), during which traditional Chinese values broke down. The following passages, compiled during the later Han Dynasty (206 B.C.E.–220 C.E.) from a number of sources, provide a glimpse into the Warring States Period and the transformation of morality and values.

LORD MU OF LU ASKED ZISI

Lord Mu of Lu asked Zisi, "Of what sort is he who can be called a loyal minister?"

Zisi said, "One who constantly cites his lord's weaknesses can be called a loyal minister."

Displeased, the lord had [Zisi] bow and retire. In an audience with Chengsun Ge, the lord said, "Before, I asked Zisi about loyal ministers, and Zisi said, 'One who constantly cites his lord's weaknesses can be called a loyal minister.' I was confused by this and did not comprehend."

Chengsun Ge said, "Oh, well spoken (by Zisi)! There have been those who have killed themselves for the sake of their lord. But there has never been one who constantly cites his lord's weaknesses. One who would kill himself for the sake of his lord is one who is committed to rank and emolument[6]; one who constantly cites his lord's weaknesses keeps rank and emolument at a distance. Practicing righteousness while keeping rank and emolument at a distance — other than Zisi, I have never heard of anyone (who does this)."

From *Hawai'i Reader in Traditional Chinese Culture*, ed. Victor H. Mair, Nancy S. Steinhardt, and Paul R. Goldin (Honolulu: University of Hawai'i Press, 2005), 143–146.

[6] **emolument**: Profit from ministerial office.

Mr. He [From *Han Fei Zi*. Excerpt]

One Mr. He of Chu obtained a jade gem from within Mount Chu; he took it and presented it to King Li. King Li had a jeweler examine it; the jeweler said, "It is (a mere) stone." The king thought (Mr.) He was a cozener,[7] so he cut off his left foot.

When King Li died, King Wu assumed the throne, and He took his gem once again to present it to King Wu. King Wu had a jeweler examine it; the jeweler said, "It is (a mere) stone." Once again, the king thought (Mr.) He was a cozener, so he cut off his right foot.

When King Wu died, King Wen assumed the throne. Then (Mr.) He wrapped his arms around his gem and wept beneath Mount Chu. After three days and three nights, his tears were exhausted, so he continued by weeping blood. The king heard of this, and sent someone to ask (He's) reason, saying, "There are many people who have had their feet cut off; why do you weep so tragically?"

He said, "I am not weeping for my feet. I am weeping because a precious jade is labeled a stone, and an honest man-of-service is dubbed a cozener. That is what I consider tragic." Then the king had his jeweler polish the gem, and this revealed how precious it was. Consequently it was named "Mr. He's jade-disk."

From *Outer Commentary to the Han Odes*

Mencius's wife was sitting by herself in a squatting position. Mencius came in through the door and saw her. He announced to his mother, "My wife is without ritual. I entreat you to expel her."

His mother said, "Why?"

He said, "She was squatting."

His mother said, "How do you know that?"

Mencius said, "I saw her."

His mother said, "Then you are without ritual, not your wife. Do the *Rites*[8] not say, 'When you are about to go through a gate, ask who is there; when you are about to ascend a hall, you must make a sound; when you are about to go through a door, you must look down, lest you surprise someone who is unprepared'? Now you went to her place of respite and privacy, going through her door without a sound. That she was seen squatting is (the result of) your lack of ritual. It is not your wife's lack of ritual."

Thereupon Mencius blamed himself and did not dare expel his wife.

---

[7] **cozener**: Con artist.
[8] ***Rites***: Confucius's *Book of Rites*.

STRATAGEMS OF THE WARRING STATES (EXCERPTS)

The state of Zhao seized the sacrificial grounds of Zhou. The King of Zhou was upset by this and told Zheng Chao. Zheng Chao said, "Lord, do not be upset. Let me take (the grounds) back with (merely) thirty pieces of gold."

The Lord of Zhou granted him (the gold). Zheng Chao presented it to the Grand Diviner of Zhao and told him about the matter of the sacrificial grounds. When the King (of Zhao) became ill, he sent for a divination. The Grand Diviner upbraided him, saying, "The sacrificial grounds of Zhou constitute an evil influence." So Zhao returned (the grounds).

When Gan Mao was Prime Minister in Qin, the King of Qin favored Gongsun Yan. One time when they were standing together at leisure, (the king) addressed (Gongsun Yan), saying, "I am about to make you Prime Minister."

One of Gan Mao's functionaries heard this while he was passing by and told Gan Mao. Gan Mao then went in to have an audience with the king. He said, "Your Majesty, you have gained a worthy Prime Minister. I venture to pay my respects and congratulate you."

The king said, "I have entrusted the state to you; why do I need another worthy Prime Minister?"

He replied, "Your Majesty, you are about to make the *xishou* [Gongsun Yan] your Prime Minister."

The king said, "How did you hear that?"

He replied, "The *xishou* told me."

The king was enraged that the *xishou* should have leaked (this information), so he banished him.

King Xuan of Jing asked his flock of ministers, saying, "I have heard that the north fears Zhao Xixu [commander-in-chief of the army]. Verily, how shall we (proceed)?"

None of the ministers answered. Then Jiang Yi said, "A tiger was seeking out the Hundred Beasts and eating them when he caught a fox. The fox said, 'You dare not eat me. Di in Heaven has made me the leader of the Hundred Beasts. If you were to eat me, you would be opposing the command of Di. If you think I am being untrustworthy, I shall walk ahead of you, and you will follow behind me. Observe whether there are any of the Hundred Beasts that dare not flee when they see me!' The tiger doubted the fox, so he walked with him. When the beasts saw them, they fled. The tiger did not know that the beasts fled because they were afraid of him, but thought they were afraid of the fox.

"Now, your Majesty, your territory is five thousand tricents square and contains a million armed (soldiers). But they have all been assigned to Zhao Xixu alone. Thus, when the north fears Zhao Xixu, in reality they fear your Majesty's armed troops, as the Hundred Beasts fear the tiger.

The King of Wei sent a beautiful woman to the King of Chu; the King of Chu was pleased by her. His wife, Zheng Xiu, knew that the king was pleased by the new woman, and that he was very kind to her. Whatever clothing or baubles (the new woman) liked, (Zheng Xiu) gave her; whatever rooms and bed-furnishings she liked, (Zheng Xiu) gave her. She was kinder to her than the king was.

The king said, "A wife serves her husband with sex, but jealousy is her essence. Now you, Zheng Xiu, know that I am pleased by the new woman, and you are kinder to her than I am. This is how a filial son would serve his parents, how a loyal minister would serve his lord."

Relying on her knowledge that the king did not consider her jealous, Zheng Xiu addressed the new woman, saying, "The king loves your beauty! Though this is so, he dislikes your nose. When you see the king, you must cover your nose." So the new woman would cover her nose whenever she went to see the king.

The king addressed Zheng Xiu, saying, "Why does the new woman cover her nose when she sees me?

Zheng Xiu said, "I know why."

The king said, "You must say it even if it is horrible."

Zheng Xiu said, "It seems she hates to smell your odor."

The king said, "Shrew!" He ordered (the new woman's) nose cut off, and would not allow anyone to disobey the command.

There was a man who presented an herb of immortality to the King of Jing. The visitor was holding it in his hand as he entered, and a Mid-Rank Servitor asked, "Can it be eaten?"

(The visitor) said, "It can."

Thereupon (the servitor) snatched it and ate it. The king was enraged and sent men to kill the Mid-Rank Servitor. The Mid-Rank Servitor sent a messenger to persuade the king, saying, "Your servant asked the visitor, and the visitor said it could be eaten; thus your servant ate it. Because of this, your servant is without guilt; the guilt is with the visitor. Furthermore, the guest was presenting an herb of immortality. If your servant eats it and you, king, kill your servant, then it must be an 'herb of mortality.' King, you will be killing a guiltless servant as well as making it plain that people deceive you." Thus the king did not kill him.

The state of Zhao was about to attack Yan. Su Dai addressed King Hui (of Zhao) on behalf of Yan, saying, "As I was coming here today, I passed the Yi River. A mussel had just come out (of its shell) to bask when a heron began to peck at its flesh; the mussel thereupon snapped closed on (the bird's) beak. The heron said, 'If it does not rain today or tomorrow, there will be a dead mussel.' The mussel said to the heron, 'If I do not come out today or tomorrow, there will be a dead heron.' Neither was willing to let the other go, and a fisherman was able to catch both of them.

"Now Zhao is about to attack Yan. Yan and Zhao will withstand each other for a long time, thereby straining their large populations. I fear that mighty Qin will be the fisherman. I request that you cook this plan through."

King Hui said, "Very well." Thereupon he desisted.

READING AND DISCUSSION QUESTIONS

1. How do the figures in these passages achieve their goals? What does this suggest about the personal traits that were valued in this time period?

2. What do these passages reveal about the nature of government in China during the Warring States Period? How did government operate? Who were the chief officials and what were their duties?

COMPARATIVE QUESTIONS

1. Compare the advice given to rulers in the *Analects, Book of Documents,* and the *Dao De Jing.* What does this suggest about the similarities and differences between Confucianism and Daoism?

2. In what ways does Legalism, illustrated in the reading from the "Five Vermin," directly attack Confucianism, as portrayed in the *Analects*?

3. Compare the sources on the Shang Dynasty ("Shang Oracle Bones" and *Book of Documents*). Do these sources agree on the nature of Shang rule?

CHAPTER 5

The Greek Experience

3500–100 B.C.E.

G reek civilization supplied Rome and much of Europe with a cultural foundation in art, literature, architecture, and philosophy. The fundamentals of Greek life and religious beliefs were laid out in poetry, the earliest form of Greek literature, during the Archaic Age (800–500 B.C.E.) by authors such as Homer, Hesiod, and Sappho, while philosophy took root under the Pre-Socratics. During the Classical Period (500–338 B.C.E.), authors including Herodotus, Thucydides, Sophocles, and Euripides created new genres such as history and drama, while philosophers such as Socrates, Plato, and Aristotle established the course of Western philosophy. Art focused on idealized portraits. After Alexander (d. 323 B.C.E.), Greek culture spread throughout Egypt and the Middle East. In this age, referred to as the Hellenistic Period (336–100 B.C.E.), innovations in science and philosophy continued, but developments in the arts remain the best known contribution of this period, as artists began to depict people in less idealized forms.

DOCUMENT 5-1

HOMER

From The Iliad: *Achilles's Anger and Its Consequences*

ca. 750 B.C.E.

Homer (ca. 800–700 B.C.E.) is the traditional name of the blind, possibly illiterate, author of the two most important epics in Greek literature, The Iliad *and the* Odyssey. The Iliad *takes place in the final year of the Trojan*

Richmond Lattimore, trans., *The Iliad of Homer* (Chicago: University of Chicago Press, 1951), 63, 330–333, 351–352, 375, 443–446.

War (ca. 1250 B.C.E.), a Greek assault against the Trojans waged to avenge
Paris of Troy's kidnapping of Helen from her husband, Menelaos, the king
of the Greek city-state of Sparta. In this passage, Achilles (Achilleus in the
translation below) becomes angry when the Achaian (Greek) king Agamemnon moves to take away a female slave whom Achilles had won in a previous
battle. The passage begins with Achilles arguing with Agamemnon.

Then looking darkly at him Achilleus of the swift feet spoke:
"O wrapped in shamelessness, with your mind forever on profit,
how shall any one of the Achaians readily obey you
either to go on a journey or to fight men strongly in battle?
I for my part did not come here for the sake of the Trojan
spearmen to fight against them, since to me they have done nothing.
Never yet have they driven away my cattle or my horses,
never in Phthia where the soil is rich and men grow great did they
spoil my harvest, since indeed there is much that lies between us,
the shadowy mountains and the echoing sea; but for your sake,
o great shamelessness, we followed, to do you favour,
you with the dog's eyes, to win your honour and Menelaos'
from the Trojans. You forget all this or else you care nothing.
And now my prize you threaten in person to strip from me,
for whom I laboured much, the gift of the sons of the Achaians.
Never, when the Achaians sack some well-founded citadel
of the Trojans, do I have a prize that is equal to your prize.
Always the greater part of the painful fighting is the work of
my hands; but when the time comes to distribute the booty
yours is far the greater reward, and I with some small thing
yet dear to me go back to my ships when I am weary with fighting.
Now I am returning to Phthia, since it is much better
to go home again with my curved ships, and I am minded no longer
to stay here dishonoured and pile up your wealth and your luxury."
        Then answered him in turn the lord of men Agamemnon:
"Run away by all means if your heart drives you. I will not
entreat you to stay here for my sake. There are others with me
who will do me honour, and above all Zeus of the counsels.
To me you are the most hateful of all the kings whom the gods love." . . .
        Meanwhile Patroklos[1] came to the shepherd of the people, Achilleus,
and stood by him and wept warm tears, like a spring dark-running

---

[1] **Patroklos**: Achilles's best friend.

that down the face of a rock impassable drips its dim water;
and swift-footed brilliant Achilleus looked on him in pity,
and spoke to him aloud and addressed him in winged words: "Why then
are you crying like some poor little girl, Patroklos,
who runs after her mother and begs to be picked up and carried,
and clings to her dress, and holds her back when she tries to hurry,
and gazes tearfully into her face, until she is picked up?
You are like such a one, Patroklos, dropping these soft tears.
Could you have some news to tell, for me or the Myrmidons?"[2] . . .
            Then groaning heavily, Patroklos the rider, you answered:
"Son of Peleus, far greatest of the Achaians, Achilleus,
do not be angry; such grief has fallen upon the Achaians.
For all those who were before the bravest in battle
are lying up among the ships with arrow or spear wounds. . . .
            "Give me your armour to wear on my shoulders into the fighting;
so perhaps the Trojans might think I am you, and give way
from their attack, and the fighting sons of the Achaians get wind
again after hard work. There is little breathing space in the fighting.
We unwearied might with a mere cry pile men wearied
back upon their city, and away from the ships and the shelters."
            So he spoke supplicating in his great innocence; this was
his own death and evil destruction he was entreating.
But now, deeply troubled, swift-footed Achilleus answered him:
"Ah, Patroklos, illustrious, what is this you are saying?
I have not any prophecy in mind that I know of;
there is no word from Zeus my honoured mother has told me,
but this thought comes as a bitter sorrow to my heart and my spirit
when a man tries to foul one who is his equal, to take back
a prize of honour, because he goes in greater authority.
This is a bitter thought to me; my desire has been dealt with
roughly. The girl the sons of the Achaians chose out for my honour,
and I won her with my own spear, and stormed a strong-fenced city,
is taken back out of my hands by powerful Agamemnon,
the son of Atreus, as if I were some dishonoured vagabond.
Still, we will let all this be a thing of the past; and it was not
in my heart to be angry forever; and yet I have said
I would not give over my anger until that time came
when the fighting with all its clamour came up to my own ships.

---

[2] **Myrmidons**: Achilles's followers.

So do you draw my glorious armour about your shoulders;
lead the Myrmidons whose delight is battle into the fighting,
if truly the black cloud of the Trojans has taken position
strongly about our ships, and the others, the Argives,[3] are bent back
against the beach of the sea, holding only a narrow division
of land, and the whole city of the Trojans has descended upon them
boldly; because they do not see the face of my helmet
glaring close; or else they would run and cram full of dead men
the water-courses; if powerful Agememnon treated me kindly. . . .
But even so, Patroklos, beat the bane aside from our ships; fall
upon them with all your strength; let them not with fire's blazing
inflame our ships, and take away our desired homecoming.
But obey to the end this word I put upon your attention
so that you can win, for me, great honour and glory
in the sight of all the Danaans,[4] so they will bring back to me
the lovely girl, and give me shining gifts in addition.
When you have driven them from the ships, come back; although later
the thunderous lord of Hera might grant you the winning of glory,
you must not set your mind on fighting the Trojans, whose delight
is in battle, without me. So you will diminish my honour." . . .

He spoke, and Patroklos was helming himself in bronze that glittered.
First he placed along his legs the beautiful greaves, linked
with silver fastenings to hold the greaves at the ankles.
Afterwards he girt on about his chest the corselet
starry and elaborate of swift-footed Aiakides.
Across his shoulders he slung the sword with the nails of silver,
a bronze sword, and above it the great shield, huge and heavy. . . .

And Patroklos charged with evil intention in on the Trojans.
Three times he charged in with the force of the running war god,
screaming a terrible cry, and three times he cut down nine men;
but as for the fourth time he swept in, like something greater
than human, there, Patroklos, the end of your life was shown forth,
since Phoibus [Apollo] came against you there in the strong encounter
dangerously, nor did Patroklos see him as he moved through
the battle, and shrouded in a deep mist came in against him
and stood behind him, and struck his back and his broad shoulders

---

[3] **Argives**: Greeks from the city-state of Argos.
[4] **Danaans**: Another word for Greeks.

with a flat stroke of the hand so that his eyes spun. Phoibos
Apollo now struck away from his head the helmet
four-horned and hollow-eyed, and under the feet of the horses
it rolled clattering, and the plumes above it were defiled
by blood and dust. Before this time it had not been permitted
to defile in the dust this great helmet crested in horse-hair;
rather it guarded the head and the gracious brow of a godlike
man, Achilleus; but now Zeus gave it over to Hektor[5]
to wear on his head, Hektor whose own death was close to him.
And in his hands was splintered all the huge, great, heavy,
iron-shod, far-shadowing spear, and away from his shoulders
dropped to the ground the shield with its shield sling and its tassels.
The lord Apollo, son of Zeus, broke the corselet upon him.
Disaster caught his wits, and his shining body went nerveless.
He stood stupidly, and from close behind his back a Dardanian
man hit him between the shoulders with a sharp javelin:
Euphorbos, son of Panthoös, who surpassed all men of his own age
with the throwing spear, and in horsemanship and the speed of his feet. He
had already brought down twenty men from their horses
since first coming, with his chariot and his learning in warfare.
He first hit you with a thrown spear, o rider Patroklos,
nor broke you, but ran away again, snatching out the ash spear
from your body, and lost himself in the crowd, not enduring
to face Patroklos, naked as he was, in close combat.

Now Patroklos, broken by the spear and the god's blow, tried
to shun death and shrink back into the swarm of his own companions.
But Hektor, when he saw high-hearted Patroklos trying
to get away, saw how he was wounded with the sharp javelin,
came close against him across the ranks, and with the spear stabbed him
in the depth of the belly and drove the bronze clean through. He fell,
thunderously, to the horror of all the Achaian people. . . .

Meanwhile the son of stately Nestor was drawing near him
and wept warm tears, and gave Achilleus his sorrowful message:
"Ah me, son of valiant Peleus; you must hear from me
the ghastly message of a thing I wish never had happened.
Patroklos has fallen, and now they are fighting over his body
which is naked. Hektor of the shining helm has taken his armour."

---

[5] **Hektor**: Troy's best warrior and Achilles's fiercest enemy.

He spoke, and the black cloud of sorrow closed on Achilleus.
In both hands he caught up the grimy dust, and poured it
over his head and face, and fouled his handsome countenance,
and the black ashes were scattered over his immortal tunic. . . .
[Angered because of the death of his friend, Achilles decides once again
to fight on the Greek side, and he confronts the Trojan champion
Hektor.]
    Pulling out the sharp sword that was slung
at the hollow of his side, huge and heavy, and gathering
himself together, he made his swoop, like a high-flown eagle
who launches himself out of the murk of the clouds on the flat land
to catch away a tender lamb or a shivering hare; so
Hektor made his swoop, swinging his sharp sword, and Achilleus
charged, the heart within him loaded with savage fury.
In front of his chest the beautiful elaborate great shield
covered him, and with the glittering helm with four horns
he nodded; the lovely golden fringes were shaken about it
which Hephaistos[6] had driven close along the horn of the helmet.
And as a star moves among stars in the night's darkening,
Hesper, who is the fairest star who stands in the sky, such
was the shining from the pointed spear Achilleus was shaking
in his right hand with evil intention toward brilliant Hektor.
He was eyeing Hektor's splendid body, to see where it might best
give way, but all the rest of the skin was held in the armour,
brazen and splendid, he stripped when he cut down the strength of
        Patroklos;
yet showed where the collar-bones hold the neck from the shoulders,
the throat, where death of the soul comes most swiftly; in this place
brilliant Achilleus drove the spear as he came on in fury,
and clean through the soft part of the neck the spearpoint was driven.
Yet the ash spear heavy with bronze did not sever the windpipe,
so that Hektor could still make exchange of words spoken.
But he dropped in the dust, and brilliant Achilleus vaunted above him:
"Hektor, surely you thought as you killed Patroklos you would be
safe, and since I was far away you thought nothing of me,
o fool, for an avenger was left, far greater than he was,
behind him and away by the hollow ships. And it was I;

---

[6] **Hephaistos**: Greek god of fire and blacksmithing.

and I have broken your strength; on you the dogs and the vultures
shall feed and foully rip you; the Achaians will bury Patroklos." . . .
"We have won ourselves enormous fame; we have killed the great Hektor
whom the Trojans glorified as if he were a god in their city."
     He spoke, and now thought of shameful treatment for glorious Hektor.
In both of his feet at the back he made holes by the tendons
in the space between ankle and heel, and drew thongs of ox-hide through
          them,
and fastened them to the chariot so as to let the head drag,
and mounted the chariot, and lifted the glorious armour inside it,
then whipped the horses to a run, and they winged their way unreluctant.
A cloud of dust rose where Hektor was dragged, his dark hair was falling
about him, and all that head that was once so handsome was tumbled
in the dust; since by this time Zeus had given him over
to his enemies, to be defiled in the land of his fathers.
     So all his head was dragged in the dust; and now his mother
tore out her hair, and threw the shining veil far from her
and raised a great wail as she looked upon her son; and his father
beloved groaned pitifully, and all his people about him
were taken with wailing and lamentation all through the city.

READING AND DISCUSSION QUESTIONS

1. Why is Achilles enraged that Agamemnon wants to take away his
    female slave? What does he threaten to do if she is taken from him?

2. What do the Greek warriors care most about? Why are they fighting?

3. How does Achilles feel when he hears Patroklos has been killed?

4. What does Achilles do to Hektor after defeating him in combat? Why
    would Achilles have treated Hektor's body in this way?

DOCUMENT 5-2

LYSIAS

On the Murder of Eratosthenes

ca. 403–380 B.C.E.

One of the innovations that resulted from a democratic style of government in Athens was the development of trials by jury. By serving as jurors, the unemployed and elderly could obtain a minimal level of subsistence. In trials, the prosecutor and defendant had to present their own cases, but they could hire famous orators to write their speeches for them. The defendant Euphiletos, who was accused of murdering Eratosthenes, gave this speech, which was written by Lysias. One of the values of the speech is that it presents everyday life without the filters of a more polished, idealized written document. The outcome of the trial is unknown.

But I think that what I must prove is that Eratosthenes seduced my wife and both corrupted her and disgraced my sons and insulted me by entering my house; and that there was neither any hostility between me and him apart from this, nor did I commit this act for money, to rise from rags to riches, nor for any other profit beyond the redress granted by the laws. So then, I shall disclose to you the whole of my story from the beginning, leaving nothing out but telling the truth. For I see this as my only means of salvation, if I am able to tell you everything that happened.

When I decided to marry, men of Athens, and I brought a wife into my house, during the early period my attitude was neither to annoy her nor to allow her too much freedom to do as she wished; I protected her to the best of my ability and kept watch as was proper. But when my child was born, from then on I trusted her and I placed all my property in her care, believing that this was the strongest bond of affection. And to begin with, men of Athens, she was the best of all women; she was a skilled and thrifty housekeeper who kept careful control over everything. But when my mother died — and her death has been the cause of all my troubles, for it was when my wife attended her funeral that she was seen by this man and eventually corrupted; he kept watch for the serving girl who used to go to market and passed messages and seduced her.

Christopher Carey, *Trials from Classical Athens* (London: Routledge, 1997), 28–31.

Now first, gentlemen (this too I must tell you), I have a small house with two floors, with the upstairs and downstairs equal in size as far as the men's and women's quarters are concerned. When our baby was born, its mother nursed it. So that my wife would not run any risk going downstairs when she had to bathe him, I lived upstairs and the women below. And this had become so normal that often my wife would go off downstairs to sleep with the baby, to give him the breast so that he wouldn't cry. And this went on for a long time, and I never once suspected, but was so gullible that I thought my own wife was the most decent woman in the city.

After a time, gentlemen, I came home unexpectedly from the country. After dinner the baby cried and howled; he was being tormented by the maid on purpose to make him, because the man was in the house — afterwards I discovered all of this. And I told my wife to go off and give the baby the breast to stop him crying. To start with she refused, as if she were pleased to see me back after a long absence. When I grew angry and told her to go she said: "Oh yes, so that you can have a go at the serving girl here! You've groped her before too when you were drunk!" I for my part laughed, while she stood up, went out and closed the door, pretending she was joking, and then turned the key. And I thought nothing of all this and suspected nothing, but went to sleep gladly, having come from the country. When it was almost daylight, she came and opened the door. When I asked why the doors banged in the night, she said that the lamp by the baby had gone out and so she had got a light from the neighbours. I said nothing, and believed that this was true. But I thought, gentlemen, that she was wearing make-up, though her brother was not yet dead thirty days. Still, even so I said nothing about the matter but went off without a word.

After this, gentlemen, time passed, and I remained in complete ignorance of my misfortunes. Then an elderly female slave came up to me; she had been sent secretly by a woman with whom Eratosthenes was having an affair — so I heard later. This woman was resentful and thought herself hard done by, because he no longer visited her frequently as before; so she kept watch until she found out the cause. This female approached me near my house, where she was looking out for me. "Euphiletos," she said, "don't think I've approached you through any desire to meddle. For the man who is insulting you and your wife is actually an enemy of ours. If you seize the girl who goes to market and works for you and put her to the test, you will discover everything. It is," she said, "Eratosthenes of Oe who is doing this. Not only has he corrupted your wife but also many others; he makes a profession of it."

With these words, gentlemen, she went off, while I was immediately thrown into confusion; everything came into my mind and I was filled with suspicion. I reflected how I was locked up in my room, and recollected that the courtyard door and outside door banged that night, something which had never happened before, and that I thought my wife was wearing make-up. All this came into my mind and I was filled with suspicion. I went home and told the serving girl to come to the market with me. I took her to the house of one of my friends and told her that I had found out everything that was going on in the house. "So," I said, "*you* have two choices, either to be whipped and thrown into a mill and never have any release from miseries of this sort, or to tell the whole truth and suffer no harm but obtain pardon from me for your offences. Tell me no lies. Speak the whole truth."

As for her, to begin with she denied it and told me to do as I wished, since she knew nothing. But when I mentioned Eratosthenes to her and said that he was the man who was visiting my wife, she was amazed, supposing that I had detailed knowledge. At that point she threw herself at my knees, and having received an assurance from me that she would suffer no harm she turned accuser, telling first of all how he approached her after the funeral, and then how she had finally served as his messenger and my wife was won over eventually, and the means by which his entry was arranged, and how at the Thesmophoria while I was in the country my wife went to the temple with his mother. And she gave me a detailed account of everything else which had taken place. . . .

After this there was an interval of four or five days . . . as I shall demonstrate with convincing evidence. But first of all I want to give you an account of what took place on the last day. I had a close friend, Sostratos, whom I met on his way from the country after sunset. I knew that having arrived so late he would find nothing he needed at home, and so I invited him to dinner. We reached my house and went upstairs and dined. When he had eaten his fill, he went off while I went to sleep. Eratosthenes, gentlemen, came in, and the serving girl woke me at once and told me that he was in the house. Telling her to watch the door, I went downstairs in silence and left the house. I called on one man after another; some I didn't catch at home, while others, I found, were not even in town. But I took as many as I could of those who were available and made my way back. We obtained torches from the nearest shop and went indoors — the door had been kept open by the serving girl. We pushed open the door of the bedroom. The first of us to enter saw him still lying beside my wife; those who entered after saw him standing naked on the bed.

I knocked him down with a blow, gentlemen; I forced his hands behind his back and tied them, and asked him why he was insulting me by entering my house. He admitted his guilt, but begged and pleaded with me not to kill him but to exact money. For my part I answered: "It is not I who shall kill you but the city's law, which you broke, because you considered it less important than your pleasures. You preferred to commit a crime such as this against my wife and my children rather than obey the laws and behave decently."

So, gentlemen, that man paid the penalty which the law prescribes for those who commit such wrongs. He was not dragged in off the street, nor did he take refuge at the hearth, as these people maintain.

READING AND DISCUSSION QUESTIONS

1. What can you learn about everyday life in a Greek family from this document? What was the role of women in the household?

2. What does this passage reveal about sexual relationships between men and women during this period?

3. How does Euphiletos justify the killing of Eratosthenes?

4. What was the role of slaves in the household? How were slaves treated?

DOCUMENT 5-3

PLATO

From Apologia

ca. 399 B.C.E.

Plato (427–347 B.C.E.), a classical Greek philosopher and founder of the Academy philosophical school, was a pupil of the philosopher Socrates (ca. 470–399 B.C.E.) and sought to preserve his mentor's contribution to Athenian life. As Socrates recorded nothing, we must rely on Plato's documentation of Socrates's teachings. In the following speech, Socrates presents his defense

---

Plato, *Apologia*, in F. J. Church, trans. *The Trial and Death of Socrates* (London: Macmillan, 1880).

in Athenian court against the charges that he was impious and corrupted the youth. It is unclear to what extent the Apologia *represents his actual words or merely Plato's reimagining of them. Although the exact date of the* Apologia *is unknown, Plato recorded this speech after Socrates's conviction and execution.*

Men of Athens, do not interrupt me with noise, even if I seem to you to be boasting; for the word that I speak is not mine, but the speaker to whom I shall refer it is a person of weight. For of my wisdom — if it is wisdom at all — and of its nature, I will offer you the god of Delphi[7] as a witness. You know Chaerephon, I fancy. He was my comrade from a youth and the comrade of your democratic party.[8] . . . Well, once he went to Delphi and made so bold as to ask the oracle this question; and, gentlemen, don't make a disturbance at what I say; for he asked if there were anyone wiser than I. Now the Pythia[9] replied that there was no one wiser. And about these things his brother here will bear you witness, since Chaerephon is dead.

But see why I say these things; for I am going to tell you from where the prejudice against me has arisen. For when I heard this, I thought to myself: "What in the world does the god mean, and what riddle is he propounding?[10] For I am conscious that I am not wise to any degree. What then does he mean by declaring that I am the wisest? He certainly cannot be lying, for that is not possible for him." And for a long time I was at a loss as to what he meant; then with great reluctance I proceeded to investigate him somewhat as follows.

I went to one of those who had a reputation for wisdom, thinking that there, if anywhere, I should prove the utterance wrong and should show the oracle "This man is wiser than I, but you said I was wisest." So examining this man — for I need not call him by name, but it was one of the public men with regard to whom I had this kind of experience, men of Athens — and conversing with him, this man seemed to me to seem to be wise to many other people and especially to himself, but not to be so; and then I tried to show him that he thought he was wise, but was not. As a result, I became hateful to him and to many of those present; and so, as I

---

[7] **Delphi**: The location of the most important oracle in the Greek world, which was dedicated to the god Apollo.

[8] **your democratic party**: Socrates did not support Athens's democratic faction.

[9] **Pythia**: The priestess at Delphi who spoke for the god Apollo.

[10] **what riddle . . . propounding?**: The Pythia at Delphi was known for answering questions with a riddle.

went away, I thought to myself, I am wiser than this man; for neither of us really knows anything fine and good, but this man thinks he knows something when he does not, whereas I, as I do not know anything, do not think I do either. I seem, then, in just this little thing to be wiser than this man at any rate, that what I do not know I do not think I know either." From him I went to another of those who were reputed to be wiser than he, and these same things seemed to me to be true; and there I became hateful both to him and to many others. . . .

Now from this investigation, men of Athens, many enmities have arisen against me, and such as are most harsh and grievous, so that many prejudices have resulted from them and I am called a wise man. For on each occasion those who are present think I am wise in the matters in which I confute someone else; but the fact is, gentlemen, it is likely that the god is really wise and by his oracle means this: "Human wisdom is of little or no value." And it appears that he does not really say this of Socrates, but merely uses my name, and makes me an example, as if he were to say: "This one of you, O human beings, is wisest, who, like Socrates, recognizes that he is in truth of no account in respect to wisdom."

Therefore I am still even now going about and searching and investigating at the god's behest anyone, whether citizen or foreigner, who I think is wise; and when he does not seem so to me, I give aid to the god and show that he is not wise. And by reason of this occupation I have no leisure to attend to any of the affairs of the state worth mentioning, or of my own, but am in vast poverty on account of my service to the god.[11]

And in addition to these things, the young men who have the most leisure, the sons of the richest men, accompany me of their own accord, find pleasure in hearing people being examined, and often imitate me themselves, and then they undertake to examine others; and then, I fancy, they find a great plenty of people who think they know something, but know little or nothing. As a result, therefore, those who are examined by them are angry with me, instead of being angry with themselves, and say that "Socrates is a most abominable person and is corrupting the youth."

And when anyone asks them "by doing or teaching what?" they have nothing to say, but they do not know, and that they may not seem to be at a loss, they say these things that are handy to say against all the philosophers, "the things in the air and the things beneath the Earth" and "not to believe in the gods" and "to make the weaker argument the stronger."

---

[11] **my service to the god**: Socrates performed his civic duty for Athens as a soldier and as an officeholder.

For they would not, I fancy, care to say the truth, that it is being made very clear that they pretend to know, but know nothing. . . . If you should say to me . . . "Socrates, this time we will not do as Anytus[12] says, but we will let you go, on this condition, however, that you no longer spend our time in this investigation or in philosophy ["love of wisdom"], and if you are caught doing so again you shall die"; if you should let me go on this condition which I have mentioned, I should say to you, "Men of Athens, I respect and love you, but I shall obey the god [Apollo] rather than you, and while I live and am able to continue, I shall never give up philosophy or stop exhorting you and pointing out the truth to any one of you whom I may meet, saying in my accustomed way: "Most excellent man, are you who are a citizen of Athens, the greatest of cities and the most famous for wisdom and power, not ashamed to care for the acquisition of wealth and for reputation and honor, when you neither care nor take thought for wisdom and truth and the perfection of your soul?" And if any of you argues the point, and says he does care, I shall not let him go at once, nor shall I go away, but I shall question and examine and cross-examine him, and if I find that he does not possess virtue, but says he does, I shall rebuke him for scorning the things that are of most importance and caring more for what is of less worth. This I shall do to whomever I meet, young and old, foreigner and citizen, but most to the citizens, inasmuch as you are more nearly related to me. For know that the god commands me to do this, and I believe that no greater good ever came to pass in the city than my service to the god. For I go about doing nothing else than urging you, young and old, not to care for your persons or your property more than for the perfection of your souls, or even so much; and I tell you that virtue does not come from money, but from virtue comes money and all other good things to man, both to the individual and to the state. If by saying these things I corrupt the youth, these things must be injurious, but if anyone asserts that I say other things than these, he says what is untrue. Therefore I say to you, men of Athens, either do as Anytus tells you, or not, and either acquit me, or not, knowing that I shall not change my conduct even if I am to die many times over. . . .

For know that if you kill me, I being such a man as I say I am, you will not injure me so much as yourselves. . . . And so, men of Athens, I am now making my defense not for my own sake, as one might imagine, but far more for yours, that you may not by condemning me err in your treatment of the gift the god gave you. For if you put me to death, you will not

---

[12] **Anytus**: The person who brought charges against Socrates.

easily find another, who, to use a rather absurd figure, attaches himself to the city as a gadfly to a horse, which, though large and well bred, is sluggish on account of his size and needs to be aroused by stinging. I think the god fastened me upon the city in some such capacity, and I go about arousing, and urging and reproaching each one of you, constantly alighting upon you everywhere the whole day long. Such another is not likely to come to you, gentlemen; but if you take my advice, you will spare me. But you, perhaps, might be angry, like people awakened from a nap, and might slap me, as Anytus advises, and easily kill me; then you would pass the rest of your lives in slumber, unless the god, in his care for you, should send someone else to sting you. And that I am, as I say, a kind of gift from the god, you might understand from this; for I have neglected all my own affairs and have been enduring the neglect of my concerns all these years, but I am always busy in your interest, coming to each one of you individually like a father or an elder brother and urging you to care for virtue; now that is not like human conduct. If I derived any profit from this and received pay for these exhortations, there would be some sense in it; but now you yourselves see that my accusers, though they accuse me of everything else in such a shameless way, have not been able to work themselves up to such a pitch of shamelessness as to produce a witness to testify that I ever exacted or asked pay of anyone. For I think I have a sufficient witness that I speak the truth, namely, my poverty. . . .

I was never any one's teacher. If any one, whether young or old, wishes to hear me speaking and pursuing my mission, I have never objected, nor do I converse only when I am paid and not otherwise, but I offer myself alike to rich and poor; I ask questions, and whoever wishes may answer and hear what I say. And whether any of them turns out well or ill, I should not justly be held responsible, since I never promised or gave any instruction to any of them;[13] but if any man says that he ever learned or heard anything privately from me, which all the others did not, be assured that he is lying.

But why then do some people love to spend much of their time with me? You have heard the reason, men of Athens; for I told you the whole truth; it is because they like to listen when those are examined who think they are wise and are not so; for it is amusing.

---

[13] **I was never any one's teacher . . . them**: Socrates contrasts himself with the Sophists who charged money for their instruction.

READING AND DISCUSSION QUESTIONS

1. How does Socrates defend himself against the charges of impiety and corrupting the youth? Do you find his argument convincing? Explain.

2. Socrates was convicted and later sentenced to death. Why might the Athenians have found him guilty?

3. How does Socrates define and seek wisdom?

4. What tactics did Socrates use to question people? Why might he have attracted so many followers? Conversely, what elements of Socrates's method might have created enemies?

> ### DOCUMENT 5-4

ARISTOTLE

From Politics

ca. 340 B.C.E.

Plato's Academy attracted a number of students, including Aristotle (384–322 B.C.E.). Following Plato's death in 347 B.C.E., Aristotle left the Academy, tutored the young Alexander before he became "the Great," and eventually founded his own school, the Lyceum in Athens. Aristotle disagreed with Plato on a number of basic philosophical points, most importantly in methodology, for Aristotle believed that direct observation and experiments were the source of true knowledge. In Politics, he compared information from numerous constitutions and sought to understand the difference between a "good" government, which enhanced everyone's life, and a "bad" government, which enriched the lives of a few.

Having established these particulars, we come to consider next the different number of governments which there are, and what they are; and first, what are their excellencies: for when we have determined this, their defects will be evident enough.

It is evident that every form of government or administration, for the words are of the same import, must contain a supreme power over the

---

Aristotle, *Politics* 3:7, 10, trans. J. E. C. Welldon (London: Macmillan, 1883), 78–79, 84.

whole state, and this supreme power must necessarily be in the hands of one person, or a few, or many; and when either of these apply their power for the common good, such states are well governed; but when the interest of the one, the few, or the many who enjoy this power is alone consulted, then ill; for you must either affirm that those who make up the community are not citizens, or else let these share in the advantages of government. We usually call a state which is governed by one person for the common good, a kingdom; one that is governed by more than one, but by a few only, an aristocracy; either because the government is in the hands of the most worthy citizens, or because it is the best form for the city and its inhabitants. When the citizens at large govern for the public good, it is called a state; which is also a common name for all other governments, and these distinctions are consonant to reason; for it will not be difficult to find one person, or a very few, of very distinguished abilities, but almost impossible to meet with the majority of a people eminent for every virtue; but if there is one common to a whole nation it is valor; for this is created and supported by numbers: for which reason in such a state that profession of arms will always have the greatest share in the government.

Now the corruptions attending each of these governments are these; a kingdom may degenerate into a tyranny, an aristocracy into an oligarchy, and a state into a democracy. Now a tyranny is a monarchy where the good of one man only is the object of government, an oligarchy considers only the rich, and a democracy only the poor; but neither of them have a common good in view. . . .

It may also be a doubt where the supreme power ought to be lodged. Shall it be with the majority, or the wealthy, with a number of proper persons, or one better than the rest, or with a tyrant? But whichever of these we prefer some difficulty will arise. For what? Shall the poor have it because they are the majority? They may then divide among themselves what belongs to the rich: nor is this unjust; because truly it has been so judged by the supreme power. But what avails it to point out what is the height of injustice if this is not? Again, if the many seize into their own hands everything which belongs to the few, it is evident that the city will be at an end. But virtue will never destroy what is virtuous; nor can what is right be the ruin of the state: therefore such a law can never be right, nor can the acts of a tyrant ever be wrong, for of necessity they must all be just; for he, from his unlimited power, compels every one to obey his command, as the multitude oppress the rich. Is it right then that the rich, the few, should have the supreme power? And what if they be guilty of the same rapine [theft] and plunder the possessions of the majority, that will be as right as the other: but that all things of this sort are wrong and unjust is evident. Well then, these of the better sort shall have it: but must not then all the other citizens live unhonored, without sharing the offices of the city; for the office of a city are its honors, and if one set of men are always in power, it is evident that the rest must be without honor. Well then, let it be with one person of all others the fittest for it: but by this means the power will be still more contracted, and a greater number than before continue unhonored. But some one may say, that it is wrong to let man have the supreme power and not the law, as his soul is subject to so many passions. But if this law appoints an aristocracy, or a democracy, how will it help us in our present doubts? For those things will happen which we have already mentioned.

READING AND DISCUSSION QUESTIONS

1. According to Aristotle, what are the different types of governments and how are they defined?

2. Aristotle believes that one of the chief problems in organizing a government is determining who should rule. How does Aristotle solve this problem and what is his argument?

3. Aristotle argues that governments tend to become corrupt; for example, a kingdom becomes a tyranny, an aristocracy becomes an oligarchy, and a state becomes a democracy. What is the problem with these corrupt governments? How might good governments be corrupted?

DOCUMENT 5-5

HERODOTUS

From Histories: *On Sparta*

ca. 450–420 B.C.E.

Herodotus is credited with inventing the composition of history. He began writing the Histories, *commonly referred to as* The Persian Wars, *in an attempt to understand the conflict between the Greeks and the Persians.*

Robert B. Strassler, ed., Andrea L. Purvis, trans., *The Landmark Herodotus: The Histories* (New York: Anchor Books, 2007), 536–537, 585–586, 592–593.

In seeking the origins and explanation of the Persian War, he interviewed eyewitnesses and journeyed to places as far as Egypt and the Middle East. For Herodotus, the conflict was between slavery and freedom, although the Persians would have understood the conflict in very different terms. The following passages describe the military capacities of the Greek city-state of Sparta, which dared to challenge the might of the Persians, led by King Xerxes, with 300 soldiers at the battle of Thermopylae.

"So tell me, will the Hellenes [Greeks] stand their ground and use force to resist me? For I think that even if all the Hellenes were assembled together, and even if they joined the peoples who dwell west of them, they still could not match me in battle, and therefore they will not stand their ground when I attack them — unless, that is, they should unite. However, I would like to hear your opinion; do tell me anything you can say about them." That was what Xerxes asked, and Demaratos[14] replied, "Sire, shall I tell you the truth or shall I say what will please you?" Xerxes ordered him to tell the truth, saying that by doing so, Demaratos would please him just as much as he had before.

Upon hearing this, Demaratos said, "Sire, since you insist that I speak the truth and say nothing for which you could later accuse me of falsehood, here it is: in Hellas [Greece], poverty is always and forever a native resident, while excellence is something acquired through intelligence and the force of strict law. It is through the exercise of this excellence that Hellas wards off both poverty and despotism. Now while I commend all the Hellenes who live in the Dorian lands,[15] what I shall next tell you applies not to all of them, but only to the Lacedaemonians.[16] First of all, there is no way that they will accept your stated intention to enslave Hellas; next, even if all the other Hellenes come to see things your way, the Spartans will certainly oppose you in battle. And you need not ask as to their number in order to consider how they could possibly do this, for if there are 1,000 of them marching out, they will fight you, and if they number more or less than that — it makes no difference — they will fight you all the same."

When Xerxes heard this, he laughed and said, "Demaratos, how can you make such a statement — that 1,000 men will fight my troops!" . . .

---

[14] **Demaratos**: A Spartan king living in exile in Persia.

[15] **Dorian lands**: Lands inhabited by Greeks, including the Spartans, who spoke the Doric dialect.

[16] **Lacedaemonians**: Spartans.

To that, Demaratos replied, "Sire, from the beginning of this conversation I knew that if I told you the truth you would not like it. But since you compelled me to speak the absolute truth, I have told you how things stand with the Spartans. . . . The Lacedaemonians are in fact no worse than any other men when they fight individually, but when they unite and fight together, they are the best warriors of all. For though they are free, they are not free in all respects, for they are actually ruled by a lord and master: law is their master, and it is the law that they inwardly fear — much more so than your men fear you. They do whatever it commands, which is always the same: it forbids them to flee from battle, and no matter how many men they are fighting, it orders them to remain in their rank and either prevail or perish. Now if I appear to you to be talking nonsense when I say this, I am quite willing to hold my tongue from now on; I said all this because you compelled me to do so. Nevertheless, sire, I hope that everything turns out in accord with your wishes." . . .

As they deliberated, Xerxes sent a mounted scout to see how many of them there were and what they were doing. While still in Thessaly, the King had heard that a small army was gathered here, and that its leaders were the Lacedaemonians and Leonidas,[17] who traced his lineage to Herakles.[18] When the scout rode up to the camp, he looked around and watched, but could not see the whole army, since some men were posted within the wall that they had rebuilt and were now guarding it, so that it was impossible for the spy to see them. But he did see those outside, whose arms were lying in front of the wall, and it just so happened that at the moment, the Lacedaemonians were the ones posted outside. The scout saw some of these men exercising and others combing their hair, which astonished him. After he had ascertained their number and every other detail, he rode back undisturbed, for no one pursued him; in fact he was practically ignored. When he returned, he reported all that he had seen to Xerxes.

Xerxes listened but could not understand: that the Lacedaemonians were really preparing to kill or be killed, to fight as much as was in their power, seemed to him to be the height of folly, the action of fools. So he sent for Demaratos son of Ariston, who was in the camp, and when Demaratos arrived, Xerxes questioned him about everything he had been told, trying to understand the meaning behind what the Lacedaemonians were doing. Demaratos answered, "You heard what I said about these men before, when we were just setting off against Hellas, and you made me a

---

[17] **Leonidas**: One of the two kings of Sparta.
[18] **Herakles**: Greek mythological hero famous for his strength.

laughingstock when you heard my view of how these matters would turn out. But it is my greatest goal to tell the truth in your presence, so hear me now once again. These men have come to fight us for control of the road, and that is really what they are preparing to do. For it is their tradition that they groom their hair whenever they are about to put their lives in danger. Now know this: if you subjugate these men and those who have remained behind in Sparta, there is no other race of human beings that will be left to raise their hands against you. For you are now attacking the most noble kingdom of all the Hellenes, and the best of men." What Demaratos said seemed quite incredible to Xerxes, and he asked for the second time how they could possibly intend to fight his whole army, since there were so few of them. Demaratos replied, "Sire, if things do not turn out just as I claim they will, treat me like a liar." But even by saying this he did not convince Xerxes. . . .

When on the fifth day, [the Hellenes] had still not gone away but were instead holding their positions in what seemed to [Xerxes] a display of reckless impudence, he lost his temper and ordered the Medes and the Kissians[19] out against them, with instructions to bring them back alive and to conduct them into his presence. The Medes charged headlong into the Hellenes, and great numbers of them fell. Although others rushed forth to replace them, even they could not drive the Hellenes away, though they, too, suffered great losses in the attempt. Indeed, the Hellenes made it clear to everyone, and especially to the King himself, that although there were many in his army, there were few real men. The fighting went on all day.

Since the Medes were suffering extremely rough treatment, they now withdrew, and the Persians under the command of Hydarnes, whom the King called the Immortals, came forth to take their place. There was every expectation that they, at least, would easily prevail, but when they joined battle with the Hellenes, they fared no better than the Medes, and indeed they suffered the very same setbacks. The fighting continued to take place in a confined space, with the Persians using shorter spears than those of the Hellenes and unable to derive any advantage from their superior numbers. The Lacedaemonians fought remarkably well, proving that they were experts in battle who were fighting among men who were not, especially whenever they would turn their backs and feign flight all together, and the barbarians, seeing this, would pursue them with much clatter and shouting; the Lacedaemonians would allow the barbarians to catch up with

---

[19] **the Medes and the Kissians**: Peoples who lived near the Persians. The Persians, Medes, and Kissians shared a common culture.

them and then suddenly turn around to face them, at which point they would slay countless numbers of them. Of the Spartans themselves, however, only a few fell there. Finally the Persians retreated, since despite all their efforts to attack by regiments or by any other means, they could not gain any ground in the pass. . . .

[A Greek traitor informed Xerxes of a path by which the Persians could flank the Greeks' position. Rather than retreating, the Spartans, supported by a group of Thespians (citizens from the Greek city-state of Thespiae), chose to fight to the death.]

Many of the barbarians fell, for the leaders of the regiments were behind them with whips, flogging each and every man and urging them ever forward. Many fell into the sea and died, but even more were trampled alive by one another. There was no counting the number of the dead. The Hellenes knew they were about to face death at the hands of the men who had come around the mountain, and so they exerted their utmost strength against the barbarians, with reckless desperation and no regard for their own lives.

By this time most of their spears had broken, so they were slaying the Persians with their swords. And it was during this struggle that Leonidas fell, the man who had proved himself the most valiant of all, and with him those other famous Spartans whose names I have learned because I think they also proved themselves to be worthy men; indeed, I have learned the names of all 300 of them. . . .

Though the Lacedaemonians and the Thespians alike proved themselves to be brave in this battle, it is said that the Spartan Dienekes proved himself to be the most valiant man of all. It is reported that before the Hellenes engaged the Medes in battle, one of the Trachinians[20] said that there were so many barbarians that whenever they shot their arrows, the sun was blocked by their number. Dienekes was not alarmed to hear this but rather, in total disregard for the vast numbers of Medes, said that what his Trachinian friend had reported was in fact good news, since it meant that while the Medes were blocking the sun, they would fight them in the shade. This saying and others like it have been left as memorials of Dienekes the Lacedaemonian.

After Dienekes, the most outstanding men in this battle are said to be two Lacedaemonian brothers, Alpheos and Maron, sons of Orsiphantos. Of the Thespians, the man who earned the highest distinction was named Dithyrambos son of Harmatides.

---

[20] **Trachinians**: Inhabitants of Trachis, which was near Thermopylae.

They were buried just where they had fallen, and for these men as well as for those who had met their end before Leonidas could send them away, an inscription was erected which says:

Three million foes were once fought right here
By four thousand men from the Peloponnese.

That inscription applied to them all, but the Spartans have one of their own:

Tell this, passerby, to the Lacedaemonians:
It is here that we lie, their commands we obey.

READING AND DISCUSSION QUESTIONS

1. How are the Spartans described? What makes them such good warriors?

2. How is Xerxes portrayed by Herodotus? Does he seem like a good ruler? Why or why not?

VIEWPOINTS
Depicting the Human Form

DOCUMENT 5-6

Zeus from Artemisium

ca. 460 B.C.E.

This bronze statue was discovered in a shipwreck off the coast of the Greek island Euboea. Bronze statues from antiquity are rare because they were normally melted down for their precious metal. This statue stands almost seven feet tall and is thought to represent Zeus. The statue probably origi-nally held a thunderbolt in its right hand and is in position to strike. Ancient

Greek statues are often figures in complete nudity, reflecting the Greeks'
comfort with the nude human form. For example, participants in athletic
competitions never wore clothes.

National Archaeological Museum, Athens.

READING AND DISCUSSION QUESTIONS

1. Describe the position of the figure's arms, legs, and head.
2. Describe this figure's emotions.
3. What does this figure tell us about Greek conceptions of their gods?

DOCUMENT 5-7

The Dying Gaul

ca. 230–220 B.C.E.

In 278 B.C.E, tribes from Gaul (modern France) invaded Greece and later attacked the Greek cities in Asia Minor. One of the Hellenistic kingdoms, Pergamum, defeated the Gauls and later set up a massive monument to commemorate their victory. The original bronze sculpture of this figure has been lost; this Roman copy was discovered during excavations in the seventeenth century. The warrior's only adornment, a torque, and his hair style identify him as a Gallic warrior.

Pinacoteca Capitolini, Palazzo Conservatori, Rome, Italy/Alinari/The Bridgeman Art Library International.

READING AND DISCUSSION QUESTIONS

1. Why is this statue called the Dying Gaul?

2. How is the statue positioned? What is the artist attempting to convey about the Gaul's feelings?

3. What emotions does this statue evoke? What might it tell us about the victors' opinion of their opponents?

COMPARATIVE QUESTIONS

1. Describe the gods in these passages. Specifically, how are the gods in Plato's *Apologia* similar to or different from those in Homer's works?

2. How do the techniques that Socrates and Aristotle used to understand the world differ?

3. What aspects of everyday life are evident in these passages? What aspects are unexamined?

4. Greek civilization is often described as "rational." In what ways do each of these passages support or challenge that characterization?

5. What is similar and different about the two images in this chapter? Which image seems to depict the idealized form and which seems more true to life? Why?

6. How does the experience of being a citizen in Sparta differ from that in Athens described in Plato's *Apologia* and Lysias's *On the Murder of Eratosthenes*?

CHAPTER 6

The World of Rome

750 B.C.E.–400 C.E.

Accoording to tradition, the twins Romulus and Remus, abandoned as infants, founded the city of Rome in 753 B.C.E. on the site where they were discovered and nurtured by a she-wolf. Rome was at first controlled by kings, the last of whom was overthrown in 509 B.C.E., but the founding of the republic put power in the hands of elected officials and the Senate. Over the next five centuries, Rome defeated Carthage and the Hellenistic states, taking complete control of the Mediterranean world. While these victories brought immense wealth to Rome, its powerful leaders plunged the republic into civil war. In 31 B.C.E., the adoptive son of Julius Caesar, who was later known as Augustus, founded the Roman Empire. The Roman Empire expanded its territory even further, moving west and north into Gaul (modern France) and Britain and eastward into Asia, while emperors consolidated power for themselves, slowly restricting the powers of the senatorial class.

DOCUMENT 6-1

The Twelve Tables

ca. 450 B.C.E.

By tradition, Roman laws were not written down and were only interpreted by the patricians (upper-class men) and the priests. In 451 B.C.E., a panel of ten men was appointed to inscribe the laws on stone, possibly to placate plebeian (lower-class) hostility to arbitrary justice. The panel initially produced ten tables and added two more in 450. The original Twelve Tables

---

Oliver J. Thatcher, ed., *The Library of Original Sources* (Milwaukee, Wis.: University Research Extension Co., 1901). Vol. 3: *The Roman World*, 9–11. Modernized by J. S. Arkenberg.

were destroyed when the city of Rome was sacked by the Gauls in the early fourth century B.C.E. and were gradually superseded by later laws. For these reasons, only fragments of the Twelve Tables survive.

Table I

1. If anyone summons a man before the magistrate, he must go. If the man summoned does not go, let the one summoning him call the bystanders to witness and then take him by force.
2. If he shirks or runs away, let the summoner lay hands on him.
3. If illness or old age is the hindrance, let the summoner provide a team. He need not provide a covered carriage with a pallet unless he chooses.
4. Let the protector of a landholder be a landholder; for one of the proletariat, let anyone that cares, be protector. . . .

6–9. When the litigants settle their case by compromise, let the magistrate announce it. If they do not compromise, let them state each his own side of the case, in the *comitium*[1] of the forum before noon. Afterwards let them talk it out together, while both are present. After noon, in case either party has failed to appear, let the magistrate pronounce judgment in favor of the one who is present. If both are present the trial may last until sunset but no later.

Table II

2. He whose witness has failed to appear may summon him by loud calls before his house every third day.

Table III

1. One who has confessed a debt, or against whom judgment has been pronounced, shall have thirty days to pay it in. After that forcible seizure of his person is allowed. The creditor shall bring him before the magistrate. Unless he pays the amount of the judgment or some one in the presence of the magistrate interferes in his behalf as protector the creditor so shall take him home and fasten him in stocks or fetters. He shall fasten him with not less than fifteen pounds of weight or, if he choose, with more. If the prisoner choose, he may

---

[1] **comitium**: A location in the forum in front of the Senate building where speeches were delivered and judicial business was conducted.

furnish his own food. If he does not, the creditor must give him a pound of meal daily; if he choose he may give him more.

2. On the third market day let them divide his body among them. If they cut more or less than each one's share it shall be no crime.

3. Against a foreigner the right in property shall be valid forever.

TABLE IV

1. A dreadfully deformed child shall be quickly killed.

2. If a father sell his son three times, the son shall be free from his father.

3. As a man has provided in his will in regard to his money and the care of his property, so let it be binding. If he has no heir and dies intestate, let the nearest agnate [male relative] have the inheritance. If there is no agnate, let the members of his gens [families belonging to one ancestral group] have the inheritance.

4. If one is mad but has no guardian, the power over him and his money shall belong to his agnates and the members of his gens.

5. A child born after ten months since the father's death will not be admitted into a legal inheritance.

TABLE V

1. Females should remain in guardianship even when they have attained their majority.

TABLE VI

1. When one makes a bond and a conveyance of property, as he has made formal declaration so let it be binding. . . .

3. A beam that is built into a house or a vineyard trellis one may not take from its place. . . .

5. *Usucapio* [obtaining ownership] of movable things requires one year's possession for its completion; but *usucapio* of an estate and buildings two years.

6. Any woman who does not wish to be subjected in this manner to the hand of her husband should be absent three nights in succession every year, and so interrupt the *usucapio* of each year.

TABLE VII

1. Let them keep the road in order. If they have not paved it, a man may drive his team where he likes. . . .

9. Should a tree on a neighbor's farm be bent crooked by the wind and lean over your farm, you may take legal action for removal of that tree.
10. A man might gather up fruit that was falling down onto another man's farm.

TABLE VIII

2. If one has maimed a limb and does not compromise with the injured person, let there be retaliation. If one has broken a bone of a freeman with his hand or with a cudgel, let him pay a penalty of three hundred coins. If he has broken the bone of a slave, let him have one hundred and fifty coins. If one is guilty of insult, the penalty shall be twenty-five coins.
3. If one is slain while committing theft by night, he is rightly slain.
4. If a patron shall have devised any deceit against his client, let him be accursed.
5. If one shall permit himself to be summoned as a witness, or has been a weigher, if he does not give his testimony, let him be noted as dishonest and incapable of acting again as witness. . . .
10. Any person who destroys by burning any building or heap of corn deposited alongside a house shall be bound, scourged [whipped], and put to death by burning at the stake provided that he has committed the said misdeed with malice aforethought; but if he shall have committed it by accident, that is, by negligence, it is ordained that he repair the damage or, if he be too poor to be competent for such punishment, he shall receive a lighter punishment. . . .
12. If the theft has been done by night, if the owner kills the thief, the thief shall be held to be lawfully killed.
13. It is unlawful for a thief to be killed by day. . . . unless he defends himself with a weapon; even though he has come with a weapon, unless he shall use the weapon and fight back, you shall not kill him. And even if he resists, first call out so that someone may hear and come up. . . .
23. A person who had been found guilty of giving false witness shall be hurled down from the Tarpeian Rock.[2] . . .
26. No person shall hold meetings by night in the city.

---

[2] **Tarpeian Rock**: A cliff located on the Capitoline Hill close to the temple of Jupiter. Those convicted of murder or treason during the republic were thrown off of it.

TABLE IX

4. The penalty shall be capital [i.e., execution] for a judge or arbiter legally appointed who has been found guilty of receiving a bribe for giving a decision.
5. Treason: he who shall have roused up a public enemy or handed over a citizen to a public enemy must suffer capital punishment.
6. Putting to death of any man, whosoever he might be unconvicted is forbidden.

TABLE X

1. None is to bury or burn a corpse in the city. . . .
3. The women shall not tear their faces nor wail on account of the funeral. . . .
5. If one obtains a crown himself, or if his chattel does so because of his honor and valor, if it is placed on his head, or the head of his parents, it shall be no crime.

TABLE XI

1. Marriages should not take place between plebeians and patricians.

TABLE XII

2. If a slave shall have committed theft or done damage with his master's knowledge, the action for damages is in the slave's name. . . .
5. Whatever the people had last ordained should be held as binding by law.

READING AND DISCUSSION QUESTIONS

1. From reading the Twelve Tables, what impression do you get of the Roman family? What power did men have over their children and wives?
2. What do these laws tell us about Roman society?
3. What was Roman justice like?

DOCUMENT 6-2

CICERO

The Defense of Marcus Caelius Rufus: Description of Clodia

56 B.C.E.

Cicero is one of the most celebrated Roman writers. A politician, he obtained the highest political office of Rome — consul — in 63 B.C.E. Despite Cicero's position, many senators looked down on him because he was a "new man" (novus homo), whose ancestors had not achieved high political office. In the Roman Republic, any citizen could present arguments in front of juries, and Cicero was widely considered one of the best lawyers available. In this speech, Cicero defends his friend Marcus Caelius Rufus, whose ex-lover, Clodia, accused Caelius of poisoning her and of killing a philosopher named Dio. Clodia happened to be the sister of one of Cicero's political enemies.

Gentlemen, the whole of the case revolves round Clodia. She is a woman of noble birth; but she also has a notorious reputation. My observations about this lady will be limited to what is necessary to refute the charge. You, Cnaeus Domitius [chairman of the tribunal], in your wisdom, must appreciate that she is the one and only person with whom we really have to concern ourselves at all. If she denies she lent Caelius gold, if she puts forward no claim that he tried to poison her, we are, I fear, guilty of disagreeable behaviour for using the name of a married Roman lady in a manner far removed from what is due to such a lady's virtue. Yet since the elimination of this woman from the case will also mean the elimination of every single charge with which Caelius is faced, we who act as his counsel are left with no alternative; if someone attacks Clodius we are obliged to show they are wrong. Indeed, my refutation would be framed in considerably more forcible terms if I did not feel inhibited by the fact that the woman's husband — sorry, I mean brother, I always make that slip — is my personal enemy. Since that is the situation, however, my language will be as moderate as I can make it, and I will go no farther than my conscience and the nature of the action render unavoidable. And indeed I never imagined I

Michael Grant, trans., *Selected Political Speeches of Cicero* (London: Penguin Books, 1969), 183–184, 191–194.

should have to engage in quarrels with women, much less with a woman who has always been widely regarded as having no enemies since she so readily offers intimacy in all directions. . . .

Let youth be permitted its fun, and tender years a measure of liberty. Allow a certain amount of amusement! Do not always give preference to logical, unbending reason. Grant that it should sometimes be overborne by the desires and pleasures of the heart, provided that in so doing the following rule and limitation be observed. A young man must be scrupulous of his own good name and not do violence to that of others. He must not squander his inheritance or become crippled by the interest on his debts. He must not destroy people's homes and reputations. He must not corrupt the uncorrupted, or blemish the virtuous, or bring scandal upon those of good repute. He must refrain from violent intimidation and stay clear of conspiracy and crime. Finally, after he has indulged his taste for entertainments and spent time on love affairs and the trivial passions of youth, he must, eventually, turn back and attend instead to his home, and the business of the Forum, and public life. For he will then have shown that satiety has caused him to discard, and experience to spurn, the things which reason had not hitherto enabled him to see in their true light. . . .

In Marcus Caelius you will find no loose living, no extravagance, no debts, no addiction to parties and low haunts, none of that vice of over-eating and over-drinking which does not diminish but grows with age. Love-making too, the taste for sexual adventures, which does not usually trouble people of reasonably strong character — for such loves are quick to bloom and fade — has never ensnared him in its toils. . . .

Surely that notorious neighbourhood on the Palatine[3] gives us a whiff of what the true facts are. Popular rumour clearly has something to tell us — and so does Baiae.[4] Yes, Baiae does not simply tell us a tale, but rings with the report that there is one woman so deeply sunk in her vicious depravities that she no longer even bothers to seek privacy and darkness and the usual veil of discretion to cover her lusts. On the contrary, she actually exults in displaying the most foully lecherous goings on amid the widest publicity and in the glaring light of day.

All the same, if anyone thinks young men ought to be forbidden affairs even with prostitutes, he is certainly very austere (that I would not deny), but he is out of touch with our present permissive age. Indeed, he is also

---

[3] **notorious neighbourhood on the Palatine**: The Palatine was the home of the wealthiest individuals in the republic.

[4] **Baiae**: A resort near Naples frequented by the wealthy Roman elite.

not in harmony with the customs of our ancestors, and the allowances which even in those times people were quite accustomed to make. For name any epoch when this was not invariably the case. When was such behaviour ever censured or forbidden? When was the permitted thing not permitted?

I will just propound a general theme, without mentioning any particular woman by name — that much I will leave open. If a woman who has no husband throws open her home to every debauchee and publicly leads the life of a whore; if she makes a habit of being entertained by men who are total strangers; if she pursues this mode of existence in the city, in her own gardens, among all the crowds at Baiae; if, in fact, she behaves in such a way that not only her general demeanour but also her dress and associates, her hot eyes and uninhibited language, her embraces and kisses, her beach parties and water parties and dinner parties, all show that she is not only a prostitute but a lewd and depraved prostitute at that; if a young man should happen to be found in the company of such a woman, then surely, Lucius Herennius,[5] you would agree that this was not so much adultery as just plain sex — not an outrage to chastity, but mere satisfaction of appetite. . . .

[After this, Cicero continues attacking Clodia based on her close connection with slaves, whose company the Romans considered beneath that of the elites.]

And, I ask, what type of slaves? For this point, too, is of considerable importance. If they belonged to Clodia, would not Caelius have known they were not living at all the ordinary life of a slave, but were enjoying a far more relaxed, undisciplined, familiar relationship with their mistress? For in a household of that sort, gentlemen, under a woman who behaves like a prostitute, where everything that happens is quite unfit to be published abroad, where abnormal lusts and excesses and unheard-of perversions and vices of every kind are rife, it is perfectly obvious and universally known that slaves are slaves no longer. For everything is delegated to them and put in their charge, they become her associates in all her loose living, they share her secrets, and they make a good bit every day from her extravagant expenditure. Was Caelius unaware of all these things? If he was as intimate with the woman as you say he was, then he must, surely, have realized she treated those slaves as her intimates too. The alternative supposition is that he was *not* so friendly with her as you allege. But, that being so, how could he have had such a close connexion with her slaves?

---

[5] **Lucius Herennius**: One of the prosecutors.

READING AND DISCUSSION QUESTIONS

1. How does Cicero describe Clodia? By implication, how would a "good" Roman woman live her life?

2. What are the characteristics of a virtuous elite male in the Roman Republic?

3. Given Cicero's defense of Marcus Caelius Rufus, would you have voted to convict or acquit him? Explain.

4. How does this passage describe the life of upper-class Romans?

DOCUMENT 6-3

PLUTARCH

On Julius Caesar, A Man of Unlimited Ambition

ca. 44 C.E.

Plutarch's Parallel Lives *served as the greatest source of knowledge about the ancient world for people of the Renaissance and for Shakespeare, even though its original intent was not to preserve history, but rather to examine moral virtues and vices. Plutarch was committed to supporting the Roman Empire and later became a priest at the Greek oracle shrine at Delphi. The following document, written about 150 years after the death of Julius Caesar, describes Roman attitudes toward the power that Julius Caesar gained following a civil war victory against the general Pompey.*

But that which brought upon him the most apparent and mortal hatred was his desire of being king,[6] which gave the common people the first occasion to quarrel with him, and proved the most specious pretence to those who had been his secret enemies all along. Those who would have procured him that title gave it out that it was foretold in the Sibyls' books[7]

Plutarch, *Parallel Lives,* "Julius Caesar," trans. John Dryden, rev. Arthur Hugh Clough (New York: Modern Library, n.d.), 888–890.

[6] **his desire of being king**: The Romans feared the tyranny of kings.
[7] **Sybils' books**: Books of prophecy that were consulted in Rome during times of crisis.

that the Romans should conquer the Parthians[8] when they fought against them under the conduct of a king, but not before. And one day, as Caesar was coming down from Alba to Rome, some were so bold as to salute him by the name of king; but he, finding the people disrelish it, seemed to resent it himself, and said his name was Caesar, not king. Upon this there was a general silence, and he passed on looking not very well pleased or contented. Another time, when the senate had conferred on him some extravagant honors, he chanced to receive the message as he was sitting on the rostra [podium], where, though the consuls [highest elected officials] and praetors [elected ministers of justice] themselves waited on him, attended by the whole body of the senate, he did not rise, but behaved himself to them as if they had been private men, and told them his honors wanted rather to be retrenched than increased. This treatment offended not only the senate, but the commonalty too, as if they thought the affront upon the senate equally reflected upon the whole republic; so that all who could decently leave him went off, looking much discomposed. Caesar, perceiving the false step he had made, immediately retired home; and laying his throat bare, told his friends that he was ready to offer this to any one would give the stroke. But afterwards he made the malady from which he suffered [epilepsy] the excuse for his sitting, saying that those who are attacked by it lose their presence of mind if they talk much standing; that they presently grow giddy, fall into convulsions, and quite lose their reason. But this was not the reality, for he would willingly have stood up to the senate, had not Cornelius Balbus, one of his friends, or rather flatterers, hindered him. "Will you not remember," said he, "you are Caesar, and claim the honor which is due to your merit?"

He gave a fresh occasion of resentment by his affront to the tribunes.[9] The Lupercalia were then celebrated, a feast at the first institution belonging, as some writers say, to the shepherds, and having some connection with the Arcadian Lycae [a mountain in Greece]. Many young noblemen and magistrates run up and down the city with their upper garments

---

[8] **Parthians**: The only civilized power on Rome's frontiers, the Parthians controlled Mesopotamia and Persia. They were famous horsemen and developed the "Parthian shot," which allowed them to shoot arrows while riding away from attackers.

[9] **tribunes**: Tribunes of the Plebs, which were originally created to defend the plebian class of citizens against the patricians who dominated the early Roman government and which could veto actions and laws they thought would harm the plebians. By the time of Caesar, the Tribunes of the Plebs were often working for their own benefit.

off, striking all they meet with thongs of hide, by way of sport; and many women, even of the highest rank, place themselves in the way, and hold out their hands to the lash, as boys in a school do to the master, out of a belief that it procures an easy labor to those who are with child, and makes those conceive who are barren. Caesar, dressed in a triumphal robe, seated himself in a golden chair at the rostra to view this ceremony. Antony [i.e., Mark Antony, Caesar's closest ally], as consul, was one of those who ran this course, and when he came into the forum, and the people made way for him, he went up and reached to Caesar a diadem wreathed with laurel [like a king's crown]. Upon this there was a shout, but only a slight one, made by the few who were planted there for that purpose; but when Caesar refused it, there was universal applause. Upon the second offer, very few, and upon the second refusal, all again applauded. Caesar finding it would not take, rose up, and ordered the crown to be carried into the capitol. Caesar's statues were afterwards found with royal diadems on their heads. Flavius and Marullus, two tribunes of the people, went presently and pulled them off, and having apprehended those who first saluted Caesar as king committed them to prison. The people followed them with acclamations, and called them by the name of Brutus, because Brutus was the first who ended the succession of kings,[10] and transferred the power which before was lodged in one man into the hands of the senate and people. Caesar so far resented this, that he displaced Marullus and Flavius; and in urging his charges against them, at the same time ridiculed the people, by himself giving the men more than once the names of Bruti and Cumaei.[11]

This made the multitude turn their thoughts to Marcus Brutus, who, by his father's side, was thought to be descended from that first Brutus, and by his mother's side from the Servilii, another noble family, being besides nephew and son-in-law to Cato. But the honors and favors he had received from Caesar took off the edge from the desires he might himself have felt for overthrowing the new monarchy. For he had not only been pardoned himself after Pompey's defeat at Pharsalia, and had procured the same grace for many of his friends, but was one in whom Caesar had a

---

[10] **was the first . . . kings:** In 509 B.C.E., Lucius Brutus removed the last king from Rome.

[11] **Bruti and Cumaei:** Both names suggest that Caesar was calling the people stupid. The name Brutus means "stupid" and people from Cumae were thought to lack intelligence.

particular confidence. He had at that time the most honorable praetorship for the year, and was named for the consulship four years after, being preferred before Cassius, his competitor. Upon the question as to the choice, Caesar, it is related, said that Cassius had the fairer pretensions, but that he could not pass by Brutus. Nor would he afterwards listen to some who spoke against Brutus, when the conspiracy against him was already afoot, but laying his hand on his body, said to the informers, "Brutus will wait for this skin of mine," intimating that he was worthy to bear rule on account of his virtue, but would not be base and ungrateful to gain it. Those who desired a change, and looked on him as the only, or at least the most proper, person to effect it, did not venture to speak with him; but in the night-time laid papers about his chair of state, where he used to sit and determine causes, with such sentences in them as, "You are asleep, Brutus," "You are no longer Brutus." Cassius, when he perceived his ambition a little raised upon this, was more insistent than before to work him yet further, having himself a private grudge against Caesar[12] for some reasons that we have mentioned in the Life of Brutus.[13] Nor was Caesar without suspicions of him, and said once to his friends, "What do you think Cassius is aiming at? I don't like him, he looks so pale." And when it was told him that Antony and Dolabella[14] were in a plot against him, he said he did not fear such fat, luxurious men, but rather the pale, lean fellows, meaning Cassius and Brutus.

READING AND DISCUSSION QUESTIONS

1. What was the Roman attitude toward Caesar becoming king? What was the difference between the views of the senators and those of the common people?

2. How did the plot against Caesar develop? What justification did Brutus and Cassius use to support their assassination of Caesar?

---

[12] **a private grudge against Caesar**: Cassius was angry that Caesar had promoted Brutus over him.

[13] **Life of Brutus**: Another one of Plutarch's *Parallel Lives*.

[14] **Dolabella**: A general who originally sided with Pompey, but later joined with Caesar, who rewarded him with the consulship.

> ### DOCUMENT 6-4

TACITUS
From The Annals: *On the Legacy of Augustus*
98 C.E.

The historian Tacitus (ca. 56–118 C.E.) was born in Gaul, moved to Rome, and held several important positions there, including the office of consul for the Roman Empire. He survived a reign of terror by the Emperor Domitian, which made him distrust the power of the Roman emperors. One of his works, The Annals, *describes the first dynasty of emperors, who succeeded the emperor Augustus. In this passage, Tacitus describes how Romans thought about the legacy of Augustus upon his death.*

On the day of the funeral soldiers stood as if forming a garrison, much to the derision of those who had seen personally or who had heard from their parents about that day of still undigested servitude and of freedom served up again unsuccessfully, when the slaughter of the dictator Caesar seemed to some the worst of acts, to others the finest. Now, they said, an elderly princeps, despite the longevity of his power, and having even provided the state with resources in the form of heirs, would evidently require protecting by military assistance to ensure that his burial was peaceful!

Afterward there was much conversation about Augustus himself, with the majority in empty wonder that the day of his first receiving command all that time ago was the same as the last of his life, and that he had ended his life in the same bedroom of the house at Nola as his father, Octavius. Also celebrated was the number of his consulships, in which he had equaled Valerius Corvus[15] and C. Marius[16] jointly; the continuation of his tribunician power for thirty-seven years; the name of "commander," acquired twenty-one times, and his other honors, whether multiplied or novel.

A. J. Woodman, trans., *Tacitus: The Annals* (Indianapolis: Hackett, 2004), 7–9.

[15] **Valerius Corvus**: Was consul six times and defeated one of Rome's earliest enemies, the Samnites.

[16] **C. Marius**: Reformed the Roman army, making it personally loyal to its commanders. He was consul seven times.

Among the perspicacious, however, his life was variously extolled or criticized. The former said that, because of devotion to his parent and the requirements of the state, in which at that time there had been no place for law, he had been driven to civil war, which could be neither prepared for nor maintained by good behavior. He had made many concessions to Antonius while avenging himself on the killers of his father, many to Lepidus;[17] after the latter had aged from apathy, and the former had been sunk by this lusts, there had been no other remedy for his disaffected fatherland than that it be ruled by one man. Yet it was neither on kingly rule nor dictatorship but on the name of "princeps" that the state had been based. The empire was cordoned by the sea of Ocean or distant streams; legions, provinces, fleets, everything was interconnected; there was legality among citizens, restraint among allies; the City itself was magnificent in its apparel; just a few things had been handled by force to ensure peace for the rest.

It was said on the other side that devotion to his parent and the times in the state had been taken up as a screen; in reality it was in a desire for domination that veterans had been mustered by his lavishness, an army procured by a juvenile in his private capacity, a consul's legions bribed, and support for the Pompeian party pretended. Subsequently, when by a decree of the fathers he had assailed the fasces and prerogative of a praetor, after the slaughter of Hirtius and Pansa[18] (whether they had been carried off by the enemy, or Pansa by poison poured into a wound and Hirtius by his own soldiers and by Caesar's engineering of guile) he had taken over the forces of both. The consulship had been extorted from an unwilling senate, and the arms which he had been given to deal with Antonius were turned against the state. The proscription of citizens and distributions of land had not been praised even by those who did them. Of course the ends of Cassius and the Bruti had been a concession to paternal antagonisms (although it was proper to forgo private hatreds for the public good); but Pompeius had been deceived by a phantom peace, Lepidus by a display of friendship; and subsequently Antonius, enticed by the Tarentine and Brundisian treaties and by a wedding to his sister,[19] had paid the penalty of

---

[17] **Lepidus**: One of Caesar's most trusted generals and a Triumvir with Antony and Octavian (later Augustus).

[18] **Hirtius and Pansa**: Consuls for the year 43. Both died fighting Antony in northern Italy, and Octavian took control of their armies.

[19] **Antonius . . . a wedding to his sister**: Antony married Octavian's sister before falling in love with Cleopatra.

a guileful relationship with his death. Peace there had been without doubt after that, but gory: there had been the Lollian and Varian disasters, and the killing at Rome of Varrones, Egnatii, and Iulli.[20]

Nor was there any abstention from family matters. Nero's wife had been abducted from him, and there was the mockery of consulting pontiffs on the question whether it was right for her to wed after conceiving but before producing a child. [. . .] and Vedius Pollio's luxuriousness.[21] Finally there was Livia,[22] her burden on the state as a mother being matched by that on the Caesars' family as a stepmother. Nothing was left with which to honor the gods, since he wished himself to be worshiped with temples and with the likenesses of a divinity by flamines and priests. Not even Tiberius had been adopted as successor through any affection or any concern for the state, but, because he had had insight into the man's arrogance and savagery, by the basest of comparisons he had sought glory for himself. (Indeed a few years before, when Augustus was again demanding tribunician power from the fathers for Tiberius, despite an honorific speech he had tossed out some comments on his demeanor, lifestyle, and habits in order to decry what he seemed to defend.)

As for his burial, once it had been completed according to custom, a temple and heavenly rituals were decreed. Prayers were then redirected toward Tiberius; and he for his part began to talk variously about the magnitude of command and his own limitations: only Divine Augustus had been mentally capable of such a great undertaking on his own; having himself been summoned by Augustus for partnership in his cares, he had learned by experience how steep, how exposed to fortune, was the burden of ruling everything. Accordingly, in a community supported by such numbers of illustrious men, it should not be the case that they tendered all things to a single individual: several would more easily carry out the responsibilities of state by sharing the labors.

---

[20] **the Lollian and Varian disasters, . . . Iulli**: Roman troops led by Lollius and Varus were defeated, and a few Roman aristocrats were executed for treason.

[21] **Vedius Pollio's luxuriousness**: Vedius Pollio was known for feeding his slaves to eels and for excessive living. He was rebuked by Augustus for the treatment of his slaves.

[22] **Livia**: Octavian married Livia while she was pregnant with her first husband's child.

READING AND DISCUSSION QUESTIONS

1. What are the two views of Augustus presented in this passage?
2. Reading between the lines, how do you think Tacitus feels about Augustus? What tone does he use to describe Augustus?
3. How does Tacitus describe Tiberius, who was Augustus's successor?

DOCUMENT 6-5

JESUS OF NAZARETH
Sermon on the Mount (Matthew, Chapter 5)
ca. 30 C.E.

Nothing was written about Jesus in his own lifetime, and later accounts of his life, chiefly the Gospels in the New Testament, were written to convey certain religious, not historical, truths about who Jesus was. The broad outlines are clear: he was born around 3 B.C.E., preached in the last years of his life, and was crucified around 33 C.E. during the reign of the Roman emperor Tiberius. Although later followers developed a new religion, Christianity, around the death of Jesus, his ethical teachings, such as those in this passage, were in line with contemporary Jewish thought.

MATTHEW 5

[1] Seeing the crowds, he went up on the mountain, and when he sat down his disciples came to him.

[2] And he opened his mouth and taught them, saying:

[3] "Blessed are the poor in spirit, for theirs is the kingdom of heaven.

[4] "Blessed are those who mourn, for they shall be comforted.

[5] "Blessed are the meek, for they shall inherit the earth.

[6] "Blessed are those who hunger and thirst for righteousness, for they shall be satisfied.

[7] "Blessed are the merciful, for they shall obtain mercy.

Matthew 5:1–48 from the *New Revised Standard Version of the Bible.*

[8] "Blessed are the pure in heart, for they shall see God.

[9] "Blessed are the peacemakers, for they shall be called sons of God.

[10] "Blessed are those who are persecuted for righteousness' sake, for theirs is the kingdom of heaven.

[11] "Blessed are you when men revile you and persecute you and utter all kinds of evil against you falsely on my account.

[12] "Rejoice and be glad, for your reward is great in heaven, for so men persecuted the prophets who were before you.

[13] "You are the salt of the earth; but if salt has lost its taste, how shall its saltness be restored? It is no longer good for anything except to be thrown out and trodden under foot by men.

[14] "You are the light of the world. A city set on a hill cannot be hid. [15] Nor do men light a lamp and put it under a bushel, but on a stand, and it gives light to all in the house. [16] Let your light so shine before men, that they may see your good works and give glory to your Father who is in heaven.

[17] "Think not that I have come to abolish the law and the prophets; I have come not to abolish them but to fulfil them. [18] For truly, I say to you, till heaven and earth pass away, not an iota, not a dot, will pass from the law until all is accomplished. [19] Whoever then relaxes one of the least of these commandments and teaches men so, shall be called least in the kingdom of heaven; but he who does them and teaches them shall be called great in the kingdom of heaven. [20] For I tell you, unless your righteousness exceeds that of the scribes and Pharisees, you will never enter the kingdom of heaven.

[21] "You have heard that it was said to the men of old, 'You shall not kill; and whoever kills shall be liable to judgment.' [22] But I say to you that every one who is angry with his brother shall be liable to judgment; whoever insults his brother shall be liable to the council, and whoever says, 'You fool!' shall be liable to the hell of fire. [23] So if you are offering your gift at the altar, and there remember that your brother has something against you, [24] leave your gift there before the altar and go; first be reconciled to your brother, and then come and offer your gift. [25] Make friends quickly with your accuser, while you are going with him to court, lest your accuser hand you over to the judge, and the judge to the guard, and you be put in prison; [26] truly, I say to you, you will never get out till you have paid the last penny.

[27] "You have heard that it was said, 'You shall not commit adultery.' [28] But I say to you that every one who looks at a woman lustfully has already committed adultery with her in his heart. [29] If your right eye causes you to sin, pluck it out and throw it away; it is better that you lose one of your members than that your whole body be thrown into hell. [30] And if your right hand causes you to sin, cut it off and throw it away; it is better that you lose one of your members than that your whole body go into hell.

[31] "It was also said, 'Whoever divorces his wife, let him give her a certificate of divorce.' [32] But I say to you that every one who divorces his wife, except on the ground of unchastity, makes her an adulteress; and whoever marries a divorced woman commits adultery.

[33] "Again you have heard that it was said to the men of old, 'You shall not swear falsely, but shall perform to the Lord what you have sworn.' [34] But I say to you, Do not swear at all, either by heaven, for it is the throne of God, [35] or by the earth, for it is his footstool, or by Jerusalem, for it is the city of the great King. [36] And do not swear by your head, for you cannot make one hair white or black. [37] Let what you say be simply 'Yes' or 'No'; anything more than this comes from evil.

[38] "You have heard that it was said, 'An eye for an eye and a tooth for a tooth.' [39] But I say to you, Do not resist one who is evil. But if any one strikes you on the right cheek, turn to him the other also; [40] and if any one would sue you and take your coat, let him have your cloak as well; [41] and if any one forces you to go one mile, go with him two miles. [42] Give to him who begs from you, and do not refuse him who would borrow from you.

[43] "You have heard that it was said, 'You shall love your neighbor and hate your enemy.' [44] But I say to you, Love your enemies and pray for those who persecute you, [45] so that you may be sons of your Father who is in heaven; for he makes his sun rise on the evil and on the good, and sends rain on the just and on the unjust. [46] For if you love those who love you, what reward have you? Do not even the tax collectors do the same? [47] And if you salute only your brethren, what more are you doing than others? Do not even the Gentiles do the same? [48] You, therefore, must be perfect, as your heavenly Father is perfect.

READING AND DISCUSSION QUESTIONS

1. Who does Jesus say is blessed?
2. What does Jesus say about his teachings and their relation to Jewish law?
3. According to Jesus, how should a person live his or her life?

VIEWPOINTS

Christianity and the Roman State

DOCUMENT 6-6

PLINY THE YOUNGER

Letters to and from the Emperor Trajan on Christians

111–113 C.E.

The Emperor Trajan sent the senator Pliny the Younger to the province of Bithynia (modern northwest Turkey) to deal with problems arising from bankrupt municipal finances and reports of illegal meetings and political activity. Pliny had previously served with distinction in the imperial service, even obtaining the political office of consul. Despite being distant from Rome, Pliny repeatedly asked the emperor for advice, as he does in this passage. In his investigations, he discovered that meetings were taking place illegally among people calling themselves Christians.

PLINY TO THE EMPEROR TRAJAN

It is my custom to refer all my difficulties to you, Sir, for no one is better able to resolve my doubts and to inform my ignorance.

Betty Radice, trans., *The Letters of the Younger Pliny* (London: Penguin Books, 1963), 293–295.

I have never been present at an examination of Christians. Consequently, I do not know the nature of the extent of the punishments usually meted out to them, nor the grounds for starting an investigation and how far it should be pressed. Nor am I at all sure whether any distinction should be made between them on the grounds of age, or if young people and adults should be treated alike; whether a pardon ought to be granted to anyone retracting his beliefs, or if he has once professed Christianity, he shall gain nothing by renouncing it; and whether it is the mere name of Christian which is punishable, even if innocent of crime, or rather the crimes associated with the name.

For the moment this is the line I have taken with all persons brought before me on the charge of being Christians. I have asked them in person if they are Christians, and if they admit it, I repeat the question a second and third time, with a warning of the punishment awaiting them. If they persist, I order them to be led away for execution; for, whatever the nature of their admission, I am convinced that their stubbornness and unshakable obstinacy ought not to go unpunished. There have been others similarly fanatical who are Roman citizens. I have entered them on the list of persons to be sent to Rome for trial.

Now that I have begun to deal with this problem, as so often happens, the charges are becoming more widespread and increasing in variety. An anonymous pamphlet has been circulated which contains the names of a number of accused persons. Amongst these I considered that I should dismiss any who denied that they were or ever had been Christians when they had repeated after me a formula of invocation to the gods and had made offerings of wine and incense to your statue[23] (which I had ordered to be brought into court for this purpose along with the images of the gods), and furthermore had reviled the name of Christ: none of which things, I understand, any genuine Christian can be induced to do.

Others, whose names were given to me by an informer, first admitted the charge and then denied it; they said that they had ceased to be Christians two or more years previously, and some of them even twenty years ago. They all did reverence to your statue and the images of the gods in the same way as the others, and reviled the name of Christ. They also declared that the sum total of their guilt or error amounted to no more

---

[23] **offerings of wine and incense to your statue**: All inhabitants of the Roman Empire were supposed to make sacrifices for the well-being of the emperor and the empire, usually of incense. Some groups, such as the Jews, were exempted.

than this: they had met regularly before dawn on a fixed day to chant verses alternately amongst themselves in honour of Christ as if to a god, and also to bind themselves by oath, not for any criminal purpose, but to abstain from theft, robbery, and adultery, to commit no breach of trust and not to deny a deposit when called upon to restore it. After this ceremony it had been their custom to disperse and reassemble later to take food of an ordinary, harmless kind; but they had in fact given up this practice since my edict, issued on your instructions, which banned all political societies. This made me decide it was all the more necessary to extract the truth by torture from two slave-women, whom they call deaconesses. I found nothing but a degenerate sort of cult carried to extravagant lengths.

I have therefore postponed any further examination and hastened to consult you. The question seems to me to be worthy of your consideration, especially in view of the number of persons endangered; for a great many individuals of every age and class, both men and women, are being brought to trial, and this is likely to continue. It is not only the towns, but villages and rural districts too which are infected through contact with this wretched cult. I think though that it is still possible for it to be checked and directed to better ends, for there is no doubt that people have begun to throng the temples which had been almost entirely deserted for a long time; the sacred rites which had been allowed to lapse are being performed again, and flesh of sacrificial victims is on sale everywhere, though up till recently scarcely anyone could be found to buy it. It is easy to infer from this that a great many people could be reformed if they were given an opportunity to repent.

Trajan's Reply to Pliny

You have followed the right course of procedure, my dear Pliny, in your examination of the cases of persons charged with being Christians, for it is impossible to lay down a general rule to a fixed formula. These people must not be hunted out; if they are brought before you and the charge against them is proved, they must be punished, but in the case of anyone who denies that he is a Christian, and makes it clear that he is not by offering prayers to our gods, he is to be pardoned as a result of his repentance however suspect his past conduct may be. But pamphlets circulated anonymously must play no part in any accusation. They create the worst sort of precedent and are quite out of keeping with the spirit of our age.

READING AND DISCUSSION QUESTIONS

1. How does Pliny describe the Christian beliefs and activities that he discovered?

2. How did Pliny investigate those who were suspected of being Christians?

3. What instructions did Trajan give to Pliny regarding the treatment of Christians?

4. What does this passage reveal about the day-to-day governing of the Roman Empire?

DOCUMENT 6-7

TERTULLIAN

From Apologia

ca. 197 C.E.

The earliest Christians originated in the Near East and the entire New Testament of the Christian Bible was composed in the koine *(common) Greek spoken throughout eastern provinces of the Roman Empire. However, by the late second century, Christianity had attracted a number of converts in the western half of the empire as well. One of these converts, Tertullian (ca. 160–240), was the first Christian of note who wrote in Latin. His most famous work, the* Apologia, *presents a defense of Christianity against Roman persecution and is excerpted below. Tertullian would exert enormous influence on later Christians in the West, including Saint Augustine (Document 8-2).*

Magistrates of the Roman Empire! You who are seated for the administration of justice in almost the highest position of the state[24] and under the gaze of everyone! If you are not allowed to conduct an open examination, face to face, into the truth regarding the Christians, if in this case alone

---

Rev. S. Thelwell, trans., *Ante-Nicene Fathers*, vol. 3 (Buffalo: The Christian Literature Publishing Co., 1885–1886). Modernized by Walter Ward.

[24] **You who are seated . . . state:** In theory, a Roman citizen could appeal a judgment made by a provincial governor to the emperor.

you fear or are ashamed to exercise your authority to conduct a public investigation with the care that justice demands, if, finally, the extreme hatred shown this group (as happened recently in the domestic courts) has been raised to such a level that it inhibits their defense, then let the truth reach your ears by the secret pathway of silent literature. . . .

If it is certain that we are the most criminal of people, why do you treat us differently from others of our kind, namely all other criminals? The same crime should receive the same treatment. When others are charged with the same crimes imputed to us, they are permitted to use their own mouths and the hired advocacy of others to plead their innocence. They have full freedom to answer the charge and to cross-examine. In fact, it is against the law to condemn anyone without a defense and a hearing. Only Christians are forbidden to say anything in defense of the truth that would clear their case and assist the judge in avoiding an injustice. All that they care about (and this by itself is enough to arouse public hatred) is a confession to bearing the name "Christian," not an investigation of the charge. Now, let us assume you are trying any other criminal. If he confesses to the crime of murder, or sacrilege, or sexual debauchery, or treason — to cite the crimes of which we stand accused — you are not content to pass sentence immediately. Rather, you weigh the relevant circumstances: the nature of the deed; how often, where, how, and when it was committed; the co-conspirators and the partners-in-crime. Nothing of this sort is done in our case. Yet, whenever that false charge is brought against us, we should equally be made to confess: How many murdered babies has one eaten? How many illicit sexual acts has one performed under cover of darkness? Which cooks and which dogs were there? Oh, how great would be the glory of that governor who should bring to light a Christian who has already devoured 100 babies!

To the contrary, we find that it is forbidden to hunt us down. When Pliny the Younger was a provincial governor and had condemned some Christians to death and had intimidated others to abandon the steadfastness of their faith, he was still concerned by their sheer numbers and worried about what to do in the future. So he consulted Trajan, the reigning emperor [ca. 98–117]. Pliny explained that, other than their obstinate refusal to offer sacrifice, he had learned nothing else about their religious ceremonies, except that they met before daybreak to sing hymns to Christ and God and to bind themselves by oath to a way of life that forbids murder, adultery, fraud, treachery, and all other crimes. Trajan then wrote back that people of this sort should not be hunted down, but, when brought to court, they should be punished.

What a decision! How inevitably self-contradictory! He declares that they should not be hunted down, as though they are innocent. Then he prescribes that they be punished, as though they are guilty. He spares them, yet he directs his anger upon them. He pretends to shut his eyes, yet he calls attention to them. Judges, why do you tie yourself up in knots? If you condemn them why not hunt them down? If you do not hunt them down, why not also find them innocent?

Throughout all the provinces, soldiers are assigned by lot to hunt down bandits. When it comes to traitors and public enemies each person is a soldier. Inquiry extends even to one's associates and confederates. The Christian alone may not be hunted down, but he may be brought to court, as if hunting down led to anything other than being haled [hauled] into court. So, you condemn someone who is haled into court, although no one wished to seek him out. He has not merited punishment, I suppose, because he is guilty, but because, forbidden to be looked for, he was found! . . .

A person shouts out, "I am a Christian." He says what he is. You want to hear what he is not. You preside to extort the truth, yet in our case alone you take infinite pains to hear a lie. "I am," he says, "what you ask if I am. Why torture me to twist the fact around? I confess, and you torture me. What would you do if I denied?" Clearly when others deny you do not readily believe them. In our case, when we deny, you immediately believe us. . . .

Inasmuch as you treat us differently from all other criminals, which you do by concentrating on disassociating us from that name (for we are cut off from the name "Christian" only if we do what non-Christians do), you must know that there is no crime whatsoever in our case. It is only a name. . . .

So much for my preface, as it were, which is intended to beat into submission the injustice of the public hatred felt for us. Now I take the stand to plead our innocence. . . .

We are said to be the worst of criminals because of our sacramental baby-killing and the baby-eating that accompanies it and the sexual license that follows the banquet, where dogs are our pimps in darkness when they overturn candles and procure a certain modesty for our impious lusts.[25] We are always spoken of in this way, yet you take no pains to investigate the charges that you have made against us for so long. If you believe them, investigate them. Otherwise, stop believing what you do not

---

[25] **where . . . impious lusts:** A rumor stated that dogs were used to extinguish the candles. Strings were attached to the dog's tails and to the candles so that when the dogs were thrown food the dogs would leap and cause the candles to fall over.

investigate. The fact that you look the other way suggests that the evil that you yourselves dare not investigate does not exist. . . .

You say, "You do not worship the [traditional Greek and Roman] gods, and you do not offer sacrifices for the emperors." It follows logically that we do not offer sacrifices for others because we do not do so even for ourselves. All of this is a consequence of our not worshipping the gods. So we are accused of sacrilege and treason. This is the chief case against us. In fact, it is the whole case. . . . Your gods we cease to worship from the moment we recognize they are not gods. So that is what you ought to require us to prove — that those gods do not exist and for that reason should not be worshipped because they deserve worship only if they are gods.

READING AND DISCUSSION QUESTIONS

1. According to Tertullian, what proof was necessary to convict someone of being a Christian? Of what crimes were Christians accused?

2. What problems does Tertullian describe concerning the persecution of Christians? How were Christian court cases unique?

3. Why did the Christians refuse to make sacrifices to the emperors? How did the Roman authorities interpret this defiance?

COMPARATIVE QUESTIONS

1. How do the writings of Plutarch and Tacitus reflect changing attitudes toward the rule of one man (king, dictator, and emperor) during different periods of Roman history?

2. How does Cicero's depiction of family and gender relations differ from that in the Twelve Tables?

3. How do Cicero's tactics in defense of Marcus Caelius Rufus compare to those in Lysias's *On the Murder of Eratosthenes* (Document 5-2)? Also compare what these documents say about the lives of women in Roman and Greek society.

4. How does Jesus reinterpret the Hebrew Law, including the Ten Commandments, in "Book of Exodus: Moses Leads the Hebrews from Egypt" (Document 2-5)?

5. What kind of relationship did Christians have with the Roman state according to Pliny and Tertullian?

CHAPTER 7

East Asia and the Spread of Buddhism

221 B.C.E.–800 C.E.

The Qin Dynasty (221–206 B.C.E.) conquered the "warring states" of China and created what Qin Shihuangdi (259–210 B.C.E.) hoped would be an empire that would last for 10,000 years. However, the brutal strategies of control espoused by Legalism, a philosophy that called for strict adherence to laws and a ruler with absolute power, ended the dynasty in just fourteen years. When the Han Dynasty (206 B.C.E.–220 C.E.) took control of China, they maintained a traditional focus on Confucianism and rejected the Qin's harsh punishments. Following the Han's collapse, nomadic groups from Central Asia took power in northern China, while southern China was ruled by a succession of unsuccessful dynasties. Buddhism became increasingly influential in this "Age of Division" (220–589 C.E.); Islam and Christianity also appeared in China but were less popular. When the Sui (581–618 C.E.) and Tang (618–907 C.E.) Dynasties reestablished formal control over all of China, neighboring societies in Korea, Tibet, Vietnam, and Japan began to imitate Chinese rule and culture.

DOCUMENT 7-1

SIMA QIAN

From the Records of the Historian:
On the Xiongnu

ca. 109–86 B.C.E.

Sima Qian is considered the founder of Chinese historical writing. By inter-viewing eyewitnesses, traveling, and collecting old records, he hoped to write a history of China and its neighbors from the beginning of Chinese civiliza-tion. He had access to official documents from his position in the imperial government, but he lost favor when he defended a scapegoat for military disasters against the Xiongnu (nomads north of China). His punishment was castration. In the following passage, Sima Qian describes the customs of the Xiongnu.

The ancestor of the Xiongnu descended from the ruler of the Xia dynasty, whose name was Qun Wei. From before the time of Emperors Yao and Shun [third millennium B.C.E.], there have been barbarians . . . living in northern uncivilized areas and wandering around herding animals. They herd mainly horses, cattle, and sheep, but also some unusual animals, such as camels, donkeys, mules, and wild horses. . . . They move around looking for water and pasture and have no walled settlements or permanent housing. They do not farm, but they do divide their land into separate holdings under different leaders. They have no writing, and all contracts are verbal. When their children can ride a sheep, they begin to use bows and arrows to shoot birds and rodents. When they are older, they shoot foxes and rabbits for food. In this way, all the young men are easily able to become archers and serve as cavalry. It is their custom when times are easy to graze their animals and hunt with the bow for their living, but when hard times come, they take up weapons to plunder and raid. This is their innate nature. Their long-range weapons are bows and arrows; they use swords and spears in close com-bat. When they have the advantage in battle, they advance, but if not, they retreat, since there is no shame in running away. They are only concerned with self-interest, knowing nothing of proper behavior or justice.

Thomas R. Martin, *Herodotus and Sima Qian: The First Great Historians of Greece and China* (Boston: Bedford/St. Martin's, 2010), 129–131.

Everyone, including the chiefs, eats the meat of their domesticated animals and wears clothing of hides and coats of fur. The men who are in their prime eat the fattiest and best food, while the elderly eat what is left over, since the Xiongnu treasure the strong and healthy but place little value on the weak and old. When his father dies, a son marries his step-mother, and when brothers die, the surviving brothers marry their widows. They have personal names but no family names or additional names. . . .

[By 221 B.C.E.] the state of Qin had finally defeated the other six states of China [to create a unified empire]. The First Emperor of Qin sent General Meng Tian with 100,000 men to attack the barbarians in the north. He won control of all the lands south of the Yellow River and made the river into a defended border. Meng Tian built forty-four walled settle-ments along the river and filled them with convicts sentenced to labor and sent to the border to do garrison duty. He also constructed the direct road from Jiuyuan to Yunyang. In this way, he used the slopes of the moun-tain and the valleys to create a defended border, erecting ramparts and fortifications at needed points. The entire line of defense stretched over two thousand miles from Lintao to Liaodong and even crossed the Yellow River, running through Yangshan and Beijia. . . .

The chief of the Xiongnu was named Touman. Too weak to resist the army of Qin, Touman had retreated to the far north, where he held out with his subjects for more than a decade. Following Meng Tian's death, the revolt of the subordinate lords against the Qin dynasty created conflict and unrest in China. The convict laborers that the Qin dynasty had sent to garrison the border seized this opportunity to return home. When the Xiongnu discovered that no one was defending the border, they crossed the Yellow River southward into their old territory and established them-selves along China's previous border.

Touman's oldest son and heir apparent as chief of the Xiongnu was named Maodun, but Touman also had a younger son from a different mother whom he had married later. Touman loved this woman very much and decided to eliminate Maodun, to make the younger son his heir. Tou-man therefore sent Maodun as a diplomatic hostage held by the Yuezhi.[1] As soon as Maodun reached the Yuezhi, Touman suddenly attacked them. They were on the verge of executing Maodun in revenge for the attack when he stole one of their best horses and got away. When he made his way home, his courage so impressed Touman that he made Maodun the commander of a cavalry unit of ten thousand men.

---

[1] **Yuezhi:** A nomadic people who lived northwest of Han China.

Maodun had arrows made that whistled in flight and trained his men to shoot their bows as they were riding. He ordered, "He who does not shoot where my whistling arrow hits will be executed!" He then went out hunting birds and animals, and if any of his men failed to shoot at what he shot at with his whistling arrow, he immediately beheaded them. Next, he shot a whistling arrow at his own favorite horse. Some of his men hesitated, not daring to shoot the horse. Maodun beheaded them. A little later, he used a whistling arrow to shoot at his favorite wife. Again, some of his men, perhaps because they were afraid, did not dare to shoot. Once more, Maodun beheaded them. Later, he went hunting with his men and shot his father's best horse. All his men shot it, too. Then Maodun knew that he could rely on his troops. Accompanying Touman on a hunting trip, he shot a whistling arrow at his father. All his followers shot where the whistling arrow struck and killed the chief. Next, Maodun murdered his stepmother, his younger brother, and all the senior officers who refused to follow his commands. So Maodun made himself the chief [in 209 B.C.E.].

READING AND DISCUSSION QUESTIONS

1. How did the Xiongnu sustain themselves? What was their society like?
2. How did Maodun take charge of the Xiongnu?
3. How might the Chinese have viewed the Xiongnu at this time?

DOCUMENT 7-2

BAN ZHAO

From Lessons for Women

ca. 80 C.E.

Although women in traditional Confucian society were regarded as subservient to men, a few women achieved distinction in their literary pursuits and roles in government. Ban Zhao (ca. 45–120 C.E.) was the daughter of

Nancy Lee Swann, trans., *Pan Chao: Foremost Woman Scholar of China* (New York: Century Co., 1932), 111–114.

a famous writer and administrator and sister to Ban Gu, who served as the court historian for Emperor He (r. 89–105 C.E.). The privileged Ban Zhao was educated at an early age. When Ban Gu died, Ban Zhao finished his history of the Han Dynasty and served as an adviser to Emperor He and the Empress Deng. Ban Zhao's best-known work, Lessons for Women, *served as an advice manual for women in China until the twentieth century.*

I, the unworthy writer, am unsophisticated, unenlightened, and by nature unintelligent, but I am fortunate both to have received not a little favor from my scholarly father, and to have had a cultured mother and instructresses upon whom to rely for a literary education as well as for training in good manners. More than forty years have passed since at the age of fourteen I took up the dustpan and the broom in the Cao family.[2] During this time with trembling heart I feared constantly that I might disgrace my parents, and that I might multiply difficulties for both the women and the men of my husband's family. Day and night I was distressed in heart, but I labored without confessing weariness. Now and hereafter, however, I know how to escape from such fears.

Being careless, and by nature stupid, I taught and trained my children without system. Consequently I fear that my son Gu may bring disgrace upon the Imperial Dynasty by whose Holy Grace he has unprecedentedly received the extraordinary privilege of wearing the Gold and the Purple,[3] a privilege for the attainment of which by my son, I a humble subject never even hoped. Nevertheless, now that he is a man and able to plan his own life, I need not again have concern for him. But I do grieve that you, my daughters, just now at the age for marriage, have not at this time had gradual training and advice; that you still have not learned the proper customs for married women. I fear that by failure in good manners in other families you will humiliate both your ancestors and your clan. I am now seriously ill, life is uncertain. As I have thought of you all in so untrained a state, I have been uneasy many a time for you. At hours of leisure I have composed . . . these instructions under the title, "Lessons for Women." In order that you may have something wherewith to benefit your persons, I wish every one of you, my daughters, each to write out a copy for yourself.

From this time on every one of you strive to practice these lessons.

---

[2] **took up the dustpan . . . family:** Ban Zhao had become a wife.
[3] **the Gold and the Purple:** The colors worn by the elite administrants of the Chinese realm.

HUMILITY

On the third day after the birth of a girl the ancients observed three customs: first to place the baby below the bed; second to give her a potsherd [shard of pottery] with which to play; and third to announce her birth to her ancestors by an offering. Now to lay the baby below the bed plainly indicated that she is lowly and weak, and should regard it as her primary duty to humble herself before others. To give her potsherds with which to play indubitably signified that she should practice labor and consider it her primary duty to be industrious. To announce her birth before her ancestors clearly meant that she ought to esteem as her primary duty the continuation of the observance of worship in the home.

These three ancient customs epitomize a woman's ordinary way of life and the teachings of the traditional ceremonial rites and regulations. Let a woman modestly yield to others; let her respect others; let her put others first, herself last. Should she do something good, let her not mention it; should she do something bad, let her not deny it. Let her bear disgrace; let her even endure when others speak or do evil to her. Always let her seem to tremble and to fear. When a woman follows such maxims as these, then she may be said to humble herself before others.

Let a woman retire late to bed, but rise early to duties; let her not dread tasks by day or by night. Let her not refuse to perform domestic duties whether easy or difficult. That which must be done, let her finish completely, tidily, and systematically. When a woman follows such rules as these, then she may be said to be industrious.

Let a woman be correct in manner and upright in character in order to serve her husband. Let her live in purity and quietness of spirit, and attend to her own affairs. Let her love not gossip and silly laughter. Let her cleanse and purify and arrange in order the wine and the food for the offerings to the ancestors. When a woman observes such principles as these, then she may be said to continue ancestral worship.

No woman who observes these three fundamentals of life has ever had a bad reputation or has fallen into disgrace. If a woman fails to observe them, how can her name be honored; how can she but bring disgrace upon herself?

HUSBAND AND WIFE

The Way of husband and wife is intimately connected with *Yin* and *Yang*,[4] and relates the individual to gods and ancestors. Truly it is the great

---

[4]**Yin and Yang**: An important concept in Chinese culture that originated in Daoism. Yin and yang are oppositional forces that are bound together and create each other.

principle of Heaven and Earth, and the great basis of human relationships. Therefore the "Rites"[5] honor union of man and woman; and in the "Book of Poetry"[6] the "First Ode" manifests the principle of marriage. For these reasons the relationship cannot but be an important one.

If a husband is unworthy, then he possesses nothing by which to control his wife. If a wife is unworthy, then she possesses nothing with which to serve her husband. If a husband does not control his wife, then the rules of conduct manifesting his authority are abandoned and broken. If a wife does not serve her husband, then the proper relationship between men and women and the natural order of things are neglected and destroyed. As a matter of fact the purpose of these two [the controlling of women by men, and the serving of men by women] is the same.

Now examine the gentlemen of the present age. They only know that wives must be controlled, and that the husband's rules of conduct manifesting his authority must be established. They therefore teach their boys to read books and study histories. But they do not in the least understand that husbands and masters must also be served, and that the proper relationship and the rites should be maintained.

Yet only to teach men and not to teach women — is that not ignoring the essential relation between them? According to the "Rites," it is the rule to begin to teach children to read at the age of eight years, and by the age of fifteen years they ought then to be ready for cultural training. Only why should it not be that girls' education as well as boys' be according to this principle?

RESPECT AND CAUTION

As *Yin* and *Yang* are not of the same nature, so man and woman have different characteristics. The distinctive quality of the *Yang* is rigidity; the function of the *Yin* is yielding. Man is honored for strength; a woman is beautiful on account of her gentleness. Hence there arose the common saying: "A man though born like a wolf may, it is feared, become a weak monstrosity; a woman though born like a mouse may, it is feared, become a tiger."

Now for self-culture nothing equals respect for others. To counteract firmness nothing equals compliance. Consequently it can be said that the Way of respect and acquiescence is woman's most important principle

---

[5] **the "Rites"**: The *Book of Rites* is one of the five classics of Confucianism. It deals with li, or "rules of conduct," and provides instructions for the correct observation of rituals.

[6] **Book of Poetry**: The *Book of Songs* is another of the five classics of Confucianism.

of conduct. So respect may be defined as nothing other than holding on to that which is permanent; and acquiescence nothing other than being liberal and generous. Those who are steadfast in devotion know that they should stay in their proper places; those who are liberal and generous esteem others, and honor and serve them.

If husband and wife have the habit of staying together, never leaving one another, and following each other around within the limited space of their own rooms, then they will lust after and take liberties with one another. From such action improper language will arise between the two. This kind of discussion may lead to licentiousness. Out of licentiousness will be born a heart of disrespect to the husband. Such a result comes from not knowing that one should stay in one's proper place.

Furthermore, affairs may be either crooked or straight; words may be either right or wrong. Straightforwardness cannot but lead to quarreling; crookedness cannot but lead to accusation. If there are really accusations and quarrels, then undoubtedly there will be angry affairs. Such a result comes from not esteeming others, and not honoring and serving them.

If wives suppress not contempt for husbands, then it follows that such wives rebuke and scold their husbands. If husbands stop not short of anger, then they are certain to beat their wives. The correct relationship between husband and wife is based upon harmony and intimacy, and conjugal love is grounded in proper union. Should actual blows be dealt, how could matrimonial relationship be preserved? Should sharp words be spoken, how could conjugal love exist? If love and proper relationship both be destroyed, then husband and wife are divided.

WOMANLY QUALIFICATIONS

A woman ought to have four qualifications: (1) womanly virtue; (2) womanly words; (3) womanly bearing; and (4) womanly work. Now what is called womanly virtue need not be brilliant ability, exceptionally different from others. Womanly words need be neither clever in debate nor keen in conversation. Womanly appearance requires neither a pretty nor a perfect face and form. Womanly work need not be work done more skillfully than that of others.

To guard carefully her chastity; to control circumspectly her behavior; in every motion to exhibit modesty; and to model each act on the best usage, this is womanly virtue.

To choose her words with care; to avoid vulgar language; to speak at appropriate times; and not to weary others with much conversation, may be called the characteristics of womanly words.

To wash and scrub filth away; to keep clothes and ornaments fresh and clean; to wash the head and bathe the body regularly; and to keep the person free from disgraceful filth, may be called the characteristics of womanly bearing.

With whole-hearted devotion to sew and to weave; to love not gossip and silly laughter; in cleanliness and order to prepare the wine and food for serving guests, may be called the characteristics of womanly work.

These four qualifications characterize the greatest virtue of a woman. No woman can afford to be without them. In fact they are very easy to possess if a woman only treasure them in her heart. The ancients had a saying: "Is Love afar off? If I desire love, then love is at hand!" So can it be said of these qualifications. . . .

IMPLICIT OBEDIENCE

Whenever the mother-in-law says, "Do not do that," and if what she says is right, unquestionably the daughter-in-law obeys. Whenever the mother-in-law says, "Do that," even if what she says is wrong, still the daughter-in-law submits unfailingly to the command.

Let a woman not act contrary to the wishes and the opinions of parents-in-law about right and wrong; let her not dispute with them what is straight and what is crooked. Such docility may be called obedience which sacrifices personal opinion. Therefore the ancient book, "A Pattern for Women," says: "If a daughter-in-law who follows the wishes of her parents-in-law is like an echo and a shadow, how could she not be praised?"

READING AND DISCUSSION QUESTIONS

1. What is the status of women in Chinese society? How does the treatment of infant daughters convey this status?

2. What are the duties of a husband and a wife?

3. What are the four qualifications to be a good woman? What does this imply about education regarding women and daughters?

4. How does this document, although written by a woman, support a patriarchal social structure?

DOCUMENT 7-3

FA-HSIEN

From A Record of Buddhistic Kingdoms

ca. 399–414 C.E.

Buddhism entered China during the early days of the Han Dynasty (202 B.C.E.–220 C.E.), when Indian merchants and missionaries traveled along the Silk Road to China, bringing the Buddhist religion with them. Fa-hsien (ca. 337–422) is possibly the most famous of the Chinese Buddhists who traveled the long distance in order to study with Indian religious scholars. Like Marco Polo, Fa-hsien recorded his journey. A Record of Buddhistic Kingdoms *describes Fa-hsien's trip to and from India and includes the description of Ceylon (modern-day Sri Lanka) excerpted below.*

The country originally had no human inhabitants, but was occupied only by spirits and nagas [dragons], with which merchants of various countries carried on a trade. When the trafficking was taking place, the spirits did not show themselves. They simply set forth their precious commodities, with labels of the price attached to them; while the merchants made their purchases according to the price; and took the things away.

Through the coming and going of the merchants (in this way), when they went away, the people of (their) various countries heard how pleasant the land was, and flocked to it in numbers till it became a great nation. The (climate) is temperate and attractive, without any difference of summer and winter. The vegetation is always luxuriant. Cultivation proceeds whenever men think fit: there are no fixed seasons for it.

When Buddha came to this country,[7] wishing to transform the wicked nagas, by his supernatural power he planted one foot at the north of the royal city, and the other on the top of a mountain, the two being fifteen yojanas apart.[8] Over the footprint at the north of the city the king built a

---

James Legge, trans., *A Record of Buddhistic Kingdoms: Being an Account by the Chinese Monk Fa-hsien of His Travels in India and Ceylon* (A.D. 399–414) *in Search of the Buddhist Books of Discipline* (New York: Paragon Book Reprint Corp., 1965).

[7] **When Buddha came . . . country**: The Buddha probably never visited Sri Lanka.
[8] **the top of a mountain . . . apart**: A reference to Adam's Peak in central Sri Lanka, which bears a rock formation known as the "sacred footprint." A yojana is approximately 8–10 miles.

large tope, 400 cubits high,[9] grandly adorned with gold and silver, and finished with a combination of all the precious substances. By the side of the top he further built a monastery, called the Abhayagiri, where there are (now) five thousand monks. There is in it a hall of Buddha, adorned with carved and inlaid works of gold and silver, and rich in the seven precious substances, in which there is an image (of Buddha) in green jade, more than twenty cubits in height, glittering all over with those substances, and having an appearance of solemn dignity which words cannot express. In the palm of the right hand there is a priceless pearl. Several years had now elapsed since Fa-hien [Fa-hsien] left the land of Han; the men with whom he had been in intercourse had all been of regions strange to him; his eyes had not rested on an old and familiar hill or river, plant or tree; his fellow-travellers, moreover, had been separated from him, some by death, and others flowing off in different directions; no face or shadow was now with him but his own, and a constant sadness was in his heart. Suddenly (one day), when by the side of this image of jade, he saw a [Chinese] merchant presenting as his offering a fan of white silk; and the tears of sorrow involuntarily filled his eyes and fell down.

A former king of the country had sent to Central India and got a slip of the patra tree,[10] which he planted by the side of the hall of Buddha, where a tree grew up to the height of about 200 cubits. As it bent on one side towards the south-east, the king, fearing it would fall, propped it with a post eight or nine spans[11] [about 3 feet] round. The tree began to grow at the very heart of the prop, where it met (the trunk); (a shoot) pierced through the post, and went down to the ground, where it entered and formed roots, that rose (to the surface) and were about four spans round. Although the post was split in the middle, the outer portions kept hold (of the shoot), and people did not remove them. Beneath the tree there has been built a vihara [monastery], in which there is an image (of Buddha) seated, which the monks and commonalty reverence and look up to without ever becoming wearied. In the city there has been reared also the vihara of Buddha's tooth,[12] on which, as well as on the other, the seven precious substances have been employed.

The king practices the Brahmanical purifications, and the sincerity of the faith and reverence of the population inside the city are also great.

---

[9] **400 cubits high**: A cubit is approximately 18 inches, so the domed monument would have topped approximately 600 feet.

[10] **patra tree**: A pippala or the Bo tree, often associated with the Buddha.

[11] **span**: The width of a human hand, about 4 inches.

[12] **Buddha's tooth**: A sacred relic of the Buddha.

Since the establishment of government in the kingdom there has been no famine or scarcity, no revolution or disorder. In the treasuries of the monkish communities there are many precious stones, and the priceless manis. One of the kings (once) entered one of those treasuries, and when he looked all round and saw the priceless pearls, his covetous greed was excited, and he wished to take them to himself by force. In three days, however, he came to himself, and immediately went and bowed his head to the ground in the midst of the monks, to show his repentance of the evil thought. As a sequel to this, he informed the monks (of what had been in his mind), and desired them to make a regulation that from that day forth the king should not be allowed to enter the treasury and see (what it contained), and that no bhikshu [male Buddhist monk] should enter it till after he had been in orders for a period of full forty years.

In the city there are many Vaisya[13] elders and Sabaean [likely Arab] merchants, whose houses are stately and beautiful. The lanes and passages are kept in good order. At the heads of the four principal streets there have been built preaching halls, where, on the eighth, fourteenth, and fifteenth days of the month, they spread carpets, and set forth a pulpit, while the monks and commonalty from all quarters come together to hear the Law. The people say that in the kingdom there may be altogether sixty thousand monks, who get their food from their common stores. The king, besides, prepares elsewhere in the city a common supply of food for five or six thousand more. When any want, they take their great bowls, and go (to the place of distribution), and take as much as the vessels will hold, all returning with them full.

The tooth of Buddha is always brought forth in the middle of the third month. Ten days beforehand the king grandly caparisons [outfits] a large elephant, on which he mounts a man who can speak distinctly, and is dressed in royal robes, to beat a large drum, and make the following proc- lamation: — "The Bodhisattva [Buddha], during three Asankhyeya-kalpas [great stretches of time], manifested his activity, and did not spare his own life. He gave up kingdom, city, wife, and son; he plucked out his eyes and gave them to another; he cut off a piece of his own flesh to ransom the life of a dove; he cut off his head and gave it as an alms; he gave his body to feed a starving tigress; he grudged not his marrow and his brains. In many such ways as these did he undergo pain for the sake of all living. And so it was, that, having become Buddha, he continued in the world for forty- five years, preaching his Law, teaching and transforming, so that those

---

[13] Vaisya: The third of the four traditional Hindu castes, usually merchants or farmers.

who had no rest found rest, and the unconverted were converted. When his connexion with the living was completed, he attained to pari-nirvana (and died). Since that event, for 1497 years, the light of the world has gone out, and all living beings have had long-continued sadness. Behold! ten days after this, Buddha's tooth will be brought forth, and taken to the Abhayagiri-vihara.[14] Let all and each, whether monks or laics [secular people], who wish to amass merit for themselves, make the roads smooth and in good condition, grandly adorn the lanes and by-ways, and provide abundant store of flowers and incense to be used as offerings to it."

When this proclamation is over, the king exhibits, so as to line both sides of the road, the five hundred different bodily forms in which the Bodhisattva has in the course of his history appeared: — here as Sudana, there as Sama; now as the king of elephants; and then as a stag or a horse.[15] All these figures are brightly colored and grandly executed, looking as if they were alive. After this the tooth of Buddha is brought forth, and is carried along in the middle of the road. Everywhere on the way offerings are presented to it, and thus it arrives at the hall of Buddha in the Abhayagiri-vihara. There monks and laics are collected in crowds. They burn incense, light lamps, and perform all the prescribed services, day and night without ceasing, till ninety days have been completed, when (the tooth) is returned to the vihara within the city. On fast-days the door of that vihara is opened, and the forms of ceremonial reverence are observed according to the rules.

Forty le [approximately one-and-a-half miles] to the east of the Abhayagiri-vihara there is a hill, with a vihara on it, called the Chaitya, where there may be 2,000 monks. Among them there is a Sramana of great virtue, named Dharma-gupta,[16] honored and looked up to by all the kingdom. He has lived for more than forty years in an apartment of stone, constantly showing such gentleness of heart, that he has brought snakes and rats to stop together in the same room, without doing one another any harm.

READING AND DISCUSSION QUESTIONS

1. How does Fa-hsien describe the king of Ceylon? Which of the king's qualities does he admire?

---

[14] **Abhayagiri-vihara**: The main temple complex in the city of Anuradhapura.
[15] **the five hundred . . . stag or a horse**: References to the Buddha's numerous reincarnations.
[16] **Dharma-gupta**: A famous Sramana, or wandering monk, in Ceylon around 400.

2. According to Fa-hsien, how did Buddhism arrive in Ceylon? What impact did its introduction have on the territory?

3. Describe the festival involving the tooth of Buddha. What role does the king play in the festival?

DOCUMENT 7-4

PRINCE TONERI

From Chronicles of Japan: *Emperor Jinmu*

ca. 720 C.E.

In 720 C.E., Prince Toneri (676–735 C.E.) completed editing a vast compilation of Japanese history, the Nihonji, *or* Chronicles. *The* Chronicles *were written in Chinese because Japan had adopted writing from China for official documents; only later did the Japanese develop a system for writing their own language. The Japanese believed that the Emperor Jinmu, the subject of this passage, lived during the seventh and sixth centuries* B.C.E. *Because records were not kept until the sixth century* C.E., *the reign of Emperor Jinmu must be thought of as a myth, although one that accurately reflects Chinese influence on Japanese society.*

The Emperor Kami Yamato Ihare-biko's personal name was Hiko-hoho-demi. He was the fourth child of Hiko-nagisa-take-u-gaya-fuki-aezu no Mikoto. His mother's name was Tama-yori-hime, daughter of the sea god. From his birth, this emperor was of clear intelligence and resolute will. At the age of fifteen he was heir to the throne. When he grew up, he married Ahira-tsu-hime, of the district of Ata in the province of Hyūga, and made her his consort. By her he had Tagishi-mimi no Mikoto and Kisu-mimi no Mikoto.

When he reached the age of forty-five, he addressed his elder brothers and his children, saying: "Of old, Our Heavenly Deities Taka-mi-musubi no Mikoto and Ō-hiru-me no Mikoto, pointing to this land of fair rice-

Wm. Theodore de Bary, ed., *Sources of East Asian Tradition.* Volume 1: *Premodern Asia* (New York: Columbia University Press, 2008), 664–665.

ears of the fertile reed-plain, gave it to Our Heavenly ancestor,[17] Hiko-ho no ninigi no Mikoto. Thereupon Hiko-ho no ninigi no Mikoto, throwing open the barrier of Heaven and clearing a cloud path, urged on his super-human course until he came to rest. At this time the world was given over to widespread desolation. It was an age of darkness and disorder. In this gloom, therefore, he fostered justice and so governed this western border. Our imperial ancestors and imperial parent, like gods, like sages, accu-mulated happiness and amassed glory. Many years elapsed. From the date when Our Heavenly ancestor descended until now it is over 1,792,470 years. But the remote regions do not yet enjoy the blessings of imperial rule. Every town has always been allowed to have its lord, and every vil-lage its chief, who, each one for himself, makes division of territory and practices mutual aggression and conflict.

"Now I have heard from the Ancient of the Sea[18] that in the east there is a fair land encircled on all sides by blue mountains. Moreover, there is there one who flew down riding in a Heavenly Rock-boat. I think that this land will undoubtedly be suitable for the extension of the Heavenly task,[19] so that its glory should fill the universe. It is, doubtless, the center of the world. The person who flew down was, I believe, Nigi-haya-hi.[20] Why should we not proceed thither, and make it the capital?"

All the imperial princes answered and said: "The truth of this is mani-fest. This thought is constantly present to our minds also. Let us go thither quickly." This was the year Kinoe Tora [fifty-first] of the Great Year.

The year Tsuchinoto Hitsuji, Spring, 3rd month, 7th day. The emperor made an order saying: "During the six years that our expedition against the east has lasted, owing to my reliance on the Majesty of Imperial Heaven, the wicked bands have met death. It is true that the frontier lands are still unpurified and that a remnant of evil is still refractory. But in the region of the Central Land,[21] there is no more wind and dust. Truly we should make a vast and spacious capital and plan it great and strong.

"At present things are in a crude and obscure condition, and the peo-ple's minds are unsophisticated. They roost in nests or dwell in caves. Their manners are simply what is customary. Now if a great man were to estab-lish laws, justice could not fail to flourish. And even if some gain should

---

[17] **Our Heavenly ancestor**: Grandfather of Jinmu; he was sent to heaven to plant rice.
[18] **Ancient of the Sea**: A god of the sea.
[19] **Heavenly task**: To extend the power of the empire.
[20] **Nigi-haya-hi**: A spirit who descended from the sky.
[21] **Central Land**: Japan; the idea is that Japan replaced China as the central kingdom.

accrue to the people, in what way would this interfere with the Sage's[22] action? Moreover, it will be well to open up and clear the mountains and forests, and to construct a palace. Then I may reverently assume the Precious Dignity and so give peace to my good subjects. Above, I should then respond to the kindness of the Heavenly Powers in granting me the kingdom, and below, I should extend the line of the imperial descendants and foster rightmindedness. Thereafter the capital may be extended so as to embrace all the six cardinal points, and the eight cords may be covered so as to form a roof. Will this not be well?

"When I observe the Kashiwa-bara plain, which lies southwest of Mount Unebi, it seems the center of the land. I must set it in order."

Accordingly he in this month commanded officers to set about the construction of an imperial residence.

READING AND DISCUSSION QUESTIONS

1. Describe Japanese society before the reign of Emperor Jinmu.
2. How did Jinmu reform Japanese society?
3. How does this document display Chinese influence on early Japan?

VIEWPOINTS
Buddhism in China

DOCUMENT 7-5

Buddha Preaching
ca. 501–580 C.E.

After the collapse of the Han Dynasty, chaos reigned in northern China. One aspect of this chaos was the entrance of new peoples into China, such as the Wei, a nomadic Turkish people who had converted to Buddhism.

---

[22] **the Sage's action:** The actions of the emperor.

As promoters of Buddhism, the Wei rulers constructed several monasteries and patronized Buddhist arts. This image comes from a cave painting from Dunhuang, China, which was located near the beginning of the Silk Road. It is just one example of how Buddhist ideas were popularized in Chinese culture. The large figure seated in the foreground is the Buddha.

Bridgeman Art Library.

READING AND DISCUSSION QUESTIONS

1. Describe this painting. What seems to be happening in it?

2. How are the figures depicted? What kind of facial expressions are they exhibiting?

3. What does the wall painting convey about the state of the visual arts in sixth-century China?

HAN YU

From Lives of the Eminent Monks: *Zhu Seng Du*

ca. 550 C.E.

Buddhism entered China during the Han Dynasty, spreading from Central Asia along the Silk Road. Although conversion to Buddhism was slow at first, later dynasties such as the Wei (386–534 C.E.) adopted and promoted Buddhism. The continued political division of China and concurrent chaos prompted many to seek spiritual refuge in the Buddha. The transformation of Buddhism so that it appealed more readily to the Chinese was a long process. Lives of the Eminent Monks, *for example, was composed in a traditional Chinese style of biography, but the content is clearly Buddhist. One of the most important features of the following life is the defense of Buddhist customs that seem to challenge traditional Chinese ways of life.*

Zhu Seng Du was originally named Wang Xi (Xuanzong) and came from Donghuan, in Guangdong, South China. He came from a lesser literati family but was a very presentable young man. When he was sixteen his spirit soared high and his character stood out among his peers. His personality was mild and he was well loved by his neighbors. He lived with his mother and was a filial son to the last letter of the Confucian code. He courted the daughter of Mr. Yang Deshen in the same village. The Yang family was also respectable. Their daughter, Tiaohua, had a comely face and proper poise. She was versed in the apocryphal literature and was the same age as Du. The day he proposed to her, she accepted. However, not soon afterwards and before the marriage was set, Tiaohua's mother died. Tiaohua's father soon followed. Meanwhile, Du's mother also passed away. Suddenly realizing the transience of this world, Du left it behind and entered a monastic order, changing his name to Seng Du, Du, the follower of Sakyamuni.[23] He left his trace beyond the world of dust and

Patricia Buckley Ebrey, ed., *Chinese Civilization and Society: A Sourcebook*, 2d ed. (New York: Free Press, 1983), 99–100.

[23] **Sakyamuni**: Another name for the Buddha.

wandered, as a student, in faraway places. Tiaohua, after having tended to the mourning rites for her parents, realized that there was no place in society for a woman like her without anyone on whom to depend, neither parents, husband, nor child. Therefore she wrote to Du, "According to the Confucian norms of filial piety the hair and skin of one's body, being something received from one's parents, should not be harmed [for example, by tonsure]. The ancestral temples should not be abandoned as you, Du, the monk, have done. Moreover, considering the teaching of Confucian society you should abandon your lofty hermit ideal, and arousing your talents make a name for yourself in the world. Through your success you should let shine the spirit and glory of your ancestors and be a comfort to those close to you, fulfilling the expectations of both man and the spirits." She also wrote five poems. . . .

Seng Du responded, "Serving the king, as demanded by Confucianism, is to assist in the ruling of one's country. That cannot be compared with pursuing the Buddhist path for all peoples. Serving one's parents means to establish a family of one's own; but that cannot be compared with following the Buddhist path for the sake of all beings in the three realms. The dictum 'Never to harm your body or hair' is the narrow advice of those committed to the world. I am ashamed that my present virtue has not extended itself to cover even that filial duty. However, small baskets of earth add up to a mountain: all beginnings are small. Thus I put on my monk's gown, drink the pure water, and laud the wisdom of the Buddhas. Although the dress of princes, the food of the eight rarities, the sound of music and the color of glories are all fine, I would not trade my lot for them. If our minds are in tune to one another, we will meet in nirvana. However, people's hearts are different, just as their faces are. Your distaste for the hermit's way is like my indifference to the world. Dear one, let this be the last parting and let all the karmic ties from ten thousand years past that brought us together end here. Time is running short. The student of the dharma must learn to daily eliminate his attachment to the world of action. Men and women of the world, however, should adapt themselves to the times. You are, in age and virtue, in your prime, so you should pursue what you desire and admire. Do not keep this man who is committed to Buddhism in your mind and thereby lose the best years of your life." Du further wrote five poems in reply. . . .

Du's mind was made up and, like a rock, it could not be swayed. Touched by his reply, Tiaohua also entered an order and became a nun.

READING AND DISCUSSION QUESTIONS

1. According to this document, what features of Buddhism were out of place in traditional Chinese culture?

2. How does Seng Du defend Buddhism against its critics?

DOCUMENT 7-7

EMPEROR WUZONG

Edict on the Suppression of Buddhism

845 C.E.

Despite Buddhism's success, or perhaps because of it, a movement within China began to advocate the removal of Buddhist influences in China. The most famous thinker of this age, Han Yu (768–824), urged a return to traditional Confucian values. Although his writings did not lead to tangible results during his lifetime, the later Emperor Wuzong (841–846) issued the following edict, which severely damaged Buddhism's standing in China but did not eliminate the religion. Ironically, Wuzong seems to have been less influenced by Confucian scholars such as Han Yu than he was by Daoist priests, who promised him immortality for eliminating the rival Buddhist belief in China.

EDICT OF THE EIGHTH MONTH

We have heard that up through the Three Dynasties the Buddha was never spoken of. It was only from the Han and Wei on that the religion of idols gradually came to prominence. So in this latter age it has transmitted its strange ways, instilling its infection with every opportunity, spreading like a luxuriant vine, until it has poisoned the customs of our nation; gradually, and before anyone was aware, it beguiled and confounded men's minds so that the multitude have been increasingly led astray. It has spread to the hills and plains of all the nine provinces and through the walls and towers of our two capitals. Each day finds its monks and followers growing

Wm. Theodore de Bary, ed., *Sources of East Asian Tradition*. Volume 1: *Premodern Asia* (New York: Columbia University Press, 2008), 585–586.

more numerous and its temples more lofty. It wears out the strength of the people with constructions of earth and wood, pilfers their wealth for ornaments of gold and precious objects, causes men to abandon their lords and parents for the company of teachers, and severs man and wife with its monastic decrees. In destroying law and injuring mankind, indeed, nothing surpasses this doctrine!

Now if even one man fails to work the fields, someone must go hungry; if one woman does not tend her silkworms, someone will be cold. At present there are an inestimable number of monks and nuns in the empire, each of them waiting for the farmers to feed him and the silkworms to clothe him, while the public temples and private chapels have reached boundless numbers, all with soaring towers and elegant ornamentation sufficient to outshine the imperial palace itself. . . .

Having thoroughly examined all earlier reports and consulted public opinion on all sides, we no longer have the slightest doubt in Our mind that this evil should be eradicated. Loyal ministers of the court and provinces have lent their aid to Our high intentions, submitting most apt proposals that We have found worthy of being put into effect. Presented with an opportunity to suppress this source of age-old evil and fulfill the laws and institutions of the ancient kings, to aid mankind and bring profit to the multitude, how could We forbear to act?

The temples of the empire that have been demolished number more than 4,600; 260,500 monks and nuns have been returned to lay life and enrolled as subject to the Twice-a-Year Tax;[24] more than 40,000 privately established temples have been destroyed, releasing 30 or 40 million *qing*[25] of fertile, top-grade land and 150,000 male and female servants who will become subject to the Twice-a-Year Tax. Monks and nuns have been placed under the jurisdiction of the Director of Aliens to make it perfectly clear that this is a foreign religion. Finally, We have ordered more than 3,000 men of the Nestorian and Mazdean[26] religions to return to lay life and to cease polluting the customs of China.

Alas, what had not been carried out in the past seemed to have been waiting for this opportunity. If Buddhism is completely abolished now, who will say that the action is not timely? Already more than 100,000 idle and unproductive Buddhist followers have been expelled, and countless of their gaudy, useless buildings destroyed. Henceforth We may guide

---

[24] **Twice-a-Year Tax**: Tax paid by all inhabitants of the Chinese Empire.

[25] *qing*: Chinese unit of land, equal to 100 square meters.

[26] **Mazdean**: A follower of Zoroastrianism.

the people in stillness and purity, cherish the principle of doing nothing [*wuwei*], order Our government with simplicity and ease, and achieve a unification of customs so that the multitudes of all realms will find their destination in Our august rule.

READING AND DISCUSSION QUESTIONS

1. How is the spread of Buddhism described? How does it conflict with the traditional activities of Chinese society?
2. How does Wuzong describe the Buddhist monks and nuns?
3. What actions did Wuzong order to suppress Buddhism?

COMPARATIVE QUESTIONS

1. What role did the Chinese government play in promoting religion throughout China?
2. How might Zhu Seng Du have responded to the emperor Wuzong's edict? What arguments would Du make?
3. How does the status and daily life of women in China as described by Ban Zhao compare to that of women in India according to *The Laws of Manu* (Document 3-5)?
4. How does Sima Qian's treatment of the Xiongnu compare to Herodotus's description of the Persian ruler Xerxes (Document 5-5)? Discuss similarities and differences.
5. What features made Buddhism successful throughout East Asia?
6. Why would people in less-developed areas of the world at this time, such as Sri Lanka and Japan, want to borrow cultural, religious, and political ideas from their more advanced neighbors?

CHAPTER 8

Continuity and Change in Europe and Western Asia

200–850

I n the fourth century, the Roman emperor Constantine legalized Chris-
tianity, and by the fifth century it was the official religion of the empire.
This change transformed the previously illegal and persecuted religion into
the most important cultural force throughout the Mediterranean world.
While Christian devotion flourished during the fifth century, the Roman
Empire at large began to disintegrate. Rome was sacked twice and by the
end of the century the western portion of the empire was in the hands of
Germanic-speaking Christian peoples such as the Goths, Lombards, and
Franks. These usurping kingdoms encouraged the spread of Christianity
into new territories, such as Saxony in modern Germany. Despite Rome's
loss of the western Mediterranean, the eastern part of the empire, called
the Byzantine Empire by modern scholars, endured until the Ottoman
Turks captured Constantinople in 1453.

DOCUMENT 8-1

EGERIA

Good Friday in Jerusalem

ca. 381–384

*The Spanish nun Egeria wrote one of the earliest Christian accounts of a
pilgrimage to the Holy Land, defined as the places mentioned in the Hebrew
Bible and Christian New Testament. Large-scale pilgrimage to the Holy
Land began after Constantine's legalization of Christianity and was inspired*

Marcelle Thiébaux, trans., *The Writings of Medieval Women: An Anthology* (New
York: Garland, 1994), 40–42.

by a trip taken by his mother, Helena, to Jerusalem. Egeria's account is representative of the role of women in the Christian church who, although they could not hold high offices such as that of bishop, were important spiritual leaders in their own communities. Here she describes the customs and worship in Jerusalem that took place on Good Friday, which commemorates the crucifixion of Jesus.

Then all the people, even the smallest children, go down to Gethsemane[1] on foot, together with the bishop. They sing hymns. There is such a great crowd of people, and they are so worn out with their nightlong vigil and weakened from each day's fasting, that they descend the steep hill to Gethsemane very slowly. They sing hymns as they go. More than two hundred church candles light their way.

When everyone has arrived in Gethsemane, the proper prayer is read first, then the hymn is sung. The gospel passage is read recounting Jesus' arrest. During the reading there is such bawling and roaring among the people, along with weeping, that it is likely that the people's groans can be heard at the far end of the city. And now they walk, singing hymns, and they arrive at the gate at an hour when they can recognize one another. From there they go through the middle of the city together. Old and young, rich and poor, all appear there on this special day when no one leaves the vigil before morning. In this manner the bishop is escorted from Gethsemane to the gate, and from the gate through the entire city to the Cross.

When they have arrived before the Cross, the day is already beginning to grow light. There, finally, they read the whole gospel account of how the Lord was led before Pilate and all that was written that Pilate said to the Lord and to the Jews.

After this the bishop speaks to the people, comforting them, since they have suffered such exertions through the night and will continue to do so during this day. He urges them not to be weary but to hope in God, since their exertions will be richly rewarded. Comforting them as much as he can, he tells them, "Go, for now, each of you to your homes, and sit down a while. Then at the second hour of the day [8 o'clock] be back here so that until the sixth hour [noon] you will be able to see the sacred wood of the Cross, trusting that it will assure future salvation for each of us. From

---

[1] **Gethsemane**: Garden in Jerusalem where Jesus's disciples prayed the night before his crucifixion.

that hour of noon on, when we must gather here again before the Cross, we must conduct readings and prayers until nightfall."

The sun has still not yet risen when the people are dismissed from the Cross. Those who are stalwart go on to pray at Sion,[2] at the pillar where the Lord was scourged. Then people go back home to rest for a little while, but before long everyone is back. A bishop's throne is set up on Golgotha,[3] behind the Cross which now stands there. The bishop is seated on his throne and a linen-covered table is placed before him. Deacons stand around the table. The silver coffer, ornamented with gold, is brought which contains the sacred wood of the true Cross. The coffer is opened and the wood of the Cross is displayed on the table together with the superscription.[4]

While the Cross is on the table, the bishop, remaining seated, holds down the ends of the holy wood with his hands. The deacons also guard it as they stand around him. They all now guard it this way for it is customary for the people to approach the table one by one, both the faithful and the catechumens.[5] They bow to the table, kiss the sacred wood, and then move along. I don't know when it was, but someone is said to have bitten off a piece of the sacred wood and stolen it. For this reason it is guarded now by the deacons who surround it, so that no one will dare to do this again.

Now all the people pass before it one by one, bowing and touching it first with the forehead, then with the eyes. Then they kiss it before they move on. No one, however, reaches out a hand to touch it.

READING AND DISCUSSION QUESTIONS

1. What rituals take place on Good Friday?
2. Why would people venerate the "True Cross"? What does the story about a person biting the "True Cross" reveal about early Christian piety?

---

[2] **Sion**: Site where Jesus was whipped by Roman soldiers.

[3] **Golgotha**: Site of Jesus's crucifixion.

[4] **the superscription**: The phrase "Jesus of Nazareth, The King of the Jews" was added to Jesus's cross by the Romans to mock him, but Christians embraced it.

[5] **catechumens**: Individuals who were learning about Christianity and on the path to joining the church.

DOCUMENT 8-2

SAINT AUGUSTINE

From City of God: A Denunciation of Paganism

ca. 413–426

No author had more influence throughout the Western Middle Ages than Saint Augustine (354–430), bishop of Hippo in his homeland of North Africa. Though he was a late convert to Christianity, Augustine became a devout Catholic in 386. His most important work, City of God, was written in response to the Goths' sack of Rome in 410. Unlike Augustine, pagans blamed the spread of the Christian faith and the rejection of the old Roman gods for sapping the strength of the Roman Empire.

Cicero,[6] a weighty man, and a philosopher in his way, when about to be made edile,[7] wished the citizens to understand that, among the other duties of his magistracy, he must propitiate Flora [honor the goddess of flowers and spring] by the celebration of games. And these games are reckoned devout in proportion to their lewdness. In another place, and when he was now consul,[8] and the state in great peril, he says that games had been celebrated for ten days together, and that nothing had been omitted which could pacify the gods: as if it had not been more satisfactory to irritate the gods by temperance, than to pacify them by debauchery; and to provoke their hate by honest living, than soothe it by such unseemly grossness. . . .

They [the pagan gods], then, are but abandoned and ungrateful wretches, in deep and fast bondage to that malign spirit, who complain and murmur that men are rescued by the name of Christ from the hellish thraldom of these unclean spirits, and from a participation in their

---

Augustine, *City of God*, 27–29, in Philip Schaff, ed., *Library of Nicene and Post-Nicene Fathers*, 1st ser. (New York, 1890), 3:41–43.

[6] **Cicero**: Roman philosopher in the first century B.C.E. (see Chapter 6) who is often considered one of the best writers in Latin.

[7] **edile**: A lower elected office in the Roman Republic.

[8] **consul**: The highest elected officer in the Roman Republic.

punishment, and are brought out of the night of pestilential ungodliness into the light of most healthful piety. Only such men could murmur that the masses flock to the churches and their chaste acts of worship, where a seemly separation of the sexes is observed; where they learn how they may so spend this earthly life, as to merit a blessed eternity hereafter; where Holy Scripture and instruction in righteousness are proclaimed from a raised platform in presence of all, that both they who do the word may hear to their salvation, and they who do it not may hear to judgment. And though some enter who scoff at such precepts, all their petulance [childish irritation] is either quenched by a sudden change, or is restrained through fear or shame. For no filthy and wicked action is there set forth to be gazed at or to be imitated; but either the precepts of the true God are recommended, His miracles narrated, His gifts praised, or His benefits implored.

This, rather, is the religion worthy of your desires, O admirable Roman race, — the progeny of your Scaevolas and Scipios, of Regulus, and of Fabricius.[9] This rather covet, this distinguish from that foul vanity and crafty malice of the devils. If there is in your nature any eminent virtue, only by true piety is it purged and perfected, while by impiety it is wrecked and punished. Choose now what you will pursue, that your praise may be not in yourself, but in the true God, in whom is no error. For of popular glory you have had your share; but by the secret providence of God, the true religion was not offered to your choice. Awake, it is now day; as you have already awaked in the persons of some in whose perfect virtue and sufferings for the true faith we glory: for they, contending on all sides with hostile powers, and conquering them all by bravely dying, have purchased for us this country of ours with their blood; to which country we invite you, and exhort you to add yourselves to the number of the citizens of this city, which also has a sanctuary of its own in the true remission of sins. Do not listen to those degenerate sons of thine who slander Christ and Christians, and impute to them these disastrous times, though they desire times in which they may enjoy rather impunity for their wickedness than a peaceful life. Such has never been Rome's ambition even in regard to her earthly country. Lay hold now on the celestial country, which is easily

---

[9] **Scaevolas . . . Fabricius:** The Scaevolas and Scipios were important families during the Roman Republic. Regulus was a consul during the Punic Wars between Rome and Carthage, and Fabricius was a general of the early republic who also served as a censor.

won, and in which you will reign truly and for ever. For there shalt thou find no vestal fire,[10] no Capitoline stone,[11] but the one true God.

No date, no goal will here ordain:

But grant an endless, boundless reign.

No longer, then, follow after false and deceitful gods; abjure them rather, and despise them, bursting forth into true liberty. Gods they are not, but malignant spirits, to whom your eternal happiness will be a sore punishment.

READING AND DISCUSSION QUESTIONS

1. How does Augustine describe the Roman pagan gods? What are his major problems with them?

2. What evidence does Augustine use to support the worship of the Christian God?

3. What do Augustine's descriptions of the pagan gods and the Christian God suggest about changing ideas of morality in the weakened Roman Empire?

DOCUMENT 8-3

SAINT BENEDICT OF NURSIA

From The Rule of Saint Benedict: *Work and Pray*

529

Christian monasticism developed in the Egyptian desert at the turn of the fourth century C.E. *as a solitary activity of self-denial. In the early fourth century, however, groups of monks began to come together to live*

E. F. Henderson, ed., *Select Historical Documents of the Middle Ages* (London: G. Bell, 1892; rept., New York: AMS Press, 1968), 274–275, 288–289, 597–598.

[10] **vestal fire**: Virgin priestesses tended a fire dedicated to Vesta, goddess of the hearth and home.

[11] **Capitoline stone**: The temple dedicated to the Roman triad of deities — Jupiter, Juno, and Minerva — was located on the Capitoline Hill, which also overlooked the Roman Forum.

in self-sufficient communities. These groups required regulation, leading to the creation of monastic "rules." Saint Benedict (480–547), who turned his country estate at Monte Cassino, Italy, into a monastery, developed the most important rule for Western European monks. It guided medieval monasticism and helped shape the early Catholic Church.

Concerning the kinds of monks and their manner of living. It is manifest that there are four kinds of monks. The cenobites are the first kind; that is, those living in a monastery, serving under a rule or an abbot. Then the second kind is that of the anchorites; that is, the hermits, — those who, not by the new fervour of a conversion but by the long probation of life in a monastery, have learned to fight against the devil, having already been taught by the solace of many. They, having been well prepared in the army of brothers for the solitary fight of the hermit, being secure now without the consolation of another, are able, God helping them, to fight with their own hand or arm against the vices of the flesh or of their thoughts.

But a third very bad kind of monks are the sarabaites, approved by no rule, experience being their teacher, as with the gold which is tried in the furnace. But, softened after the manner of lead, keeping faith with the world by their works, they are known through their tonsure to lie to God. These being shut up by twos or threes, or, indeed, alone, without a shepherd, not in the Lord's but in their own sheep-folds — their law is the satisfaction of their desires. For whatever they think good or choice, this they call holy; and what they do not wish, this they consider unlawful. But the fourth kind of monks is the kind which is called gyratory. During their whole life they are guests, for three or four days at a time, in the cells of the different monasteries, throughout the various provinces; always wandering and never stationary, given over to the service of their own pleasures and the joys of the palate, and in every way worse than the sarabaites. Concerning the most wretched way of living of all of such monks it is better to be silent than to speak. These things therefore being omitted, let us proceed, with the aid of God, to treat of the best kind, the cenobites. . . .

Concerning the utensils or property of the monastery. For the belongings of the monastery in utensils, or garments, or property of any kind, the abbot shall provide brothers of whose life and morals he is sure; and to them as he shall see fit he shall consign the different things to be taken care of and collected. Concerning which the abbot shall keep a list, so that when in turn the brothers succeed each other in the care of the things assigned, he may know what he gives or what he receives. If moreover any one have soiled or treated negligently the property of the monastery, he shall be rebuked; but if he do not amend, he shall be subjected to the discipline of the Rule.

Whether the monks should have any thing of their own. More than any thing else is this special vice to be cut off root and branch from the monastery, that one should presume to give or receive anything without the order of the abbot, or should have anything of his own. He should have absolutely not anything: neither a book, nor tablets, nor a pen — nothing at all. — For indeed it is not allowed to the monks to have their own bodies or wills in their own power. But all things necessary they must expect from the Father of the monastery; nor is it allowable to have anything which the abbot did not give or permit. All things shall be common to all, as it is written: "Let not any man presume or call anything his own." But if any one shall have been discovered delighting in this most evil vice: being warned once and again, if he do not amend, let him be subjected to punishment. . . .

Concerning the daily manual labor. Idleness is the enemy of the soul. And therefore, at fixed times, the brothers ought to be occupied in manual labor; and again, at fixed times, in sacred reading. Therefore we believe that, according to this disposition, both seasons ought to be arranged; so that, from Easter until the Calends of October,[12] going out early, from the first until the fourth hour they shall do what labor may be necessary. Moreover, from the fourth hour until about the sixth, they shall be free for reading. After the meal of the sixth hour, moreover, rising from table, they shall rest in their beds with all silence; or, perchance, he that wishes to read may so read to himself that he do not disturb another. And the nona[13] shall be gone through with more moderately about the middle of the eighth hour; and again they shall work at what is to be done until Vespers.[14] But, if the exigency or poverty of the place demands that they be occupied by themselves in picking fruits, they shall not be dismayed: for then they are truly monks if they live by the labors of their hands; as did also our fathers and the apostles. Let all things be done with moderation, however, on account of the faint-hearted. . . . [There follows a slightly different schedule for the winter months from October to Easter.] But in the days of Lent,[15] from dawn until the third full hour, they shall be free for their readings; and, until the tenth full hour, they shall do the labor that is enjoined on them. In which days of Lent they shall all receive separate

---

[12] **Calends of October**: The first day of the month of October.

[13] **nona**: The second meal of the day.

[14] **Vespers**: Evening prayers.

[15] **Lent**: The forty days leading up to Easter, normally spent in self-denial, fasting, and prayer.

books from the library; which they shall read entirely through in order. These books are to be given out on the first day of Lent. Above all there shall certainly be appointed one or two elders, who shall go round the monastery at the hours in which the brothers are engaged in reading, and see to it that no troublesome brother chance to be found who is open to idleness and trifling, and is not intent on his reading; being not only of no use to himself, but also stirring up others. If such a one — may it not happen — be found, he shall be admonished once and a second time. If he do not amend, he shall be subject under the Rule to such punishment that the others may have fear. . . . On feeble or delicate brothers such a labor or art is to be imposed, that they shall neither be idle, nor shall they be so oppressed by the violence of labor as to be driven to take flight. Their weakness is to be taken into consideration by the abbot.

READING AND DISCUSSION QUESTIONS

1. What are the four kinds of monks? Which did Benedict consider the best kind?
2. Describe the daily life of a monk.
3. Why might there be so much emphasis on reading in the monastery?
4. What objects were monks allowed to own? Why would Benedict have wanted to limit the items owned by monks?

DOCUMENT 8-4

ZACHARIAH OF MITYLENE
From Syriac Chronicle
ca. 569

Zachariah of Mitylene (465/6–536), was born near Gaza and was trained in Greek rhetoric in Alexandria and in Roman law in Beirut. He served in Constantinople but became the bishop of Mitylene on the island of Lesbos, off the coast of modern Turkey. His works do not survive in Greek but do

Michael Maas, *Readings in Late Antiquity: A Sourcebook* (London: Routledge, 2000), 291–292.

exist in a Syriac translation and summary produced in northern Iraq. This
passage describes the actions of the Sassanid Persian king, Kavadh, during
an invasion of the eastern Roman territories in northern Mesopotamia. It
demonstrates the complex religious situation of the period, when different
Christian groups were competing for authority.

But Kavadh, who succeeded (Piroz) in the kingdom, and his nobles cherished hatred against the Romans, saying that they had caused the incursion of the Huns, and the pillage and the devastation of their country. And Kavadh gathered an army and went out against Theodosiopolis in Armenia of the Romans, and subdued the city; and he treated its inhabitants mercifully, because he had not been insulted by them. . . . And in the month of October he reached Amida of Mesopotamia. But though he assailed it with fierce assaults of sharp arrows and with battering-rams, which thrust the wall to overthrow it, and roofs of skin which protected those who brought together the materials for the besiegers' mound and raised it up and made it equal in height with the wall, for three months, day after day, yet he could not take the city by storm; while his own people were suffering much hardship through work and fighting, and he was constantly hearing in his ears the insults of disorderly men on the wall, and their ridicule and mockery, and he was reduced to great straits.

When Kavadh and his army had been defeated in the various assaults which they had made upon the city, and a large number of his soldiers had perished, his hands were weakened; and he asked that a small gift of silver should be given to him and he would withdraw from the city. But Leontius, the governor, and Paul Bar Zainab the steward, by the messengers whom they sent to Kavadh, demanded from him the price of the garden vegetables which his army had eaten, as well as for the corn and wine which they gathered and brought away from the villages. And when he was greatly grieved at this and was preparing to withdraw in disgrace, Christ appeared to him in a vision of the night, as he himself afterwards related it, and said to him that within three days He would deliver up to him [Kavadh] the inhabitants of the city, because they had sinned against him. . . .

[The siege was successful.]

And after three days and three nights the slaughter ceased by the king's demand. And men went in to guard the treasures of the Church and of the great men of the city, that the king might have whatever was found in them. But the order also was given that the corpses of those who were slain in the streets and of those whom they had crucified should be collected and brought round to the northern side of the city, so that the king, who was on the south side, might enter in. And they were collected, and they were numbered as they were brought out, eighty thousand. . . . And the king entered the treasury of the Church, and seeing there an image of the Lord Jesus, depicted in the likeness of a Galilean, he asked who it was. And they answered him, "It is God"; and he bowed his head before it, and said, "He it was Who said to me, 'Stay and receive from Me the city and its inhabitants, for they have sinned against me.'" . . .

But the gold and silver belonging to the great men's houses, and the beautiful garments, were collected together and given to the king's treasurers. But they also took down all the statues of the city, and the sundials, and the marble; and they collected the bronze and everything that pleased them, and they placed them upon wooden rafts that they made and sent them by the river Tigris . . . But the king sought for the chiefs and great men of the city . . . They clothed Leontius and Cyrus[16] in filthy garments, and put swine-ropes on their necks, and made them carry pigs, and led them about proclaiming and exposing them, and saying, "Rulers who do not rule their city well nor restrain its people from insulting the king, deserve such insult as this." But at last the great men, and all the chief craftsmen, were bound and brought together, and set apart as the king's captives; and they were sent to his country with the military escort which brought them down. But influential men of the king's army drew near and said to him, "Our kinsmen and brethren were killed in battle by the inhabitants of the city," and they asked him that one-tenth of the men should be given to them for the exaction of vengeance. And they brought them together and counted them, and gave to them in proportion from the men; and they put them to death, killing them in all sorts of ways.

READING AND DISCUSSION QUESTIONS

1. According to this account, why did the Persians attack Roman territory?
2. Describe the Persian treatment of the defeated inhabitants of the city.
3. How did Kavadh claim to have taken the city?
4. Kavadh was not a Christian, so why might Zachariah have blamed the victory of Kavadh on the sins of the Christian inhabitants?

---

[16] **Cyrus**: Bishop of the city.

VIEWPOINTS

Justinian's Deeds and His Critics

DOCUMENT 8-5

PROCOPIUS

From The Secret History

ca. 550–562

In addition to legalizing Christianity, Constantine constructed a new capital city in the eastern Mediterranean, Constantinople (modern-day Istanbul). Constantinople and the eastern Roman Empire survived the collapse of the western empire. This empire became influenced by Greek culture and is called the Byzantine Empire by scholars. One of the foremost emperors of the Byzantine Empire was Justinian, who was the subject of many writings by the contemporary historian Procopius, who worked for Justinian's general Belisarius. Procopius wrote many works praising Justinian, such as On Buildings, *but his* Secret History *launches a vicious assault on Justinian and his inner circle. As such, it must have circulated secretly during Justinian's life.*

When Justinian ascended the throne it took him a very little while to bring everything into confusion. Things hitherto forbidden by law were one by one brought into public life, while established customs were swept away wholesale, as if he had been invested with the forms of majesty on condition that he would change all things to new forms. Long established offices were abolished, and new ones set up to run the nation's business; the laws of the land and the organization of the army were treated in the same way, not because justice required it or the general interest urged him to it, but merely that everything might have a new look and might be associated with his name. If there was anything which he was not in a

G. A. Williamson, trans., *Procopius: The Secret History* (London: Penguin Books, 1966, 1981), 94–95, 101–103.

position to transform then and there, even so he would at least attach his own name to it.

Of the forcible seizure of property and the murder of his subjects he could never have enough: when he had looted innumerable houses of wealthy people he was constantly on the look-out for others, immediately squandering on one foreign tribe or another, or on crazy building schemes, all that he had amassed by his earlier looting. And when he had without any excuse got rid of thousands and thousands of people, or so it would seem, he promptly devised schemes for doing the same to others more numerous still.

At that time the Romans were at peace with all other nations; so not knowing how to satisfy his lust for blood Justinian kept flinging all the foreign nations at each other's throats; and sending for the chieftains of the Huns, though he had no reason at all, with senseless prodigality he flung vast sums into their laps, making out, if you please, that these were pledges of friendship. This he was stated to have done even when Justin was on the throne.[17] They for their part, having received this windfall, used to send some of their brother-chieftains at the head of their men, urging them to make sudden raids into the Emperor's territory, so that they too might be in a position to exact a price for peace from the man who for no reason at all was prepared to pay for it. These chiefs at once began the enslavement of the Roman Empire, and all the time they were in the Emperor's pay. Their example was immediately followed by others, who joined in the pillaging of the unfortunate Romans, and on top of the pillage received as a reward for their inroads the extravagant largesse of the Emperor. Thus, in short, from year's end to year's end they all took turns to plunder and pillage everything within their reach. For these native races have many groups of chieftains, and the war was passed from one group to another in rotation as a result of Justinian's inexcusable prodigality; it could never come to an end, but went on circling round itself month after month, year after year. And so no single patch of ground, mountain, cave, or anything else on Roman soil, escaped being pillaged at this time, and many places were actually overrun five times or more. These calamities, however, and all those suffered at the hands

---

[17] **even when Justin was on the throne**: Justin was Justinian's uncle and the ruler of the empire just prior to Justinian. According to Procopius, Justinian played an important role in developing policy during Justin's reign.

of Medes, Saracens, Slavs, Antae,[18] and other foreign nations, have been recounted in my earlier volumes; but as I said in the first paragraph of the present volume, it is essential that I should make clear now where the responsibility lay for all that happened. . . .

Until the "Nika" insurrection[19] took place, they were content to annex the estates of the well-to-do one at a time; but after it took place, as I related in an earlier volume, from then on they confiscated at a single stroke the possessions of nearly all the senators. On all movable property and on the most attractive landed estates they laid their hands just as they fancied; but they set aside properties liable to oppressive and crushing taxation, and with sham generosity *sold* them to their previous owners! These in consequence were throttled by the tax-collectors and reduced to penury by the never-ending interest on their debts, dragging out a miserable existence that was no more than a lingering death.

In view of all this I, like most of my contemporaries, never once felt that these two were human beings: they were a pair of blood-thirsty demons and what the poets call "plaguers of mortal men." For they plotted together to find the easiest and swiftest means of destroying all races of men and all their works, assumed human shape, became man-demons, and in this way convulsed the whole world. Proof of this could be found in many things, but especially in the power manifested in their doings. For the actions of demons are unmistakably different from those of human beings. In the long course of time there have doubtless been many men who by chance or by nature have inspired the utmost fear, and by their unaided efforts have ruined cities or countries or whatever it might be; but to bring destruction on all mankind and calamities on the whole world has been beyond the power of any but these two, who were, it is true, aided in their endeavours by chance, which collaborated in the ruin of mankind; for earthquakes, pestilences, and rivers that burst their banks brought wide-

---

[18] **Medes, Saracens, Slavs, Antae:** All foreign peoples. *Medes* is another name for the Persians (see Document 8-4). *Saracens* was a derogatory term for nomads along the desert frontiers in the Middle East. Slavs were nomadic groups who settled in central Europe. The Antae were a nomadic group related to the Slavs.

[19] **"Nika" insurrection:** In 532, riots began at the chariot races in Constantinople's hippodrome. The riots almost pushed Justinian out of the city, and many important buildings, such as Hagia Sophia (see Document 8-6) were damaged. In the end, Justinian retained his throne through bribery and the slaughter of thousands.

spread destruction at this time, as I shall explain shortly. Thus it was not by human but by some very different power that they wrought such havoc.

It is said that Justinian's own mother told some of her close friends that he was not the son of her husband Sabbatius or of any man at all. For when she was about to conceive she was visited by a demon, who was invisible but gave her a distinct impression that he was really there with her like a man in bodily contact with a woman. Then he vanished like a dream.

Some of those who were in the Emperor's company late at night, conversing with him (evidently in the Palace) — men of the highest possible character — thought that they saw a strange demonic form in his place. One of them declared that he more than once rose suddenly from the imperial throne and walked round and round the room; for he was not in the habit of remaining seated for long. And Justinian's head would momentarily disappear, while the rest of his body seemed to continue making these long circuits. The watcher himself, thinking that something had gone seriously wrong with his eyesight, stood for a long time distressed and quite at a loss. But later the head returned to the body, and he thought that what a moment before had been lacking was, contrary to expectation, filling out again. A second man said that he stood by the Emperor's side as he sat, and saw his face suddenly transformed to a shapeless lump of flesh: neither eyebrows nor eyes were in their normal position, and it showed no other distinguishing feature at all; gradually, however, he saw the face return to its usual shape. I did not myself witness the events I am describing, but I heard about them from men who insist that they saw them at the time.

READING AND DISCUSSION QUESTIONS

1. How does Procopius describe Justinian?

2. What policies did Justinian pursue? Did Procopius feel that these policies were in the interest of the Byzantine state?

3. How does Procopius describe Justinian's relationship with other world leaders? What was the impact of these policies?

4. Explain how Procopius wrote some works that praised Justinian, while also authoring this work. What do you think was the purpose of *The Secret History*?

DOCUMENT 8-6

Hagia Sophia

537

At the beginning of Justinian's reign, rioters in the Nika revolt burned Hagia Sophia, the church dedicated to Holy Wisdom. Justinian decided to replace it with an extravagant structure and spared no expense. The crowning achievement was the large dome, designed by Anthemius of Tralles, which Procopius described as seeming to be "suspended from heaven by a fabled golden chain." When the church was dedicated, Justinian claimed to have outdone Solomon's construction of the first temple of Jerusalem. The structure awed all visitors to Constantinople for centuries, and when the Ottomans took the city in 1453, they converted it into a mosque and added the minarets that can be seen in this image.

Murat Taner/Getty Images.

READING AND DISCUSSION QUESTIONS

1. Describe the structure of the Hagia Sophia.
2. Why would Justinian have wanted to build such an impressive church?
3. How did the Ottomans appropriate the structure for Islam?

DOCUMENT 8-7

EINHARD

From The Life of Charlemagne

829–836

During the collapse of the western half of the Roman Empire in the fifth century, the Franks took control of northern Gaul (now called France). By the middle of the eighth century, the Franks had become the most powerful of the Germanic kingdoms. Charlemagne (747–814), or Charles the Great, amassed such a large empire in what is now France, Germany, and Italy that he was crowned Roman Emperor on Christmas Day in 800 by Pope Leo III, who was seeking allies against the Byzantine Empire. One of Charlemagne's closest friends and advisers, Einhard, composed these passages, which describe Charlemagne's building projects and his personal characteristics

However much energy Charlemagne may have expended in enlarging his realm and conquering foreign nations, and despite all the time which he devoted to this preoccupation, he nevertheless set in hand many projects which aimed at making his kingdom more attractive and at increasing public utility. Some of these projects he completed. Outstanding among these, one might claim, are the great church of the Holy Mother of God at Aachen, which is a really remarkable construction, and the bridge over the Rhine at Mainz, which is five hundred feet long, this being the width of the river at that point. The bridge was burned down just one year before Charlemagne's death. He planned to rebuild it in stone instead of wood, but his death followed so quickly that the bridge could not be restored in time. He also began the construction of two magnificent palaces: one not far from the city of Mainz, near the township called Ingelheim; and the other at Nimeguen, on the River Waal, which flows along the southern shore of the Betuwa peninsula. More important still was the fact that he commanded the bishops and churchmen in whose care they were to restore sacred edifices which had fallen into ruin through their very antiquity, wherever he discovered them throughout the whole of his kingdom;

Lewis Thorpe, trans., *Two Lives of Charlemagne: Einhard and Notker the Stammerer* (London: Penguin Books, 1969), 71, 78–80.

and he instructed his representatives to see that these orders were carried out. . . .

He was moderate in his eating and drinking, and especially so in drinking; for he hated to see drunkenness in any man, and even more so in himself and his friends. All the same, he could not go long without food, and he often used to complain that fasting made him feel ill. He rarely gave banquets and these only on high feast days, but then he would invite a great number of guests. His main meal of the day was served in four courses, in addition to the roast meat which his hunters used to bring in on spits and which he enjoyed more than any other food. During his meal he would listen to a public reading or some other entertainment. Stories would be recited for him, or the doings of the ancients told again. He took great pleasure in the books of Saint Augustine and especially in those which are called *The City of God*.

He was so sparing in his use of wine and every other beverage that he rarely drank more than three times in the course of his dinner. In summer, after his midday meal, he would eat some fruit and take another drink; then he would remove his shoes and undress completely, just as he did at night, and rest for two or three hours. During the night he slept so lightly that he would wake four or five times and rise from his bed. When he was dressing and putting on his shoes he would invite his friends to come in. Moreover, if the Count of the Palace told him that there was some dispute which could not be settled without the Emperor's personal decision, he would order the disputants to be brought in there and then, hear the case as if he were sitting in tribunal and pronounce a judgement. If there was any official business to be transacted on that day, or any order to be given to one of his ministers, he would settle it at the same time.

He spoke easily and fluently, and could express with great clarity whatever he wanted to say. He was not content with his own mother tongue, but took the trouble to learn foreign languages. He learnt Latin so well that he spoke it as fluently as his own tongue; but he understood Greek better than he could speak it. He was eloquent to the point of sometimes seeming almost garrulous.

He paid the greatest attention to the liberal arts; and he had great respect for men who taught them, bestowing high honours upon them. When he was learning the rules of grammar he received tuition from Peter the Deacon of Pisa, who by then was an old man, but for all other subjects he was taught by Alcuin, surnamed Albinus, another Deacon, a man of the Saxon race who came from Britain and was the most learned man anywhere to be found. Under him the emperor spent much time and effort in studying rhetoric, dialectic and especially astrology. He applied himself to mathematics and traced the course of the stars with great attention and care. He also tried to learn to write. With this object in view he used to keep writing-tablets and notebooks under the pillows on his bed, so that he could try his hand at forming letters during his leisure moments; but, although he tried very hard, he had begun too late in life and he made little progress.

Charlemagne practised the Christian religion with great devotion and piety, for he had been brought up in this faith since earliest childhood. This explains why he built a cathedral of such great beauty at Aachen, decorating it with gold and silver, with lamps, and with lattices and doors of solid bronze. He was unable to find marble columns for his construction anywhere else, and so he had them brought from Rome and Ravenna.

As long as his health lasted he went to church morning and evening with great regularity, and also for early-morning Mass, and the late-night hours. He took the greatest pains to ensure that all church ceremonies were performed with the utmost dignity, and he was always warning the sacristans to see that nothing sordid or dirty was brought into the building or left there. He donated so many sacred vessels made of gold and silver, and so many priestly vestments, that when service time came even those who opened and closed the doors, surely the humblest of all church dignitaries, had no need to perform their duties in their everyday clothes.

He made careful reforms in the way in which the psalms were chanted and the lessons read. He was himself quite an expert at both of these exercises, but he never read the lesson in public and he would sing only with the rest of the congregation and then in a low voice.

He was most active in relieving the poor and in that form of really disinterested charity which the Greeks call *eleemosyna*. He gave alms not only in his own country and in the kingdom over which he reigned, but also across the sea in Syria, Egypt, Africa, Jerusalem, Alexandria and Carthage. Wherever he heard that Christians were living in want, he took pity on their poverty and sent them money regularly. It was, indeed, precisely for this reason that he sought the friendship of kings beyond the sea, for he hoped that some relief and alleviation might result for the Christians living under their domination.

READING AND DISCUSSION QUESTIONS

1. What features of Charlemagne's personal habits would have made him a good ruler?
2. Describe Charlemagne's personality. What were his religious beliefs?
3. What does this source tell us about life in post-Roman Europe?

COMPARATIVE QUESTIONS

1. What do the documents in this chapter reveal about the political, cultural, and religious changes that had taken place since the time of ancient Rome (Chapter 6)?
2. What values did Christians profess, according to Egeria and Saints Augustine and Benedict? How might these values have affected their society?
3. Are there any ways in which Augustine may have been influenced by Tertullian (Document 6-7)? How do their attitudes toward paganism differ?
4. What does this chapter reveal about the foreign relations between kingdoms after the collapse of the western Roman Empire?
5. Compare Procopius's description of Justinian in *The Secret History* with the construction of the Hagia Sophia. In what ways does the Hagia Sophia confirm Procopius's description, and in what ways does this building challenge Procopius?
6. Why does Procopius's description of Justinian seem so different from Einhard's description of Charlemagne? Compare the two rulers.

CHAPTER 9

The Islamic World

600–1400

I n the sixth century, the city of Mecca rose to prominence in the Arabian peninsula because of the popularity of its religious shrine, the Ka'ba, and its trade with the Byzantine and Persian Empires. The Prophet Muhammad (ca. 570–632) began his adult life working Mecca's caravans, but on turning forty he began to have revelations that formed the basis for the Qur'an. In 622, Muhammad was forced out of Mecca and led his followers to Medina, where he settled disputes between Jewish merchant groups and eventually became the leader of the city. Muhammad later captured the city of Mecca and united the nomadic tribes of the Arabian peninsula. Under Muhammad's successors, the caliphs, Islamic armies conquered the Middle East, North Africa, Spain, and portions of northern India. In so doing, the Muslims encountered Jews and Christians — honored as fellow "people of the book" — as well as polytheists, whom they persecuted. During the Umayyad (661–750) and the Abbasid (750–1258) Dynasties, the Islamic caliphate dominated the world in economic activity, scientific development, and culture.

VIEWPOINTS

Islam and the People of the Book

DOCUMENT 9-1

MUHAMMAD

Qur'an: Muslim Devotion to God

ca. 650

The Prophet Muhammad urged "submission" (Islam) to God (Allah) and he demanded that the nomadic Arab tribes of the Arabian peninsula convert from polytheism. His revelations (Qur'an) delivered by the angel Gabriel accepted the authority of Jewish prophets and the teachings of Jesus, who was considered a prophet. However, Islamic faith holds that the Jewish and Christian scriptures are corrupt versions of God's teachings, which appear in their purest form in the Qur'an. While Muhammad lived, the Qur'an was passed orally or in short written sections, but during the reign of the caliph Uthman (644–656), these fragments were collected into a unified document.

IN THE NAME OF GOD, THE COMPASSIONATE, THE MERCIFUL

Praise be to God, the Lord of the Worlds!

The Compassionate, the Merciful!

King of the day of judgment!

Thee we worship, and Thee we ask for help.

Guide us in the straight way,

The way of those to whom Thou art gracious;

Not of those upon whom is Thy wrath, nor of the erring.

In the name of the merciful and compassionate God. That is the book! there is no doubt therein; a guide to the pious, who believe in the unseen,

N. J. Dawood, trans., *The Koran: With a Parallel Arabic Text* (London: Penguin Books, 1990), 28–29, 76–77, 81.

and are steadfast in prayer, and of what we have given them expend in alms; who believe in what is revealed to thee, and what was revealed before thee, and of the hereafter they are sure. These are in guidance from their Lord, and these are the prosperous.

Verily, those who misbelieve, it is the same to them if ye warn them or if ye warn them not, they will not believe. God has set a seal upon their hearts and on their hearing; and on their eyes is dimness, and for them is grievous woe. There are, indeed, those among men who say, "We believe in God and in the last day"; but they do not believe. They would deceive God and those who do believe; but they deceive only themselves and they do not perceive. In their hearts is a sickness, and God has made them still more sick, and for them is grievous woe because they lied. . . .

And if ye are in doubt of what we have revealed unto our servant, then bring a chapter like it, and call your witnesses other than God if ye tell truth. But if ye do it not, and ye shall surely do it not, then fear the fire, whose fuel is men and stones, prepared for misbelievers. But bear the glad tidings to those who believe and work righteousness, that for them are gardens beneath which rivers flow. Whenever they are provided with fruit therefrom they say, "This is what we were provided with before, and they shall be provided with the like; and there are pure wives for them therein, and they shall dwell therein for aye [forever]." . . .

IN THE NAME OF GOD, THE COMPASSIONATE, THE MERCIFUL

Have we not made the earth as a bed? And the mountains as tent-pegs? and created you in pairs, and made you sleep for rest, and made the night for a mantle, and made the day for breadwinning, and built above you seven firmaments, and put therein a burning lamp, and sent down water pouring from the squeezed clouds to bring forth grain and herb withal, and gardens thick with trees?

Lo! the Day of Decision is appointed — the day when there shall be a blowing of the trumpet, and ye shall come in troops, and the heavens shall be opened, and be full of gates, and the mountains shall be removed, and turn into [mist]. Verily hell lieth in wait, the goal for rebels, to abide therein for ages; they shall not taste therein coolness nor drink, save scalding water and running sores, — a meet reward! Verily they did not expect the reckoning, and they denied our signs with lies; but everything have we recorded in a book: —

Then the people of the right hand — what people of good omen! And the people of the left hand — what people of ill omen! And the outstrippers, still outstripping: — these are the nearest [to God], in gardens of delight; a crowd of the men of yore, and a few of the latter days; upon inwrought couches, reclining thereon face to face. Youths ever young shall go unto them round about with goblets and ewers [pitchers] and a cup of flowing wine, — their heads shall not ache with it, neither shall they be confused; and fruits of their choice, and flesh of birds of their desire; and damsels with bright eyes like hidden pearls, — a reward for what they have wrought. They shall hear no folly therein, nor any sin, but only the greeting, "Peace! peace!"

And the people of the right hand — what people of good omen! Amid thornless lote-trees,[1] and bananas laden with fruit, and shade outspread, and water flowing, and fruit abundant, never failing, nor forbidden, . . . But the people of the left hand — what people of ill omen! — amid burning wind and scalding water, and a shade of black smoke, not cool or grateful! Verily before that they were prosperous; but they persisted in the most grievous sin, and used to say, "When we have died, and become dust and bones, shall we indeed be raised again, and our fathers, the men of yore." Say: Verily those of yore and of the latter days shall surely be gathered to the trysting-place of a day which is known. Then ye, O ye who err and call it a lie, shall surely eat of the tree of Zakkum,[2] and fill your bellies with it, and drink upon it scalding water, — drink like the thirsty camel: — this shall be their entertainment on the Day of Judgment! . . .

On Violence, Unbelievers, and the People of the Book

In the month of Ramaḍān the Qur'an was revealed, a book of guidance for mankind with proofs of guidance distinguishing right from wrong. Therefore whoever of you is present in that month let him fast. But he who is ill or on a journey shall fast a similar number of days later on.

God desires your well-being, not your discomfort. He desires you to fast the whole month so that you may magnify God and render thanks to Him for giving you His guidance.

If My servants question you about Me, tell them that I am near. I answer the prayer of the suppliant when he calls to Me; therefore let them answer My call and put their trust in Me, that they may be rightly guided.

---

[1] **lote-trees**: Mythical trees representing the boundary between humans and Allah and beyond which no mortal can pass; they mark the uppermost limit of human knowledge.
[2] **Zakkum**: A tree in hell that causes a burning sensation when eaten. People in hell are forced to eat from it.

It is now lawful for you to lie with your wives on the night of the fast; they are a comfort to you as you are to them. God knew that you were deceiving yourselves. He has relented towards you and pardoned you. Therefore you may now lie with them and seek what God has ordained for you. Eat and drink until you can tell a white thread from a black one in the light of the coming dawn. Then resume the fast till nightfall and do not approach them, but stay at your prayers in the mosques.

These are the bounds set by God: do not approach them. Thus He makes known His revelations to mankind that they may guard themselves against evil.

Do not devour one another's property by unjust means, nor bribe the judges with it in order that you may wrongfully and knowingly usurp the possessions of other men.

They question you about the phases of the moon. Say: "They are seasons fixed for mankind and for the pilgrimage."

Righteousness does not consist in entering your dwellings from the back.[3] The righteous man is he that fears God. Enter your dwellings by their doors and fear God, so that you may prosper.

Fight for the sake of God those that fight against you, but do not attack them first. God does not love aggressors.

Slay them wherever you find them. Drive them out of the places from which they drove you. Idolatry is more grievous than bloodshed. But do not fight them within the precincts of the Holy Mosque unless they attack you there; if they attack you put them to the sword. Thus shall the unbelievers be rewarded: but if they mend their ways, know that God is forgiving and merciful.

Fight against them until idolatry is no more and God's religion reigns supreme. But if they desist, fight none except the evil-doers.

A sacred month for a sacred month: sacred things too are subject to retaliation. If anyone attacks you, attack him as he attacked you. Have fear of God, and know that God is with the righteous.

Give generously for the cause of God and do not with your own hands cast yourselves into destruction. Be charitable; God loves the charitable.

Make the pilgrimage and visit the Sacred House for His sake. If you cannot, send such offerings as you can afford and do not shave your heads until the offerings have reached their destination. But if any of you is ill or

---

[3] **entering your dwellings from the back**: The pre-Islamic Arabs would enter their houses from the back when they had completed a pilgrimage.

suffers from an ailment of the head, he must do penance either by fasting or by almsgiving or by offering a sacrifice. . . .

The People of the Book ask you to bring down for them a book from heaven. Of Moses they demanded a harder thing than that. They said to him: "Show us God distinctly." And for their wickedness the thunderbolt smote them. They worshipped the calf after clear signs had been revealed to them; yet We forgave them that, and bestowed on Moses clear authority.

When We made a covenant with them We raised the Mount above them and said: "Enter the gates in adoration. Do not break the Sabbath." We took from them a solemn covenant. But they broke their covenant, denied the revelations of God, and killed the prophets unjustly. They said: "Our hearts are sealed."

It is God who has sealed their hearts, on account of their unbelief. They have no faith, except a few of them.

They denied the truth and uttered a monstrous falsehood against Mary. They declared: "We have put to death the Messiah, Jesus son of Mary, the apostle of God." They did not kill him, nor did they crucify him, but they thought they did.

God made a covenant with the Israelites and raised among them twelve chieftains. God said: "I shall be with you. If you attend to your prayers and render the alms levy; if you believe in My apostles and assist them and give God a generous loan, I shall forgive you your sins and admit you to gardens watered by running streams. But he that hereafter denies Me shall stray from the right path."

But because they broke their covenant We laid on them Our curse and hardened their hearts. They have tampered with words out of their context and forgotten much of what they were enjoined. You will ever find them deceitful, except for a few of them. But pardon them and bear with them. God loves those who do good.

With those who said they were Christians We made a covenant also, but they too have forgotten much of what they were exhorted to do. Therefore We stirred among them enmity and hatred, which shall endure till the Day of Resurrection, when God will declare to them all that they have done.

People of the Book! Our apostle has come to reveal to you much of what you have hidden of the Scriptures, and to forgive you much. A light has come to you from God and a glorious Book, with which God will guide to the paths of peace those that seek to please Him; He will lead them by His will from darkness to the light; He will guide them to a straight path.

Unbelievers are those who declare: "God is the Messiah, the son of Mary." Say: "Who could prevent God, if He so willed, from destroying the Messiah, the son of Mary, his mother, and all the people of the earth? God has sovereignty over the heavens and the earth and all that lies between them. He creates what He will; and God has power over all things."

The Jews and the Christians say: "We are the children of God and His loved ones." Say: "Why then does He punish you for your sins? Surely you are mortals of His own creation. He forgives whom He will and punishes whom He pleases. God has sovereignty over the heavens and the earth and all that lies between them. All shall return to Him."

Those that disagreed about him were in doubt concerning him; they knew nothing about him that was not sheer conjecture; they did not slay him for certain. God lifted him up to Him; God is mighty and wise. There is none among the People of the Book but will believe in him before his death; and on the Day of Resurrection he will bear witness against them.

Because of their iniquity, We forbade the Jews wholesome things which were formerly allowed them; because time after time they have debarred others from the path of God; because they practise usury — although they were forbidden it — and cheat others of their possessions. Woeful punishment have We prepared for those that disbelieve. But those of them that have deep learning, and those that truly believe in what has been revealed to you and what was revealed before you; who attend to their prayers and render the alms levy and have faith in God and the Last Day — these shall be richly recompensed.

We have revealed Our will to you as We revealed it to Noah and to the prophets who came after him; as We revealed it to Abraham, Ishmael, Isaac, Jacob, and the tribes; to Jesus, Job, Jonah, Aaron, Solomon and David,[4] to whom We gave the Psalms. Of some apostles We have already told you, but there are others of whom We have not yet spoken (God spoke directly to Moses): apostles who brought good news to mankind and admonished them, so that they might have no plea against God after their coming. God is mighty and wise.

---

[4] **Abraham, Ishmael, . . . Solomon and David**: People mentioned in the Hebrew Bible.

READING AND DISCUSSION QUESTIONS

1. How is God (Allah) described in these passages? What Muslim religious practices do they reveal?

2. What is the fate for believers and unbelievers? In what ways does this contradict or support the idea of a compassionate, merciful God?

3. What does this selection say about religious violence? What about nonreligious violence?

4. How does the Qur'an describe Jews and Christians? How does this selection criticize their beliefs? How is Islam connected to Judaism and Christianity?

DOCUMENT 9-2

MUHAMMAD

The Constitution of Medina: Muslims and Jews at the Dawn of Islam

ca. 625

In 622, Muhammad was invited by the Jewish tribes of Yathrib (Medina) to settle disputes that caused continual fighting among them. Because Muhammad's teaching faced growing persecution in Mecca, his entire community followed him to Medina. This "flight" (hijra) marks the beginning of the Islamic calendar. Muhammad became the most important leader in Medina as many of the Jewish tribes converted to Islam. Around 625, Muhammad and the remaining Jewish tribes signed the following treaty, which was originally recorded by the eighth-century Arabic historian Ibn Ishaq and preserved in the text of the ninth-century writer Ibn Hisham.

The Messenger of God [Muhammad] wrote a document, concerning the emigrants from Mecca and the helpers of Medina, in which he reconciled

---

J. A. Williams, *Themes in Islamic Civilization* (Berkeley and Los Angeles: University of California Press, 1971), 11–15.

the Jews and covenanted with them, letting them act freely in the religion and possessions which they had, and stated reciprocal obligations.

IN THE NAME OF GOD, THE MERCIFUL, THE COMPASSIONATE!

This document is from Muhammad the Prophet, governing relations among the Believers and the Muslims of Quraysh [Mecca] and Yathrib (Medina) and those who followed them and joined with them and struggled with them.

1. They are one Community (*umma*) to the exclusion of all other men. . . .
11. The Believers shall not desert any poor person among them, but shall pay his redemption or blood-money, as is proper.
12. No Believer shall seek to turn the auxiliary of another Believer against him.
13. God-fearing Believers will be against whoever among them is rebellious or whoever seeks to sow injustice or sin or enmity among the Believers; every man's hand shall be against him, though he were the son of one of them.
14. No Believer shall kill a Believer for the sake of an unbeliever, or aid an unbeliever against a Believer.
15. The protection of God is one: even the least of them may extend it to a stranger. The Believers are friends to each other, to the exclusion of all other men.
16. The Jews who follow us shall have aid and equality, except those who do wrong or aid the enemies of the Muslims.
17. The peace of the Believers is one: no Believer shall make peace separately where there is fighting for God's sake. Conditions (of peace) must be just and equitable to all.
18. In every raid, the riders shall ride close together.
19. And the Believers shall avenge one another's blood, if shed for God's sake, for the God-fearing have the best and strongest guidance.
20. No idolator [polytheist] (of Medina) shall take Qurayshi property or persons under his protection, nor shall he turn anyone against a Believer.
21. Whoever kills a Believer shall also be killed, unless the next of kin of the slain man is otherwise satisfied, and the Believers shall be against him altogether; no one is permitted to act otherwise.

22. No Believer who accepts this document and believes in God and Judgment is permitted to aid a criminal or give him shelter. The curse of God and His wrath on the Day of Judgment shall fall upon whoever aids or shelters him, and no repentance or compensation shall be accepted from him if he does.

23. Whenever you differ about a case, it shall be referred to God and to Muhammad.

24. The Jews shall bear expenses with the Muslims as long as they fight along with them.

25. The Jews of the Banu 'Awf [one Jewish tribe] are one community with the Believers; the Jews have their religion and the Muslims have theirs. This is so for them and their clients, except for one who does wrong or treachery; he hurts only himself and his family. . . .

46. Everyone shall have his portion from the side to which he belongs; the Jews of al-Aws [another Jewish tribe], their clients and themselves, are in the same position as the people of this document. Honorable dealing is without treachery.

47. Whoever acquires any (guilt) does not acquire it for any but himself. God is the most just and loyal fulfiller of what is in this document. This writing will not protect a wrongdoer or a traitor. Whoever goes out is safe, and he who stays at home is safe in the town, unless he has done wrong or treachery. God is the protecting neighbor (jar) of whoever does good and fears Him, and Muhammad is the Messenger of God. Verily God is wrathful when His covenant is broken. Peace be upon you.

READING AND DISCUSSION QUESTIONS

1. What is the role of religion in administering justice for Muhammad and the tribes of Medina?

2. How is the relationship between Jews and Muslims defined here? What could negatively affect that relationship?

3. Muhammad, unlike Jesus, was a secular ruler in addition to being a religious teacher. How may this have affected his teachings?

ABRAHAM BEN YIJU

From Cairo Geniza: *Letter to Joseph*

1153

In the late 1800s, thousands of fragmentary documents from the Islamic period were discovered in a Cairo synagogue. Many of the texts were written by Jewish merchants in Hebrew script, but the language of the documents is Arabic. These documents were stored in a Geniza (sacred storeroom) because the Hebrew script was considered holy and could not be destroyed. The family of merchants represented in the texts traded with communities in India, central Asia, southern Arabia, and throughout the Mediterranean, as revealed in this letter, sent by Abraham in Fustat (modern-day Cairo) to his brother Joseph in Sicily. The discovery of these texts completely changed the way that scholars interpreted the economic history of this period and Muslim-Jewish relationships.

In Your name, O Merciful.
This is my letter to you, my dear, nob[le] brother and lord . . . , may God prolong your life and preserve you and keep you! May he unite us in the near future in the best of circumstances, fulfilling our happiest hopes in His grace and favor, for He is omnipotent!

You will be pleased to know that I had sent you a number of letters, which, however, came into the possession of Mevassēr, who did not make the effort to forward them to you. Then, he came to Aden, and I exerted myself for him beyond my ability, until I found out that I had gotten myself into trouble. However, it would take too much time to explain my experience with him.

Now, my brother, it has pleased God, the Exalted, to ordain my safe arrival in Fustat. *Let them praise the Lord for His steadfast love* and I have already heard that [you have a grown son . . .] who is *learned in Torah*, and two other sons. [I am in the possession of × thousand and ×] hundred dinars

---

S. D. Goitein and Mordechai A. Friedman, *India Traders of the Middle Ages: Documents from the Cairo Geniza* (Leiden: Brill, 2007), 728–732.

and am well-off. [. . . Out in India] two children were born to me, pleasant as the twigs of sweet basil. [The younger died in India.] The firstborn died in Aden. . . . I have no words to describe him. . . . I have left a daughter, his sister, li[ke . . . She will receive] all my money. Now by God [when my letter arrives,] send your [eldest] son [. . .] so that we have joy from her and from him and marry [them. . . . While] in Aden, Sheikh Khalaf b. Bundār [had asked me for her hand] for his son, and she stayed three years in their house. However, I called the engagement off, when I heard about your son Surūr, because I said: "My brother's son has more rights (to her) than strangers." When I brought her to Egypt, many asked me for her hand. I am writing you this, so that you should know. Saying less about this would have been enough.

I sent you with Sulaymān b. Siṭrūn a bale (*shikāra*), called *surra*, containing pepper and ginger, in a mixture, weighing exactly one *qintār* and fifteen *ratl*.[5] May God ordain that it arrives safely and comes into your hand safely! However, do not deal with it as you did with the pepper, which I had sent you and which you lost through incompetence.

Your letters to me should reach me in Fustat, God willing. Let your son Surūr carry the letters. Were it not now the time of the sailing of the *Salībiyya* (winds), I would have sent more for you [[and sons]] and your sons. Sulaymān and Abraham will explain to you my situation and the troubles I have.

As to Mevassēr, he is not a man, he is indolent, possessed of a hard heart. I gave him all he needed, although I got into trouble (through him). By these lines, I lost one thousand and forty dinars[6] and suffered also losses on my way to Fustat, six hundred dinars.

Receive for your noble self the best greetings, and to your three sons — may God preserve them! — the best greetings, and she who is with you, their mother, is greeted by me with the best greetings.

---

[5] **one *qintār* and fifteen *ratl*:** A *ratl* is equal to a pound; a *qintār* is 100 ratl.
[6] **dinars:** The common currency in Islamic lands.

READING AND DISCUSSION QUESTIONS

1. What does this document reveal about family life and personal relationships between merchants at this time?

2. What information does the merchant mention about his trading activities?

3. What places are mentioned in the document? What can you infer about the possibility of travel in this period?

DOCUMENT 9-4

BENJAMIN BEN JONAH OF TUDELA
From Book of Travels

ca. 1159–1172

By the twelfth century, cultures throughout the Mediterranean were coming into contact with one another, largely as a consequence of the Crusades that began in 1095. Following in the paths of merchant vessels from Italian city-states and Crusader armies, travelers and pilgrims began to cross from Europe to the Middle East. One such traveler, Benjamin ben Jonah of Tudela, left his home in Christian-controlled Spain and visited Jewish communities throughout Europe and the Middle East. Benjamin's record of his journeys, the Book of Travels, *describes the social and religious customs at his various stops.*

Baghdad [is] . . . the royal residence of the Caliph[7] Emir al-Muminin al-Abbasi (1160–1170) of the family of Muhammad [Abbasid Dynasty]. He is at the head of the Muslim religion, and all the kings of Islam obey him; he occupies a similar position to that held by the pope over the Christians. He has a palace in Baghdad three miles in extent, wherein is a great park with all varieties of trees, fruit-bearing and otherwise, and all

---

Benjamin ben Jonah, *The Itinerary of Benjamin of Tudela*, trans. Marcus N. Adler (London: H. Frowde, 1907), 35–42.

[7] **Caliph**: A successor of Muhammad; the title denotes the secular and religious leader of the Islamic community, or *umma*.

manner of animals. . . . There the great king, al-Abbasi the Caliph holds his court, and he is kind unto Israel [the Jewish people], and many belonging to the people of Israel are his attendants; he knows all languages, and is well versed in the Law of Israel. He reads and writes the holy language [Hebrew]. . . . He is truthful and trusty, speaking peace to all men. . . .

In Baghdad there are about forty thousand Jews,[8] and they dwell in security, prosperity, and honor under the great Caliph, and among them are great sages, the heads of Academies engaged in the study of the Law [Jewish law: the Torah and the Talmud]. In this city there are ten Academies. . . . And at the head of them all is Daniel the son of Hisdai, who is styled "Our Lord the Head of the Captivity of all Israel." He possesses a book of pedigrees going back as far as David, King of Israel (ca. 1000–965 B.C.E.). The Jews call him "Our Lord, Head of the Captivity," and the Muslims call him "Saidna ben Daoud," ["Lord, son of David"] and he has been invested with authority over all the congregations of Israel at the hands of the Emir al-Muminin, the Lord of Islam. For thus Muhammad [not the Prophet, but a later Abbasid ruler of Baghdad] commanded concerning him and his descendants; and he granted him a seal of office over all the congregations that dwell under his rule, and ordered that every one, whether Muslim or Jew, or belonging to any other nation in his dominion, should rise up before him and salute him, and that any one who should refuse to rise up should receive one hundred stripes [public lashes].

And every fifth day when he goes to pay a visit to the great Caliph, horsemen, gentiles as well as Jews, escort him, and heralds proclaim in advance, "Make way before our Lord, the son of David, as is due unto him," the Arabic words being "Amilu tarik la Saidna ben Daud." He is mounted on a horse, and is attired in robes of silk and embroidery with a large turban on his head. . . . Then he appears before the Caliph and kisses his hand, and the Caliph rises and places him on a throne which Muhammad had ordered to be made for him, and all the Muslim princes who attend the court of the Caliph rise up before him. And the Head of the Captivity is seated on his throne opposite to the Caliph, in compliance with the command of Muhammad. . . . The authority of the Head of the Captivity extends over all the communities of Shinar,[9] Persia, Khurasan,

---

[8] **forty thousand Jews:** Some of these Jews were the descendants of families deported by Nebuchadnezzar during the Babylonian captivity (586–537 B.C.E.).

[9] **the communities of Shinar:** The Head of the Captivity's reach extended through great stretches of Mesopotamia, Northeastern Iran, around the Black Sea, all the way to a city in central Asia along the Silk Road, then to Tibet and India.

and Sheba which is El-Yemen, and Diyar Kalach and the land of Aram Naharaim, and over the dwellers in the mountains of Ararat and the land of the Alans. . . . His authority extends also over the land of Siberia, and the communities in the land of the Togarmim unto the mountains of Asveh and the land of Gurgan, the inhabitants of which are called Gurganim who dwell by the river Gihon, and these are the Girgashites [Nubians and Ethiopians] who follow the Christian religion. Further it extends to the gates of Samarkand, the land of Tibet, and the land of India. In respect of all these countries the Head of the Captivity gives the communities power to appoint Rabbis and Ministers who come unto him to be consecrated and to receive his authority. They bring him offerings and gifts from the ends of the earth. He owns hospices, gardens, and plantations in Babylon, and much land inherited from his fathers, and no one can take his possessions from him by force. He has a fixed weekly revenue arising from the hospices of the Jews, the markets and the merchants, apart from that which is brought to him from far-off lands. The man is very rich, and wise in the Scriptures as well as in the Talmud,[10] and many Israelites dine at his table every day.

At his installation, the Head of the Captivity gives much money to the Caliph, to the Princes, and to the Ministers. On the day that the Caliph performs the ceremony of investing him with authority, he rides in the second of the royal carriages, and is escorted from the palace of the Caliph to his own house with timbrels and fifes. The Exilarch [leader of the exile, Daniel the son of Hisdai] appoints the Chiefs of the Academies by placing his hand upon their heads, thus installing them in their office. The Jews of the city are learned men and very rich.

In Baghdad there are twenty-eight Jewish Synagogues, situated either in the city itself or in al-Karkh on the other side of the Tigris; for the river divides the metropolis into two parts. The great synagogue of the Head of the Captivity has columns of marble of various colors overlaid with silver and gold, and on these columns are sentences of the Psalms in golden letters. And in front of the ark are about ten steps of marble; on the topmost step are the seats of the Head of the Captivity and of the Princes of the House of David. The city of Baghdad is twenty miles in circumference, situated in a land of palms, gardens and plantations, the like of which is not to be found in the whole land of Shinar.

---

[10] **Talmud**: Writings that date after the Torah, but have a high authority. One collection was written in Babylon during the captivity, and the other was compiled later in Palestine.

READING AND DISCUSSION QUESTIONS

1. What is the relationship between the Jewish and Muslim communities of Baghdad as described by Benjamin ben Jonah?

2. Describe the Jewish community and the social status of Daniel the son of Hisdai.

3. In this account, Benjamin ben Jonah appears to have exaggerated the power of the caliph, who had delegated authority to sultans throughout the caliphate. Why might ben Jonah have portrayed the caliphate as more powerful than it really was?

4. What seems to be ben Jonah's opinion of Baghdad? What does it suggest about the purpose of his travels?

DOCUMENT 9-5

Courtyard of the Virgins, the Alcazar of Seville

ca. 1200–1364

Muslim armies entered Spain in 711, and quickly conquered the entire Iberian Peninsula. When the Ummayad Dynasty was overthrown around 750, one of the surviving royal members took control of Spain, and from that point forward, Spain was not controlled by the Islamic Caliphate again. Al-Andalus, as Spain was known at the time, produced a vibrant mixing of cultures – Christian, Jewish, and Muslim – until 1492, when the last Muslim territory, Granada, was conquered by Christians. The image here depicts the Alcazar, a palace originally constructed by Muslim rulers of Seville but remodeled by later Christian conquerors. Christians claimed that it was in the Courtyard of the Virgins that the sultan received virgins in tribute from Christians.

Alessandro Rizzoli/Shutterstock.com.

READING AND DISCUSSION QUESTIONS

1. How is the palace decorated? What portions of the decoration could be attributed to the Muslims, and what could be attributed to the Christians?

2. Describe the architectural structure. Is there any influence of earlier building styles in this image?

DOCUMENT 9-6

IBN KHALDŪN

From Prolegomenon to History: On Shi'ite Succession

1377

Ibn Khaldūn (1332–1406) was one of the most learned people of his day and is credited as being one of the first scholars of sociology, demography, economics, and the philosophy of history. Born in North Africa, he received a traditional Muslim education in the Qur'an. At age twenty he began a career working for Muslim rulers in North Africa and Spain. He later became a professor in Egypt and even negotiated with the Mongol general Timur. His Prolegomenon to History *is considered the first book on the philosophy of history. In this passage, he describes the Shi'ite view of succession after the death of Muhammad. In Islam, Sunnis such as Ibn Khaldūn often consider Shi'ites a heretical group.*

SHĪ'AH TENETS CONCERNING THE QUESTION OF THE IMAMATE[11]

It should be known that, linguistically, *Shī'ah* means "companions and followers." In the customary usage of old and modern jurists and speculative theologians, the word is used for the followers and descendants of

---

Franz Rosenthal, trans., *Ibn Khaldūn, the Muqaddimah: An Introduction to History* (New York: Pantheon, 1958), 403–408.

[11] **imamate:** The lead Muslim religious authority.

'Alī. The tenet on which they all agree is that the imamate is not a general (public) interest to be delegated to the Muslim nation for consideration and appointment of a person to fill it. (To the Shī'ah,) it is a pillar and fundamental article of Islam. No prophet is permitted to neglect it or to delegate (the appointment of an imam) to the Muslim nation. It is incumbent upon him to appoint an imam for the (Muslims). The imam cannot commit sins either great or small. 'Alī is the one whom Muhammad appointed. The (Shī'ah) transmit texts (of traditions) in support of (this belief), which they interpret so as to suit their tenets. The authorities on the Sunnah and the transmitters of the religious law do not know these texts. Most of them are supposititious, or some of their transmitters are suspect, or their (true) interpretation is very different from the wicked interpretation that (the Shī'ah) give to them. . . .

Another tradition of this sort is the following statement of (Muhammad): "Your best judge is 'Alī." Imamate means exclusively the activity of judging in accordance with the divine laws. (The activity of) judging and being a judge is (what is) meant by "the people in authority" whom God requires us to obey in the verse of the Qur'ān: "Obey God, and obey the Messenger and the people in authority among you." Therefore, 'Alī and no other was arbitrator in the question of the imamate on the day of the Saqīfah.[12]

Another statement of this sort is the following statement by (Muhammad): "He who renders the oath of allegiance to me upon his life is my legatee and the man who will be in charge of this authority here after me." Only 'Alī rendered the oath of allegiance to him (in this manner).

An implied (argument), according to the Shī'ah, is the fact that the Prophet sent 'Alī to recite the *sūrat al-Barā'ah*[13] at the festival (in Mecca) when it had (just) been revealed. He first sent Abū Bakr with it. Then it was revealed to Muhammad that "a man from you," — or: ". . . from your people" — "should transmit it." Therefore, he sent 'Alī to transmit it. As they say, this proves that 'Alī was preferred (by Muhammad). Furthermore, it is not known that Muhammad ever preferred anyone to 'Alī, while he preferred Usāmah b. Zayd and 'Amr b. al-'Āṣ to both Abū Bakr and 'Umar[14] during two different raids. According to (the Shī'ah), all these things prove that 'Alī and no one else was appointed (by Muhammad) to

---

[12] **Saqīfah**: The council that decided who would succeed Muhammad.

[13] *sūrat al-Barā'ah*: Ninth chapter in the Qur'an, issued during a time of war.

[14] **Abū Bakr and 'Umar**: Abū Bakr was the first successor of Muhammad, 'Umar the second.

the caliphate. However, some of the statements quoted are little known, and others require an interpretation very different from that which (the Shī'ah) give.

Some (Shī'ah) hold the opinion that these texts prove both the personal appointment of 'Alī and the fact that the imamate is transmitted from him to his successors. They are the Imāmīyah. They renounce the two *shaykhs* (Abū Bakr and 'Umar), because they did not give precedence to 'Alī and did not render the oath of allegiance to him, as required by the texts quoted. The Imāmīyah do not take the imamates (of Abū Bakr and 'Umar) seriously. But we do not want to bother with transmitting the slanderous things said about (Abū Bakr and 'Umar) by (Imāmīyah) extremists. They are objectionable in our opinion and (should be) in theirs. . . .

The Shī'ah differ in opinion concerning the succession to the caliphate after 'Alī. Some have it passed on among the descendants of Fāṭimah[15] in succession, through testamentary determination (*naṣṣ*). We shall mention that later on. They (who believe this) are called the Imāmīyah, with reference to their statement that knowledge of the imam and the fact of his being appointed are an article of the faith. That is their fundamental tenet. . . .

Some (Shī'ah) consider as successors to the imamate, after 'Alī — or after his two sons, Muḥammad's grandsons (al-Ḥasan and al-Ḥusayn), though they disagree in this respect — (al-Ḥasan's and al-Ḥusayn's) brother, Muḥammad b. al-Ḥanafīyah, and then the latter's children. They are the Kaysānīyah, so named after Kaysān, a client of ('Alī's).

There are many differences among these sects which we have omitted here for the sake of brevity.

There are also (Shī'ah) sects that are called "Extremists" (*ghulāh*). They transgress the bounds of reason and the faith of Islam when they speak of the divinity of the imams. They either assume that the imam is a human being with divine qualities, or they assume that he is God in human incarnation. This is a dogma of incarnation that agrees with the Christian tenets concerning Jesus. 'Alī himself had these (Shī'ah) who said such things about him burned to death. Muḥammad b. al-Ḥanafīyah was very angry with al-Mukhtār b. Abī 'Ubayd when he learned that al-Mukhtār had suggested something along these lines concerning him. He cursed

---

[15] **Fāṭimah:** Daughter of Muhammad and wife to Ali.

and renounced al-Mukhtār openly. Ja'far aṣ-Ṣādiq did the same thing with people about whom he had learned something of the sort.

Some (Shī'ah) extremists say that the perfection the imam possesses is possessed by nobody else. When he dies, his spirit passes over to another imam, so that this perfection may be in him. This is the doctrine of metempsychosis.

Some extremists stop $(w - q - f)$ with one of the imams and do not go on. (They stop with the imam) whom they consider (to have been) appointed as the (last one). They (who believe this) are the Wāqifīyah. Some of them say that the (last imam) is alive and did not die, but is removed from the eyes of the people. As a proof for that (theory), they adduce the problem of al-Khiḍr.[16] . . .

The extremist Imāmīyah, in particular the Twelvers, hold a similar opinion. They think that the twelfth of their imams, Muḥammad b. al-Ḥasan al-'Askarī, to whom they give the epithet of al-Mahdī, entered the cellar of their house in al-Ḥillah and was "removed" when he was imprisoned (there) with his mother. He has remained there "removed." He will come forth at the end of time and will fill the earth with justice. The Twelver Shī'ah refer in this connection to the tradition found in the collection of at-Tirmidhī regarding the Mahdī. The Twelver Shī'ah are still expecting him to this day. Therefore, they call him "the Expected One." Each night after the evening prayer, they bring a mount and stand at the entrance to the cellar where (the Mahdī is "removed"). They call his name and ask him to come forth openly. They do so until all the stars are out. Then, they disperse and postpone the matter to the following night. They have continued that custom to this time.

Some of the Wāqifīyah say that the imam who died will return to actual life in this world. They adduce as a proof (for the possibility of this assumption) the story of the Seven Sleepers, the one about the person who passed by a village, and the one about the murdered Israelite who was beaten with the bones of the cow that (his people) had been ordered to slaughter, all of them stories included in the Qur'ān. They further adduce similar wonders that occurred in the manner of (prophetical) miracles. However, it is not right to use those things as proof for anything except where they properly apply.

---

[16] **al-Khiḍr**: "The Green One," thought to be a companion of Moses. He was said to have obtained eternal life and illumination directly from God.

READING AND DISCUSSION QUESTIONS

1. Who do Shi'ites think should have been the successor of Muhammad?

2. What, according to the Wāqifīyah, happened to the last of the imams?

3. How does Ibn Khaldūn feel about the Shi'ites? Is Ibn Khaldūn a trustworthy source about their beliefs? Why or why not?

COMPARATIVE QUESTIONS

1. How does the nature of the Muslims' relationship to God compare to that of the Jews (Document 2-5) and Christians (Documents 6-5 and 8-2)?

2. How does Islam view non-Muslims? What day-to-day evidence of Muslim-Jewish and Muslim-Christian relations is revealed in this chapter?

3. Drawing on these documents, what evidence is there to explain the success of Islam? What factors might have influenced people to convert to Islam?

4. How does the architectural style of the Courtyard of the Virgins at the Alcazar of Seville compare to the Hagia Sophia (Document 8-6)? What are the notable similarities and differences?

CHAPTER 10

African Societies and Kingdoms

1000 B.C.E.–1500 C.E.

T he history of Africa is as richly diverse as the continent itself. By the fifteenth century, Islam was dominant in the north, several major kingdoms had emerged in the west, and the Bantu-speaking people had migrated through the interior of the continent. Although written records for the period are often from the perspective of outsiders, such as Muslim merchants, they nonetheless point to the vitality and strength of African culture and society. The selections for this chapter reveal the critical role that trade routes played in the development of Africa, bringing African societies into contact with one another and connecting Africa to the larger world. The readings also document the introduction of Islam and Christianity to the continent, both of which significantly influenced the direction of the early kingdoms of Africa.

DOCUMENT 10-1

EZANA, KING OF AKSUM

Stele of Ezana

ca. 325

Trade was essential to the development of the kingdom of Aksum in north-western Ethiopia, which served as a critical hub for trade routes between India and the Mediterranean, as well as between Africa and the Arabian peninsula. Aksum was also significant for its adoption of Christianity, which the kingdom maintained even after the introduction of Islam into Africa.

Stuart Munro-Hay, *Aksum: An African Civilisation of Late Antiquity* (Edinburgh: Edinburgh University Press, 1991), 227–229.

King Ezana of Aksum (r. 330–356) converted to Christianity during his reign and conquered his Nubian neighbors. Ezana ordered the inscription of a stele, excerpted below, to document these major events of his reign.

By the might of the Lord of Heaven who in the sky and on earth holds power over all beings, Ezana, son of Ella Amida, Bisi Halen, king of Aksum, Himyar, Raydan, Saba, Salhin, Tsiyamo, Beja and of Kasu, king of kings, son of Ella Amida, never defeated by the enemy.

May the might of the Lord of Heaven, who has made me king, who reigns for all eternity, invincible, cause that no enemy can resist me, that no enemy may follow me!

By the might of the Lord of All I campaigned against the Noba when the Noba peoples revolted and boasted. "They will not dare to cross the Takaze" said the Noba people. When they had oppressed the Mangurto, Hasa and Barya peoples, and when the blacks fought the red people and they broke their word for the second and third times and put their neighbours to death without mercy, and pillaged our messengers and the envoys whom I sent to them to admonish them, and they plundered them of what they had including their lances; when finally, having sent new messengers to whom they did not wish to listen but replied by refusals, scorn, and evil acts; then I took the field.

I set forth by the might of the Lord of the Land and I fought at the Takaze and the ford Kemalke. Here I put them to flight, and, not resting, I followed those who fled for twenty-three days during which I killed some everywhere they halted. I made prisoners of others and took booty from them. At the same time those of my people who were in the field brought back captives and booty.

At the same time I burnt their villages, both those with walls of stone and those of straw. My people took their cereals, bronze, iron and copper and overthrew the idols in their dwellings, as well as their corn and cotton, and threw them themselves into the river Seda (Blue Nile). Many lost their lives in the river, no-one knows the number. At the same time my people pierced and sank their boats which carried a crowd of men and women.

And I captured two notables who had come as spies, mounted on camels, by name Yesaka and Butala, and the chief Angabene. The following nobles were put to death: Danoko, Dagale, Anako, Haware. The soldiers had wounded Karkara, their priest, and took from him a necklace of silver and a golden box. Thus five nobles and a priest fell.

I arrived at the Kasu, fought them and took them prisoner at the confluence of the rivers Seda and Takaze. And the day after my arrival I sent into the field the columns Mahaza, Hara, Damawa, Falha, and Sera, along the Seda going up to their cities with walls of stone and of straw; their cities with walls of stone are Alwa and Daro. And my troops killed and took prisoners and threw them into the water and they returned home safe and sound after terrifying their enemies and vanquishing them thanks to the power of the Lord of the Land.

Next, I sent the columns of Halen, Laken, Sabarat, Falha and Sera along the Seda, going down towards the four towns of straw of the Noba and the town of Negus. The towns of the Kasu with walls of stone which the Noba had taken were Tabito(?), Ferroti; and the troops penetrated to the territory of the Red Noba and my peoples returned safe after taking prisoners and booty, and killing by the might of the Lord of Heaven.

And I erected a throne at the confluence of the rivers Seda and Takaze opposite the town with walls of stone which rises on this peninsula.

And behold what the Lord of Heaven has given me; prisoners, 214 men, 415 women, total 629; killed, 602 men, 156 women and children, total 758, and adding the prisoners and killed 1,387. The booty came to 10,560 head of cattle and 51,050 sheep.

And I set up a throne here in Shado by the might of the Lord of Heaven who has helped me and given me supremacy. May the Lord of Heaven reinforce my reign. And, as he has now defeated my enemies for me, may he continue to do so wherever I go. As he has now conquered for me, and has submitted my enemies to me, I wish to reign in justice and equity, without doing any injustice to my peoples. And I put this throne which I have raised under the protection of the Lord of Heaven, who has made me king, and that of the Earth (Meder) which bears it. And if anyone is found to root it up, deface it or displace it, let him and his race be rooted up and extirpated. They shall be cast out of the country. And I have raised this throne by the power of the Lord of Heaven. . . .

In the faith of God and the power of the Father, son and Holy Spirit who saved for me the kingdom, by the faith of his son Jesus Christ who has helped me and will always help me.

I Azanas king of the Aksumites, and Himyarites, and Reeidan and of the Sabaeans and of Sileel and of Khaso and of the Beja and of Tiamo, Bisi Alene, son of Ella Amida servant of Christ thank the Lord my God, and I am unable to state fully his favours because my mouth and my mind cannot (embrace) all the favours which he has given me, for he has given me strength and power and favoured me with a great name through his son in whom I believed. And he made me the guide of all my kingdom because of my faith in Christ by his will and in the power of Christ, for he has guided me. And I believe in him and he became to me a guide. I went out to fight the Noba because there cried out against them, the Mangartho and Khasa and Atiaditai and Bareotai saying that "the Noba have ground us down; help us because they have troubled us by killing." And I left by the power of Christ the God in whom I have believed and he has guided me and I departed from Aksum on the eighth day, a Saturday, of the Aksumite month of Magabit having faith in God and arrived in Mambarya and there I fed my army.

READING AND DISCUSSION QUESTIONS

1. What role did Christianity play in Ezana's conquests?
2. Describe Ezana as a conqueror. How did he view the people and territories that he conquered? Why did Ezana attack his neighbors?

VIEWPOINTS

Outsiders' Views of Sub-Saharan Africa

DOCUMENT 10-2

ABU UBAYDALLAH AL-BAKRI

From The Book of Routes and Realms

ca. 1067–1068

For centuries, the expansive Sahara desert isolated northern and western Africa from each other. In the fifth century C.E.*, the introduction of the Arabian camel allowed for the establishment of regular trade routes across the Sahara. This trans-Sahara trade accelerated in the seventh and eight centuries as Arab Muslim forces conquered North Africa and turned to the western*

N. Levtzion and J. F. P. Hopkins, eds., *Corpus of Early Arabic Sources for West African History*, trans. J. R. Hopkins (Cambridge: Cambridge University Press, 1981), 78–83, 85–87.

Sudan region for gold and slaves. In exchange for their precious goods, West Africans received items such as horses and salt, as well as exposure to the tenets of the Islamic faith. Excepted here are accounts by a Spanish Muslim of the West African kingdoms of Ghana and Mali.

Ghana is a title given to their kings; the name of the region is Awkar, and their king today, namely in the year 460, is Tunka Manin. He ascended the throne in 455 [1063 c.e.]. The name of his predecessor was Basi and he became their ruler at the age of 85. He led a praiseworthy life on account of his love of justice and friendship for the Muslims. At the end of his life he became blind, but he concealed this from his subjects and pretended that he could see. When something was put before him he said: "This is good" or "This is bad." His ministers deceived the people by indicating to the king in cryptic words what he should say, so that the commoners could not understand. Basi was a maternal uncle of Tunka Manin. This is their custom and their habit, that the kingship is inherited only by the son of the king's sister. He has no doubt that his successor is a son of his sister, while he is not certain that his son is in fact his own, and he is not convinced of the genuineness of his relationship to him. This Tunka Manin is powerful, rules an enormous kingdom, and possesses great authority. . . .

Around the king's town are domed buildings and groves and thickets where the sorcerers of these people, men in charge of the religious cult, live. In them too are their idols and the tombs of their kings. These woods are guarded and none may enter them and know what is there. In them also are the king's prisons. If somebody is imprisoned there no news of him is ever heard. The king's interpreters, the official in charge of his treasury and the majority of his ministers are Muslims. Among the people who follow the king's religion[1] only he and his heir apparent (who is the son of his sister) may wear sewn clothes. All other people wear robes of cotton, silk, or brocade, according to their means. All of them shave their beards, and women shave their heads. . . .

Their religion is paganism and the worship of idols. When their king dies they construct over the place where his tomb will be an enormous dome of wood. Then they bring him on a bed covered with a few carpets and cushions and place him beside the dome. At his side they place his ornaments, his weapons, and the vessels from which he used to eat and

---

[1] **the king's religion:** The king was not a Muslim. He followed the traditional religion of the Soninke.

drink, filled with various kinds of food and beverages. They place there too the men who used to serve his meals. They close the door of the dome and cover it with mats and furnishings. Then the people assemble, who heap earth upon it until it becomes like a big hillock and dig a ditch around it until the mound can be reached at only one place.

They make sacrifices to their dead and make offerings of intoxicating drinks.

On every donkey-load of salt when it is brought into the country their king levies one golden dinar, and two dinars when it is sent out. From a load of copper the king's due is five mithqals,[2] and from a load of other goods ten mithqals. The best gold found in his land comes from the town of Ghiyaru, which is eighteen days' traveling distant from the king's town over a country inhabited by tribes of the Sudan whose dwellings are continuous.

The nuggets found in all the mines of his country are reserved for the king, only this gold dust being left for the people. But for this the people would accumulate gold until it lost its value. The nuggets may weigh from an ounce to a pound. It is related that the king owns a nugget as large as a big stone. . . .

The king of Ghana, when he calls up his army, can put 200,000 men[3] into the field, more than 40,000 of them archers. . . .

On the opposite bank of the Nil [the Niger River] is another great kingdom, stretching a distance of more than eight days' marching, the king of which has the title of *Daw*. The inhabitants of this region use arrows when fighting. Beyond this country lies another called Malal [later Mali], the king of which is known as *al-musulmani* ["the Muslim"]. He is thus called because his country became afflicted with drought one year following another; the inhabitants prayed for rain, sacrificing cattle till they had exterminated almost all of them, but the drought and the misery only increased. The king had as his guest a Muslim who used to read the Quran and was acquainted with the Sunna [Islamic traditions]. To this man the king complained of the calamities that assailed him and his people. The man said: "O King, if you believed in God (who is exalted) and testified that He is One, and testified as to the prophetic mission of Muhammad (God bless him and give him peace) and if you accepted all

---

[2] **dinar . . . mithqals**: A dinar was a standard gold coin in the Islamic kingdom. It weighed one *mithqal*, or 4.72 grams.

[3] **200,000 men**: Surely an exaggeration. Ghana had no standing army.

the religious laws of Islam, I would pray for your deliverance from your plight and that God's mercy would envelop all the people of your country and that your enemies and adversaries might envy you on that account." Thus he continued to press the king until the latter accepted Islam and became a sincere Muslim. The man made him recite from the Quran some easy passages and taught him religious obligations and practices which no one may be excused from knowing. Then the Muslim made him wait till the eve of the following Friday [the Islamic day of rest], when he ordered him to purify himself by a complete ablution, and clothed him in a cotton garment which he had. The two of them came out towards a mound of earth, and there the Muslim stood praying while the king, standing at his right side, imitated him. Thus they prayed for a part of the night, the Muslim reciting invocations and the king saying "Amen." The dawn had just started to break when God caused abundant rain to descend upon them. So the king ordered the idols to be broken and expelled the sorcerers from his country. He and his descendants after him as well as his nobles were sincerely attached to Islam, while the common people of his kingdom remained polytheists. Since then their rulers have been given the title of *al-musulmani*.

READING AND DISCUSSION QUESTIONS

1.   What evidence does al-Bakri provide to suggest that the king of Ghana wielded significant power and authority in his territory?

2.   Describe the presence of Islam in Ghana. Who practiced Islam? How was the spread of Islam encouraged? What potential obstacles were there to the growth of Islam in Ghana?

3.   Why did the king of Mali convert to Islam? What did he need to do in order to convert?

DOCUMENT 10-3

ABŪ HĀMID MUHAMMAD
AL-ANDALUSĪ AL-GHARNĀTĪ
From Gift of the Spirit
ca. 1120–1170

The Muslim traveler Abū Hāmid Muhammad al-Andalusī al-Gharnātī (ca. 1080–1170) was born in Spain but left in his twenties, never to return. He visited numerous Muslim-controlled regions of the world, such as North Africa, Egypt, Syria, and Central Asia. It is unknown if he actually visited sub-Saharan Africa. Regardless, he preserves much information that was circulating about sub-Saharan Africa, but he embellishes it with legends and writings from previous authors, including those of the Greeks. He is principally known for being a major source for Zakariya al-Qazwini (Document 14-4).

The inhabited earth has an extent of one hundred years' travelling of which fourteen belong to the various peoples of the Sūdān. Their country lies next to the Upper West (*al-Maghrib al-A'lā*), which adjoins Ṭanja, stretching along the Sea of Darkness[4] (*Baḥr al Ẓulumāt*).

It is said that kings of five of their tribes have adopted Islam. The nearest of them is Ghāna, where gold of extraordinary [purity] (*al-dhahab al-tibr al-ghāya*) grows in the sand, and is in abundance. Merchants carry to them on camels blocks of rock salt. They set out from a town called Sijilmāsa, at the farthest end of the Upper West. They travel over sands like seas, led by guides who direct themselves over the wastes according to the stars and the mountains. They carry supplies for six months with them. When they arrive in Ghāna, they sell the salt at one weight for one weight of gold, or sometimes they sell it at one weight for two weights or more, according to whether traders are many or few.

The people of Ghāna, of all the Sūdān, have the best way of living, are the best looking, and have the least crinkled hair. They possess intelligence and understanding, and they go on the Pilgrimage to Mecca.

N. Levtzion and J. F. P. Hopkins, eds., J. F. P. Hopkins, trans., *Corpus of Early Arabic Sources for West African History* (New York: Cambridge University Press, 1981), 132–134.

[4] **Sea of Darkness**: The Atlantic Ocean.

As for the Fāwah (var. Qitāwa), the Qūqū, the Malī, the Takrūr and the Ghadāmis,[5] they are brave people but there are no blessings in their lands, nor anything good, nor do they possess religion or intelligence. The worst of them are the Qūqū, who have short necks, flattened noses, and red eyes. Their hair is like peppercorns, and their smell is abominable, resembling burnt horn. They shoot arrows poisoned with the blood of yellow snakes. Within one hour the flesh begins to fall off the bones of anyone struck with such an arrow, be it elephant or any other animal. For these people vipers and all other kinds of snakes are like fish, which they eat, paying no attention to the venom of the vipers and serpents, with the exception of the yellow snake which is found in their country. This they fear, and take its blood for their arrows. Their bows, which I have seen in the Maghrib, are short and so are their arrows. I saw that their bows have strings made from the fibres of a tree that grows in their country. Their arrows are short, each one span in length, and have points made of tree thorns as strong as iron, which they fasten to their arrows with the fibres of a tree. [When shooting] they [can] hit the pupil of the eye. They are the worst kind of the Sūdān. The other Sūdān are useful as slaves and labourers, but not the Qūqū, who have no good qualities, except in war. They possess small wooden tablets, with holes partly drilled through them, on which they whistle, and produce strange tones, thus causing all sorts of snakes, vipers and serpents to come out. Then they take these reptiles and eat them. Some of them tie these snakes round their middles as one ties a cummerbund, others use a long serpent in the guise of a turban, and enter the market, while nobody pays attention [to them]. Then they take off their clothes and throw upon people various serpents and vipers. People give them something to go away, for otherwise they would throw some of these snakes into their shops.

Various kinds of goatskins dyed in a marvellous manner are exported from the land of the Sūdān, each skin being tough, thick and pliant, and in a pleasing colour from violet to black. One skin may weigh twenty *mann*. They are used to make boots for kings. They do not let the water through, nor do they damage easily or perish, despite their pliability and softness and their pleasant smell. One such skin is sold for ten dinars. The thread with which the shoe is sown perishes, but the leather does not, nor does it crack. It may be washed in a bath of hot water, and again becomes as new. The owner may have inherited it from his grandfather through his father. It is one of the marvels of the world.

---

[5] **Fāwah . . . Ghadāmis**: Peoples of the Sudan; the Ghadāmis, however, were from North Africa.

In the country of these people lives an animal called *lamṭ*, resembling a big bull. It has horns like spears, stretching along its back, and growing as long as its body. If it strikes an animal with them, the latter is killed instantly. It has a broad neck, and from its hide shields called *al-daraq al-lamṭiyya* are made, called after the animal. The shields are three cubits long, light and pliable, and cannot be pierced by an arrow, nor does a sword make any impression on them. They are white like paper, and they are one of the best kinds of shield, being flat like a flat cake of bread, and cover the knight and his horse.

In the land of the Sūdān exist people without heads. They are mentioned by al-Shaʿbī in his book *Siyar al-Mulūk [Rules for Kings]*. It is also said that in the deserts of the Maghrib there are a people of the progeny of Adam, consisting solely of women. There are no men among them, nor does any of the male sex live in that land. These women enter a certain water by which they become pregnant. Each woman gives birth to a girl, never to a boy. Tubbaʿ Dhū 'l-Manār arrived in their country when he was trying to reach the Darkness (*al-ẓulumāt*), which Dhū 'l-Qarnayn had entered. God knows best. And [it is also said] that his son, Ifrīqisūn b. Tubbaʿ Dhū 'l-Manār was the one who founded the town of Ifrīqiya, and called it after himself. And that his father, Tubbaʿ, reached Wādī al-Sabt (the River of Saturday), which is a river in the Maghrib, where sands flow like flood-water, and no living being may enter it without perishing. When he reached there, he hastened back. As for Dhū 'l-Qarnayn, on his arrival there he stayed until the day of Saturday, when the flow of the sand stopped, and then he crossed it, and marched until he reached the Darkness. This is what is said, but God knows best. These headless people have eyes in their shoulders, and mouths in their chests. They form many nations, and are numerous like beasts. They reproduce and do not harm anyone, and they have no intelligence. God knows best.

READING AND DISCUSSION QUESTIONS

1. How does al-Gharnātī describe the people of Ghana and their neighbors?

2. How does he describe the people of Sudan?

3. Which account seems more credible, and why?

4. Would al-Gharnātī be likely to describe either of these groups as "civilized"? Why or why not?

DOCUMENT 10-4

IBN BATTUTA

From Travels in Asia and Africa

ca. 1325–1354

Ibn Battuta (1304–1368) was a Muslim explorer from Tangier, Morocco. At the age of twenty-one, he left home to make the traditional Muslim pilgrimage to Mecca, a journey that sparked his abiding interest in travel. Ibn Battuta became an explorer and spent more than three decades visiting much of the Islamic world, as well as India, East Asia, and parts of Europe, which he recorded extensively. Excerpted here are his impressions of the east coast of Africa, his description of the treacherous trip across the Sahara desert, and his thoughts on the Kingdom of Mali.

IBN BATTUTA SAILS ALONG THE EAST COAST OF AFRICA

I took ship at Aden, and after four days at sea reached Zayla [Zeila, on the Somalian coast], the town of the Berberah, who are a black people. Their land is a desert extending for two months' journey from Zayla to Maqdashaw [Mogadishu]. Zayla is a large city with a great bazaar, but it is the dirtiest, most abominable, and most stinking town in the world. The reason for the stench is the quantity of its fish and the blood of the camels that they slaughter in the streets. When we got there, we chose to spend the night at sea, in spite of its extreme roughness, rather than in the town, because of its filth.

THE TOWN OF MOGADISHU IN SOMALIA

On leaving Zayla we sailed for fifteen days and came to Maqdasha [Mogadishu], which is an enormous town. Its inhabitants are merchants and have many camels, of which they slaughter hundreds every day [for food]. When a vessel reaches the port, it is met by sumbuqs, which are small boats, in each of which are a number of young men, each carrying a covered dish containing food. He presents this to one of the merchants on the ship saying "This is my guest," and all the others do the same. Each merchant on disembarking goes only to the house of the young man who is his host, except those who have made frequent journeys to the town and know

Ibn Battuta, *Travels in Asia and Africa 1325–1354*, trans. and ed. H. A. R. Gibb (London: Broadway House, 1929), 110–112, 317–323.

its people well; these live where they please. The host then sells his goods for him and buys for him, and if anyone buys anything from him at too low a price, or sells to him in the absence of his host, the sale is regarded by them as invalid. This practice is of great advantage to them.

We stayed there [in Mogadishu] three days, food being brought to us three times a day, and on the fourth, a Friday, the qadi [judge] and one of the wazirs [chief ministers] brought me a set of garments. We then went to the mosque and prayed behind the [sultan's] screen. When the Shaykh [elder] came out I greeted him and he bade me welcome. He put on his sandals, ordering the qadi and myself to do the same, and set out for his palace on foot. All the other people walked barefooted. Over his head were carried four canopies of colored silk, each surmounted by a golden bird. After the palace ceremonies were over, all those present saluted and retired. . . .

Ibn Battuta Prepares to Cross the Sahara

At Sijilmasa [at the edge of the desert] I bought camels and a four months' supply of forage for them. Thereupon I set out on the 1st Muharram of the year 53 [February 13, 1352] with a caravan including, amongst others, a number of the merchants of Sijilmasa.

The Saltworks at the Oasis of Taghaza

After twenty-five days [from Sijilmasa] we reached Taghaza, an unattractive village, with the curious feature that its houses and mosques are built of blocks of salt, roofed with camel skins. There are no trees there, nothing but sand. In the sand is a salt mine; they dig for the salt, and find it in thick slabs, lying one on top of the other, as though they had been tool-squared and laid under the surface of the earth. A camel will carry two of these slabs.

No one lives at Taghaza except the slaves of the Massufa tribe, who dig for the salt; they subsist on dates imported from Dar'a and Sijilmasa, camels' flesh, and millet imported from the Negrolands. The blacks come up from their country and take away the salt from there. At Iwalatan a load of salt brings eight to ten mithqals; in the town of Malli [Mali] it sells for twenty to thirty, and sometimes as much as forty. The blacks use salt as a medium of exchange, just as gold and silver is used [elsewhere]; they cut it up into pieces and buy and sell with it. The business done at Taghaza, for all its meanness, amounts to an enormous figure in terms of hundred-weights of gold-dust.

We passed ten days of discomfort there, because the water is brackish and the place is plagued with flies. Water supplies are laid in at Taghaza for the crossing of the desert which lies beyond it, which is a ten-nights' journey with no water on the way except on rare occasions. We indeed had the good fortune to find water in plenty, in pools left by the rain. One day we found a pool of sweet water between two rocky prominences. We quenched our thirst at it and then washed our clothes. Truffles are plentiful in this desert and it swarms with lice, so that people wear string necklaces containing mercury, which kills them.

DEATH IN THE DESERT

At that time we used to go ahead of the caravan, and when we found a place suitable for pasturage we would graze our beasts. We went on doing this until one of our party was lost in the desert; after that I neither went ahead nor lagged behind. We passed a caravan on the way and they told us that some of their party had become separated from them. We found one of them dead under a shrub, of the sort that grows in the sand, with his clothes on and a whip in his hand. The water was only about a mile away from him.

THE OASIS OF TISARAHLA, WHERE THE CARAVAN HIRES A DESERT GUIDE

We came next to Tisarahla, a place of subterranean water-beds, where the caravans halt. They stay there three days to rest, mend their waterskins, fill them with water, and sew on them covers of sackcloth as a precaution against the wind.

From this point the "takshif" is despatched. The "takshif" is a name given to any man of the Massufa tribe who is hired by the persons in the caravan to go ahead to Iwalatan, carrying letters from them to their friends there, so that they may take lodgings for them. These persons then come out a distance of four nights' journey to meet the caravan, and bring water with them. Anyone who has no friend in Iwalatan writes to some merchant well known for his worthy character who then undertakes the same services for him.

It often happens that the "takshif" perishes in this desert, with the result that the people of Iwalatan know nothing about the caravan, and all or most of those who are with it perish. That desert is haunted by demons; if the "takshif" be alone, they make sport of him and disorder his mind, so that he loses his way and perishes. For there is no visible road or track in these parts, nothing but sand blown hither and thither by the wind. You see hills of sand in one place, and afterwards you will see them moved to quite another place. The guide there [sic] is one who has made the journey frequently in both directions, and who is gifted with a quick intelligence. I remarked, as a strange thing, that the guide whom we had was blind in one eye, and diseased in the other, yet he had the best knowledge of the road of any man. We hired the "takshif" on this journey for a hundred gold mithqals; he was a man of the Massufa. On the night of the seventh day [from Tasarahla] we saw with joy the fires of the party who had come out to meet us.

THE CARAVAN REACHES THE OASIS OF WALATA

Thus we reached the town of Iwalatan [Walata, in modern-day Mauritania] after a journey from Sijilmasa of two months to a day. Iwalatan is the northernmost province of the blacks, and the sultan's representative there was one Farba Husayn, "farba" meaning deputy. When we arrived there, the merchants deposited their goods in an open square, where the blacks undertook to guard them, and went to the farba. He was sitting on a carpet under an archway, with his guards before him carrying lances and bows in their hands, and the headmen of the Massufa behind him. The merchants remained standing in front of him while he spoke to them through an interpreter, although they were close to him, to show his contempt for them. It was then that I repented of having come to their country, because of their lack of manners and their contempt for the whites.

I went to visit Ibn Badda, a worthy man of Sala [Sallee, in modern-day Morocco], to whom I had written requesting him to hire a house for me, and who had done so. Later on the mushrif [inspector] of Iwalatan, whose name was Mansha Ju, invited all those who had come with the caravan to partake of his hospitality. At first I refused to attend, but my companions urged me very strongly, so I went with the rest. The repast was served — some pounded millet mixed with a little honey and milk, put in a half calabash[6] shaped like a large bowl. The guests drank and retired. I said to them, "Was it for this that the black invited us?" They answered, "Yes; and it is in their opinion the highest form of hospitality." This convinced me that there was no good to be hoped for from these people, and I made up my mind to travel [back to Morocco at once] with the pilgrim caravan from Iwalatan. Afterwards, however, I thought it best to go to see the capital of their king [of the kingdom of Mali].

LIFE AT WALATA

My stay at Iwalatan lasted about fifty days; and I was shown honor and entertained by its inhabitants. It is an excessively hot place, and boasts a few small date-palms, in the shade of which they sow watermelons. Its water comes from underground waterbeds at that point, and there is plenty of mutton to be had. The garments of its inhabitants, most of whom belong to the Massufa tribe, are of fine Egyptian fabrics.

---

[6] **calabash**: Bottle gourd.

Their women are of surpassing beauty, and are shown more respect than the men. The state of affairs amongst these people is indeed extraordinary. Their men show no signs of jealousy whatever; no one claims descent from his father, but on the contrary from his mother's brother. A person's heirs are his sister's sons, not his own sons. This is a thing which I have seen nowhere in the world except among the Indians of Malabar. But those are heathens; these people are Muslims, punctilious in observing the hours of prayer, studying books of law, and memorizing the Koran. Yet their women show no bashfulness before men and do not veil themselves, though they are assiduous in attending the prayers. Any man who wishes to marry one of them may do so, but they do not travel with their husbands, and even if one desired to do so her family would not allow her to go.

The women there have "friends" and "companions" amongst the men outside their own families, and the men in the same way have "companions" amongst the women of other families. A man may go into his house and find his wife entertaining her "companion" but he takes no objection to it. One day at Iwalatan I went into the qadi's house, after asking his permission to enter, and found with him a young woman of remarkable beauty. When I saw her I was shocked and turned to go out, but she laughed at me, instead of being overcome by shame, and the qadi said to me, "Why are you going out? She is my companion." I was amazed at their conduct, for he was a theologian and a pilgrim [to Mecca] to boot. I was told that he had asked the sultan's permission to make the pilgrimage that year with his "companion" — whether this one or not I cannot say — but the sultan would not grant it.

READING AND DISCUSSION QUESTIONS

1. What impact did trade routes have on the East African coast? What measures did trade cities take to ensure that they benefited from commerce in the area?

2. What were some of the dangers of crossing the Sahara? How did travelers and merchants protect themselves from these dangers?

3. As Ibn Battuta's chronicle makes clear, despite the introduction of Islam, local traditions persisted in the kingdom of Mali. What were some of these traditions? What does Ibn Battuta think of them?

From Epic of Sundiata

ca. 1250

Very little literature of West Africa was written down prior to European imperialism in the nineteenth century; instead, literature and culture were handed down orally. This passage, a selection from the Epic of Sundiata, *was passed on by oral poets called griots. The* Epic of Sundiata *covers the life of Mali's first ruler, Sundiata Keita (ca. 1217–1255), and contains a wealth of information about the rise of Mali's power and everyday life in the kingdom. This passage narrates the wedding ceremony between Nare Maghan and Sogolon, Sundiata's parents.*

At the home of the king's old aunt, the hairdresser of Nianiba[7] was plaiting Sogolon Kedjou's hair. As she lay on her mat, her head resting on the hairdresser's legs, she wept softly, while the king's sisters came to chaff her, as was the custom.

"This is your last day of freedom; from now onwards you will be our woman."

"Say farewell to your youth," added another.

"You won't dance in the square any more and have yourself admired by the boys," added a third.

Sogolon never uttered a word and from time to time the old hairdresser said, "There, there, stop crying. It's a new life beginning, you know, more beautiful than you think. You will be a mother and you will know the joy of being a queen surrounded by your children. Come now, daughter, don't listen to the gibes of your sisters-in-law." In front of the house the poetesses who belonged to the king's sisters chanted the name of the young bride.

During this time the festivity was reaching its height in front of the king's enclosure. Each village was represented by a troupe of dancers and

---

D. T. Niane, *Sundiata: An Epic of Old Mali*, G. D. Pickett, trans. (London: Longmans, Green, 1965), 10–12.

[7] **Nianiba:** The capital city.

musicians; in the middle of the courtyard the elders were sacrificing oxen which the servants carved up, while ungainly vultures, perched on the great silk-cotton tree, watched the hecatomb with their eyes.

Sitting in front of the palace, Naré Maghan listened to the grave music of the "bolon"[8] in the midst of his courtiers. Doua,[9] standing amid the eminent guests, held his great spear in his hand and sang the anthem of Mandingo kings. Everywhere in the village people were dancing and singing and members of the royal family [evinced] their joy, as was fitting, by distributing grain, clothes, and even gold. Even the jealous Sassouma Bérété took part in this largesse and, among other things, bestowed fine loin-cloths on the poetesses.

But night was falling and the sun had hidden behind the mountain. It was time for the marriage procession to form up in front of the house of the king's aunt. The tam-tams had fallen silent. The old female relatives of the king had washed and perfumed Sogolon and now she was dressed completely in white with a large veil over her head.

Sogolon walked in front held by two old women. The king's relatives followed and, behind, the choir of young girls of Mali sang the bride's departure song, keeping time to the songs by clapping their hands. The villagers and guests were lined up along the stretch of ground which separated the aunt's house from the palace in order to see the procession go by. When Sogolon had reached the threshold of the king's antechamber one of his young brothers lifted her vigorously from the ground and ran off with her towards the palace while the crowd cheered.

The women danced in front of the palace of the king for a long while, then, after receiving money and presents from members of the royal family, the crowd dispersed and night darkened overhead.

"She will be an extraordinary woman if you manage to possess her." Those were the words of the old woman of Do,[10] but the conqueror of the buffalo had not been able to conquer the young girl. It was only as an afterthought that the two hunters, Oulani and Oulamba, had the idea of giving her to the king of Mali.

That evening, then, Naré Maghan tried to perform his duty as a husband but Sogolon repulsed his advances. He persisted, but his efforts were

---

[8] **bolon**: A three-stringed instrument that was played during wartime.

[9] **Doua**: A griot (bard).

[10] **old woman of Do**: Do was a nearby, powerful land.

in vain and early the next morning Doua found the king exhausted, like a man who had suffered a great defeat.

"What is the matter, my king?" asked the griot.

"I have been unable to possess her — and besides, she frightens me, this young girl. I even doubt whether she is a human being; when I drew close to her during the night her body became covered with long hairs and that scared me very much. All night long I called upon my wraith[11] but he was unable to master Sogolon's."

All that day the king did not emerge and Doua was the only one to enter and leave the palace. All Nianiba seemed puzzled. The old women who had come early to seek the virginity pagne[12] had been discreetly turned away. And this went on for a week.

Naré Maghan had vainly sought advice from some great sorcerers but all their tricks were powerless in overcoming the wraith of Sogolon. But one night, when everyone was asleep, Naré Maghan got up. He unhooked his hunter's bag from the wall and, sitting in the middle of the house, he spread on the ground the sand which the bag contained. The king began tracing mysterious signs in the sand; he traced, effaced and began again. Sogolon woke up. She knew that sand talks, but she was intrigued to see the king so absorbed at dead of night. Naré Maghan stopped drawing signs and with his hand under his chin he seemed to be brooding on the signs. All of a sudden he jumped up, bounded after his sword which hung above his bed, and said, "Sogolon, Sogolon, wake up. A dream has awakened me out of my sleep and the protective spirit of the Mandingo kings has appeared to me. I was mistaken in the interpretation I put upon the words of the hunter who led you to me. The jinn[13] has revealed to me their real meaning. Sogolon, I must sacrifice you to the greatness of my house. The blood of a virgin of the tribe of Kondé must be spilt, and you are the Kondé virgin whom fate has brought under my roof. Forgive me, but I must accomplish my mission. Forgive the hand which is going to shed your blood."

"No, no — why me? — no, I don't want to die."

"It is useless," said the king. "It is not me who has decided."

---

[11] **my wraith**: Each person in West Africa was thought to have a spirit double.

[12] **virginity pagne**: A blood-stained cloth that proved that the marriage was consummated and the bride had been a virgin.

[13] **jinn**: A genie, in some cultures thought to be evil, but this does not seem to be the case here.

He seized Sogolon by the hair with an iron grip, but so great had been her fright that she had already fainted. In this faint, she was congealed in her human body and her wraith was no longer in her, and when she woke up, she was already a wife. That very night, Sogolon conceived.

READING AND DISCUSSION QUESTIONS

1. Describe the wedding ceremony.
2. What did a woman give up when she got married in Mali? What does the passage convey about the status of women in Mali society?
3. What religious beliefs are present in this account?

DOCUMENT 10-6

Sankore Mosque, Timbuktu

ca. 1400

The growth of Islam in sub-Saharan Africa meant that people needed to learn to read the Qur'an and interpretations of it. This need for education and the influence of learned Muslim scholars led to the creation of the first universities in Africa. One of the most famous was founded in Timbuktu. The Sankore Mosque was constructed in the typical fashion of Timbuktu, using clay lined with wooden stakes, because clay structures require regular maintenance, and the wooden stakes allowed the building to be repaired again and again. Unlike European universities, here students selected one teacher and remained with him until they completed their education. Although quality inevitably varied among teachers, those who taught at Sankore were considered the best in sub-Saharan Africa during the sixteenth century.

Travel Ink/Getty Images.

READING AND DISCUSSION QUESTIONS

1. Describe this structure. What is its visual effect?
2. What does this building suggest about the importance of education in West Africa in this period?

COMPARATIVE QUESTIONS

1. What role did the introduction of Christianity and Islam play in the development of the kingdoms of Aksum, Ghana, and Mali? How did these religions influence the actions of the kings? How did they influence the economies of the territories?

2. Describe al-Bakri's, al-Gharnāti's, and Ibn Battuta's impressions of the sub-Saharan kingdoms of Ghana and Mali. What do they admire about these kingdoms? What local traditions do they criticize?

3. Identify the trade routes mentioned in the documents by al-Bakri and Ibn Battuta. What were the economic and cultural repercussions for Africa of such trade routes?

4. How does the role of women in society in these passages compare to other societies that you have read about, such as India and China?

5. How is the Sankore Mosque similar to or different from the Courtyard of the Virgins at the Alcazar of Seville (Document 9-5) or the Hagia Sophia (Document 8-6)?

CHAPTER 11

The Americas

2500 B.C.E.–1500 C.E.

W ritten records of premodern societies in both Africa and the Americas typically come from the perspective of outsiders. While Muslim explorers and merchants created a record of African civilizations, European conquerors and missionaries wrote accounts of the American experience. These same Europeans also destroyed much of the writings of native American civilizations to discourage traditional practices and beliefs that opposed the spread of Christianity. This chapter explores the cultures of the Western Hemisphere, specifically the Mississippian societies of North America, the Mayans and Mexica of Mesoamerica, and the Inca in South America. European colonization of these peoples was so successful that little evidence from the precontact period survives. Thus, the most important information concerning these societies comes from discoveries in archaeological excavations or from the writings of Europeans, some of whom attempted to preserve native languages and cultures.

DOCUMENT 11-1

Stele 4, Ixtutz, Guatemala

780

Beginning with Olmec civilization (1500–300 B.C.E.), Mesoamerica was the scene of an extensive urban society comprising several complex states. The succeeding civilization, the Maya (300–900 C.E.), inherited much from the Olmecs but continued to develop notions of kingship and writing. The decipherment of Mayan was a complex process that was unlocked only after World War II and continues to this day. Because Spanish bishops and rulers wished to eradicate Maya culture, almost every book in Mayan was destroyed, leaving only archaeological discoveries, such as this source, for analysis. This document contains the original Mayan glyphs from a stele (pillar) set up in the city-state at Ixtutz, the transliteration of the glyphs, and an English translation.

STELA 4 (A1-B5), IXTUTZ, GUATEMALA: TRANSLITERATION, TRANSCRIPTION, AND TRANSLATION

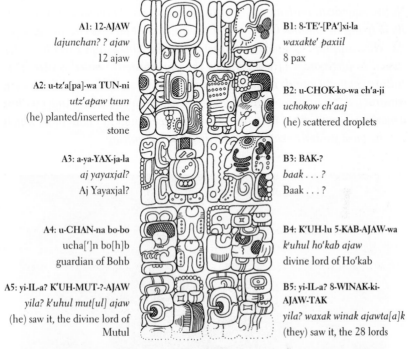

A1: 12-AJAW
lajunchan? ? ajaw
12 ajaw

A2: u-tz'a[pa]-wa TUN-ni
utz'apaw tuun
(he) planted/inserted the
stone

A3: a-ya-YAX-ja-la
aj yayaxjal?
Aj Yayaxjal?

A4: u-CHAN-na bo-bo
ucha[']n bo[h]b
guardian of Bohb

A5: yi-IL-a? K'UH-MUT-?-AJAW
yila? k'uhul mut[ul] ajaw
(he) saw it, the divine lord of
Mutul

B1: 8-TE'-[PA']xi-la
waxakte' paxiil
8 pax

B2: u-CHOK-ko-wa ch'a-ji
uchokow ch'aaj
(he) scattered droplets

B3: BAK-?
baak . . . ?
Baak . . . ?

B4: K'UH-lu 5-KAB-AJAW-wa
k'uhul ho'kab ajaw
divine lord of Ho'kab

B5: yi-IL-a? 8-WINAK-ki-
AJAW-TAK
yila? waxak winak ajawta[a]k
(they) saw it, the 28 lords

"On 12 *ajaw* 8 *pax* (2 December 780), Aj Yayaxjal? Baak ?, guardian of Bohb, divine lord of Ho'kab, planted the stone and scattered droplets. It was seen/witnessed by the divine lord of Mutul and by the 28 lords."

Harri Kettunen and Christophe Helmke/WAYEB.

READING AND DISCUSSION QUESTIONS

1. Describe the individual Mayan glyphs. How do they compare to other forms of writing with which you are familiar?

2. What might this stele commemorate? Who erected it?

3. What does this stele reveal about Maya religious beliefs and political structure?

Maize Grinder Effigy Pipe

ca. 1200

While societies in Mesoamerica were constructed around urban centers, Native American settlement in North America was characterized by a variety of living conditions. One of the largest and most famous cultural groups, the Mississippian, was located at first along the Mississippi River but later spread to large areas of what is now the southeastern United States. This culture created mounds on which homes, temples, and other buildings were constructed. This ceremonial tobacco pipe depicting a maize grinder within a mortar was unearthed from the famous Spiro mounds in Oklahoma, which are the most westerly expression of Mississippian culture.

Werner Forman/Art Resource, N.Y.

READING AND DISCUSSION QUESTIONS

1. What is this figure doing? What might that suggest about Mississippian culture?

2. How is the fact that this object is a pipe significant for understanding Mississippian culture?

DOCUMENT 11-3

PEDRO DE CIEZA DE LEÓN
From Chronicles: *On the Inca*
ca. 1535

From the fifteenth to the early sixteenth century, the large Inca empire in western South America spanned an area that included modern-day Peru. Compared to other civilizations in the Americas, the Inca had a sophisticated bureaucracy. Their empire had four provinces that were each headed by a governor who reported back to the king, or Sapa Inca (God Emperor). In the following account, Pedro de Cieza de León (1520–1554), a Spanish conquistador who came to admire the Inca culture, describes the administration of the empire. In the case of the Inca, historians are particularly dependent on the Spanish record because no civilization from South America developed a form of writing.

It is told for a fact of the rulers of this kingdom that in the days of their rule they had their representatives in the capitals of all the provinces, . . . for in all these places there were larger and finer lodgings than in most of the other cities of this great kingdom, and many storehouses. They served as the head of the provinces or regions, and from every so many leagues around the tributes were brought to one of these capitals, and from so many others, to another. This was so well organized that there was not a village that did not know where it was to send its tribute. In all these capitals the Incas had temples of the sun, mints, and many silversmiths who did

---

Pedro de Cieza de León, *Chronicles*, from *The Incas of Pedro de Cieza de León*, ed. Victor Wolfgang von Hagen, trans. Harriet de Onis (Norman: University of Oklahoma Press, 1959), 165–167, 169–174, 177–178.

nothing but work rich pieces of gold or fair vessels of silver; large garrisons were stationed there, and, as I have said, a steward or representative who was in command of them all, to whom an accounting of everything that was brought in was made, and who, in turn, had to give one of all that was issued. And these governors could in no way interfere with the jurisdiction of another who held a similar post, but within his own, if there were any disorder or disturbance, he had authority to punish it[s perpetrators], especially if it were in the nature of a conspiracy or a rebellion, or failure to obey the Inca [i.e., Sapa Inca], for full power resided in these governors. And if the Incas had not had the foresight to appoint them and to establish the *mitimaes*,[1] the natives would have often revolted and shaken off the royal rule; but with the many troops and the abundance of provisions, they could not effect this unless they had all plotted such treason or rebellion together. This happened rarely, for these governors who were named were of complete trust, all of them *Orejones* [elite, and typically blood relations of the king], and most of them had their holdings, or *chacaras*, in the neighborhood of *Cuzco* [the capital city], and their homes and kinfolk. If one of them did not show sufficient capacity for his duties, he was removed and another put in his place.

When one of them came to Cuzco on private business or to see the Inca, he left a lieutenant in his place, not one who aspired to the post, but one he knew would faithfully carry out what he was ordered to do and what was best for the service of the Inca. And if one of these governors or delegates died while in office, the natives at once sent word to the Inca how and of what he had died, and even transported the body by the post road if this seemed to them advisable. The tribute paid by each of these districts where the capital was situated and that turned over by the natives, whether gold, silver, clothing, arms, and all else they gave, was entered in the accounts of . . . [those] who kept the *quipus* [knotted strings used for accounting] and did everything ordered by the governor in the matter of finding the soldiers or supplying whomever the Inca ordered, or making delivery to Cuzco; but when they came from the city of Cuzco to go over the accounts, or they were ordered to go to Cuzco to give an accounting, the accountants themselves gave it by the quipus, or went to give it where there could be no fraud, but everything had to come out right. Few years went by in which an accounting of all these things was not made. . . .

---

[1] **establish the *mitimaes*:** A reference to the practice of relocating the populations of recently conquered territories. By moving the population of the empire around, the Inca hoped to break down local customs and practices and create a unified culture for the entire empire.

Realizing how difficult it would be to travel the great distances of their land where every league and at every turn a different language was spoken, and how bothersome it would be to have to employ interpreters to understand them, these rulers, as the best measure, ordered and decreed, with severe punishment for failure to obey, that all the natives of their empire should know and understand the language of Cuzco, both they and their women. This was so strictly enforced that an infant had not yet left its mother's breast before they began to teach it the language it had to know. And although at the beginning this was difficult and many stubbornly refused to learn any language but their own, the Incas were so forceful that they accomplished what they had proposed, and all had to do their bidding. This was carried out so faithfully that in the space of a few years a single tongue was known and used in an extension of more than 1,200 leagues, yet, even though this language was employed, they all spoke their own [languages], which were so numerous that if I were to list them it would not be credited. . . .

[The Indians] had a method of knowing how the tributes of food supplies should be levied on the provinces when the Lord-Inca came through with his army, or was visiting the kingdom; or, when nothing of this sort was taking place, what came into the storehouses and what was issued to the subjects, so nobody could be unduly burdened. . . . This involved the quipus, which are long strands of knotted strings, and those who were the accountants and understood the meaning of these knots could reckon by them expenditures or other things that had taken place many years before. By these knots they counted from one to ten and from ten to a hundred, and from a hundred to a thousand. On one of these strands there is the account of one thing, and on the other of another, in such a way that what to us is a strange, meaningless account is clear to them. In the capital of each province there were accountants whom they called *quipu-camayocs*, and by these knots they kept the account of the tribute to be paid by the natives of that district in silver, gold, clothing, flocks, down to wood and other more insignificant things, and by these same quipus at the end of a year, or ten, or twenty years, they gave a report to the one whose duty it was to check the account so exact that not even a pair of sandals was missing. . . .

The *Orejones* of Cuzco who supplied me with information are in agreement that in olden times, in the days of the Lord-Incas, all the villages and provinces of Peru were notified that a report should be given to the rulers and their representatives each year of the men and women who had died, and all who had been born, for this was necessary for the levying of the tributes as well as to know how many were available for war and those who could assume the defense of the villages. This was an easy matter, for each province at the end of the year had a list by the knots of the quipus of all the people who had died there during the year, as well as of those who had been born. At the beginning of the new year they came to Cuzco, bringing their quipus, which told how many births there had been during the year, and how many deaths. This was reported with all truth and accuracy, without any fraud or deceit. In this way the Inca and the governors knew which of the Indians were poor, the women who had been widowed, whether they were able to pay their taxes, and how many men they could count on in the event of war, and many other things they considered highly important.

As this kingdom was so vast, as I have repeatedly mentioned, in each of the many provinces there were many storehouses filled with supplies and other needful things; thus, in times of war, wherever the armies went they drew upon the contents of these storehouses, without ever touching the supplies of their confederates or laying a finger on what they had in their settlements. And when there was no war, all this stock of supplies and food was divided up among the poor and the widows. These poor were the aged, or the lame, crippled, or paralyzed, or those afflicted with some other diseases; if they were in good health, they received nothing. Then the storehouses were filled up once more with the tributes paid the Inca. If there came a lean year, the storehouses were opened and the provinces were lent what they needed in the way of supplies; then, in a year of abundance, they paid back all they had received. Even though the tributes paid to the Inca were used only for the aforesaid purposes, they were employed to advantage, for in this way their kingdom was opulent and well supplied.

No one who was lazy or tried to live by the work of others was tolerated; everyone had to work. Thus on certain days each lord went to his lands and took the plow in hand and cultivated the earth, and did other things. Even the Incas themselves did this to set an example, for everybody was to know that there should be nobody so rich that, on this account, he might disdain or affront the poor. And under their system there was none such in all the kingdom, for, if he had his health, he worked and lacked for nothing; and if he was ill, he received what he needed from the storehouses. And no rich man could deck himself out in more finery than the poor, or wear different clothing, except the rulers and headmen, who, to maintain their dignity, were allowed great freedom and privilege, as well as the *Orejones*, who held a place apart among all the peoples.

READING AND DISCUSSION QUESTIONS

1. Describe the Inca bureaucracy. How did it enable the king to rule this large territory?

2. What role did the *quipu* [khipu] play in the administration of the Inca Empire?

3. Cieza mentions a law requiring that every person in the empire learn the Inca language. What does this law tell you about the priorities of the Inca government?

4. What services did the Inca government provide for the people of the empire? How were they able to offer such services?

DOCUMENT 11-4

DIEGO DURÁN

From Book of the Gods and Rites

ca. 1576–1579

The Mexica, or Aztecs, occupied a large section of modern-day central Mexico. Like their Mayan and Toltec predecessors in the area, the Mexica practiced human sacrifice. This tradition drew on Mesoamerican creation myths, which often involved gods making the first sacrifice by offering their own blood in order to create humanity. Victims of human sacrifice were usually captured enemy soldiers sold in slave markets. In this excerpt, the Dominican priest Diego Durán (1537–1588) describes the role of the marketplace in Mexica society, as well as the practice of human sacrifice.

The markets in this land were all enclosed by walls and stood either in front of the temples of the gods or to one side. Market day in each town was considered a main feast in that town or city. And thus in that small shrine where the idol of the market stood were offered ears of corn, chili, tomatoes, fruit, and other vegetables, seeds, and breads — in sum, everything

---

Diego Durán, *Book of the Gods and Rites and the Ancient Calendar*, trans. Fernando Horcasitas and Doris Heyden (Norman: Oklahoma University Press, 1971), 137–139, 273–280, 284–286.

sold in the *tianguiz* [marketplace]. Some say that (these offerings) were left there until they spoiled; others deny this, saying that all was gathered up by the priests and ministers of the temples.

But, to return to what I said about the market day being a feast day, the following is the truth. One day I was informed in a personal way, and now I shall tell what took place between me and a lord of a certain village. When I begged him to finish a part of the church that was under construction, he answered: "Father, do you not know that tomorrow is a great feast in this town? How can you expect them to work? Leave it for another day." Then, very carefully, I looked at the calendar to see which saint's day it was, and I found none. Laughing at me, (the lord) said: "Do you not know that tomorrow is the feast of the *tianguiz* of this town? (Do you not know) that not a man or a woman will fail to pay it its due honor?" From these words I realized (how important) a feast and solemnity the market is for them. . . .

Furthermore, a law was established by the state prohibiting the selling of goods outside the market place. Not only were there laws and penalties connected with this, but there was a fear of the supernatural, of misfortune, and of the ire and wrath of the god of the market. No one ventured, therefore, to trade outside (the market limits), and the custom has survived until these days. Many a time have I seen a native carry two or three hens or a load of fruit for sale in the market. On the road he meets a Spaniard who wants to buy them from him. The Spaniard offers the price which he would have received in the market. The native refuses and is unwilling to sell, even though he would save himself a league or two of walking. He begs the Spaniard to go to the market place to buy them there. . . . Even today, though they are Christians, the awe and fear of their ancient law is still strong. It must also be said that the planting of this awe and nonsense in these people brought a certain income from all that which was sold in the markets (in the form of taxes), which was divided between the lord and the community.

In this land the sovereigns had set up a regulation regarding the markets: they were to take the form of fairs or markets specializing in the selling of certain things. Some markets, therefore, became famous and popular for these reasons: it was commanded that slaves were to be sold at the fair in Azcapotzalco and that all the people of the land who had slaves for sale must go there and to no other place to sell. The same can be said of Itzocan. Slaves could be sold in these two places only. It was at these two fairs that slaves were sold so that those who needed them would go there and no other place to buy. In other places, such as Cholula, it was ordered that the merchandise must consist of jewels, precious stones, and fine featherwork. At others, such as Tetzcoco, cloth and fine gourds were sold, together with exquisitely worked ceramics, splendidly done in the native way. . . .

I would like to say some things regarding the slaves sold in the two markets I have mentioned, Azcapotzalco and Itzocan. Some things worthy of remembering can be said about these slaves. In the first place, it should be known that in honor of the gods (as has been noted) men and women were slain on all the feast days. Some of these were slaves bought in the market place for the special purpose of representing gods. When they had performed the representation, when those slaves had been purified and washed — some for an entire year, others for forty days, others for nine, others for seven — after having been honored and served in the name of the god they impersonated, at the end they were sacrificed by those who owned them.

Captives of another type were those taken as prisoners in war. These served exclusively as sacrifices for the man who had impersonated the god whose feast was being celebrated. Thus these were called the "delicious food of the gods." I do not have to deal with all of these, but only with the slaves who were sold in the market place for having broken the law or for the reasons I shall describe later. These were bought by rich merchants and by important chieftains, some to glorify their own names and others to fulfill their customary vows.

The masters took the slaves to the *tianguiz*: some took men, others women, others boys or girls, so that there would be variety from which to choose. So that they would be identified as slaves, they wore on their necks wooden or metal collars with small rings through which passed rods about one yard long. In its place I shall explain the reason for putting these collars on them. At the site where these slaves were sold (which stood at one side of the *tianguiz*, according to market regulations) the owners kept (the slaves) dancing and singing so that merchants would be attracted by the charm of their voices and their (dance) steps and buy them quickly. If one possessed this facility, therefore, he found a master immediately. This was not the case for those who lacked grace and were inept in these things. Thus they were presented many times at market places without anyone paying attention to them, though (occasionally) some bought them to make use of them (as domestic servants), since they were unfit to represent the gods. Singers and dancers were in demand because when they were garbed in the raiment of the gods they went about singing and dancing in the streets and the houses during the time of their impersonation. They entered (the houses) and the temples and (climbed to) the flat roofs of the royal houses and those of their masters. They were given all the pleasures and joys of the world — foods, drink, feasts — as if they had been the gods themselves. So it was that the merchants wished that, aside from being good dancers and singers, they were healthy, without blemish or deformity. . . . (These slaves) were therefore made to strip, and were examined from head to foot, member by member. They were forced to extend their hands and lift their feet (as is done today with) Negro (slaves), to determine whether they were crippled. If one was found healthy, he was bought; otherwise, no. For it was desired that the slaves to be purified to represent the gods (this ceremony belonging to their rites, religion and precepts) were healthy and without blemish, just as we read in the Holy Writ about the sacrifices of the Old Testament which were to be without blemish. These slaves were not strangers or foreigners or prisoners of war, as some have declared, but were natives of the same town.

READING AND DISCUSSION QUESTIONS

1. What rules did the Mexica government establish to regulate the marketplaces?

2. What role did the markets play in Mexica society? Why would work stop on the day of the market?

3. How were slaves selected for human sacrifice? What qualities did they need to exhibit?

4. How were slaves treated before being sacrificed?

VIEWPOINTS

The Importance of the Ball Game in Maya Society

DOCUMENT 11-5

ANTONIO DE HERRERA Y TORDESILLAS

On the Maya Ball Game Tlachtli

ca. 1598

The Maya ball game tlachtli *had social, political, and religious significance. Tlachtli courts were some of the most important structures in Maya cities. Their size demonstrated the power and authority of the city, while decorative carvings highlighted key aspects of Maya religion and myth. Tlachtli players tried to pass a rubber ball through tall rings without touching the ball with their hands. While winners became heroes, losers were typically sacrificed to the Maya gods. The following description of this Mesoamerican sport was written by an official court historian to King Philip II of Spain.*

The game was called "Tlachtli," which is the same as "Trinquete" in Spanish. The ball was made of the gum from a tree which grows in the hot country. This tree, when tapped, exudes some large white drops, which soon congeal and when mixed and kneaded become as black as pitch: of this material the balls are made, and, although heavy and hard to the hand, they bound and rebound as lightly as footballs, and are indeed better, as there is no need to inflate them. They do not play for "chases" but to make a winning stroke — that is, to strike the ball against or to hit it over the wall which the opposite party defend. The ball may be struck with any part of the body, either such part as is most convenient or such as each player is most skillful in using. Sometimes it is arranged that it should count against any player who touches the ball otherwise than with his

Alfred Percival Maudslay, A *Glimpse at Guatemala* (London: John Murray, 1899), 205–206.

hip, for this is considered by them to show the greatest skill, and on this account they would wear a piece of stiff raw hide over the hips, so that the ball might better rebound. The ball might be struck as long as it bounded, and it made many bounds one after the other, as though it were alive.

They played in parties, so many on each side, and for such a stake as a parcel of cotton cloths, more or less, according to the wealth of the players. They also played for articles of gold and for feathers, and at times staked their own persons. The place where they played was a court on the level of the ground, long, narrow, and high, but wider above than below, and higher at the sides than at the ends. So that it should be better to play in, the court was well cemented, and the walls and floors made quite smooth. In the side walls were fixed two stones like millstones, with a hole pierced through the middle, through which there was just room for the ball to pass, and the player who hit the ball through the hole won the game; and as this was a rare victory, which few gained, by the ancient custom and law of the game, the victor had a right to the mantles of all the spectators. . . .

To those who saw the feat performed for the first time it seemed like a miracle, and they said that a player who had such good luck would become a thief or an adulterer, or would die soon. And the memory of such a victory lasted many days, until it was followed by another, which put it out of mind.

READING AND DISCUSSION QUESTIONS

1. How did Maya society recognize and reward the winners of the ball game? What does this recognition suggest about the role of the ball game in Maya society?

2. Describe the ball game court. What does the court suggest about the building capabilities of the Mayans?

DOCUMENT 11-6

FATHER FRANCISCO XIMÉNEZ
From the Popol Vuh
ca. 1701–1703

As the Spanish were so successful at destroying the precontact cultural heritages of the Native Americans, it is often necessary to use much later sources to understand native societies. Some Spanish clergy, however, attempted to collect and preserve aspects of native culture, and because of the actions of a Dominican priest, Father Francisco Ximénez, a remarkable document known as the Popol Vuh *has survived. It is thought to have originated with a native Maya text from the mid-sixteenth century. This passage describes how the twin heroes, Hun-Hunahpú and Vucub-Hunahpú, died.*

And having gone to play ball on the road to Xibalba,[2] they [Hun-Hunahpú and Vucub-Hunahpú] were overheard by Hun-Camé and Vucub-Camé, the lords of Xibalba.

"What are you doing on earth? Who are they who are making the earth shake, and making so much noise? Go and call them! Let them come here to play ball. Here we will overpower them! We are no longer respected by them. They no longer have consideration, or fear of our rank, and they even fight above our heads," said all the lords of Xibalba.

All of them held a council. Those called Hun-Camé and Vucub-Camé were the supreme judges. All the lords had been assigned their duties. Each one was given his own authority by Hun-Camé and Vucub-Camé.

They were, then, Xiquiripat and Cuchumaquic lords of these names. They were the two who caused the shedding of blood of the men.

Others were called Ahalpuh and Ahalganá, also lords. And their work was to make men swell and make pus gush forth from their legs and stain their faces yellow, what is called Chuganal. Such was the work of Ahalpuh and Ahalganá.

Delia Goetz and Sylvanus G. Morely, from the translation of Adrián Recimos, *Popol Vuh: The Sacred Book of the Ancient Quiché Maya* (Norman: University of Oklahoma Press, 1950), 109–113, 116–118.

[2] **Xibalba**: The underworld, commonly translated as "the place of fear."

Others were Lord Chamiabac and Lord Chamiaholom, constables of Xibalba, whose staffs were of bone. Their work was to make men waste away until they were nothing but skin and bone and they died, and they carried them with their stomach and bones stretched out. This was the work of Chamiabac and Chamiaholom, as they were called.

Others were called Lord Ahalmez and Lord Ahaltocob; their work was to bring disaster upon men, as they were going home, or in front of it, and they would be found wounded, stretched out, face up, on the ground, dead. This was the work of Ahalmez and Ahaltocob, as they were called.

Immediately after them were other lords named Xic and Patán whose work it was to cause men to die on the road, which is called sudden death, making blood to rush to their mouths until they died vomiting blood. The work of each one of these lords was to seize upon them, squeeze their throats and chests, so that the men died on the road, making the blood rush to their throats when they were walking. This was the work of Xic and Patán.

And having gathered in council, they discussed how to torment and wound Hun-Hunahpú and Vucub-Hunahpú. What the Lords of Xibalba coveted were the playing implements of Hun-Hunahpú and Vucub-Hunahpú — their leather pads and rings and gloves and crown and masks which were the playing gear of Hun-Hunahpú and Vucub-Hunahpú. . . .

The messengers of Hun-Camé and Vucub-Camé arrived immediately.

"Go, Ahpop Achih!" they were told. "Go and call Hun-Hunahpú and Vucub-Hunahpú. Say to them, 'Come with us. The lords say that you must come.' They must come here to play ball with us so that they shall make us happy, for really they amaze us. So, then, they must come," said the lords. "And have them bring their playing gear, their rings, their gloves, and have them bring their rubber balls, too," said the lords. "Tell them to come quickly," they told the messengers. . . .

Hun-Hunahpú and Vucub-Hunahpú went immediately and the messengers took them on the road. Thus they were descending the road to Xibalba, by some very steep stairs. . . .

Immediately they arrived at the House of Gloom. There was only darkness within the house. Meanwhile the Lords of Xibalba discussed what they should do.

"Let us sacrifice them tomorrow, let them die quickly, quickly, so that we can have their playing gear to use in play," said the Lords of Xibalba to each other.

Well, their fat-pine sticks were round and were called *zaquitoc*, which is the pine of Xibalba. Their fat-pine sticks were pointed and filed and were as bright as bone; the pine of Xibalba was very hard.

Hun-Hunahpú and Vucub-Hunahpú entered the House of Gloom. There they were given their fat-pine sticks, a single lighted stick which Hun-Camé and Vucub-Camé sent them, together with a lighted cigar for each of them which the lords had sent. They went to give them to Hun-Hunahpú and Vucub-Hunahpú.

They found them crouching in the darkness when the porters arrived with the fat-pine sticks and the cigars. As they entered, the pine sticks lighted the place brightly.

"Each of you light your pine sticks and your cigars; come and bring them back at dawn, you must not burn them up, but you must return them whole; this is what the lords told us to say." So they said. And so they were defeated. They burned up the pine sticks, and they also finished the cigars which had been given to them.

There were many punishments in Xibalba; the punishments were of many kinds.

The first was the House of Gloom, Quequma-ha, in which there was only darkness.

The second was Xuxulim-ha, the house where everybody shivered, in which it was very cold. A cold, unbearable wind blew within.

The third was the House of Jaguars, Balami-ha, it was called, in which there were nothing but jaguars which stalked about, jumped around, roared, and made fun. The jaguars were shut up in the house.

Zorzi-há, the House of Bats, the fourth place of punishment was called. Within this house there were nothing but bats which squeaked and cried and flew around and around. The bats were shut in and could not get out.

The fifth was called Chayim-há, the House of Knives, in which there were only sharp, pointed knives, silent or grating against each other in the house.

There were many places of torture in Xibalba, but Hun-Hunahpú and Vucub-Hunahpú did not enter them. We only mention the names of these houses of punishment.

When Hun-Hunahpú and Vucub-Hunahpú came before Hun-Camé and Vucub-Camé, they said: "Where are my cigars? Where are my sticks of fat pine which I gave you last night?"

"They are all gone, Sir."

"Well. Today shall be the end of your days. Now you shall die. You shall be destroyed, we will break you into pieces and here your faces will stay hidden. You shall be sacrificed," said Hun-Camé and Vucub-Camé.

They sacrificed them immediately and buried them in the Pucbal-Chah, as it was called. Before burying them, they cut off the head of Hun-Hunahpú, and buried the older brother together with the younger brother.

"Take the head and put it in that tree which is planted on the road," said Hun-Camé and Vucub-Camé. And having put the head in the tree, instantly the tree, which had never borne fruit before the head of Hun-Hunahpú was placed among its branches, was covered with fruit. And this calabash tree, it is said, is the one which we now call the head of Hun-Hunahpú.

Hun-Camé and Vucub-Camé looked in amazement at the fruit on the tree. The round fruit was every where; but they did not recognize the head of Hun-Hunahpú; it was exactly like the other fruit of the calabash tree. So it seemed to all of the people of Xibalba when they came to look at it.

According to their judgment, the tree was miraculous, because of what had instantly occurred when they put Hun-Hunahpú's head among its branches. And the Lords of Xibalba said:

"Let no one come to pick this fruit. Let no one come and sit under this tree!" they said, and so the Lords of Xibalba resolved to keep everybody away.

The head of Hun-Hunahpú did not appear again, because it had become one and the same as the fruit of the gourd tree. Nevertheless, a girl heard the wonderful story. Now we shall tell about her arrival.

READING AND DISCUSSION QUESTIONS

1.   What is the significance of the ball game in this passage?
2.   Describe the Maya gods as they appear in this passage.

COMPARATIVE QUESTIONS

1. From the documents in this chapter, what can be said about the similarities and differences in culture and religion in the Americas before contact with Europeans?

2. Taking into consideration the depictions of the Mexica marketplace and the Maya ball game, what benefits did entertainment provide to the civilizations of the Americas?

3. What role did law play in Mexica and Inca society? According to Durán and Cieza de León, how successful were the rulers of these civilizations in enforcing laws?

4. Compare the sources in this chapter to those on Africa (Chapter 10). Because most of the material from both chapters is written from the perspective of outsiders, can it be trusted? Why or why not? How might the information in such sources be verified?

5. How do the gods and the underworld in the *Popol Vuh* compare to those in *The Epic of Gilgamesh* (Document 2-1)?

6. Compare the depiction of the human form in Mississippian culture with that of the Greeks (Documents 5-6 and 5-7).

CHAPTER 12

Cultural Exchange in Central and Southern Asia

to 1400

D uring the medieval period, the climate of Central and Southern Asia was one of contact and transformation. While Indian merchants sailed throughout Southeast Asia introducing Buddhism and Hinduism, Muslim merchants and, later, Muslim armies brought their own religion into India. In Central Asia, nomadic groups of Turks and Mongols began to abandon their traditional transitory lifestyles as they came into contact with settled civilizations. The Mongols evolved into cultural brokers who facilitated the exchange of people and ideas throughout their far-reaching empire. The Mongols never conquered India, allowing Indian traditions to develop as a complex blend of Hindu and Islamic customs. The sources in this chapter examine the changes underway in Central and Southern Asia from approximately the fourth to the fifteenth centuries, with a special emphasis on the Mongol experience and empire.

DOCUMENT 12-1

From The Secret History of the Mongols

ca. 1227–1251

In 1206, a Mongol warrior named Temüjin united the nomadic tribes north of the Great Wall of China and received the title Chinggis Khan. Under his leadership, the Mongols swept into northern China and Central Asia. After Temüjin's death in 1227, his successors expanded into the Middle East and Russian Asia. Only one account of Chinggis Khan's early life survives,

Igor de Rachewiltz, trans., *The Secret History of the Mongols: A Mongolian Epic Chronicle of the Thirteenth Century* (Leiden: Brill, 2004), 1:13–15, 26–28, 48–50.

The Secret History of the Mongols, *written at an unknown time in the thirteenth century by an unknown writer. Although originally written in Mongolian, the surviving text is a transliteration in Chinese characters that was created in the fourteenth century to teach Chinese diplomats the Mongolian language.*

When Temüjin was nine years old, Yisügei Ba'atur[1] set out to go to the Olqunu'ut people, relatives of Mother Hö'elün, taking Temüjin with him and saying, "I shall ask his maternal uncles for a girl in marriage for him." On the way, between Mount Čekčer and Mount Čiqurqu, he met Dei Sečen of the Onggirat.

Dei Sečen said, "Quda[2] Yisügei, in whose direction are you going, coming this way? Yisügei Ba'atur said, "I have come here on my way to the Olqunu'ut people, the maternal uncles of this my son, to ask for a girl in marriage for him." Dei Sečen said, "This son of yours is a boy
> Who has fire in his eyes,
> Who has light in his face.

"Quda Yisügei, I had a dream last night, I did. A white gerfalcon clasping both sun and moon in its claws flew to me and perched on my hand. I told the people about this dream of mine, saying, 'Before, when I looked, I could only see the sun and the moon from afar; now this gerfalcon has brought them to me and has perched on my hand. He has alighted, all white. Just what sort of good thing does this show?' I had my dream, quda Yisügei, just as you were coming here bringing your son. I had a dream of good omen. What kind of dream is it? The august spirit of you, Kiyat people, has come in my dream and has announced your visit.
> "With us, the Onggirat people, from old days,
> To have the good looks of our granddaughters
> And the beauty of our daughters is enough:
> We do not strive for dominion.
> For those of you who have become qa'an [Khan, ruler],
> We have our daughters with beautiful cheeks
> Ride on a large cart to which we harness
> A black male camel.
> We trot them off to the qa'an,
> And seat them by him on the qatun's seat[3]

---

[1] **Yisügei Ba'atur**: Temüjin's father.
[2] **quda**: A term the parents of the bride and bridegroom used to describe each other and to symbolize the joining of their families.

We do not strive for dominion, nor for people.
We lift our good-looking daughters,
We have them ride on a carriage with front seat;
We harness a dark male camel,
We lead them off to the qa'an,
And seat them on the throne, at his side.
From old days, the Onggirat people
Have the qatuns as shields,
Have their daughters as intercessors.
We live thanks to the good looks
Of our granddaughters
And the beauty of our daughters.
With our boys, when they seek a bride,
One looks at the wealth of our camp;
With our girls, when they are sought as brides,
One considers only their beauty.

Quda Yisügei, let us go to my tent. My daughter is still small, take a look at her, quda!" So said Dei Sečen, and having led him to his tent he made him dismount.

When Yisügei saw his daughter, he saw a girl
Who had light in her face,
Who had fire in her eyes.

He was pleased with her. She was ten years old, one year older than Temüjin, and her name was Börte. Yisügei spent the night there, and the following morning, when he requested his daughter for Temüjin, Dei Sečen said, "If I gave her away after much asking on your part, you would respect me; if I gave her away without much asking, you would despise me. But the fate of a girl is not to grow old in the family in which she was born. I will give you my daughter, and you, for your part, leave your son here as my son-in-law." . . .

One day some robbers came and stole the eight horses, the light-bay geldings, that were standing by the tent and made off with them before their very eyes. Temüjin and his brothers sighted the robbers, but being on foot fell behind.

Belgütei was then away marmot-hunting on a short-tailed, short-haired chestnut horse. He arrived on foot in the evening after sunset, leading behind him the short-tailed, short-haired chestnut horse, which was so laden down with marmots that it staggered. When he was told that

---

[3] **qatun's seat**: The seat closest to the bridegroom.

robbers had stolen the light-bay geldings, Belgütei said, "I will go after them!" Qasar said, "You cannot cope with them, I will go after them!" Temüjin said, "Neither of you can cope with them, I will go after them!" Temüjin got on the short-haired chestnut horse and went off in pursuit of the light-bay geldings, following the tracks left in the grass.

He spent three days and nights tracking, and in the early morning of the fourth day he met on the way a brisk lad milking mares in a large herd of horses. When Temüjin inquired about the light-bay geldings, the lad said, "This morning, before sunrise, eight horses — light-bay geldings — were driven past here. I will show you their trail." He made Temüjin leave the short-haired chestnut horse there, set him on a white horse with a black back, and he himself rode a fast dun mare. And without even going to his tent, he put down his leather bucket and pail, concealing them in the grass.

"Friend," he said, "you came to me being in great trouble, but men's troubles are the same for all. I will be your companion. My father is called Naqu Bayan. I am his only son and my name is Bo'orču."

They spent three days and nights following the trail of the light-bay geldings. Then, in the evening of the fourth day, just as the sun was setting on the hills, they came upon people in a circular camp. They saw the eight horses, the light-bay geldings, standing at the edge of that large camp, grazing.

Temüjin said, "Friend, you stay here. As for me — the light-bay geldings are those there — I will go and drive them off!" Bo'orču said, "I came with you as your companion. How can I stay here?" They raced in together and drove the light-bay geldings off.

The men came after them in separate groups and began to pursue them. Away from the rest, one man on a white horse and holding a pole-lasso drew closer and caught up with them. Bo'orču said, "Friend, give me the bow and arrows. I'll trade shots with him!" Temüjin said, "I am afraid you'll come to harm because of me. I'll trade shots with him!" He swung around and they began to shoot arrows at each other. The man on the white horse stood up, aiming at him with his pole-lasso. His companions, who had fallen behind, caught up with him, but the sun sank, dusk came down and those men behind, overtaken by darkness, halted and were left behind altogether.

They rode all that night and then rode for three more days and nights before they reached their destination. Temüjin said, "Friend, would I ever have got these horses of mine back without you? Let's share them. How many do you say you'll take?" Bo'orču said, "I became your companion because you, a good friend, were in trouble and approached me, and I wished to be of help to a good friend. Am I now to take the horses as booty? My father is called Naqu Bayan. I am the only son of Naqu Bayan. The property of my father is ample for me. I won't take the horses. What sort of help would my help be? I won't take them.". . .

Then Naqu Bayan said, . . . "Temüjin, if you become lord of the people, how will you please me for this augury?" Temüjin said, "If it is indeed given to me to rule over the people as you say, I will make you a leader of ten thousand."

Qorči[4] said, "What kind of happiness is it for me, the man who foretold so many great affairs, merely to become the leader of ten thousand? Make me a leader of ten thousand, but in addition allow me to take freely beautiful and fine girls from among the people, and let me have thirty as wives. And again, whatever I say, heed me closely!"

The Geniges, with Qunan at their head, also came as one camp. Then came Dāritai Otčigin — also one camp. From the Jadaran came also Mulqalqu. And the Ünjin and the Saqayit came — also one camp. When Temüjin had parted company in this way from Jamuqa and had moved further on, setting up camp at Ayil Qaraqana by the Kimurqa Stream, there came, also separating from Jamuqa, the sons of Sorqatu Jürki of the Jürkin, Sača Beki and Taiču — one camp; then the son of Nekün Taiši, Qučar Beki — one camp; and the son of Qutula Qan, Altan Otčigin — one camp. These, then, left Jamuqa and moved on, and when Temüjin set up camp at Ayil Qaraqana by the Kimurqa Stream, they joined camp with him. From there they went on, and camped at Kökö Na'ur of Mount Qara Jirügen by the Senggür Stream in the Gürelgü Mountains.

Altan, Qučar and Sača Beki, all of them having agreed among themselves, said to Temüjin, "We shall make you qan. When you, Temüjin, become qan, we

> As vanguard shall speed
> After many foes: for you
> Fine-looking maidens and ladies of rank,
> Palatial tents, and from foreign people
> Ladies and maidens with beautiful cheeks,
> And geldings with fine croups
> At the trot we shall bring.
> When in a battue we hunt the cunning
> Wild beasts, for you

---

[4] **Qorči**: Brother of one of Temüjin's closest companions, Jamuqa.

We shall go ahead and round them up.
For you we shall drive the beasts of the steppe
Until their bellies press together;
For you we shall drive the beasts of the steep banks
Until their thighs press together.
In the days of war,
If we disobey your commands,
Deprive us of all our goods and belongings, and
Our noble wives, and cast
Our black heads on the ground!
In the days of peace,
If we violate your counsel,
Cut us off from our retainers and possessions, and
Our wives, and cast us
Out into the wilderness!"
Thus they pledged their word and in
This way they swore the oath of loyalty,
and made Temüjin qan, naming him Činggis Qa'an.

Having become qa'an, Činggis ordered the younger brother of Bo'orču, Ögölei Čerbi, to carry a quiver, Qači'un Toqura'un to carry a quiver, and the two brothers Jetei and Doqolqu Čerbi each to carry a quiver.

Önggür, Söyiketü Čerbi and Qada'an Daldurqan then spoke, saying,
"We shall not let you go without
Your morning drinks;
We shall not neglect your drinks
In the evening!"
And so they became stewards. Then Degei spoke:
"In making broth
Of a two-year-old wether,[5]
I shall not fail in the morning,
I shall not be remiss at night.
I shall tend pied sheep,
And shall fill the bottom of the cart with them.
I shall tend brown sheep,
And shall fill the sheep-fold with them.
I was a base and greedy man: now
I shall tend sheep,
And tripe shall I eat!"

---

[5] **wether**: A goat.

READING AND DISCUSSION QUESTIONS

1. What does this selection reveal about the workings of Mongolian society, especially regarding marriage customs?
2. What was the role of dreams and omens in Mongolian culture?
3. What was expected of Mongol leaders and their followers?

VIEWPOINTS

The Mongols and Their Conquests

DOCUMENT 12-2

Epitaph for the Honorable Menggu

ca. 1272

The Mongol conquest of China took part in stages and was not complete until the 1270s. The Mongols chose to continue using the established system of administration in China, but they distrusted local Chinese officials and the bureaucrats themselves. To watch the activities of the Chinese officials, the Mongols placed outsiders in key positions. Many were Mongols, such as the official described here, but many were imported from Central Asia and the Middle East. It is not known who wrote this epitaph, but it is thought to have been a Chinese official.

EPITAPH FOR THE HONORABLE MENGGU, GREAT GENERAL OF HUAIYUAN, GOVERNOR OF HUAIMENG ROUTE, AND MILITARY ADMINISTRATOR OF SEVERAL ARMIES

Emperor Taizu [Chinggis Khan] received the mandate of Heaven and subjugated all regions. When Emperor Taizong [Ogodei Khan] succeeded, he revitalized the bureaucratic system and made it more efficient

---

Patricia Buckley Ebrey, ed., *Chinese Civilization and Society: A Sourcebook*, 2d ed. (New York: Free Press, 1993), 192–194.

and organized. At court, one minister supervised all the officials and helped the emperor rule. In the provinces, commanderies and counties received instructions from above and saw that they got carried out. Prefects and magistrates were as a rule appointed only after submitting [to the Mongols]. Still one Mongol, called the governor, was selected to supervise them. The prefects and magistrates all had to obey his orders. The fortune of the common people and the quality of the government both were entirely dependent on the wisdom of the governor.

Zhangde, one of the ten routes,[6] is crucial to communication between north and south. In the fourth month of 1236, the court deemed Menggu capable of handling Zhangde, so promoted him from the post of legal officer of the troops of Quduqu to be its governor. At the time, the Jin[7] had fallen only three years earlier. The common people were not yet free of the army, the injured had not yet recovered, those who had fled had not yet returned, and the residents were not yet contented. Because regulations were lax, the soldiers took advantage of their victory to plunder. Even in cities and marketplaces, some people kept their doors closed in the daytime. As soon as Menggu arrived, he took charge. Knowing the people's grievances, he issued an order, "Those who oppress the people will be dealt with according to the law. Craftsmen, merchants, and shopkeepers, you must each go about your work with your doors open, peaceably attending to your business without fear. Farmers, you must be content with your lands and exert yourselves diligently according to the seasons. I will instruct or punish those who mistreat you." After this order was issued, the violent became obedient and no one any longer dared violate the laws. Farmers in the fields and travelers on the roads felt safe, and people began to enjoy life.

In the second month of 1238, Wang Rong, prefect of Huaizhou, rebelled. The grand preceptor and prince ordered Menggu to put down this rebellion, telling him to slaughter everyone. Menggu responded, "When the royal army suppresses rebels, those who were coerced into joining them ought to be pardoned, not to mention those who are entirely innocent." The prince approved his advice and followed it. When Wang Rong surrendered, he was executed but the region was spared. The

---

[6] **the ten routes**: The Mongols transformed the adminstration of China by basing it on population size. One route equaled 100,000 households. Ten routes equaled a province.

[7] **the Jin**: Dynasty that ruled northern China from 1115 to 1234. The Jin were originally from north of the Great Wall in modern-day Manchuria.

residents, with jugs of wine and burning incense, saw Menggu off tearfully, unable to bear his leaving. Forty years later when he was put in charge of Henei, the common people were delighted with the news, saying, "We will all survive — our parents and relatives through marriage all served him before."

In 1239 locusts destroyed all the vegetation in Xiang and Wei, so the people were short of food. Menggu reported this to the great minister Quduqu who issued five thousand piculs[8] of army rations to save the starving. As a consequence no one had to flee or starve.

During the four years from 1240 to 1243, the great southern campaigns took place. Wherever the armies passed, the local officials complained. Menggu, through loyal and diligent preparations, was able to supply the troops without hurting the people.

In 1247 some previously pacified cities in the Huai and Han areas rose in revolt. Refugees fled north and south. Border generals and local officials joined the fray, fighting and plundering. Menggu, by establishing trust, was able to gather together more than ten thousand households and settle them down as commoners. Even children were included.

At that time the harvest failed for several years in a row, yet taxes and labor services were still exacted. Consequently, three or four of every ten houses was vacant. Menggu ordered the officials to travel around announcing that those who returned to their property would be exempt from taxes and services for three years. That year seventeen thousand households returned in response to his summons.

In the first month of 1248 Zhu Ge, a bandit from Huizhou, organized a gang and rebelled. The military officers were planning to go overboard in their response to this, but Menggu declared, "The state has honored me, enriched me, delegated control of the troops to me, and entrusted the fate of the region to me. Does it want me to pacify the bandits or become a bandit myself? There is no need to act recklessly. If the bandits are not caught or the rebellion not suppressed, I will accept the responsibility." He then personally led the troops, capturing thirty-eight bandits at Heilu Mountain, and restoring peace to the local population. By fall there were no more rebels. When the bandit Xie Zhiquan rebelled in the third month of 1249, he pacified him the same way.

General Chagan recognized Menggu's honesty and humanity. Whenever the other circuits condemned prisoners to death, he had Menggu conduct the review investigation. Innumerable times, Menggu relied on

---

[8]**piculs**: Weight equal to how much a man could carry on his shoulder.

the law to redress grievances and reduce penalties. Ten years before, a peasant in Anyang had offended a noble and been ordered to turn over six young girls. Menggu ordered the noble official Alachur to marry them all out to commoners. There was a drought in the summer of 1250. After Menggu prayed for rain, moisture became adequate.

In the spring of 1262, Li Tan revolted and sent his henchmen to far away places disguised as mounted couriers. They traveled through many routes, east and west, the officials unable to recognize them. Menggu discovered them and got them to admit their treacherous conspiracy, thus defeating them. When there was a drought in 1263, Menggu prayed for rain and it rained. That year he was given the title Brilliant and August General and made governor of Zhongshan prefecture. In 1270 he was transferred and became governor of Hezhong prefecture. In the spring of 1274 he was allowed to wear the golden tiger tablet in recognition of his long and excellent service, his incorruptibility, and the repute in which he was held where he had served. He was advanced out of order to great general of Huaiyuan, governor of Huaimeng route, and military administrator of several armies. On the 29th of the second month he died of illness in the main room of his private residence at the age of seventy-one.

Menggu was a Mongol, and when young was called Mongol Baer. His father was Xibaer, his mother Lengla. He had six wives . . . , seven sons, . . . six daughters. . . . Seven years after he was buried, Naohai and his other sons recorded Menggu's virtuous government service for an epitaph and came to ask me to write the inscription.

Alas! When I think about all the government officials of the past and present, I come to the realization that the greedy ones are invariably oppressive and the honest ones are invariably incorrupt, the connection between their virtues and their administrative behavior as automatic as shape to shadow or sound to echo. Those who are greedy are not satisfied; not satisfied, they take by force, not caring how much they harm the world. Those who are honest do not take what is not theirs, no matter how slight it might be. How would they harm others to benefit themselves? The house where Menggu lived when he governed Zhangde nearly forty years ago, and the fields from which he obtained food then, were just adequate to keep out the wind and rain and supply enough to eat. When he died there were no estates or leftover wealth to leave his sons or grandsons. Therefore they had to model themselves on him and concentrate on governing in a way that would bring peace and safety, show love for the people, and benefit all. They have no need to be ashamed even if compared to the model officials of the Han and Tang dynasties.

READING AND DISCUSSION QUESTIONS

1. How is the governor Menggu described in this passage? What might this reveal about Chinese attitudes toward the Mongols?

2. What can this document reveal about how the Mongol system of government worked in China?

3. What were Menggu's duties?

DOCUMENT 12-3

LIU GUANDAO

Khubilai Khan Hunting

1280

The Mongol campaign to conquer China was not complete until the reign of Chinggis Khan's grandson, Khubilai Khan. In 1271, Khubilai declared himself emperor of China and inaugurated a new dynasty called the Yuan. In doing so, he began imitating Chinese styles of rule and propaganda, including commissioning portraits of himself in the Chinese style. One such portrait is this painting by Liu Guandao (1264–1294), who was primarily known for his landscapes and paintings of Buddhist and Daoist figures. Khubilai is located in the center of the figures, wearing the imperial robe.

Opposite: Kubilai Khan (1214–1294) Hunting, Yuan Dynasty (ink and color on silk) (see 110534 & 226021 for detail), Liu Kuan-tao (fl. 1270–1300) (attr. to)/National Palace Museum, Taipei, Taiwan/The Bridgeman Art Library International.

READING AND DISCUSSION QUESTIONS

1. Describe the figures' relationship to the landscape in this painting.
2. What are the figures doing? How are they dressed?
3. How does this painting conform with and deviate from Chinese landscape paintings from the Song Era (Document 13-3)?

DOCUMENT 12-4

MARCO POLO

From Travels: *Description of the World*

ca. 1298

Marco Polo (ca. 1253–1324) was an Italian merchant who traveled through Central Asia to China. He served as a government official for many years in the court of Khubilai Khan. Upon returning to Europe in 1295 — approximately twenty-five years after he began his journey — Polo wrote a popular book describing his adventures. Although historians have at times doubted the veracity of some of Polo's claims, his Travels nonetheless provide an important record of Central Asia during the time of the Mongols. In this excerpt, Polo describes his journey along the Asian trade routes known as the Silk Road, including his crossing of the challenging Taklamakan Desert.

Let us turn next to the province of Yarkand [on the southwestern border of the Taklamakan Desert], five days' journey in extent. The inhabitants follow the law of Mahomet,[9] and there are also some Nestorian Christians. They are subject to the Great Khan's nephew, of whom I have already spoken. It is amply stocked with the means of life, especially cotton. But,

Marco Polo, from *The Travels of Marco Polo*, trans. Ronald Latham (London: Penguin, 1958), 82–85, 87–88.

[9] **Mahomet**: Western Europeans mistakenly believed that Muslims worshipped a god named Mahomet, or Muhammad, who is in fact the founder of the Islamic religion and believed to be a prophet of God.

since there is nothing here worth mentioning in our book, we shall pass on to Khotan,[10] which lies towards the east-north-east.

Khotan is a province eight days' journey in extent, which is subject to the Great Khan. The inhabitants all worship Mahomet. It has cities and towns in plenty, of which the most splendid, and the capital of the kingdom, bears the same name as the province, Khotan. It is amply stocked with the means of life. Cotton grows here in plenty. It has vineyards, estates, and orchards in plenty. The people live by trade and industry; they are not at all warlike.

Passing on from here we come to the province of Pem, five days' journey in extent, towards the east-north-east. Here too the inhabitants worship Mahomet and are subject to the Great Khan. It has villages and towns in plenty. The most splendid city and the capital of the province is called Pem. There are rivers here in which are found stones called jasper and chalcedony [both are quartz] in plenty. There is no lack of the means of life. Cotton is plentiful. The inhabitants live by trade and industry.

The following custom is prevalent among them. When a woman's husband leaves her to go on a journey of more than twenty days, then, as soon as he has left, she takes another husband, and this she is fully entitled to do by local usage. And the men, wherever they go, take wives in the same way.

You should know that all the provinces I have described, from Kashgar to Pem and some way beyond, are provinces of Turkestan [i.e., the area of Central Asia inhabited by Turks].

I will tell you next of another province of Turkestan, lying east-north-east, which is called Charchan. It used to be a splendid and fruitful country, but it has been much devastated by the Tartars [Mongols]. The inhabitants worship Mahomet. There are villages and towns in plenty, and the chief city of the kingdom is Charchan.[11] There are rivers producing jasper and chalcedony, which are exported for sale in Cathay and bring in a good profit; for they are plentiful and of good quality.

All this province is a tract of sand; and so is the country from Khotan to Pem and from Pem to here. There are many springs of bad and bitter water, though in some places the water is good and sweet. When it happens that an army passes through the country, if it is a hostile one,

---

[10] **Khotan**: A city along a Silk Road trading route located on the southern border of the Taklamakan Desert.

[11] **Charchan**: This was the next major city along the trade route.

the people take flight with their wives and children and their beasts two or three days' journey into the sandy wastes to places where they know that there is water and they can live with their beasts. And I assure you that no one can tell which way they have gone, because the wind covers their tracks with sand, so that there is nothing to show where they have been, but the country looks as if it had never been traversed by man or beast. That is how they escape from their enemies. But, if it happens that a friendly army passes that way, they merely drive off their beasts, because they do not want to have them seized and eaten; for the armies never pay for what they take. And you should know that, when they harvest their grain, they store it far from any habitation, in certain caves among these wastes, for fear of the armies; and from these stores they bring home what they need month by month.

After leaving Charchan, the road runs for fully five days through sandy wastes, where the water is bad and bitter, except in a few places where it is good and sweet; and there is nothing worth noting in our book. At the end of the five days' journey towards the east-north-east, is a city which stands on the verge of the Great Desert. It is here that men take in provisions for crossing the desert. Let us move on accordingly and proceed with our narrative.

The city I have mentioned, which stands at the point where the traveler enters the Great Desert, is a big city called Lop, and the desert is called the Desert of Lop. The city is subject to the Great Khan, and the inhabitants worship Mahomet. I can tell you that travelers who intend to cross the desert rest in this town for a week to refresh themselves and their beasts. At the end of the week they stock up with a month's provisions for themselves and their beasts. Then they leave the town and enter the desert.

This desert is reported to be so long that it would take a year to go from end to end; and at the narrowest point it takes a month to cross it. It consists entirely of mountains and sand and valleys. There is nothing at all to eat. But I can tell you that after traveling a day and a night you find drinking water [at an oasis] — not enough water to supply a large company, but enough for fifty or a hundred men with their beasts. And all the way through the desert you must go for a day and a night before you find water. And I can tell you that in three or four places you find the water bitter and brackish; but at all the other watering-places, that is, twenty-eight in all, the water is good. Beasts and birds there are none, because they find nothing to eat. But I assure you that one thing is found here, and that a very strange one, which I will relate to you.

The truth is this. When a man is riding by night through this desert and something happens to make him loiter and lose touch with his companions, by dropping asleep or for some other reason, and afterwards he wants to rejoin them, then he hears spirits talking in such a way that they seem to be his companions. Sometimes, indeed, they even hail him by name. Often these voices make him stray from the path, so that he never finds it again. And in this way many travelers have been lost and have perished. And sometimes in the night they are conscious of a noise like the clatter of a great cavalcade of riders away from the road; and, believing that these are some of their own company, they go where they hear the noise and, when day breaks, find they are victims of an illusion and in an awkward plight. And there are some who, in crossing this desert, have seen a host of men coming towards them and, suspecting that they were robbers, have taken flight; so, having left the beaten track and not knowing how to return to it, they have gone hopelessly astray. Yes, and even by daylight men hear these spirit voices, and often you fancy you are listening to the strains of many instruments, especially drums, and the clash of arms. For this reason bands of travelers make a point of keeping very close together. Before they go to sleep they set up a sign pointing in the direction in which they have to travel. And round the necks of all their beasts they fasten little bells, so that by listening to the sound they may prevent them from straying off the path.

That is how they cross the desert, with all the discomfort of which you have heard. . . .

Now I will tell you of some other cities, which lie towards the northwest near the edge of this desert.

The province of Kamul, which used to be a kingdom, contains towns and villages in plenty, the chief town being also called Kamul.[12] The province lies between two deserts, the Great Desert and a small one three days' journey in extent. The inhabitants are all idolaters [Buddhists] and speak a language of their own. They live on the produce of the soil; for they have a superfluity of foodstuffs and beverages, which they sell to travelers who pass that way. They are a very gay folk, who give no thought to anything but making music, singing and dancing, and reading and writing according to their own usage, and taking great delight in the pleasures of the body. I give you my word that if a stranger comes to a house here to seek

---

[12] **Kamul**: Known today as Hami, this city is located along the northern route, which Polo is apparently describing from secondhand accounts.

hospitality he receives a very warm welcome. The host bids his wife do everything that the guest wishes. Then he leaves the house and goes about his own business and stays away two or three days. Meanwhile the guest stays with his wife in the house and does what he will with her, lying with her in one bed just as if she were his own wife; and they lead a gay life together. All the men of this city and province are thus cuckolded by their wives; but they are not the least ashamed of it. And the women are beautiful and vivacious and always ready to oblige.

Now it happened during the reign of Mongu Khan,[13] lord of the Tartars, that he was informed of this custom that prevailed among the men of Kamul of giving their wives in adultery to outsiders. Mongu thereupon commanded them under heavy penalties to desist from this form of hospitality. When they received this command, they were greatly distressed; but for three years they reluctantly obeyed. Then they held a council and talked the matter over, and this is what they did. They took a rich gift and sent it to Mongu and entreated him to let them use their wives according to the traditions of their ancestors; for their ancestors had declared that by the pleasure they gave to guests with their wives and goods they won the favor of their idols and multiplied the yield of their crops and their tillage. When Mongu Khan heard this he said: "Since you desire your own shame, you may have it." So he let them have their way. And I can assure you that since then they have always upheld this tradition and uphold it still.

READING AND DISCUSSION QUESTIONS

1. What were some of the dangers of traveling the Silk Road?

2. Describe the role of the Mongols in the areas that Polo visits. What impact did the Mongol presence have in these territories?

3. Consider the story Polo tells regarding the wives of Kamul. What does the response of the Great Khan say about the political strength of the Mongol leader in his empire?

---

[13] **Mongu Khan:** Brother of Khubilai Khan, who was Great Khan from 1251 to 1259.

VATSYAYANA

From the Kamasutra: *About a Wife*

ca. 150–1200

Most Westerners know of the Kamasutra *as a manual of sexual positions, but the text actually examines all facets of love, including this selection on the duties of a wife. Most scholars have dated the original text to the second century* C.E., *but it was revised and expanded in subsequent centuries. Traditionally, the text was said to have been recited by the doorkeeper of the Hindu god Shiva after hearing Shiva making love to his consort, Parvati. Whatever its origin, the* Kamasutra *was an immensely popular text throughout medieval India.*

On the Manner of Living of a Virtuous Woman, and of Her Behaviour During the Absence of Her Husband

A virtuous woman, who has affection for her husband, should act in conformity with his wishes as if he were a divine being, and with his consent should take upon herself the whole care of his family. She should keep the whole house well cleaned, and arrange flowers of various kinds in different parts of it, and make the floor smooth and polished so as to give the whole a neat and becoming appearance. She should surround the house with a garden, and place ready in it all the materials required for the morning, noon and evening sacrifices. Moreover she should herself revere the sanctuary of the Household Gods, for says Gonardiya,[14] "nothing so much attracts the heart of a householder to his wife as a careful observance of the things mentioned above."

Towards the parents, relations, friends, sisters, and servants of her husband she should behave as they deserve. In the garden she should plant beds of green vegetables, bunches of the sugar cane, and clumps of the fig tree, the mustard plant, the parsley plant, the fennel plant, . . . She should also have seats and arbours made in the garden, in the middle of which a well, tank or pool should be dug.

The Kama Sutra of Vatsyayana (1883 for the Kama Shastra Society of London and Benares), 97–100.

[14] **Gonardiya**: An author of a Sanskrit grammar.

The wife should always avoid the company of female beggars, female buddhist mendicants, unchaste and roguish women, female fortune tellers and witches. As regards meals she should always consider what her husband likes and dislikes, and what things are good for him, and what are injurious to him. When she hears the sounds of his footsteps coming home she should at once get up, and be ready to do whatever he may command her, and either order her female servant to wash his feet, or wash them herself. When going anywhere with her husband, she should put on her ornaments, and without his consent she should not either give or accept invitations, or attend marriages and sacrifices, or sit in the company of female friends, or visit the temples of the gods. And if she wants to engage in any kind of games or sports, she should not do it against his will. In the same way she should always sit down after him, and get up before him, and should never awaken him when he is asleep. The kitchen should be situated in a quiet and retired place, so as not to be accessible to strangers, and should always look clean.

In the event of any misconduct on the part of her husband, she should not blame him excessively, though she be a little displeased. She should not use abusive language towards him, but rebuke him with conciliatory words, whether he be in the company of friends or alone. Moreover, she should not be a scold, for says Conardiya [Gonardiya], "there is no cause of dislike on the part of a husband so great as this characteristic in a wife." Lastly she should avoid bad expressions, sulky looks, speaking aside, standing in the doorway, and looking at passers-by, conversing in the pleasure groves, and remaining in a lonely place for a long time; and finally she should always keep her body, her teeth, her hair and everything belonging to her tidy, sweet, and clean.

When the wife wants to approach her husband in private her dress should consist of many ornaments, various kinds of flowers, and a cloth decorated with different colours, and some sweet-smelling ointments or unguents. But her every-day dress should be composed of a thin, close-textured cloth, a few ornaments and flowers, and a little scent, not too much. She should also observe the fasts and vows of her husband, and when he tries to prevent her doing this, she should persuade him to let her do it.

At appropriate times of the year, and when they happen to be cheap, she should buy earth, bamboos, firewood, skins, and iron pots, as also salt and oil. Fragrant substances, vessels made of the fruit of the plant wrightea antidy senterica, or oval leaved wrightea, medicines, and other things which are always wanted, should be obtained when required and kept in a secret place of the house. The seeds of the radish, the potato, the common beet, the Indian wormwood, the mangoe, the cucumber, the egg plant, the kushmanda, the pumpkin gourd, the surana, [the] bignonia indica, the sandal wood, the premma spinosa, the garlic plant, the onion, and other vegetables, should be bought and sown at the proper seasons.

The wife, moreover, should not tell to strangers, the amount of her wealth, nor the secrets which her husband has confided to her. She should surpass all the women of her own rank in life in her cleverness, her appearance, her knowledge of cookery, her pride, and her manner of serving her husband. The expenditure of the year should be regulated by the profits. The milk that remains after the meals should be turned into ghee or clarified butter. Oil and sugar should be prepared at home; spinning and weaving should also be done there; and a store of ropes and cords, and barks of trees for twisting into ropes should be kept. She should also attend to the pounding and cleaning of rice, using its small grain and chaff in some way or other. She should pay the salaries of the servants, look after the tilling of the fields, and keeping of the flocks and herds, superintend the making of vehicles, and take care of the rams, cocks, quails, parrots, starlings, cuckoos, peacocks, monkeys, and deer; and finally adjust the income and expenditure of the day. The worn-out clothes should be given to those servants who have done good work, in order to show them that their services have been appreciated, or they may be applied to some other use. The vessels in which wine is prepared, as well as those in which it is kept, should be carefully looked after, and put away at the proper time. All sales and purchases should also be well attended to. The friends of her husband she should welcome by presenting them with flowers, ointment, incense, betel leaves, and betel nut. Her father-in-law and mother-in-law she should treat as they deserve, always remaining dependant on their will, never contradicting them, speaking to them in few and not harsh words, not laughing loudly in their precence, and acting with their friends and enemies as with her own. In addition to the above she should not be vain, or too much taken up with her enjoyments. She should be liberal towards her servants, and reward them on holidays and festivals; and not give away anything without first making it known to her husband.

Thus ends the manner of living of a virtuous woman.

During the absence of her husband on a journey the virtuous woman should wear only her auspicious ornaments, and observe the fasts in honour of the gods. While anxious to hear the news of her husband, she should look after her household affairs. She should sleep near the elder women of the house, and make herself agreeable to them. She should look after and keep in repair the things that are liked by her husband, and continue the works that have been begun by him. To the abode of her relations she should not go except on occasions of joy and sorrow, and then she should go in her usual travelling dress, accompanied by her husband's servants, and not remain there for a long time. The fasts and feasts should be observed with the consent of the elders of the house. The resources should be increased by making purchases and sales according to the practice of the merchants, and by means of honest servants, superintended by herself. The income should be increased, and the expenditure diminished as much as possible. And when her husband returns from his journey, she should receive him at first in her ordinary clothes, so that he may know in what way she has lived during his absence, and should bring to him some presents, as also materials for the worship of the Deity.

READING AND DISCUSSION QUESTIONS

1. According to the *Kamasutra*, how should a virtuous wife act?
2. What is the ideal relationship between a husband and a wife, according to this text?
3. What features of this text might have helped make the *Kamasutra* so popular? How might women have viewed the text compared to men?

DOCUMENT 12-6

MAULANA BURHĀN UD-DĪN MARGHĪNĀNĪ
From Guidance: *Alms, Marriage, and Testimony*
ca. 1197

The Islamic religion began to arrive via merchants in the seventh century C.E., *and the later advance of Muslim armies into Pakistan and India between the eighth and twelfth centuries led to centuries of Islamic control over northern India. Many converted, but many retained their traditional religion. The Muslims of India followed a school of Islamic law called Hanafi, which was*

Wm. Theodore de Bary et al., eds., *Sources of Indian Tradition* (New York: Columbia University Press, 1958), 407–410.

*codified by the author Maulana Burhān ud-dīn Marghīnānī, who was born
in what is now Uzbekistan. His* Guidance (al-Hidāyah) *remains one of the
most important reference guides to Islamic law.*

THE ALMS TAX

Alms-giving is an ordinance of God, incumbent upon every person who is
free, sane, adult, and a Muslim, provided he be possessed, in full property,
of such estate or effects as are termed in the language of the law a minimum, and that he has been in possession of the same for the space of one
complete year. . . . The reason of this obligation is found in the word of
God, who has ordained it in the Qur'ān, saying, "Bestow alms." The same
injunction occurs in the traditions, and it is moreover universally admitted.
The reason for freedom being a requisite condition is that this is essential to
the complete possession of property. The reason why sanity of intellect and
maturity of age are requisite conditions shall be hereafter demonstrated.
The reason why the Muslim faith is made a condition is that the rendering
of alms is an act of piety, and such cannot proceed from an infidel.

OF THE DISBURSEMENT OF ALMS, AND OF THE PERSONS TO WHOSE USE IT IS TO BE APPLIED

The objects of the disbursement of alms are of eight different descriptions:
first, the needy; secondly, the destitute; thirdly, the collector of alms; . . .
fourthly, slaves [upon whom alms are bestowed in order to enable them,
by fulfilling their contract (i.e., by procuring their purchase price) to procure their freedom]; fifthly, debtors not possessed of property amounting
to a legal minimum; sixthly, in the service of God; seventhly, travelers;
and eighthly, the winning over of hearts. And those eight descriptions are
the original objects of the expenditure of alms, being particularly specified as such in the Qur'ān; and there are, therefore, no other proper or
legal objects of its application. With respect to the last, however, the law
has ceased to operate, since the time of the Prophet, because he used
to bestow alms upon them as a bribe or gratuity to prevent them from
molesting the Muslims, and also to secure their occasional assistance; but
when God gave strength to the faith, and to its followers, and rendered the
Muslims independent of such assistance, the occasion of bestowing this
gratuity upon them no longer remained; and all the doctors[15] unite in this
opinion. . . .

---

[15] **all the doctors**: All of the Muslim judges.

POLYGAMY

It is lawful for a freeman to marry four wives, whether free or slaves; but it is not lawful for him to marry more than four, because God has commanded in the Qur'ān, saying: "Ye may marry whosoever women are agreeable to you, two, three, or four," and the numbers being thus expressly mentioned, any beyond what is there specified would be unlawful. Shāfi'ī[16] alleges a man cannot lawfully marry more than one woman of the description of slaves, from his tenet as above recited, that "the marriage of freemen with slaves is allowable only from necessity"; the text already quoted is, however, in proof against him, since the term "women" applies equally to free women and to slaves.

TESTIMONY

In all rights, whether of property or otherwise, the probity of the witness, and the use of the word *shahādat* [evidence] is requisite; even in the case of the evidence of women with respect to birth, and the like; and this is approved; because *shahādat* is testimony, since it possesses the property of being binding; whence it is that it is restricted to the place of jurisdiction; and also, that the witness is required to be free; and a Muslim. If, therefore, a witness should say: "I know," or "I know with certainty," without making use of the word *shahādat*, in that case his evidence cannot be admitted. With respect to the probity of the witness, it is indispensable, because of what is said in the Qur'ān: "Take the evidence of two just men."

The testimony of *zimmīs* [protected unbelievers] with respect to each other is admissible, notwithstanding they be of different religions. Mālik[17] and Shāfi'ī have said that their evidence is absolutely inadmissible, because, as infidels are unjust, it is requisite to be slow in believing anything they may advance, God having said [in the Qur'ān]: "When an unjust person tells you anything, be slow in believing him"; whence it is that the evidence of an infidel is not admitted concerning a Muslim; and consequently, that an infidel stands [in this particular] in the same predicament with an apostate. The arguments of our doctors upon this point are twofold. First, it is related of the Prophet, that he permitted and held lawful the testimony of some Christians concerning others of their sect. Secondly, an infidel having power over himself, and his minor children,

---

[16] **Shāfi'ī**: Founder of a ninth-century school of thought on Sunni Islamic jurisprudence.

[17] **Mālik**: Founder of an eighth-century school of thought on Sunni Islamic jurisprudence.

is on that account qualified to be a witness with regard to his own sect; and the depravity which proceeds from his faith is not destructive of this qualification, because he is supposed to abstain from everything prohibited in his own religion, and falsehood is prohibited in every religion. It is otherwise with respect to an apostate, as he possesses no power, either over his own person, or over that of another; and it is also otherwise with respect to a *zimmī* in relation to a Muslim, because a *zimmī* has no power over the person of a Muslim. Besides, a *zimmī* may be suspected of inventing falsehoods against a Muslim from the hatred he bears to him on account of the superiority of the Muslims over him.

READING AND DISCUSSION QUESTIONS

1. Why must Muslims give alms to the poor? Who should receive the alms?
2. What are the Islamic laws regarding marriage?
3. Who is allowed to give testimony? What does this reveal about the relationship between Muslims and "People of the Book"?

COMPARATIVE QUESTIONS

1. What do these documents reveal about what values were prized by the Mongols? Is there any discernible change in values between their time as nomads and their time as rulers?
2. Characterize Mongol rule over Central and East Asia. How effective does Mongol rule appear to have been?
3. How do the duties of a wife in the *Kamasutra* compare to Ban Zhao's ideas about the duties of a wife in China (Document 7-2)?

CHAPTER 13

States and Cultures in East Asia

800–1400

Throughout the medieval period, East Asia saw unprecedented economic growth, created sophisticated governments, and experienced a cultural boom. China drove this development and led in technological innovations such as mastering the printing press and perfecting the compass for overseas navigation. The Song Dynasty (960–1279) in particular advanced new forms of governance through the creation of an elite corps of educated civil servants and established thriving trade with its neighbors in Southeast Asia and beyond. China's vitality granted it tremendous influence over its neighbors, including Korea, Vietnam, and Japan. The sources in this chapter focus on the economic successes of China during the medieval period, as well as its cultural developments, and include accounts from Heian Japan (794–1185) and the Kamakura period (1185–1333), high points in the development of Japanese government and culture.

VIEWPOINTS

Feudalism and Society in Medieval Japan

DOCUMENT 13-1

MURASAKI SHIKIBU

From The Tale of Genji

ca. 1021

Heian Japan (794–1185) developed a culturally vibrant aristocratic society — one in which women played remarkably important roles, especially in literary endeavors. During this period, the Japanese developed a phonetic writing system that appealed to women who often lacked the education needed to master the more complicated Chinese-based writing system. Court society soon benefited from the entertainments of significant female writers such as Murasaki Shikibu, the author of the narrative masterpiece The Tale of Genji. *In the excerpts below, the characters of the story discuss how to pick a good wife and the role of women in marriage.*

They talked on, of the varieties of women.

"A man sees women, all manner of them, who seem beyond reproach," said the guards officer, "but when it comes to picking the wife who must be everything, matters are not simple. The emperor has trouble, after all, finding the minister who has all the qualifications. A man may be very wise, but no man can govern by himself. Superior is helped by subordinate, subordinate defers to superior, and so affairs proceed by agreement and concession. But when it comes to choosing the woman who is to be in charge of your house, the qualifications are altogether too many. A merit is balanced by a defect, there is this good point and that bad point, and

---

Murasaki Shikibu, *The Tale of Genji*, trans. Edward Seidensticker (New York: Alfred A. Knopf, 1976).

even women who though not perfect can be made to do are not easy to find. I would not like to have you think me a profligate who has to try them all. But it is a question of the woman who must be everything, and it seems best, other things being equal, to find someone who does not require shaping and training, someone who has most of the qualifications from the start. The man who begins his search with all this in mind must be reconciled to searching for a very long time."

"There are those who display a womanly reticence to the world, as if they had never heard of complaining. They seem utterly calm. And then when their thoughts are too much for them they leave behind the most horrendous notes, the most flamboyant poems, the sort of keepsakes certain to call up dreadful memories, and off they go into the mountains or to some remote seashore. When I was a child I would hear the women reading romantic stories, and I would join them in their sniffling and think it all very sad, all very profound and moving. Now I am afraid that it suggests certain pretenses.

"It is very stupid, really, to run off and leave a perfectly kind and sympathetic man. He may have been guilty of some minor dereliction, but to run off with no understanding at all of his true feelings, with no purpose other than to attract attention and hope to upset him — it is an unpleasant sort of memory to have to live with. She gets drunk with admiration for herself and there she is, a nun. When she enters her convent she is sure that she has found enlightenment and has no regrets for the vulgar world.

"Her women come to see her. 'How very touching,' they say. 'How brave of you.'

"But she no longer feels quite as pleased with herself. The man, who has not lost his affection for her, hears of what has happened and weeps, and certain of her old attendants pass this intelligence on to her. 'He is a man of great feeling, you see. What a pity that it should have come to this.' The woman can only brush aside her newly cropped hair[1] to reveal a face on the edge of tears. She tries to hold them back and cannot, such are her regrets for the life she has left behind; and the Buddha is not likely to think her one who has cleansed her heart of passion. Probably she is in more danger of brimstone now in this fragile vocation than if she had stayed with us in our sullied world.

---

[1] **newly cropped hair**: Buddhist nuns were expected to cut off their hair upon entering the convent.

"The bond between husband and wife is a strong one. Suppose the man had hunted her out and brought her back. The memory of her acts would still be there, and inevitably, sooner or later, it would be cause for rancor. When there are crises, incidents, a woman should try to overlook them, for better or for worse, and make the bond into something durable. The wounds will remain, with the woman and with the man, when there are crises such as I have described. It is very foolish for a woman to let a little dalliance upset her so much that she shows her resentment openly. He has his adventures — but if he has fond memories of their early days together, his and hers, she may be sure that she matters. A commotion means the end of everything. She should be quiet and generous, and when something comes up that quite properly arouses her resentment she should make it known by delicate hints. The man will feel guilty and with tactful guidance he will mend his ways. Too much lenience can make a woman seem charmingly docile and trusting, but it can also make her seem somewhat wanting in substance. We have had instances enough of boats abandoned to the winds and waves. Do you not agree?"

Tô no Chûjô nodded. "It may be difficult when someone you are especially fond of, someone beautiful and charming, has been guilty of an indiscretion, but magnanimity produces wonders. They may not always work, but generosity and reasonableness and patience do on the whole seem best."

READING AND DISCUSSION QUESTIONS

1. According to the characters, how is the selection of a wife similar to the emperor selecting a minister? Why is picking a wife more difficult?

2. What do the characters believe is the proper reaction of a wife when she learns of a "little dalliance" by her husband? In what ways, if any, may she show her disapproval?

3. Can the characters' views regarding the proper role of women in Japanese society be taken at face value? In what ways does the knowledge that the author of *The Tale of Genji* was a woman change its meaning?

4. Given the lack of educational opportunities for Heian Japanese women, who do you suppose was Shikibu's audience?

From The Tale of the Heike
ca. 1250

The Tale of the Heike *narrates the battle for power at the end of the twelfth century between two rival families, the Taira (Heike) and the Minamoto (Genji), in which the Minamoto, from the east, win convincingly. There was no single author of this work; rather, as with the poems by Homer (see Chapter 5), it seems that countless bards and storytellers added and altered tales as they saw fit before the work was assembled into one document in the middle of the thirteenth century. The tales themselves tend to be episodic in nature, as in the passages excerpted here. First the hero, Atsumori, is defeated, and then the entire Tairan force is destroyed.*

The Death of Atsumori

When the Heike were routed at Ichi no tani, and their nobles and courtiers were fleeing to the shore to escape in their ships, Kumagai Naozane came riding along a narrow path onto the beach, with the intention of intercepting one of their great captains. Just then his eye fell on a single horseman who was attempting to reach one of the ships in the offing. The horse he rode was dappled-gray, and its saddle glittered with gold mounting. Not doubting that he was one of the chief captains, Kumagai beckoned to him with his war fan, crying out: "Shameful! to show an enemy your back. Return! Return!"

The warrior turned his horse and rode back to the beach, where Kumagai at once engaged him in mortal combat. Quickly hurling him to the ground, he sprang upon him and tore off his helmet to cut off his head, when he beheld the face of a youth of sixteen or seventeen, delicately powdered and with blackened teeth,[2] just about the age of his own son

---

Donald Keene, ed., *Anthology of Japanese Literature from the Earliest Era to the Mid-Nineteenth Century* (New York: Grove Press, 1955), 179–184.

[2] **delicately powdered and with blackened teeth**: It was believed impolite to show one's teeth, so courtiers would often color their teeth black. Pale faces were considered most beautiful, so the elite would also powder their faces.

and with features of great beauty. "Who are you?" he asked. "Tell me your name, for I would spare your life."

"Nay, first say who you are," replied the young man.

"I am Kumagai Naozane of Musashi, a person of no particular importance."

"Then you have made a good capture," said the youth. "Take my head and show it to some of my side, and they will tell you who I am."

"Though he is one of their leaders," mused Kumagai, "if I slay him it will not turn victory into defeat, and if I spare him, it will not turn defeat into victory. When my son Kojirō was but slightly wounded at Ichi no tani this morning, did it not pain me? How this young man's father would grieve to hear that he had been killed! I will spare him."

Just then, looking behind him, he saw Doi and Kajiwara coming up with fifty horsemen. "Alas! look there," he exclaimed, the tears running down his face, "though I would spare your life, the whole countryside swarms with our men, and you cannot escape them. If you must die, let it be by my hand, and I will see that prayers are said for your rebirth in Paradise."

"Indeed it must be so," said the young warrior. "Cut off my head at once."

Kumagai was so overcome by compassion that he could scarcely wield his blade. His eyes swam and he hardly knew what he did, but there was no help for it; weeping bitterly he cut off the boy's head. "Alas!" he cried, "what life is so hard as that of a soldier? Only because I was born of a warrior family must I suffer this affliction! How lamentable it is to do such cruel deeds!" He pressed his face to the sleeve of his armor and wept bitterly. Then, wrapping up the head, he was stripping off the young man's armor when he discovered a flute in a brocade bag. "Ah," he exclaimed, "it was this youth and his friends who were amusing themselves with music within the walls this morning. Among all our men of the Eastern Provinces I doubt if there is any one of them who has brought a flute with him. How gentle the ways of these courtiers!"

When he brought the flute to the Commander, all who saw it were moved to tears; he discovered then that the youth was Atsumori, the youngest son of Tsunemori, aged sixteen years. From this time the mind of Kumagai was turned toward the religious life.

THE FIGHT AT DAN NO URA

Yoshitsune [General of the Minamoto clan], after his victory at Yashima, crossed over to Suwo to join his brother. Just at this time the High Priest of Kumano, who was under great obligations to the Heike, suddenly had a change of heart and hesitated as to which side he should support. He went to the shrine of Imakumano at Tanabe and spent seven days in retirement there, having sacred dances performed and praying before the deity. He received as a result an oracle commanding him to adhere to the white [Genji] banner, but he was still doubtful. He then held a cockfight before the shrine, with seven white cocks and seven red ones; the red cocks were all beaten and ran away. He therefore made up his mind to join the Genji.

Assembling all his retainers, to the number of some two thousand men, and embarking them on two hundred ships of war, he put the emblem of the deity of the shrine on board his ship, and painted the name of the Guardian God on the top of his standard. When this vessel with its divine burden approached the ships of the Genji and Heike at Dan no ura both parties saluted it reverently, but when it was seen to direct its course toward the fleet of the Genji the Heike could not conceal their chagrin. To the further consternation of the Heike, Michinobu of the province of Iyo also came rowing up with a hundred and fifty large ships and went over to the fleet of their enemies.

Thus the forces of the Genji went on increasing, while those of the Heike grew less. The Genji had some three thousand ships, and the Heike one thousand, among which were some of Chinese build. Thus, on the twenty-fourth day of the third month of 1185, at Ta no ura in the province of Bungo and at Dan no ura in the province of Nagato, began the final battle of the Genji and the Heike.

Both sides set their faces against each other and fought grimly without a thought for their lives, neither giving an inch. But as the Heike had on their side an emperor endowed with the Ten Virtues and the Three Sacred Treasures of the Realm,[3] things went hard with the Genji and their hearts were beginning to fail them, when suddenly something that they at first took for a cloud but soon made out to be a white banner floating in the breeze came drifting over the two fleets from the upper air, and finally settled on the stern of one of the Genji ships, hanging on by the rope.

---

[3] the Ten Virtues . . . Treasures of the Realm: The emperor, therefore, had not committed the ten sins and held the sword, mirror, and jewels of the kingdom.

When he saw this, Yoshitsune, regarding it as a sign from the Great Bodhisattva Hachiman,[4] removed his helmet and after washing his hands did obeisance; his men all followed his example. Just then a shoal of thousands of dolphins appeared and made straight for the ships of the Heike. One of the Heike generals called a diviner and said, "There are always many dolphins about here, but I have never seen so many before; what may it portend?" "If they turn back," replied the diviner, "the Genji will be destroyed, but if they go on our own side will be in danger." No sooner had he finished speaking than the dolphins dived under the Heike ships and passed on.

As things had come to this pass, Shigeyoshi, who for three years had been a loyal supporter of the Heike, made up his mind that all was lost, and suddenly forsook his allegiance and deserted to the enemy.

The strategy of the Heike had been to put the stoutest warriors on board the ordinary fighting ships and the inferior soldiers on the big ships of Chinese build; the Genji would be induced to attack the big ships, thinking that the commanders were on board them, and the Heike could then surround and destroy them. But when Shigeyoshi went over and joined the Genji he revealed this plan to them, with the result that they left the big ships alone and concentrated their attacks on the smaller ones, which bore the Heike champions. Later on the men of Shikoku and Kyushu all left the Heike in a body and went over to the Genji. Those who had so far been their faithful retainers now turned their bows against their lords and drew their swords against their own masters. On one shore the heavy seas beat on the cliff so as to forbid any landing, while on the other stood the serried ranks of the enemy waiting with leveled arrows to receive them. And so on this day the struggle for supremacy between the Genji and the Heike was at last decided.

Meanwhile the Genji warriors sprang from one Heike vessel to the other, shooting and cutting down the sailors and helmsmen, — who left their posts and flung themselves in panic to the bottom of the ships. Tomomori rowed in a small boat to the Imperial vessel and cried out, "You see what affairs have come to! Clean up the ship, and throw everything unsightly into the sea!" He ran about the ship from bow to stern, sweeping and cleaning and gathering up the dust with his own hands. "How goes the

---

[4] **Hachiman:** Originally the Shinto god of war, but in this period considered a bodhisattva.

battle, Tomomori?" asked the court ladies. "Oh, you'll soon see some rare gallants from the east," he replied, bursting into loud laughter. "What? Is this a time for joking?" they answered, and they lifted up their voices and wept aloud.

Then the Lady Nii, who had already resolved what she would do, donned a double outer dress of dark gray mourning and tucking up her long skirts put the Sacred Jewel under her arm and the Sacred Sword in her sash. She took the Emperor in her arms and said, "Though I am but a woman, I will not fall into the hands of the enemy. I will accompany our Sovereign Lord. Let those of you who will, follow me." She moved softly to the gunwale of the vessel.

The Emperor was seven years old that year but looked much older than his age. He was so lovely that he seemed to shed a brilliant radiance about him, and his long black hair hung loose far down his back. With a look of surprise and anxiety on his face he asked the Lady Nii, "Where are you going to take me?"

She turned to the youthful sovereign, with tears streaming down her cheeks, and answered, "Perhaps Your Majesty does not know that he was reborn to the Imperial throne in this world as a result of the merit of the Ten Virtues practiced in former lives. Now, however, some evil karma claims you. Turn to the east and bid farewell to the deity of the Great Shrine of Ise and then to the west and say the *nembutsu*,[5] that Amida Buddha and the Holy Ones may come to welcome you to the Pure Western Land. Japan is small as a grain of millet, but now it is a vale of misery. There is a pure land of happiness beneath the waves, another capital where no sorrow is. It is there that I am taking my Sovereign."

She comforted him, and bound up his long hair in his dove-colored robe. Blinded with tears, the child sovereign put his beautiful little hands together. He turned first to the east to say farewell of the deity of Ise and then to the west to repeat the *nembutsu*. The Lady Nii took him tightly in her arms and with the words, "In the depths of the ocean is our capital," sank with him at last beneath the waves.

---

[5] *nembutsu*: Prayer to the Amida Buddha. It was thought that prayer to him would allow one to enter into the Pure Western Land.

READING AND DISCUSSION QUESTIONS

1. What values were prized among the Japanese warrior elite?

2. Why did the imperial family commit suicide?

3. The Heike were the losers in a civil war, and yet the victors allowed these tales to circulate. Why would they permit this? Why was *The Tale of the Heike* so popular?

4. How does this document demonstrate the importance of Buddhist philosophy in Japan?

DOCUMENT 13-3

MA YUAN

Song Dynasty Landscape

960–1279

The Song Dynasty (960–1279) marked a period of important economic, political, and cultural transformations in Chinese society. Among these changes was the development of Neo-Confucianism, which blended elements of Daoism, Confucianism, and Buddhism. The suppression of Buddhism had failed, so during the Song it was completely integrated into Chinese society. Artistic endeavors such as painting also show the influence of Neo-Confucianism. This image by Ma Yuan (1190–1235) is representative of the landscape style popular during the Song.

Willows and Distant Mountains, Song Dynasty (960–1279) (ink and watercolor on silk), Ma Yuan (1190–1235)/Private Collection/The Bridgeman Art Library International.

READING AND DISCUSSION QUESTIONS

1. Describe this painting. How are humans depicted? By implication, what is the place of humans in the natural world, according to the artist?

2. How does this painting portray the continuing influence of Buddhism and Daoism on Chinese culture?

DOCUMENT 13-4

CHAU JU-KUA
On the Arab People of Quanzhou
ca. 1250

The commercial growth of Song China was not confined to its borders. China conducted extensive international trade through ongoing traffic along the Silk Road and the use of sea routes through Southeast Asia that connected China to the Islamic world. The following account describes China's trading partners through the eyes of Chau Ju-Kua (1170–1228), a customs inspector of the southern port city of Quanzhou. Although Chau's knowledge was probably not firsthand, his descriptions hint at the important role that Arab merchants played in facilitating international trade.

TA-SHÏ [ARABS]

The Ta-shï are to the west and north (or north-west) of Ts'üan-chóu [Quanzhou] at a very great distance from it, so that the foreign ships find it difficult to make the voyage there direct. After these ships have left Ts'üan-chóu they come in some forty days to Lan-li, where they trade. The following year they go to sea again, when with the aid of the regular wind they take some sixty days to make the journey.

The products of the country are for the most part brought to San-fo-ts'i [another port in Sumatra], where they are sold to merchants who forward them to China.

This country of the Ta-shï is powerful and warlike. Its extent is very great, and its inhabitants are pre-eminent among all foreigners for their distinguished bearing.

The climate throughout a large part of it is cold, snow falling to a depth of two or three feet; consequently rugs are much prized.

The capital of the country, called Mi-sü-li, is an important centre for the trade of foreign peoples. . . .

Chau Ju-Kua: His Work on the Chinese and Arab Trade in the Twelfth and Thirteenth Centuries, Entitled Chu-fan-chi, trans. Friedrich Hirth and W. W. Rockhill (St. Petersburg: Printing Office of the Imperial Academy of Sciences, 1911), 114–116, 124–125, 154–155.

The streets are more than fifty feet broad; in the middle is a roadway twenty feet broad and four feet high for the use of camels, horses, and oxen carrying goods about. On either side, for the convenience of pedestrians' business, there are sidewalks paved with green and black flagstones of surpassing beauty.

The dwellings of the people are like those of the Chinese, with this difference that here thin flagstones are used instead of tiles.

The food consists of rice and other cereals; mutton stewed with fine strips of dough is considered a delicacy. The poor live on fish, vegetables and fruits only; sweet dishes are preferred to sour. Wine is made out of the juice of grapes, and there is also the drink *ssï*, a decoction of sugar and spices. By mixing of honey and spices they make a drink *meï-ssï-ta-hu*, which is very heating.

Very rich persons use a measure instead of scales in business transactions in gold or silver. The markets are noisy and bustling, and are filled with great store of gold and silver damasks, brocades, and such like wares. The artisans have the true artistic spirit.

The king, the officials and the people all serve Heaven. They have also a Buddha by the name of Ma-hia-wu [Muhammad]. Every seven days they cut their hair and clip their finger nails. At the New Year for a whole month they fast and chant prayers. Daily they pray to Heaven five times.

The peasants work their fields without fear of inundations or droughts; a sufficiency of water for irrigation is supplied by a river whose source is not known. During the season when no cultivation is in progress, the level of the river remains even with the banks; with the beginning of cultivation it rises day by day. Then it is that an official is appointed to watch the river and to await the highest water level, when he summons the people, who then plough and sow their fields. When they have had enough water, the river returns to its former level.

There is a great harbour in this country, over two hundred feet deep, which opens to the south-east on the sea, and has branches connecting with all quarters of the country. On either bank of the harbour the people have their dwellings and here daily are held fairs, where crowd boats and wagons, all loaded with hemp, wheat, millet, beans, sugar, meal, oil, firewood, fowls, sheep, geese, ducks, fish, shrimps, date-cakes, grapes and other fruits.

The products of the country consist in pearls, ivory, rhinoceros horns, frankincense, ambergris, putchuck, cloves, nutmegs, benzoin, aloes, myrrh, dragon's-blood, . . . borax, opaque and transparent glass, . . . shell, coral,

cat's-eyes, gardenia flowers, rose-water, nut-galls, yellow wax, soft gold brocades, camel's-hair cloth, . . . and foreign satins.

The foreign traders who deal in these merchandise, bring them to
San-fo-ts'i and to Fo-lo-an to barter. . . .

MA-KIA [MECCA]

The country of Ma-kia is reached if one travels from the country of Ma-lo-
pa for eighty days westward by land.

This is the place where the Buddha Ma-hia-wu was born. In the
House of the Buddha the walls are made of jade stone (or precious stones)
of every colour. Every year, when the anniversary of the death of the Buddha comes round, the people from all countries of the Ta-shï assemble
here, when they vie with each other in bringing presents of gold, silver,
jewels and precious stones. Then also is the House adorned anew with silk
brocade.

Farther off there is the tomb of the Buddha. Continually by day and
night there is at this place such a brilliant refulgence that no one can
approach it; he who does loses his sight.

Whosoever in the hour of his death rubs his breast with dirt taken
from this tomb, will, they say, be restored to life again by the power of the
Buddha. . . .

MU-LAN-P'I [MULANPI, SOUTHERN SPAIN]

The country of Mu-lan-p'i is to the west of the Ta-shï country. There is a
great sea, and to the west of this sea there are countless countries, but Mu-
lan-p'i is the one country which is visited by the big ships of the Ta-shï.
Putting to sea from T'o-pan-ti in the country of Ta-shï, after sailing due
west for full an hundred days, one reaches this country. A single one of
these (big) ships of theirs carries several thousand men, and on board they
have stores of wine and provisions, as well as weaving looms. If one speaks
of big ships, there are none so big as those of Mu-lan-p'i.

The products of this country are extraordinary; the grains of wheat
are three inches long, the melons six feet round, enough for a meal for
twenty or thirty men. The pomegranates weigh five catties, the peaches
two catties, citrons over twenty catties, salads weigh over ten catties and
have leaves three or four feet long. Rice and wheat are kept in silos for tens
of years without spoiling. Among the native products are foreign sheep,
which are several feet high and have tails as big as a fan. In the spring-time
they slit open their bellies and take out some tens of catties of fat, after

which they sew them up again, and the sheep live on; if the fat were not removed, (the animal) would swell up and die.

If one travels by land (from Mu-lan-p'i) two hundred days journey, the days are only six hours long. In autumn if the west wind arises, men and beasts must at once drink to keep alive, and if they are not quick enough about it they die of thirst.

READING AND DISCUSSION QUESTIONS

1. What Islamic religious practices does Chau describe? In what ways does Chau's experience with Buddhism influence his understanding of Islam?

2. What are some of the goods traded along the routes that Chau describes? How is trade encouraged along these routes?

DOCUMENT 13-5

Statistical Tables on Chinese Civil Service Exams

2000

Although civil service exams were first administered during the Han Dynasty, it was not until the Song Dynasty that passing the exams became the chief requirement for potential officials in the Chinese court. The impact of these exams on the culture of China cannot be underestimated, because being a civil servant was one of the most desired occupations in China. The exams were a series of grueling essays, based on a Confucian curriculum, which demanded advanced education. These tables were compiled by the modern scholar Benjamin Elman, who used the extensive records of exams as the raw data. Virtually none of the exams have been translated into English.

Benjamin A. Elman, A *Cultural History of Civil Examinations in Late Imperial China* (Berkeley: University of California Press, 2000), Tables 1.5, 2.2, 5.2, 5.22.

TABLE 13.1
Chin-shih[11] by Reign Period During the Ming Dynasty

Reign Name	Reign Years	Duration in Years	No. of Exams	No. of *Chin-shih*	*Chin-shih* by Year
Hung-wu	1368–99	31	6	933	30
Chian-wen	1399–1402	3	1	110	37
Yung-lo	1403–25	22	8	1,849	84
Hung-hsi	1425–26	1	0	0	0
Hsuan-te	1426–36	10	3	300	30
Cheng-t'ung	1436–50	14	5	650	46
Ching-t'ai	1450–57	7	2	549	78
T'ien-shun	1457–65	8	3	694	87
Ch'eng-hua	1465–88	23	8	2,398	104
Hung-chih	1488–1506	18	6	1,798	100
Ch'eng-te	1506–22	16	5	1,800	113
Chia-ching	1522–67	45	15	4,924	105
Lung-ch'ing	1567–73	6	2	799	133
Wan-li	1573–1620	47	16	5,082	108
Kuang-tsung	1620–21	1	0	0	0
T'ien-ch'i	1621–28	7	2	700	100
Ch'ung-chen	1628–45	17	6	1,950	115
Early Ming	1368–1450	82	23	3,636	44
Later Ming	1451–1644	193	65	20,958	109
Total	1368–1644	276	89[a]	24,594 (24,536)[b]	89

Source: Huang Kuang-liang, *Ch'ing-tai k'o-chii chih-tu chih yen-chiu* (Research on the Ch'ing dynasty civil examination system) (Taipei: Chia-hsin Cement Co. Cultural Foundation, 1976), pp. 72–81. Cf. Ping-ti Ho, *The Ladder of Success in Imperial China* (New York: Columbia University Press, 1962), p. 189.

[a] There were two palace examinations in 1397.
[b] Revising Huang's *chin-shih* figures from supplementary data, we can increase his total to 24,536 *chin-shih* during the Ming dynasty. Ping-ti Ho gives 24,594.

---

[11] **chin-shih**: Those who passed the exam and were qualified to begin their career in the civil service.

TABLE 13.2

Ming Dynasty Ratio of Graduates to Candidates in Metropolitan
Examinations, 1371–1601, with Comparisons to T'ang and Sung Ratios

Year	Candidates	Graduates	%
T'ang *chin-shih*	1,000	10–20	1–2
T'ang *ming-ching*[12]	2,000	20–40	1–2
977	5,200	500	9.6
1044	South		100: 1 ratios
	North		10: 1 ratios
1124	15,000	800	5.3
1371	200	120	60.0
1409	3,000	350	11.7
1439	1,000	100	10.0
1451	2,200	200	9.1
1475	4,000	300	7.5
1499	3,500	300	8.6
1520	3,600	350	9.7
1526	3,800	300	7.9
1549	4,500	320	7.1
1574	4,500	300	6.7
1601	4,700	300	6.4

Sources: *Wen-hsien t'ung-k'ao* (Comprehensive analysis of civil institutions), compiled by Ma Tuan-lin, in *Shih-t'ung* (Ten comprehensive encyclopedias) (Shanghai
Commercial Press, 1936), 30.284; *Huang-Ming ch'eng-shih tien-yao lu* (Digest of
records of metropolitan examinations during the Ming dynasty) (late Ming edition);
Hui-shih lu, 1559, 1562, 1568.

---

[12] **ming-ching**: Degrees offered in the knowledge of classical Chinese books, especially the Five Confucian classics.

TABLE 13.3

Social Origins of Candidates for Ming-Ch'ing Metropolitan (M)
and Palace (P) Civil Examinations

Year/Exam	Status Total	Commoner No.	Commoner %	Military No.	Military %	Official[a] No.	Official[a] %	Special, etc.[b] No.	Special, etc.[b] %
1411/P	84[c]	70	83	10	12	1	1	2	2
1436/P	100	76	76	19	19	2	2	1	1
1499/P	300	165	55	88	29	15	5	19	6
1508/P	349	196	56	89	25	21	6	31	9
1541/P	298	177	59	77	26	11	4	26	9
1547/P	300	181	60	79	26	11	4	22	7
1598/P	292	186	64	80	27	10	3	14	5
1604/P	308	188	61	82	27	10	3	23	7
1622/M	412	245	59	80	19	15	4	17	4
1649/P	143	114	80	18	13	4	3	6	4
1651/P	57	35	61	5	9	0	0	0	0

Sources: *Hui-shih t'ung-nien ch'ih-lu*, 1622; *Teng-k'o lu*, 1411, 1436, 1499, 1508, 1541, 1547, 1598, 1604, 1649; *T'ing-shih ch'ih-lu*, 1651.

[a] "Official" (*kuan*) as a status in the Ming dynasty applied to military officers and their families. See Ho, *The Ladder of Success*, pp. 68–69.
[b] "Special" includes: medical (*i*, salt (*yen-tsao*), and artisan (*chiang*) households.
[c] For the entries under "Status Total" the information is incomplete. For example, of the 84 graduates in 1411, one does not give sufficient information to determine social background.

TABLE 13.4

Age of *Chin-shih* on Palace Examination During the Ming Dynasty

Age	1472 No.	1472 %	1529 No.	1529 %
Under 20 *sui*	1	0.4	6	1.9
21–25 *sui*	10	4.0	45	13.9
26–30 *sui*	47	18.8	67	20.7
31–35 *sui*	97	38.8	101	31.2
36–40 *sui*	72	28.8	67	20.7
41–45 *sui*	20	8.0	31	9.6
46–50 *sui*	3	1.2	6	1.8
Over 50 *sui*	0	0.0	0	0.0
Total	250	100	323	100

Source: Chien-Chin-sung, *Ming-tai wen-hsueh p'i-p'ing yen-chiu*
(Research on Ming dynasty literary criticism) (Taipei: Student Book-
store, 1989), p. 44; *Chin-shih t'ung-nien pien-lan lu*, 1529.

READING AND DISCUSSION QUESTIONS

1. Based on these statistics, what sorts of people took the exams?

2. What might account for the wide variation in the number and percentages of applicants who passed the exams during the Ming and earlier periods?

3. What do these statistics reveal about the nature of Chinese government?

4. What do these tables convey about the importance of education in China?

DOCUMENT 13-6

Widows Loyal Unto Death

ca. 1754

The ordained and practical roles of women in medieval China present several contradictions. Surviving records suggest that women were active members of society — serving as midwives, living as Buddhist nuns, and helping their families run businesses — yet several popular practices existed that constrained the lives of women, such as the right of husbands to take concubines and the custom of binding the feet of elite women. One of the more destructive traditions, described in the stories below, was the idea that widows should give up their lives after the deaths of their husbands in order to demonstrate their personal virtue.

Xu Sungjie, daughter of Xu Yuanyan, married Chen Boshan at the age of seventeen. When her husband was gravely ill, he told her to remarry because she had no son. At his death, she embraced him and cried bitterly. After the coffin was closed, she hanged herself to die with her husband. The official Bai Bi was impressed with her fidelity and so arranged for her burial and had a banner with the inscription "filial piety and propriety" displayed at her door.

From Patricia Buckley Ebrey, ed. and trans., *Chinese Civilization and Society: A Sourcebook* (New York: Free Press, 1993), 253–255.

Lin Shunde, the daughter of the prefect Lin Jin, was engaged to Sun Mengbi. When Mengbi died, she was with her father at his post. Once the announcement of her fiance's death reached her, she put on mourning dress and wept to tell her parents that she wished to go to his home. Her parents packed for her and told her to behave properly. On arriving there, she performed the rituals for her first meeting with her parents-in-law, then she made an offering at her fiance's coffin. After he was buried, she served her mother-in-law for the rest of her life. The local official inscribed a placard with "She hurried to the funeral of a husband she had never seen. Suffering cold and frost, she swore not to remarry." . . .

Fu Xiajie was the wife of Chen Banghuai. Her husband was taken hostage by some bandits. She supported herself by making hemp cloth. After a long time someone told her that her husband had died. She was spinning at the time. She then immediately entered her bedroom and hanged herself.

Wu Jinshun was the wife of Sun Zhen. On the first anniversary of her husband's death, she was so forlorn that she died of grief.

Zhang Zhongyu was engaged to Chen Shunwei, who died prematurely when Zhongyu was eighteen. When she learned of his death, she decided to hurry to the Chen family. Her parents tried to stop her, but she cried and said, "Once you betrothed me to the Chen family, I became a daughter-in-law of the Chen family." So, she hurried to attend her fiance's funeral and bow to her mother-in-law. Then, she cut her hair and removed her ornaments. She lived a secluded life. In the first month of the xinsi year [1461], there was a fire in her neighborhood. She leaned herself against her husband's coffin, wanting to be burned up with her husband. Suddenly a wind came and extinguished the fire. Only her house survived. On the sixth day of the sixth month of the wuzi year [1468], a large army approached. People in the county fled helter-skelter. Zhongyu remained to guard the coffin, keeping a knife with her. When the army arrived the next day, she showed the banner and the tablet from the previous official. The soldiers recognized her righteousness, and general Bai attached his order on the door so that no other soldiers would enter her house. One day she became severely ill and told her mother-in-law, "Don't let any men put their hands on me when I am shrouded after I die. Use the money in the small box that I earned by splicing and spinning to bury me with my husband." Then she died.

Sun Yinxiao was the daughter of Sun Keren and married Lin Zengqing at the age of seventeen. Lin, who made his living fishing, drowned after they had been married for only two months. Sun was determined to kill herself. After the mourning period was over, she made a sacrifice with utmost grief. That night, she dressed carefully and bound a wide girdle round the beam to hang herself. When the magistrate Xu Jiadi heard of this, he paid a visit to offer a sacrifice to her soul.

Wang Yingjie was the wife of Qiu Bianyu. She was widowed at nineteen before bearing any children. As a consequence she decided to die. Her family had long been rich and her dowry was particularly ample. She gave it all to her husband's younger brother so that in the future he could arrange for an heir to succeed to her husband. Then she ceased eating. Her mother forced her to stop, so she had no alternative but to pretend to eat and drink as usual. When her mother relaxed her vigilance, she hanged herself.

Wang Jingjie, whose family had moved to Nantai, married Fu Yan, a candidate for the examinations. Yan studied so hard that he got ill and died. When Wang learned of this, she emptied out her savings and gave it to her father-in-law to pay for her husband's funeral, asking him to do it properly. The evening after he was buried, her brother came to console her and she asked how her parents were doing. Her brother slept in another room. At dawn, when the members of the family got up, they kept shouting to her, but she did not answer. When they pried open her door, she was already dead, having hanged herself. She was solemnly facing the inside, standing up straight. She was twenty-one.

Zhang Xiujie married He Liangpeng when she was eighteen. Before a year had passed, he became critically ill. He asked her what she would do, and she pointed to Heaven and swore to follow her husband in death. Since she wished to commit suicide, the other family members had to prevent her. After several months, their only son died of measles. Zhang wept and said, "It is my fate. I had been living for him." That night she hanged herself.

Huang Yijie was engaged to Chen Rujing from Changle who lived in Lianjiang. Before they were married, he died. When she was fifteen, she heard of it and was saddened by it. As she slowly understood what it meant, streams of tears rolled down her cheeks. Without her knowledge a matchmaker arranged a new engagement. In the fifth month of the bingyin year [1506], her first fiance's mother came to call. Huang followed the courtesies appropriate to a daughter-in-law when she went out to meet her, and they both expressed their grief, not holding back. After a while she asked her mother-in-law why she had come, and she told her that she had heard of the new engagement and so had come to get the brideprice back. The girl was startled and thought, "Could this be true?

Only in extremely unfortunate circumstances is a dead man's wife sold." She told her mother-in-law, "Fortunately not much has been done with it. Let me make a plan." Disoriented, for a long time she sat, not saying a word. Then she asked her mother-in-law to stay for the night and told her everything she wanted to say. She gave her the hairpins and earrings she had received as betrothal gifts, saying, "Keep these to remember your son by." At dusk, her mother-in-law took her leave, and the girl, weeping, saw her to the gate. She then took a bath, combed her hair, and changed into new clothes. Those things done, she took a knife and cut her throat. The first cut did not sever it, so she had to cut it again before she died. In the morning when her family found her body, there were traces of three cuts.

READING AND DISCUSSION QUESTIONS

1. How did a widow demonstrate her virtue and integrity after the death of her husband? To whom was she obligated after the death of her husband?

2. How did accounts like this one perpetuate the practice of widows committing suicide?

COMPARATIVE QUESTIONS

1. Compare and contrast the reading "Widows Loyal Unto Death" with *The Tale of Genji*. In what ways did Chinese and Japanese societies have similar expectations for wives? In what ways did those expectations differ?

2. Both Marco Polo (Document 12-4) and Chau Ju-Kua describe the Islamic world and its people from the perspective of outsiders. What are their impressions of Islam? What do their accounts suggest about the role of religion in the development of commercial relationships?

3. Compare the ideals that these sources indicate for men in Japan and China during this period. How were these ideals similar, and how were they different?

CHAPTER 14

Europe in the Middle Ages

850–1450

A fter the division of Charlemagne's empire in 843, Europe entered a period known as the Middle Ages. Although later Renaissance scholars dismissively labeled this time the "Dark Ages" preceding their own cultural boom, in truth the Middle Ages witnessed a dynamic restructuring of Europe's political, social, and religious life. Europe's kings slowly consolidated their territories and their claim to power, while the introduction of feudalism and manorialism brought stability and order to European society. Although the medieval European experience was extremely diverse because of increased foreign encroachment, catastrophic outbreaks of disease, and civil and international warfare, the thriving Christian Church was a prominent and unifying element of society. Together, the church, territorial leaders, and scholars guided society toward the development of a distinct European way of life and identity.

DOCUMENT 14-1

From Domesday Book

1085–1086

The bureaucracies of medieval Europe were in a state of infancy when William, Duke of Normandy, conquered England in 1066. William, known henceforth as the Conqueror, commissioned a census of property in England in an attempt to determine how much tax was paid to his predecessor, and how much should be owed to him. It became known as the Domesday Book,

---

Caroline Thorn and Frank Thorn, eds., Caroline Thorn, trans., *Domesday Book: 8 Somerset* (Chichester, U.K.: Phillimore, 1980), entry 21.

domesday *meaning "the day of judgment," because the verdict of the book
could not be appealed. It is full of statistical information, but does not make
a compelling read. This short section describes the property of Roger of Courseulles in the county of Somerset.*

LAND OF ROGER OF COURSEULLES

Roger of Courseulles holds CURRY (Mallet)[1] from the King.
Brictric held it before 1066; it paid tax for 3½ hides.[2]
Land for 4 ploughs, of which 1 hide is in lordship; 2 ploughs
there; 2 slaves;
> 11 villagers and 7 smallholders with 3½ ploughs & 2½ hides.
> Meadow, 12 acres; pasture, 5 acres; woodland, ½ league
>> in both length and width. 1 cob; 9 pigs; 23 sheep.

The value was £4; now 100s.[3]

Roger holds CURRY (Mallet) himself. Ceolric held it before 1066;
it paid tax for 3½ hides. Land for 4 ploughs, of which 1 hide
is in lordship; 1 plough there, with 1 slave;
> 10 villagers and 7 smallholders with 3½ ploughs & 2½ hides.
> Meadow, 10 acres; pasture, 5 acres; woodland, ½ league
>> in length and width. 8 pigs; 22 sheep.

The value was £4; now 100s.
Roger holds these two lands as one manor.

Robert holds NEWTON from Roger. Elaf held it before 1066;
it paid tax for 3 virgates[4] of land. Land for 1 plough,
which is there, with
> 1 villager, 5 smallholders and 2 slaves.
> Woodland, 6 acres. 21 cattle; 20 pigs; 50 sheep.

Value 20s; when Roger acquired it, 10s.

Robert holds HADWORTHY from Roger. Algar held it before 1066;
it paid tax for 1 hide. Land for 1½ ploughs. 2 slaves.

---

[1] CURRY (Mallet): A village in Somerset, England.
[2] hides: A unit of land for taxation purposes; it was not based on measurement but on
the productivity of the land.
[3] 100s: One hundred shillings. Twenty shillings equaled a pound.
[4] virgates: A unit of land equal to a quarter of a hide.

In lordship 2 virgates & 1 plough.
1 villager and 9 smallholders (have) the rest of the land & ½ plough.
Meadow, 4 acres; woodland, 7 acres; pasture, 36 acres.
1 cob; 15 cattle.
The value was 15s; now 20s.
Of this hide W(alter) of Douai has 1 virgate of land.

Geoffrey of Vautortes holds PERRY from Roger. Four thanes held it before 1066; it paid tax for 1 hide and 1 furlong. Land for 2 ploughs. In lordship 1 plough; 3 virgates.
2 villagers and 5 smallholders with 1 plough & 1 virgate & 1 furlong.
Meadow, 33 acres; pasture, 43 acres; woodland, 37 acres.
1 cow; 2 pigs; 12 sheep.
Value 30s; when Roger acquired it, as much.

READING AND DISCUSSION QUESTIONS

1. What does this document reveal about the feudal system?
2. What was the impact of the Conquest of 1066 on the ownership of land?
3. How could this document be used to reconstruct the economy of England in this period?

VIEWPOINTS
The Crusades

DOCUMENT 14-2

FULCHER OF CHARTRES
From A History of the Expedition to Jerusalem: *The Call for Crusade*
ca. 1100–1127

The Frenchman (Frank) Fulcher of Chartres (ca. 1059–1127) was an eye-witness to the First Crusade and its aftermath. He traveled with the Crusade across Asia Minor and participated in the siege of Edessa. When his lord, Baldwin I, became King of Jerusalem, Fulcher moved to Jerusalem and probably continued writing until his death. This passage describes Pope Urban II's call to Christians to go on crusade to the Holy Land, the place where Jesus lived. Fulcher may have been present at this event, but he does not explicitly say so.

The Council Held at Clermont. In the year 1095 after the Incarnation of Our Lord, while Henry the so-called emperor was reigning in Germany and King Philip in France, evils of all kinds multiplied throughout Europe because of vacillating faith. Pope Urban II then ruled in the city of Rome. He was a man admirable in life and habits who strove prudently and vigorously to raise the status of Holy Church ever higher and higher.

Moreover he saw the faith of Christendom excessively trampled upon by all, by the clergy as well as by the laity, and peace totally disregarded, for the princes of the lands were incessantly at war quarreling with someone or other. He saw that people stole worldly goods from one another, that many captives were taken unjustly and were most barbarously cast into foul prisons and ransomed for excessive prices, or tormented there by three evils, namely hunger, thirst, and cold, and secretly put to death, that holy places were violated, monasteries and villas consumed by fire, nothing mortal spared, and things human and divine held in derision.

Frances Rita Ryan, trans., Harold S. Fink, ed., *Fulcher of Chartres: A History of the Expedition to Jerusalem, 1095–1127* (New York: W. W. Norton, 1969), 61–62, 65–67.

When he heard that the interior part of Romania [modern Turkey] had been occupied by the Turks and the Christians subdued by a ferociously destructive invasion, Urban, greatly moved by compassionate piety and by the prompting of God's love, crossed the mountains and descended into Gaul and caused a council to be assembled in Auvergne at Clermont, as the city is called. This council, appropriately announced by messengers in all directions, consisted of 310 members, bishops as well as abbots carrying the crozier [staff of office].

On the appointed day Urban gathered them around himself and in an eloquent address carefully made known the purpose of the meeting. In the sorrowing voice of a suffering church he told of its great tribulation. He delivered an elaborate sermon concerning the many raging tempests of this world in which the faith had been degraded as was said above.

Then as a suppliant he exhorted all to resume the powers of their faith and arouse in themselves a fierce determination to overcome the machinations of the devil, and to try fully to restore Holy Church, cruelly weakened by the wicked, to its honorable status as of old. . . .

Urban's Exhortation Concerning a Pilgrimage to Jerusalem. When these and many other matters were satisfactorily settled, all those present, clergy and people alike, spontaneously gave thanks to God for the words of the Lord Pope Urban and promised him faithfully that his decrees would be well kept. But the pope added at once that another tribulation not less but greater than that already mentioned, even of the worst nature, was besetting Christianity from another part of the world.

He said, "Since, oh sons of God, you have promised Him to keep peace among yourselves and to faithfully sustain the rights of Holy Church more sincerely than before, there still remains for you, newly aroused by Godly correction, an urgent task which belongs to both you and God, in which you can show the strength of your good will. For you must hasten to carry aid to your brethren dwelling in the East, who need your help for which they have often entreated.

"For the Turks, a Persian people, have attacked them, as many of you already know, and have advanced as far into Roman territory as that part of the Mediterranean which is called the Arm of St. George. They have seized more and more of the lands of the Christians, have already defeated them in seven times as many battles, killed or captured many people, have destroyed churches, and have devastated the kingdom of God. If you allow them to continue much longer they will conquer God's faithful people much more extensively.

"Wherefore with earnest prayer I, not I, but God exhorts you as heralds of Christ to repeatedly urge men of all ranks whatsoever, knights as well as foot-soldiers, rich and poor, to hasten to exterminate this vile race from our lands and to aid the Christian inhabitants in time.

"I address those present; I proclaim it to those absent; moreover Christ commands it. For all those going thither there will be remission of sins if they come to the end of this fettered life while either marching by land or crossing by sea, or in fighting the pagans. This I grant to all who go, through the power vested in me by God.

"Oh what a disgrace if a race so despicable, degenerate, and enslaved by demons should thus overcome a people endowed with faith in Almighty God and resplendent in the name of Christ! Oh what reproaches will be charged against you by the Lord Himself if you have not helped those who are counted like yourselves of the Christian faith!

"Let those," he said, "who are accustomed to wantonly wage private war against the faithful march upon the infidels in a war which should be begun now and be finished in victory. Let those who have long been robbers now be soldiers of Christ. Let those who once fought against brothers and relatives now rightfully fight against barbarians. Let those who have been hirelings for a few pieces of silver [Matth. 27:3] now attain an eternal reward. Let those who have been exhausting themselves to the detriment of body and soul now labor for a double glory. Yea on the one hand will be the sad and the poor, on the other the joyous and the wealthy; here the enemies of the Lord, there His friends.

"Let nothing delay those who are going to go. Let them settle their affairs, collect money, and when winter has ended and spring has come, zealously undertake the journey under the guidance of the Lord."

READING AND DISCUSSION QUESTIONS

1. According to Fulcher, what was the political situation in Europe and the Middle East prior to the call to go on crusade?

2. How does Pope Urban II describe the Muslims? Why does he ask Christians to go to the Holy Land?

3. What benefits would Crusaders get from going on crusade, according to Urban?

4. Based on what Urban says, how might the Crusades have benefited European society?

DOCUMENT 14-3

NICETAS CHONIATES
From Annals
1170–1207

*Nicetas Choniates (1155–1216) was a Byzantine government official who
wrote a comprehensive history of the Byzantine Empire during the time of
the Crusades. His firsthand account of the sacking of Constantinople by
the Crusaders of Western Europe is the most extensive in existence. Poor
planning and financing of the Fourth Crusade (1202–1204) had prompted
the Crusaders to set their sights on the wealthy Byzantine capital of Constantinople. When the dust finally settled, the attack had devastated the
once mighty Byzantine Empire and irrevocably damaged the relationship
between the Latin and Greek branches of Christianity.*

The enemy, who had expected otherwise, found no one openly ventur-
ing into battle or taking up arms to resist; they saw that the way was open
before them and everything there for the taking. The narrow streets were
clear and the crossroads unobstructed, safe from attack, and advantageous
to the enemy. The populace, moved by the hope of propitiating them, had
turned out to greet them with crosses and venerable icons of Christ as was
customary during festivals of solemn processions. But their disposition was
not at all affected by what they saw, nor did their lips break into the slightest
smile, nor did the unexpected spectacle transform their grim and frenzied
glance and fury into a semblance of cheerfulness. Instead, they plundered
with impunity and stripped their victims shamelessly, beginning with their
carts. Not only did they rob them of their substance but also the articles
consecrated to God; the rest fortified themselves all around with defensive
weapons as their horses were roused at the sound of the war trumpet.

What then should I recount first and what last of those things dared
at that time by these murderous men? O, the shameful dashing to earth
of the venerable icons and the flinging of the relics of the saints, who had
suffered for Christ's sake, into defiled places! How horrible it was to see the
Divine Body and Blood of Christ [i.e., the consecrated bread and wine of

Harry J. Magoulias, trans., *O City of Byzantium: Annals of Niketas Chronicles*, 198,
with the permission of Wayne State University Press (Detroit, 1984), 314–316.

the Eucharist] poured out and thrown to the ground! These forerunners of Antichrist,[5] chief agents and harbingers of his anticipated ungodly deeds, seized as plunder the precious chalices and patens; some they smashed, taking possession of the ornaments embellishing them, and they set the remaining vessels on their tables to serve as bread dishes and wine goblets. Just as happened long ago, Christ was now disrobed and mocked, his garments were parted, and lots were cast for them by this race; and although his side was not pierced by the lance, yet once more streams of Divine Blood poured to the earth.

The report of the impious acts perpetrated in the Great Church [the Hagia Sophia] are unwelcome to the ears. The table of sacrifice, fashioned from every kind of precious material and fused by fire into one whole — blended together into a perfection of one multicolored thing of beauty, truly extraordinary and admired by all nations — was broken into pieces and divided among the despoilers, as was the lot of all the sacred church treasures, countless in number and unsurpassed in beauty. They found it fitting to bring out as so much booty the all-hallowed vessels and furnishings which had been wrought with incomparable elegance and craftsmanship from rare materials. In addition, in order to remove the pure silver which overlay the railing of the bema [where Mass is performed], the wondrous pulpit and the gates, as well as that which covered a great many other adornments, all of which were plated with gold, they led to the very sanctuary of the temple itself mules and asses with packsaddles; some of these, unable to keep their feet on the smoothly polished marble floors, slipped and were pierced by knives so that the excrement from the bowels and the spilled blood defiled the sacred floor. Moreover, a certain silly woman laden with sins . . . the handmaid of demons, the workshop of unspeakable spells and reprehensible charms, waxing wanton against Christ, sat upon the synthronon [throne for the head of the Greek church] and intoned a song, and then whirled about and kicked up her heels in dance.

It was not that these crimes were committed in this fashion while others were not, or that some acts were more heinous than others, but that the most wicked and impious deeds were perpetrated by all with one accord. Did these madmen, raging thus against the sacred, spare pious matrons and girls of marriageable age or those maidens who, having chosen a life of chastity, were consecrated to God? Above all, it was a difficult and arduous

---

[5] **Antichrist**: According to Christian belief, the Antichrist was a false Christ who would appear in the guise of the true Christ before the Second Coming and cause chaos.

task to mollify the barbarians with entreaties and to dispose them kindly towards us, as they were highly irascible and bilious and unwilling to listen to anything. Everything incited their anger, and they were thought fools and became a laughingstock. He who spoke freely and openly was rebuked, and often the dagger would be drawn against him who expressed a small difference of opinion or who hesitated to carry out their wishes.

The whole head was in pain. There were lamentations and cries of woe and weeping in the narrow ways, wailing at the crossroads, moaning in the temples, outcries of men, screams of women, the taking of captives, and the dragging about, tearing in pieces, and raping of bodies heretofore sound and whole. They who were bashful of their sex were led about naked, they who were venerable in their old age uttered plaintive cries, and the wealthy were despoiled of their riches. Thus it was in the squares, thus it was on the corners, thus it was in the temples, thus it was in the hiding places; for there was no place that could escape detection or that could offer asylum to those who came streaming in.

O Christ our Emperor, what tribulation and distress of men at that time! The roaring of the sea, the darkening and dimming of the sun, the turning of the moon into blood, the displacement of the stars — did they not foretell in this way the last evils? Indeed, we have seen the abomination of desolation stand in the holy place, rounding off meretricious and petty speeches and other things which were moving definitely, if not altogether, contrariwise to those things deemed by Christians as holy and ennobling the word of faith.

Such then, to make a long story short, were the outrageous crimes committed by the Western armies against the inheritance of Christ. Without showing any feelings of humanity whatsoever, they exacted from all their money and chattel, dwellings and clothing, leaving to them nothing of all their goods. Thus behaved the brazen neck, the haughty spirit, the high brow, the evershaved and youthful cheek, the bloodthirsty right hand, the wrathful nostril, the disdainful eye, the insatiable jaw, the hateful heart, the piercing and running speech practically dancing over the lips. More to blame were the learned and wise among men, they who were faithful to their oaths, who loved the truth and hated evil, who were both more pious and just and scrupulous in keeping the commandments of Christ than we "Greeks." Even more culpable were those who had raised the cross to their shoulders, who had time and again sworn by it and the sayings of the Lord to cross over Christian lands without bloodletting, neither turning aside to the right nor inclining to the left, and to take up arms against the Saracens and to stain red their swords in their blood; they who had sacked Jerusalem, and had taken an oath not to marry or to have sexual intercourse with women as long as they carried the cross on their shoulders, and who were consecrated to God and commissioned to follow in his footsteps.

In truth, they were exposed as frauds. Seeking to avenge the Holy Sepulcher,[6] they raged openly against Christ and sinned by overturning the Cross with the cross they bore on their backs, not even shuddering to trample on it for the sake of a little gold and silver. By grasping pearls, they rejected Christ, the pearl of great price, scattering among the most accursed of brutes the All-Hallowed One. The sons of Ismael [Muslims] did not behave in this way, for when the Latins overpowered Sion [Jerusalem] the Latins showed no compassion or kindness to their race. Neither did the Ismaelites neigh after Latin women, nor did they turn the cenotaph of Christ[7] into a common burial place of the fallen, nor did they transform the entranceway of the life-bringing tomb into a passageway leading down into Hades, nor did they replace the Resurrection with the Fall.

Rather, they allowed everyone to depart in exchange for the payment of a few gold coins; they took only the ransom money and left to the people all their possessions, even though these numbered more than the grains of sand. Thus the enemies of Christ dealt magnanimously with the Latin infidels, inflicting upon them neither sword, nor fire, nor hunger, nor persecution, nor nakedness, nor bruises, nor constraints. How differently, as we have briefly recounted, the Latins treated us who love Christ and are their fellow believers, guiltless of any wrong against them.

READING AND DISCUSSION QUESTIONS

1. According to Nicetas, what was the primary objective of the Crusaders?

2. Nicetas writes of the Crusaders, "In truth, they were exposed as frauds." What does he mean by this statement? How were the Crusaders frauds?

3. Nicetas compares the sacking of Constantinople by the Western Crusaders with earlier experiences with Muslim conquerors. How were the actions of the Crusaders different from those of the Muslims?

---

[6] **Holy Sepulcher**: The site in Jerusalem where Christians believe Jesus was crucified.
[7] **cenotaph of Christ**: The monument marking the site of the Holy Sepulcher.

DOCUMENT 14-4

ZAKARIYA AL-QAZWINI

From Monuments of the Lands:
An *Islamic View of the West*

1275–1276

Zakariya al-Qazwini (1203–1283) was born in Persia and served as a professor of Islamic law who also cultivated interests in astronomy and geography. A prolific writer, he is best known for two works: Wonders of the Created Things *and* Monuments of the Lands (Athar al-bilad). Monuments *is a geographical text compiled from other sources, which suggests that al-Qazwini did not actually visit many of the peoples and places that he describes. In this passage, he describes "Frank-land," as the Muslims called Western Europe, in the aftermath of the Crusades.*

Frank-land, a mighty land and a broad kingdom in the realms of the Christians. Its cold is very great, and its air is thick because of the extreme cold. It is full of good things and fruits and crops, rich in rivers, plentiful of produce, possessing tillage and cattle, trees and honey. There is a wide variety of game there and also silver mines. They forge very sharp swords there, and the swords of Frank-land are keener than the swords of India.

Its people are Christians, and they have a king possessing courage, great numbers, and power to rule. He has two or three cities on the shore of the sea on this side,[8] in the midst of the lands of Islam, and he protects them from his side. Whenever the Muslims send forces to them to capture them, he sends forces from his side to defend them. His soldiers are of mighty courage and in the hour of combat do not even think of flight, rather preferring death. But you shall see none more filthy than they. They are a people of perfidy and mean character. They do not cleanse or bathe themselves more than once or twice a year, and then in cold water, and they do not wash their garments from the time they put them on until they

---

Zakariya al-Qazwini, *Islam from the Prophet Muhammed to the Capture of Constantinople,* ed. and trans. Bernard Lewis, Volume 2: *Religion and Society* (New York: Walker, 1987), 2:123.

[8] **He has two or three . . . on this side**: Lands in the Middle East captured during the Crusades.

fall to pieces. They shave their beards, and after shaving they sprout only a revolting stubble. One of them was asked as to the shaving of the beard, and he said, "Hair is a superfluity. You remove it from your private parts, so why should we leave it on our faces?"

READING AND DISCUSSION QUESTIONS

1. How does al-Qazwini describe the Frankish lands?
2. How does al-Qazwini describe the Frankish people?
3. What do his descriptions tell us about Muslim values?

DOCUMENT 14-5

CHRÉTIEN DE TROYES
The Knight of the Cart
1177–1181

Among the most famous works of the medieval period are the stories of the knights of King Arthur. Although the outline of the stories existed previously, Chrétien de Troyes added many well-known features, such as the love affair between Lancelot and Queen Guinevere, the subject of this excerpt, and the search for the Holy Grail. Chrétien's works describe the concept of chivalry — the knightly moral code — and courtly love — secret romantic, often Platonic, affairs.

Meanwhile Lancelot came riding up swiftly. As soon as the king saw him, he ran to kiss and embrace him; his joy so lightened him that he felt as if he had wings. But his joy was cut short by the thought of those who had taken and bound Lancelot. The king cursed the hour in which they

William W. Kibler, trans., *Arthurian Romances by Chrétien de Troyes* (London: Penguin Books, 1991), 262–265.

had come and wished them all dead and damned. They answered only that they thought he would have wanted Lancelot. "Though you may think that," replied the king, "none the less it displeases me. Worry not for Lancelot — you have brought him no shame. No! But I, who promised him safe conduct, am dishonoured. In all events the shame is mine, and you will find it no light matter if you try to escape from me."

When Lancelot perceived his anger, he did his very best to make peace and was finally able to do so. Then the king led him to see the queen. This time the queen did not let her eyes lower towards the ground but went happily up to him and had him sit beside her, honouring him with her kindest attentions. Then they spoke at length of everything that came into their minds; they never lacked subject matter, with which Love supplied them in abundance. When Lancelot saw how well he was received, and that anything he said pleased the queen, he asked her in confidence: "My lady, I wonder why you acted as you did when you saw me the other day and would not say a single word to me. You nearly caused my death, yet at that moment I did not have enough confidence to dare to question you, as I do now. My lady, if you will tell me what sin it was that caused me such distress, I am prepared to atone for it at once."

"What?" the queen replied. "Were you not shamed by the cart,[9] and frightened of it? By delaying for two steps you showed your great unwillingness to climb into it. That, to tell the truth, is why I didn't wish to see you or speak with you."

"In the future, may God preserve me from such sin," said Lancelot, "and may He have no mercy upon me if you are not completely right. My lady, for God's sake, accept my penance at once; and if ever you could pardon me, for God's sake tell me so!"

"Dear friend, may you be completely forgiven," said the queen. "I absolve you most willingly."

"My lady," said he, "I thank you. But I cannot tell you in this place all that I would like to. If it were possible, I'd gladly speak with you at greater leisure."

The queen indicated a window to him with a glance, not by pointing.

"Tonight when everyone within is asleep, you can come to speak with me at that window. Make your way first through the orchard. You cannot

---

[9] **Were you not shamed by the cart**: A hangman's cart. For a knight to ride in the hangman's cart would have been seen as very disgraceful, both because knights rode their own horses and not in carts and because only criminals would have ridden in the cart.

come inside or be with me: I shall be inside and you without. It is impossible for you to get inside, and I shall be unable to come to you, except by words or by extending my hand. But out of love for you I will stay by the window until the morning, if that pleases you. We cannot come together because Kay the seneschal, suffering from the wounds that cover him, sleeps opposite me in my room. Moreover, the door is always locked and guarded. When you come, be careful that no informer see you."

"My lady," said Lancelot, "I'll do everything possible to ensure that no one will observe my coming who might think evil of it or speak badly of us." Having set their tryst, they separated joyfully. On leaving the room, Lancelot was so full of bliss that he did not recall a single one of his many cares. But night was slow in coming, and this day seemed longer to him, for all his anticipation, than a hundred others or even a whole year. He ached to be at the tryst, if only night would come. At last, dark and sombre night conquered day's light, wrapped it in her covering, and hid it beneath her cloak. When Lancelot saw the day darkening, he feigned fatigue and weariness, saying that he had been awake a long while and needed repose. You who have behaved in a similar manner will be able to understand that he pretended to be tired and went to bed because there were others in the house; but his bed had no attraction for him, and nothing would have made him sleep. He could not have slept, nor had he the courage, nor would he have wanted to dare to fall asleep.

He crept out of bed as soon as possible. He was not at all disappointed that there was no moon or star shining outside, nor any candle, lamp, or lantern burning within the house. He moved slowly, careful not to disturb anyone; everyone thought he slept throughout the night in his bed. Alone and unobserved, he went straight to the orchard. He had the good fortune to discover that a part of the orchard wall had recently fallen. Through this breach he quickly passed and continued until he reached the window, where he stood absolutely silent, careful not to cough or sneeze, until the queen approached in a spotless white shift. She had no dress or coat over it, only a short mantle of scarlet and marmot fur.

When Lancelot saw the queen leaning upon the window ledge behind the thick iron bars, he greeted her softly. She returned his greeting promptly, since she had great desire for him, as did he for her. They did not waste their time speaking of base or tiresome matters. They drew near to one another and held each other's hands. They were vexed beyond measure at being unable to come together, and they cursed the iron bars. But Lancelot boasted that, if the queen wished it, he could come in to her: the iron bars would never keep him out.

The queen responded: "Can't you see that these bars are too rigid to bend and too strong to break? You could never wrench or pull or bend them enough to loosen them."

"My lady," he said, "don't worry! I don't believe that iron could ever stop me. Nothing but you yourself could keep me from coming in to you. If you grant me your permission, the way will soon be free; but if you are unwilling, then the obstacle is so great that I will never be able to pass."

"Of course I want you with me," she replied. "My wishes will never keep you back. But you must wait until I am lying in my bed, in case some noise might reveal your presence, for we would be in grave trouble if the seneschal sleeping here were to be awakened by us. So I must go now, for if he saw me standing here he'd see no good in it."

"My lady," said Lancelot, "go then, but don't worry about my making any sound. I plan to separate the bars so smoothly and effortlessly that no one will be awakened."

At that the queen turned away, and Lancelot prepared and readied himself to unbar the window. He grasped the iron bars, strained, and pulled until he had bent them all and was able to free them from their fittings. But the iron was so sharp that he cut the end of his little finger to the quick and severed the whole first joint of the next finger; yet his mind was so intent on other matters that he felt neither the wounds nor the blood dripping from them.

Although the window was quite high up, Lancelot passed quickly and easily through it. He found Kay still asleep in his bed. He came next to that of the queen; Lancelot bowed low and adored her, for in no holy relic did he place such faith. The queen stretched out her arms towards him, embraced him, clasped him to her breast, and drew him into the bed beside her, showing him all the love she could, inspired by her heartfelt love. But if her love for him was strong, he felt a hundred thousand times more for her. Love in the hearts of others was as nothing compared with the love he felt in his. Love had taken root in his heart, and was so entirely there that little was left over for other hearts.

Now Lancelot had his every wish: the queen willingly sought his company and affection, as he held her in his arms and she held him in hers. Her love-play seemed so gentle and good to him, both her kisses and caresses, that in truth the two of them felt a joy and wonder the equal of which has never been heard or known. But I shall let it remain a secret forever, since it should not be written of: the most delightful and choicest pleasure is that which is hinted at, but never told.

Lancelot had great joy and pleasure all that night, but the day's arrival sorrowed him deeply, since he had to leave his sweetheart's side. So deep was the pain of parting that getting up was a true martyrdom, and he suffered a martyr's agony: his heart repeatedly turned back to the queen where she remained. Nor was he able to take it with him, for it so loved the queen that it had no desire to desert her. His body left, but his heart stayed. Lancelot went straight to the window, but he left behind enough of his body that the sheets were stained and spotted by the blood that dripped from his fingers. As Lancelot departed he was distraught, full of sighs and full of tears. It grieved him that no second tryst had been arranged, but such was impossible. Regretfully he went out of the window through which he had entered most willingly. His fingers were badly cut. He straightened the bars and replaced them in their fittings so that, from no matter what angle one looked, it did not seem as if any of the bars had been bent or removed. On parting, Lancelot bowed low before the bedchamber, as if he were before an altar. Then in great anguish he left.

On the way back to his lodging he did not encounter anyone who might recognize him. He lay down naked on his bed without rousing anyone. And then for the first time, to his surprise, he noticed his wounded fingers; but he was not the least upset, for he knew without doubt that he had cut himself pulling the iron bars from the window casing. Therefore he did not grow angry with himself, since he would rather have had his two arms pulled from his body than not have entered through the window. Yet, if he had so seriously injured himself for any other purpose, he would have been most upset and distressed.

READING AND DISCUSSION QUESTIONS

1. Describe the relationship between Lancelot and Guinevere.
2. Why did Lancelot not feel his injury until the morning?
3. What does this passage suggest about the status of women in medieval society?

DOCUMENT 14-6

KING JOHN OF ENGLAND

From Magna Carta: *The Great Charter of Liberties*

1215

In many ways, the Magna Carta is a traditional feudal document. A contract between King John of England (r. 1199–1216) and his barons, the Magna Carta represents an effort by England's rebellious nobility to ensure that the King could not make unfair demands of his vassals. However, the importance of the contract exceeds its feudal origins. It became the founding document for the development of justice and law in England and helped give rise to ideas such as the rule of law and due process.

John, by the grace of God, king of England, lord of Ireland, duke of Normandy and Aquitaine, and count of Anjou, to the archbishops, bishops, abbots, earls, barons . . . and faithful subjects, greeting. . . .

We have . . . granted to all free men of our kingdom, for ourselves and our heirs, for ever, all the liberties written below, to be had and held by them and their heirs of us and our heirs. . . .

No widow shall be forced to marry so long as she wishes to live without a husband, provided that she gives security not to marry without our consent if she holds [a fief] of us, or without the consent of her lord of whom she holds, if she holds of another.

No scutage [payment in lieu of performing military service] or aid shall be imposed in our kingdom unless by common counsel of our kingdom, except for ransoming our person, for making our eldest son a knight, and for once marrying our eldest daughter; and for these only a reasonable aid shall be levied. . . .

Neither we nor our bailiffs will take, for castles or other works of ours, timber which is not ours, except with the agreement of him whose timber it is.

David C. Douglas and Harry Rothwell, eds., *English Historical Documents*, vol. 3 (London: Eyre and Spottiswoode, 1975), 316–321; Ernest F. Henderson, trans. and ed., *Select Historical Documents of the Middle Ages* (London: George Bell and Sons, 1892), 146–148. Reprinted by AMS Press, New York, 1968.

We will not hold for more than a year and a day the lands of those convicted of felony, and then the lands shall be handed over to the lords of the fiefs.

No free man shall be arrested or imprisoned or disseised [dispossessed] or outlawed or exiled or in any way victimized, neither will we attack him or send anyone to attack him, except by the lawful judgment of his peers or by the law of the land.

To no one will we sell, to no one will we refuse or delay right or justice.

We will not make justices, constables, sheriffs, or bailiffs save of such as know the law of the kingdom and mean to observe it well. . . .

Moreover all the subjects of our realm, clergy as well as laity, shall, as far as pertains to them, observe, with regard to their vassals, all these aforesaid customs and liberties which we have decreed shall, as far as pertains to us, be observed in our realm with regard to our own.

Inasmuch as, for the sake of God, and for the bettering of our realm, and for the more ready healing of the discord which has arisen between us and our barons, we have made all these aforesaid concessions, — wishing them to enjoy for ever entire and firm stability, we make and grant to them the following security: that the barons, namely, may elect at their pleasure twenty five barons from the realm, who ought, with all their strength, to observe, maintain and cause to be observed, the peace and privileges which we have granted to them and confirmed by this our present charter. In such wise, namely, that if we, or our justice, or our bailiffs, or any one of our servants shall have transgressed against any one in any respect, or shall have broken some one of the articles of peace or security, and our transgression shall have been shown to four barons of the aforesaid twenty five: those four barons shall come to us, or, if we are abroad, to our justice, showing to us our error; and they shall ask us to cause that error to be amended without delay. And if we do not amend that error, or, we being abroad, if our justice do not amend it within a term of forty days from the time when it was shown to us or, we being abroad, to our justice: the aforesaid four barons shall refer the matter to the remainder of the twenty five barons, and those twenty five barons, with the whole land in common, shall distrain and oppress us in every way in their power, — namely, by taking our castles, lands and possessions, and in every other way that they can, until amends shall have been made according to their judgment. Saving the persons of ourselves, our queen and our children. And when amends shall have been made they shall be in accord with us as they had been previously. And whoever of the land wishes to do so, shall swear that in carrying out all the aforesaid measures he will obey the mandates of the aforesaid twenty five barons, and that, with them, he will oppress us to the extent of his power. And, to any one who wishes to do so, we publicly and freely give permission to swear; and we will never prevent any one from swearing. Moreover, all those in the land who shall be unwilling, themselves and of their own accord, to swear to the twenty five barons as to distraining and oppressing us with them: such ones we shall make to swear by our mandate, as has been said. And if any one of the twenty five barons shall die, or leave the country, or in any other way be prevented from carrying out the aforesaid measures, — the remainder of the aforesaid twenty five barons shall choose another in his place, according to their judgment, who shall be sworn in the same way as the others. Moreover, in all things entrusted to those twenty five barons to be carried out, if those twenty five shall be present and chance to disagree among themselves with regard to some matter, or if some of them, having been summoned, shall be unwilling or unable to be present: that which the majority of those present shall decide or decree shall be considered binding and valid, just as if all the twenty five had consented to it. And the aforesaid twenty five shall swear that they will faithfully observe all the foregoing, and will cause them to be observed to the extent of their power. And we shall obtain nothing from any one, either through ourselves or through another, by which any of those concessions and liberties may be revoked or diminished. And if any such thing shall have been obtained, it shall be vain and invalid, and we shall never make use of it either through ourselves or through another.

And we have fully remitted to all, and pardoned, all the ill-will, anger and rancour which have arisen between us and our subjects, clergy and laity, from the time of the struggle. Moreover we have fully remitted to all, clergy and laity, and — as far as pertains to us — have pardoned fully all the transgressions committed, on the occasion of that same struggle, from Easter of the sixteenth year of our reign until the re-establishment of peace. In witness of which, moreover, we have caused to be drawn up for them letters patent of lord Stephen, archbishop of Canterbury, lord Henry, archbishop of Dublin, and the aforesaid bishops and master Pandulf, regarding that surety and the aforesaid concessions.

Wherefore we win and firmly decree that the English church shall be free, and that the subjects of our realm shall have and hold all the aforesaid liberties, rights and concessions, duly and in peace, freely and quietly, fully and entirely, for themselves and their heirs, from us and our heirs, in all matters and in all places, forever, as has been said. Moreover it has been sworn, on our part as well as on the part of the barons, that all these above mentioned provisions shall be observed with good faith and without evil intent. The witnesses being the above mentioned and many others. Given through our hand, in the plain called Runnimede between Windsor and Stanes, on the fifteenth day of June, in the seventeenth year of our reign.

READING AND DISCUSSION QUESTIONS

1. What practices of the king did the Magna Carta specifically prohibit? Under what conditions could the king engage in these practices?

2. What are some of the legal rights that the Magna Carta guarantees for individuals?

3. What redress did nobles have if the king failed to live up to this agreement?

4. How were the twenty-five barons empowered to enforce the charter to be chosen? How were they to decide on an action if they were not unanimous?

DOCUMENT 14-7

THOMAS AQUINAS

From Summa Theologica: *Can It Be Demonstrated That God Exists?*

1268

The development of the university was one of the most significant changes that occurred during the Middle Ages in Europe. Universities allowed for a flowering of European scholarship. Thomas Aquinas (ca. 1225–1274) was a Dominican priest and professor at the University of Paris. Aquinas practiced Scholasticism, using logic and reason to provide explanations for beliefs usually accepted on faith. In his massive Summa Theologica, *Aquinas*

Thomas Aquinas, *Summa Theologica*, q. 2, art. 2, pt. 1, trans. Fathers of the English Dominican Province (London: Burns, Oates & Washbourne, 1912, reprinted in 1981 by Christian Classics, Westminster, Md.).

assembled a compendium for all knowledge regarding theology. The excerpt below is a perfect example of the Scholastic method. In it, Aquinas asks if it can be proven that God exists and then cites authorities, such as biblical passages, in order to provide a reasoned solution to the query.

We proceed thus to the Second Article: —

Objection 1. It seems that the existence of God cannot be demonstrated. For it is an article of faith that God exists. But what is of faith cannot be demonstrated, because a demonstration produces scientific knowledge; whereas faith is of the unseen (Heb. xi. 1). Therefore it cannot be demonstrated that God exists.

Obj. 2. Further, the essence is the middle term of demonstration. But we cannot know in what God's essence consists, but solely in what it does not consist; as Damascene[10] says (*De Fid. Orth.* i. 4). Therefore we cannot demonstrate that God exists.

Obj. 3. Further, if the existence of God were demonstrated, this could only be from His effects. But His effects are not proportionate to Him, since He is infinite and His effects are finite; and between the finite and infinite there is no proportion. Therefore, since a cause cannot be demonstrated by an effect not proportionate to it, it seems that the existence of God cannot be demonstrated.

On the contrary, The Apostle says: *The invisible things of Him are clearly seen, being understood by the things that are made* (Rom. i. 20). But this would not be unless the existence of God could be demonstrated through the things that are made; for the first thing we must know of anything is, whether it exists.

I answer that, Demonstration can be made in two ways: One is through the cause, and is called *a priori,* and this is to argue from what is prior absolutely. The other is through the effect, and is called a demonstration *a posteriori;* this is to argue from what is prior relatively only to us. When an effect is better known to us than its cause, from the effect we proceed to the knowledge of the cause. And from every effect the existence of its proper cause can be demonstrated, so long as its effects are better known to us; because since every effect depends upon its cause, if the effect exists, the cause must pre-exist. Hence the existence of God, in so far as it is not self-evident to us, can be demonstrated from those of His effects which are known to us.

---

[10] **Damascene**: Saint John, bishop of Damascus after the Muslim conquest of the Near East.

Reply Obj. 1. The existence of God and other like truths about God, which can be known by natural reason, are not articles of faith, but are preambles to the articles; for faith presupposes natural knowledge, even as grace presupposes nature, and perfection supposes something that can be perfected. Nevertheless, there is nothing to prevent a man, who cannot grasp a proof, accepting, as a matter of faith, something which in itself is capable of being scientifically known and demonstrated.

Reply Obj. 2. When the existence of a cause is demonstrated from an effect, this effect takes the place of the definition of the cause in proof of the cause's existence. This is especially the case in regard to God, because, in order to prove the existence of anything, it is necessary to accept as a middle term the meaning of the word, and not its essence, for the question of its essence follows on the question of its existence. Now the names given to God are derived from His effects; consequently, in demonstrating the existence of God from His effects, we may take for the middle term the meaning of the word "God."

Reply Obj. 3. From effects not proportionate to the cause no perfect knowledge of that cause can be obtained. Yet from every effect the existence of the cause can be clearly demonstrated, and so we can demonstrate the existence of God from His effects; though from them we cannot perfectly know God as He is in His essence.

READING AND DISCUSSION QUESTIONS

1. In what ways does the *Summa Theologica* represent the medieval synthesis of Christian theology and classical philosophy?

2. Does Aquinas believe it can be shown that God exists? What is his argument?

COMPARATIVE QUESTIONS

1. Taking all of the documents in this chapter into consideration, what role did Christianity play in medieval Europe? What signs are there that a secular society was developing?

2. Compare the accounts of the Crusades. How might Pope Urban II respond to the accounts of the Crusades, compared to his original intentions?

3. Are the basic ideas behind the Crusades in keeping with Thomas Aquinas's rational methods?

4. How might Nicetas have responded to the Magna Carta? What might he have thought of European notions of justice?

5. How does the status of women in "The Knight of the Cart" compare to that of women in earlier periods of European history, such as Rome (Document 6-2) or Greece (Document 5-2)?

CHAPTER 15

Europe in the Renaissance and Reformation

1350–1600

The devastation of plague and warfare that marked the late Middle Ages stimulated Europe's economy by condensing wealth in the cities and creating an impetus for diversifying and revolutionizing business practices to adjust to a drastic labor shortage. Europeans were hopeful for a new beginning, a wish that came to fruition with the Renaissance, French for "rebirth." Originating in the commercial centers of Italy in the fourteenth century, the Renaissance was a cultural movement that spread throughout Europe. Renaissance writers and artists struck out in new directions and declared a definitive break from their medieval heritage. They looked to the classical past for inspiration and praised the abilities and achievements of human beings. In the sixteenth century, a second break came in the form of the Protestant Reformation (ca. 1517–1648), which splintered the Christian church in the West. The following documents reveal the vibrant cultures of the Renaissance and Reformation and address the new attitudes and ideas articulated by their leading thinkers.

The Intellectual Origins of the Renaissance

DOCUMENT 15-1

PETRARCH

Letters

ca. 1354, 1360

The Renaissance arose in the affluent city-states of northern Italy, where a spirit of civic engagement flourished. Instead of stressing careers in medicine or law as in the medieval university, northern Italian academics, called humanists, wanted to educate men to think and speak well. Selections from the letters of Petrarch, considered the father of humanism, are excerpted here. The letters demonstrate the role played by the rediscovery of literature from ancient Greece, as well as the continuing importance of the Christian religion.

THANKS FOR A MANUSCRIPT OF HOMER IN GREEK

[To Nicholas Sygeros]

I rejoice in possessing such a friend as you, wherever you may be. But your living voice, which could both rouse and sate my burning thirst for learning, no longer sounds in my ears. Without it your Homer is dumb to me, or rather I am deaf to him. Nevertheless I rejoice at his mere physical presence; often I clasp him to my bosom and say with a sigh: "O great man, how gladly would I hear you speak! But death has stopped one of my ears, and hateful remoteness has blocked the other."[1] Nevertheless I am very grateful to you for your magnificent gift.

I have long had a copy of Plato; it came to me from the west, rather remarkably. He was the prince of philosophers, as you know. I am not

David Thompson, ed., *Petrarch: A Humanist Among Princes* (New York: Harper & Row, 1971), 132–133, 179–181.

[1] **death has stopped . . . blocked the other**: This refers to two of Petrarch's Greek tutors.

afraid that you, with your intelligence, will object, like certain scholastics, to this statement. Cicero himself would not object, nor Seneca nor Apuleius nor Plotinus, that great Platonist, nor in later times our Ambrose and Augustine.[2] Now by your bounty the prince of Greek poets joins the prince of philosophers. Who would not rejoice and glory in housing such guests? I have indeed of both of them all that has been translated into Latin from their own tongue. But it is certainly a pleasure, though no advantage, to regard the Greeks in their own dress. Nor have the years robbed me of all hope of making progress in your language; after all, we see that Cato made great strides in Greek at a very advanced age.

If you want anything that I can provide, feel free to call upon me without hesitation. You will see that I call freely upon you. And since the success of prayer begets still bolder prayers, I ask you to send me, if available, a Hesiod; and send me, I beg, Euripides.

So farewell, worthiest of men. And since my name is well known in the west, not for my merits but by the favor of men or of fortune, may you be pleased to mention it among the illustrious men of the Oriental palace. Thus may the Emperor of Constantinople not disdain one whom the Roman Caesar[3] cherishes.

HE TURNS FROM PROFANE TO RELIGIOUS LITERATURE

[To Francesco Nelli]

I noticed in a letter of yours that you were pleased at my mixture of sacred and secular themes, and that you thought Saint Jerome would have been likewise pleased. You mention the charm of variety, the beauty of structure, the force of association. What can I reply? You must make your own judgments, and certainly you are not easily or commonly deceived, except that well-wishers readily err, and often are eager to do so.

But putting all this to one side, let me speak of myself and of my new but serious enthusiasm, which turns my thoughts and my writings to sacred literature. Let the supercilious laugh, who are revolted by the austerity of holy words, as the modest garb of a chaste matron repels those who are used to the flaunting colors of light women. I think that the Muses and Apollo will not merely grant me permission, they will applaud, that after giving my youth to studies proper to that age, I should devote my riper years to more important matters. Nor am I to be criticized, if I, who so

---

[2] **Seneca . . . Augustine**: Petrarch refers to three other Roman philosophers, then to two early Christian thinkers. Cato was also a Roman.

[3] **Roman Caesar**: Petrarch indicates he is better at Latin than at Greek.

often used to rouse by night to work for empty fame and celebrate the futile lauds of men, should now arise at midnight to recite the lauds of my creator, and devote the hours proper to quiet and repose to him who shall neither slumber nor sleep while he keepeth Israel; nor is he content with universal custodianship, but he watches over me personally and is solicitous for my welfare. I am clearly conscious of this, and all men capable of gratitude must feel the same. He cares for each individual as if he were forgetful of mankind *en masse*; and so he rules the mass as if he were careless of each individual. Thus I have it firmly in mind that if it be heaven's will I shall spend the rest of my life in these studies and occupations. In what state could I better die than in loving, remembering, and praising him, without whose constant love I should be nothing, or damned, which is less than nothing? And if his love for me should cease, my damnation would have no end.

I loved Cicero, I admit, and I loved Virgil. I delighted in their thought and expression so far that I thought nothing could surpass them. I loved many others also of the troop of great writers, but I loved Cicero as if he were my father, Virgil as my brother. My admiration, my familiarity with their genius, contracted in long study, inspired in me such love for their persons that you may think it hardly possible to feel a like affection for living men. Similarly I loved, of the Greeks, Plato and Homer. When I compared their genius with that of our own masters I was often in despair of sound judgment.

But now I must think of more serious matters. My care is more for my salvation than for noble language. I used to read what gave me pleasure, now I read what may be profitable. This is my state of mind, and it has been so for some time. I am not just beginning this practice, and my white hair warns me that I began none too soon. Now my orators shall be Ambrose, Augustine, Jerome, Gregory;[4] my philosopher shall be Paul, my poet David.[5] You remember that years ago, in the first eclogue of my *Bucolicum carmen*[6] I contrasted him with Homer and Virgil, and I left the victory among them undecided. But now, in spite of my old deep-rooted habit, experience and the shining revelation of truth leave me in no doubt as to the victor. But although I put the Christian writers first, I do not reject the others. (Jerome said that he did so, but it seems to me from the imitative style of his writing that he actually approved them.) I seem able to love

---

[4] **Jerome, Gregory**: Jerome translated the Bible into Latin and was the author of numerous works; Gregory was a famous pope.
[5] **my poet David**: David, king of Jerusalem, thought to have written the Psalms.
[6] *Bucolicum carmen*: A series of twelve poems written in Latin.

both groups at once, provided that I consciously distinguish between those I prefer for style and those I prefer for substance. Why should I not act the prudent householder, who assigns part of his furniture for use and another for ornament, who appoints some of his slaves to guard his son, and others to provide the son with sport? Both gold and silver are kinds of money, and you must know their value and not confound them. Especially since those ancient writers demand nothing of me except that I do not let them fall into oblivion. Happy that I have spent upon them my early studies, they now let me give all my time to more important matters.

Since I had already come of myself to this conclusion, I shall now so act the more confidently thanks to your encouragement. If circumstances require, I shall practice, for style, Virgil and Cicero, and I shall not hesitate to draw from Greece whatever Rome may seem to lack. But for the direction of life, though I know much that is useful in the classics, I shall still use those counselors and guides to salvation, in whose faith and doctrine there can be no suspicion of error. First among them in point of merit will David always be to me, the more beautiful for his naivety, the more profound, the more vigorous, for his purity. I want to have his Psalter always at hand during my waking hours where I may steal a glance at it; and I want to have it beneath my pillow when I sleep and when I come to die. I think that such an outcome will be no less glorious for me than was the act of Plato, greatest of philosophers, in keeping the *Mimes* of Sophron[7] under his pillow.

Farewell, and remember me.

READING AND DISCUSSION QUESTIONS

1. How do these letters demonstrate the importance of Greek and Latin texts to the development of the Renaissance? Why would Petrarch want to read Homer in the original Greek?

2. What were Petrarch's thoughts on the value of Christianity to the humanists?

3. What were the advantages of studying the Greek and Latin classics? What about Christian literature?

4. What kind of person would Petrarch consider ideal? How would this person act and think?

---

[7] **Mimes of Sophron**: Sophron was the first writer of mimes, crude comedic performances.

DOCUMENT 15-2

PICO DELLA MIRANDOLA
From On the Dignity of Man
1486

Most of the literature written during the Renaissance was composed by wealthy elites, as is true in most of human history. Without the need to work for a living, the Renaissance authors could spend their time educating themselves. They often learned many languages; Pico della Mirandola, for example, learned Latin, Greek, Arabic, and Hebrew. By combining influences from literature in all these languages, Pico attempted, in his 900 Questions, to synthesize all of human knowledge, religious and secular, through the lens of Plato's philosophy. His most famous writing, On the Dignity of Man, *argued that humans have the capacity to rationally understand the world. In this excerpt, he defends the vocation of philosophy and his right to discuss his 900 Questions publicly.*

These are the reasons, most reverend fathers, that have not merely inspired me but compelled me to the study of philosophy. I was certainly not going to state them, except as a reply to those accustomed to condemning the study of philosophy in princes especially, or more generally, in men of ordinary fortune. Already (and this is the misfortune of our age) all this philosophizing makes for contempt and contumely [insulting treatment] rather than for honor and glory. This destructive and monstrous opinion that no one, or few, should philosophize, has much invaded the minds of almost everybody. As if it were absolutely nothing to have the causes of things, the ways of nature, the reason of the universe, the counsels of God, the mysteries of heaven and earth very certain before our eyes and hands, unless someone could derive some benefit from it or acquire profit for himself. It has already reached the point that now (what sorrow!) those only are considered wise who pursue the study of wisdom for the sake of money; so that one may see chaste Pallas,[8] who stays among men by a gift of the gods, chased out, hooted, hissed; who loves and befriends her does not have her unless she, as it were prostituting herself and receiving

Charles Glenn Wallis, trans., *Pico della Mirandola: On the Dignity of Man* (Indianapolis: Bobbs-Merrill, 1965), 17–19.

[8] **Pallas**: Athena, the goddess of wisdom.

a pittance for her deflowered virginity, bring back the ill-bought money to her lover's money-box. I say all these things not without great grief and indignation, not against the princes, but against the philosophers of this age, who believe and preach that there should be no philosophizing because there is no money for philosophers, no prizes awarded them; as if they did not show by this one word that they are not philosophers. Since their whole life is set on money-making or ambition, they do not embrace the knowledge of truth for itself. I shall give myself this credit and shall not blush to praise myself in this respect, that I have never philosophized for any reason other than for the sake of philosophizing, that I have neither hoped nor sought from my studies, from my lucubrations [studies], any other gain or profit than cultivation of soul and knowledge of truth, always so greatly desired by me. I have always been so desirous of this truth and so much in love with it that, abandoning all care of public and private affairs, I gave my whole self over to the leisure of contemplating, from which no disparaging of the envious, no curses from the enemies of wisdom, have been able so far or will be able later to frighten me away. Philosophy herself has taught me to weigh things rather by my own conscience than by the judgments of others, and to consider not so much whether I should be badly spoken of as whether I myself should say or do anything bad. In fact, I was not ignorant, most reverend fathers, that this disputation of mine will be as pleasant and enjoyable to all you who delight in good arts and have wished to honor it with your most august presence, as it will be heavy and burdensome to many others; and I know that there are some who have condemned my undertaking before this, and who condemn it now under many names. Thus there are usually no fewer, not to say more, growlers who carry on well and in a holy way against virtue, than there are who do so wickedly and wrongly against vice.

There are some who do not approve of this whole class of disputes and this practice of debating in public about letters, asserting that it makes rather for the display of talent and learning than for acquiring knowledge. There are some who do not disapprove of this type of exercise, but who do not approve of it at all in my case, because I at my age, in only my twenty-fourth year, have dared, in the most famous city, in the largest assembly of the most learned men, in the apostolic senate,[9] to propose a disputation on the sublime mysteries of Christian theology, on the loftiest questions of philosophy, on unknown teachings. Others who give me leave to dispute are unwilling to give me leave to dispute about nine hundred questions, saying in slander

---

[9] **apostolic senate**: A body made up of the most famous Christian saints and theologians.

that the proposal was made as needlessly and ambitiously as it was beyond my powers. I should have immediately surrendered to their objections if the philosophy which I profess had so taught me; and now, at her teaching me, I would not answer if I believed this disputation among us were set up for brawling and quarreling. Consequently, let every intent of detraction and irritation depart, and let malice, which, Plato writes, is always absent from the divine chorus, also depart from our minds. And let us learn in friendly fashion whether I ought to dispute, and on so many questions.

First, to those who slander this practice of disputing publicly, I am not going to say much, except that this crime, if they judge it a crime, is the joint work not only of all you very excellent doctors — who have often discharged this office not without very great praise and glory — but also of Plato and Aristotle and the most upright philosophers of every age, together with me. To them it was most certain that they had nothing better for reaching the knowledge of the truth which they sought than that they be very often in the exercise of disputing. As through gymnastics the forces of the body are strengthened, so doubtless in this, as it were, literary gymnasium, the forces of the soul become much stronger and more vigorous. I would not believe that the poets signified anything else to us by the celebrated arms of Pallas, or the Hebrews when they say *barzel*, iron, is the symbol of wise men, than that this sort of contest is very honorable, exceedingly necessary for gaining wisdom. Perhaps that is why the Chaldaeans,[10] too, desire that at the birth of him who is to become a philosopher, Mars should behold Mercury with triangular aspect, as if to say that if you take away these encounters, these wars, then all philosophy will become drowsy and sleepy.

READING AND DISCUSSION QUESTIONS

1. What does Pico say about the study of philosophy? Why might he argue that one should not be paid for being a philosopher?

2. How does he defend his ability to synthesize all human knowledge?

3. What kinds of examples and influences from the ancient world does Pico cite?

---

[10] **Chaldaeans:** The Greeks and Romans called astronomers from Mesopotamia *Chaldaeans* and associated them with magic. They were most famous for the development of astrology.

DOCUMENT 15-3

MEO DI BETTO AND BENEDETTO DI MEIO
A Tuscan Peasant's Memoir
1450–1453

The economic and cultural changes of the Renaissance touched all corners of Italian society, including the peasantry. Between 1450 and 1502, two members of a Tuscan peasant family, Meo di Betto and his son Benedetto di Meio, kept careful records of their business dealings. Although Benedetto was able to read, neither man could write. Their records, therefore, were written by many different people, but all the records were recorded in two account books. These documents, which were discovered in the early 1980s, are important because they provide information about rural life during the Renaissance.

(*Page 1*) + 1450. On the 6th of March, Meio di Betto from Montealbuccio paid to us, Francesco and Tomaso Luti, 7 lire, 10 soldi for pasturing five oxen in the year 1450.

(*Page 1v*) Today, May 20th, I Chompanio di Teio received thirty lire for a young heifer I sold, and I am satisfied and fully paid; which money we got from Beto del Masaritia.

(*Page 2*) 1451. On this day, December 4th, I, Ghuccio di Pietro di Iacomo received six lire, 12 soldi, 6 denari from Benedetto di Meio di Betto, of Montalbuccio, as payment for money the aforesaid Meio owed me, which he had got from us a long time ago. And I declare myself fully paid for all dealings I have had with him up to today.

(*Page 2v*) A memoir of how on the 18th of March 1451 Betto di Meio di Betto of Montalbuccio paid 55 lire, 16 soldi as taxes for the piles of wood and dead wood and hay he took from the Selva in this year, to me Lorenzo di Filipo, official of the 24th, as is recorded in the woodland register on page 11 and on page 122: 55 lire, 16 soldi. In addition he paid me, Lorenzo, seven lire, ten soldi as a downpayment for 5 oxen, recorded on page 84.

(*Page 3*) + Christ 1452. Pietro and Gionta di Iachomo di Gionta must have thirty-eight lire on June 8th, which are for a heifer he had from mine.

Duccio Balestracci, *The Renaissance in the Fields*, Paolo Squatriti and Betsy Merideth, trans. (University Park: The Pennsylvania State University Press, 1984), 102–104.

And they got on this day thirty-eight lire in cash, and Betto [gave] cash to Pietro.

(*Page 3v*) + Christ, mcccclii. Biagio di Guido Tholomei must have twenty-four lire, ten soldi, which are for a heifer I bought from Ghino di Lenzo, his sharecropper at Badia Ymola, which I got on June 11th.

(*Page 4*) + 1452. I, Pietro di Pauolo, mayor of Casciano, declare I received from Benetto di Meio, as the annual tax for the Palio festival, on account of their property at Casciano, five soldi.

I, Michele d'Antonio, mayor of Casciano, admit I received 5 s[oldi], 4 d[inaro] from Benedetto di Meio as his share of the Palio celebrations for 1453.

(*Page 4v*) On the 20th day of September, 1452, Betto di Meio di Betto paid twenty lire in cash to Lorenzo di Filipo, official of the 24th. For his lime kiln for 1451. They are recorded in an entry on page 129.

(*Page 5*) 1452. On the 22nd of October I, friar Tomasso di Lottino, admit I received eight lire, 10 soldi in cash from Benedetto di Meio di Betto, paid by him into my own hand as rent for the house in the neighborhood of Laterino, for which he owes, by common consent, twelve lire per year. He has had it for eight and a half months, that is, he began paying on the 29th day of September 1452. On the feast of St. Michael he returned the key.

On the 28th of September [1452], I, Tomaxo di Giovanni Franci, received five fiorini, which were granted to me by Meio di Beto called Massarizia on account of his loan from Mariano Tomaxi, treasury official.

(*Page 5v*) + 1452. Benedetto di Meo di Betto of Montalbuccio must give thirty-two lire as rent for the lands we possess at Laterino and for all the trees, that is, for their fruits and the vineyard, with our half of the wine reserved, to be brought to Siena in his vehicle with us paying the toll, as proved by a writ of my own hand which he holds, including all houses and cellars in this rent.

There are records on page 6.

He has given as downpayment for several items in this house and farm 19 lire, twelve soldi, as revealed in his document, written by my own hand on January 17th 1452.

(*Page 6*) 1452. Betto di Meio di Betto from Montalbuccio paid nine lire for the pasturage of six oxen to me, Francesco di Lippo from Urbino, for 1452.

On the x day of March, Betto di Meio di Betto paid fourteen lire to us, Gheri Bolghanii, as shown in the calculations on page 76.

On the 14th day of July, we, Gheri Bolghanii and associates, received seventeen lire and 0 soldi, entered on page 76 in the book of calculations, which Betto paid.

(Page 6v) + 1453. On the xxiiii day of November Meo di Betto paid four lire, 0 soldi to us, Bernardo Saracini and company, which were recorded on page 4 of the book of forced loans and on page 154.

Benedetto di Meo di Betto has thirty-two lire to pay as rent for the land of the vineyard, that is for the property in Laterino called "the Ghodiuolo," that belongs to San Galgano abbey, as recorded on page 5.

He has paid in part as recorded on the same page.

He has paid eight lire, 19 soldi, 4 denari in cash to me, Don Giovanni, on December 13th, 1453, for the year ending on All Hallows 1453.

He owes us twenty-two soldi for early grapes he sold.

READING AND DISCUSSION QUESTIONS

1. What kinds of business dealings are recorded in this account?
2. What can you learn about peasant life from this source? What were Meo and Benedetto's obligations to society and the state?

DOCUMENT 15-4

NICCOLÒ MACHIAVELLI

From The Prince: *Power Politics During the Italian Renaissance*

1513

The writings of Niccolò Machiavelli (1469–1527) represent the culmination of Renaissance humanism. Although most humanists looked to classical and historical examples to direct political reform in their own times, Machiavelli, a Florentine diplomat, was less of an idealist and more of a pragmatist. In The Prince, *which was circulated only privately until after his death, the author advised rulers to think of governance as a process that demanded practical responses to the often fluctuating circumstances created by human frailties.*

Philip Smith, ed., *Niccolò Machiavelli: The Prince* (New York: Dover, 1992), 43–46.

Of Cruelty and Clemency, and Whether It Is Better to Be Loved or Feared

. . . I say that every Prince should desire to be accounted merciful and not cruel. Nevertheless, he should be on his guard against the abuse of this quality of mercy. Cesare Borgia[11] was reputed cruel, yet his cruelty restored Romagna [a region in northeastern Italy], unified it, and brought it to order and obedience; so that if we look at things in their true light, it will be seen that he was in reality far more merciful than the people of Florence, who, to avoid the imputation of cruelty, suffered Pistoja[12] to be torn to pieces by factions.

A Prince should therefore disregard the reproach of being thought cruel where it enables him to keep his subjects united and obedient. For he who quells disorder by a very few signal examples will in the end be more merciful than he who from too great leniency permits things to take their course and so to result in rapine and bloodshed; for these hurt the whole State, whereas the severities of the Prince injure individuals only.

And for a new Prince, of all others, it is impossible to escape a name for cruelty, since new States are full of dangers. Wherefore Virgil, by the mouth of Dido, excuses the harshness of her reign on the plea that it was new, saying: —

A fate unkind, and newness in my reign
Compel me thus to guard a wide domain.

Nevertheless, the new Prince should not be too ready of belief, nor too easily set in motion; nor should he himself be the first to raise alarms; but should so temper prudence with kindliness that too great confidence in others shall not throw him off his guard, nor groundless distrust render him insupportable.

And here comes in the question whether it is better to be loved rather than feared, or feared rather than loved. It might perhaps be answered that we should wish to be both; but since love and fear can hardly exist together, if we must choose between them, it is far safer to be feared than loved. For of men it may generally be affirmed that they are thankless, fickle, false, studious to avoid danger, greedy of gain, devoted to you while you are able

---

[11] **Cesare Borgia:** An illegitimate son of Pope Alexander VI, he led papal military forces, and even created his own kingdom.

[12] **Pistoja:** A city-state near Florence that was destroyed by fighting among its own citizens.

to confer benefits upon them, and ready, as I said before, while danger is distant, to shed their blood, and sacrifice their property, their lives, and their children for you; but in the hour of need they turn against you. The Prince, therefore, who without otherwise securing himself builds wholly on their professions is undone. For the friendships which we buy with a price, and do not gain by greatness and nobility of character, though they be fairly earned are not made good, but fail us when we have occasion to use them.

Moreover, men are less careful how they offend him who makes himself loved than him who makes himself feared. For love is held by the tie of obligation, which, because men are a sorry breed, is broken on every whisper of private interest; but fear is bound by the apprehension of punishment which never relaxes its grasp.

Nevertheless a Prince should inspire fear in such a fashion that if he do not win love he may escape hate. For a man may very well be feared and yet not hated, and this will be the case so long as he does not meddle with the property or with the women of his citizens and subjects. And if constrained to put any to death, he should do so only when there is manifest cause or reasonable justification. But, above all, he must abstain from the property of others. For men will sooner forget the death of their father than the loss of their patrimony. Moreover, pretexts for confiscation are never to seek, and he who has once begun to live by rapine always finds reasons for taking what is not his; whereas reasons for shedding blood are fewer, and sooner exhausted.

But when a Prince is with his army, and has many soldiers under his command, he must needs disregard the reproach of cruelty, for without such a reputation in its Captain, no army can be held together or kept under any kind of control. Among other things remarkable in Hannibal this has been noted, that having a very great army, made up of men of many different nations and brought to light in a foreign country, no dissension ever arose among the soldiers themselves, nor any mutiny against their leader, either in his good or in his evil fortunes. This we can only ascribe to the transcendent cruelty, which, joined with numberless great qualities, rendered him at once venerable and terrible in the eyes of his soldiers; for without this reputation for cruelty these other virtues would not have produced the like results.

Unreflecting writers, indeed, while they praise his achievements, have condemned the chief cause of them; but that his other merits would not by themselves have been so efficacious we may see from the case of Scipio, one of the greatest Captains, not of his own time only but of all times of which we have record, whose armies rose against him in Spain from no other cause than his too great leniency in allowing them a freedom inconsistent with military strictness. With which weakness Fabius Maximus taxed him in the Senate House, calling him the corrupter of the Roman soldiery. Again, when the Locrians[13] were shamefully outraged by one of his lieutenants, he neither avenged them, nor punished the insolence of his officer; and this from the natural easiness of his disposition. So that it was said in the Senate by one who sought to excuse him, that there were many who knew better how to refrain from doing wrong themselves than how to correct the wrong-doing of others. This temper, however, must in time have marred the name and fame even of Scipio, had he continued in it, and retained his command. But living as he did under the control of the Senate, this hurtful quality was not merely disguised, but came to be regarded as a glory.

Returning to the question of being loved or feared, I sum up by saying, that since his being loved depends upon his subjects, while his being feared depends upon himself, a wise Prince should build on what is his own, and not what rests with others. Only, as I have said, he must do his utmost to escape hatred.

How Princes Should Keep Faith

Every one understands how praiseworthy it is in a Prince to keep faith, and to live uprightly and not craftily. Nevertheless, we see from what has taken place in our own days that Princes who have set little store by their word, but have known how to overreach men by their cunning, have accomplished great things, and in the end got the better of those who trusted to honest dealing.

Be it known, then, that there are two ways of contending, one in accordance with the laws, the other by force; the first of which is proper to men, the second to beasts. But since the first method is often ineffectual, it becomes necessary to resort to the second. A Prince should, therefore, understand how to use well both the man and the beast. And this lesson has been covertly taught by the ancient writers, who relate how Achilles and many others of these old Princes were given over to be brought up and trained by Chiron the Centaur, since the only meaning of their having for instructor one who was half man and half beast is, that it is necessary for a Prince to know how to use both natures, and that the one without the other has no stability.

---

[13] **Locrians**: Citizens of the Greek city-state Locris.

But since a Prince should know how to use the beast's nature wisely, he ought of beasts to choose both the lion and the fox; for the lion cannot guard himself from the toils, nor the fox from wolves. He must therefore be a fox to discern toils, and a lion to drive off wolves.

To rely wholly on the lion is unwise; and for this reason a prudent Prince neither can nor ought to keep his word when to keep it is hurtful to him and the causes which led him to pledge it are removed. If all men were good, this would not be good advice, but since they are dishonest and do not keep faith with you, you, in return, need not keep faith with them; and no prince was ever at a loss for plausible reasons to cloak a breach of faith. Of this numberless recent instances could be given, and it might be shown how many solemn treaties and engagements have been rendered inoperative and idle through want of faith in Princes, and that he who was best known to play the fox has had the best success.

It is necessary, indeed, to put a good colour on this nature, and to be skilful in simulating and dissembling. But men are so simple, and governed so absolutely by their present needs, that he who wishes to deceive will never fail in finding willing dupes. One recent example I will not omit. Pope Alexander VI had no care or thought but how to deceive, and always found material to work on. No man ever had a more effective manner of asseverating [affirming], or made promises with more solemn protestations, or observed them less. And yet, because he understood this side of human nature, his frauds always succeeded.

It is not essential, then, that a Prince should have all the good qualities which I have enumerated above, but it is most essential that he should seem to have them; I will even venture to affirm that if he has and invariably practises them all, they are hurtful, whereas the appearance of having them is useful. Thus, it is well to seem merciful, faithful, humane, religious, and upright, and also to be so; but the mind should remain so balanced that were it needful not to be so, you should be able and know how to change to the contrary.

And you are to understand that a Prince, and most of all a new Prince, cannot observe all those rules of conduct in respect whereof men are accounted good, being often forced, in order to preserve his Princedom, to act in opposition to good faith, charity, humanity, and religion. He must therefore keep his mind ready to shift as the winds and tides of Fortune turn, and, as I have already said, he ought not to quit good courses if he can help it, but should know how to follow evil courses if he must.

A Prince should therefore be very careful that nothing ever escapes his lips which is not replete with the five qualities above named, so that to see and hear him, one would think him the embodiment of mercy, good faith, integrity, humanity, and religion. And there is no virtue which it is more necessary for him to seem to possess than this last; because men in general judge rather by the eye than by the hand, for every one can see but few can touch. Every one sees what you seem, but few know what you are, and these few dare not oppose themselves to the opinion of the many who have the majesty of the State to back them up.

Moreover, in the actions of all men, and most of all of Princes, where there is no tribunal to which we can appeal, we look to results. Wherefore if a Prince succeeds in establishing and maintaining his authority, the means will always be judged honourable and be approved by every one. For the vulgar are always taken by appearances and by results, and the world is made up of the vulgar, the few only finding room when the many have no longer ground to stand on.

A certain Prince of our own days, whose name it is as well not to mention, is always preaching peace and good faith, although the mortal enemy of both; and both, had he practised them as he preaches them, would, oftener than once, have lost him his kingdom and authority.

READING AND DISCUSSION QUESTIONS

1. Why does Machiavelli say that a good ruler must "be skilful in simulating and dissembling"? What advantages does the ability to deceive give to the ruler?

2. How does Machiavelli view human nature? How does this idea of human nature affect his ideas regarding governance?

3. Like other humanists, Machiavelli often looked to history for guidance. What examples from the past does he reference? What lessons does Machiavelli draw from these examples?

4. Are Machiavelli's instructions moral or immoral? To what extent does he seem influenced by Christianity?

MARTIN LUTHER

From Address to the Christian Nobility of the German Nation

1520

Martin Luther (1483–1546) was an Augustinian monk from eastern Germany whose translation of the Bible contributed to the development of the modern German language. In penning his Ninety-five Theses *(1517) criticizing the Catholic Church's sale of indulgences, which allowed for the remission of sins without penance, Luther became the father of the Protestant Reformation. Some scholars argue that the theses, which Luther enclosed in a letter to a German archbishop, were posed in a format traditionally used as an invitation to debate and that their author could not have foreseen the consequences of his dissension, which led to his excommunication from the Catholic Church in 1521. In the following reading, Luther attacks the extravagance and corruption of the Catholic hierarchy.*

OF THE MATTERS TO BE CONSIDERED IN THE COUNCILS

Let us now consider the matters which should be treated in the councils, and with which popes, cardinals, bishops, and all learned men should occupy themselves day and night, if they love Christ and His Church. But if they do not do so, the people at large and the temporal powers must do so, without considering the thunders of their excommunications. For an unjust excommunication is better than ten just absolutions, and an unjust absolution is worse than ten just excommunications. Therefore let us rouse ourselves, fellow-Germans, and fear God more than man, that we be not answerable for all the poor souls that are so miserably lost through the wicked, devilish government of the Romanists, and that the dominion of the devil should not grow day by day, if indeed this hellish government can grow any worse, which, for my part, I can neither conceive nor believe.

Harry Emerson Fosdick, ed., *Great Voices of the Reformation: An Anthology* (New York: Modern Library, 1952), 109–111, 114–115.

1. It is a distressing and terrible thing to see that the head of Christendom, who boasts of being the vicar of Christ and the successor of St. Peter, lives in a worldly pomp that no king or emperor can equal, so that in him that calls himself most holy and most spiritual there is more worldliness than in the world itself. He wears a triple crown, whereas the mightiest kings only wear one crown. If this resembles the poverty of Christ and St. Peter, it is a new sort of resemblance. They prate of its being heretical to object to this; nay, they will not even hear how unchristian and ungodly it is. But I think that if he should have to pray to God with tears, he would have to lay down his crowns; for God will not endure any arrogance. His office should be nothing else than to weep and pray constantly for Christendom and to be an example of all humility.

However this may be, this pomp is a stumbling-block, and the pope, for the very salvation of his soul, ought to put it off, for St. Paul says, "Abstain from all appearance of evil" (I Thess. v. 21), and again, "Provide things honest in the sight of all men" (II Cor. viii. 21). A simple mitre would be enough for the pope: wisdom and sanctity should raise him above the rest; the crown of pride he should leave to antichrist, as his predecessors did some hundreds of years ago. They say, He is the ruler of the world. This is false; for Christ, whose viceregent and vicar he claims to be, said to Pilate, "My kingdom is not of this world" (John xviii. 36). But no viceregent can have a wider dominion than his Lord, nor is he a viceregent of Christ in His glory, but of Christ crucified, as St. Paul says, "For I determined not to know anything among you save Jesus Christ, and Him crucified" (II Cor. ii. 2), and "Let this mind be in you, which was also in Christ Jesus, who made Himself of no reputation, and took upon Himself the form of a servant" (Phil. ii. 5, 7). Again, "We preach Christ crucified" (I Cor. i.). Now they make the pope a viceregent of Christ exalted in heaven, and some have let the devil rule them so thoroughly that they have maintained that the pope is above the angels in heaven and has power over them, which is precisely the true work of the true antichrist.

2. What is the use in Christendom of the people called "cardinals"? I will tell you. In Italy and Germany there are many rich convents, endowments, fiefs, and benefices, and as the best way of getting these into the hands of Rome, they created cardinals, and gave them the sees, convents, and prelacies, and thus destroyed the service of God. That is why Italy is almost a desert now: the convents are destroyed, the sees consumed, the revenues of the prelacies and of all the churches drawn to Rome; towns are decayed, the country and the people ruined, because there is no more

any worship of God or preaching; why? Because the cardinals must have all the wealth. No Turk could have thus desolated Italy and overthrown the worship of God.

Now that Italy is sucked dry, they come to Germany and begin very quietly; but if we look on quietly Germany will soon be brought into the same state as Italy. We have a few cardinals already. What the Romanists mean thereby the drunken Germans are not to see until they have lost everything — bishoprics, convents, benefices, fiefs, even to their last farthing. Antichrist must take the riches of the earth, as it is written (Dan. xi. 8, 39, 43). They begin by taking off the cream of the bishoprics, convents, and fiefs; and as they do not dare to destroy everything as they have done in Italy, they employ such holy cunning to join together ten or twenty prelacies, and take such a portion of each annually that the total amounts to a considerable sum. The priory of Würzburg gives one thousand guilders; those of Bamberg, Mayence, Treves, and others also contribute. In this way they collect one thousand or ten thousand guilders, in order that a cardinal may live at Rome in a state like that of a wealthy monarch. . . .

This precious roman avarice has also invented the practice of selling and lending prebends[14] and benefices on condition that the seller or lender has the reversion, so that if the incumbent dies, the benefice falls to him that has sold it, lent it, or abandoned it; in this way they have made benefices heritable property, so that none can come to hold them unless the seller sells them to him, or leaves them to him at his death. Then there are many that give a benefice to another in name only, and on condition that he shall not receive a farthing. It is now, too, an old practice for a man to give another a benefice and to receive a certain annual sum, which proceeding was formerly called simony. And there are many other such little things which I cannot recount; and so they deal worse with the benefices than the heathens by the cross dealt with Christ's clothes.

But all this that I have spoken of is old and common at Rome. Their avarice has invented another device, which I hope will be the last and choke it. The pope has made a noble discovery, called *Pectoralis Reservatio*, that is, "mental reservation" — *et propius motus*, that is, "and his own will and power." The matter is managed in this way: Suppose a man obtains a benefice at Rome, which is confirmed to him in due form; then comes another, who brings money, or who has done some other service of which the less said the better, and requests the pope to give him the same

---

[14] **prebends**: A stipend paid by the Catholic Church to the clergy.

benefice: then the pope will take it from the first and give it him. If you say, that is wrong, the Most Holy Father must then excuse himself, that he may not be openly blamed for having violated justice; and he says "that in his heart and mind he reserved his authority over the said benefice," whilst he never had heard of or thought of the same in all his life. Thus he has devised a *gloss* which allows him in his proper person to lie and cheat and fool us all, and all this impudently and in open daylight, and nevertheless he claims to be the head of Christendom, letting the evil spirit rule him with manifest lies.

This wantonness and lying reservation of the popes has brought about an unutterable state of things at Rome. There is a buying and a selling, a changing, blustering and bargaining, cheating and lying, robbing and stealing, debauchery and villainy, and all kinds of contempt of God, that antichrist himself could not rule worse. Venice, Antwerp, Cairo, are nothing to this fair and market at Rome, except that there things are done with some reason and justice, whilst here things are done as the devil himself could wish. And out of this ocean a like virtue overflows all the world. Is it not natural that such people should dread a reformation and a free council, and should rather embroil all kings and princes than that their unity should bring about a council? Who would like his villainy to be exposed?

READING AND DISCUSSION QUESTIONS

1. How does Martin Luther describe the papal court? Why does it anger him so?

2. What problems does Luther say were caused by the expansion of the Catholic hierarchy though the appointment of cardinals?

3. Why does Luther attack the selling and lending of prebends and benefices by the Catholic Church?

4. Based on this reading, why might Luther have been excommunicated by the Catholic Church?

DOCUMENT 15-6

JOHN CALVIN
From Instruction in Faith
1537

John Calvin (1509–1564) received a Catholic education but came to reject the authority of the Catholic Church around 1529, while studying at the University of Bourges. He went on to publish a number of texts about Christian theology during the Reformation and is seen as the principal thinker of Calvinism, which stresses predestination and God's role as ultimate authority. This selection comes from his Instruction in Faith, *which is a condensation of his more famous* Institutes. *The* Instruction in Faith *was intended to be read by the common person. It therefore describes how individuals should understand his theology in their daily lives.*

WE APPREHEND CHRIST THROUGH FAITH

Just as the merciful Father offers us the Son through the word of the Gospel, so we embrace him through faith and acknowledge him as given to us. It is true that the word of the Gospel calls all to participate in Christ, but a number, blinded and hardened by unbelief, despise such a unique grace. Hence, only believers enjoy Christ; they receive him as sent to them; they do not reject him when he is given, but follow him when he calls them.

ELECTION AND PREDESTINATION

Beyond this contrast of attitudes of believers and unbelievers, the great secret of God's counsel must necessarily be considered. For, the seed of the word of God takes root and brings forth fruit only in those whom the Lord, by his eternal election, has predestined to be children and heirs of the heavenly kingdom. To all the others (who by the same counsel of God are rejected before the foundation of the world) the clear and evident preaching of truth can be nothing but an odor of death unto death. Now, why does the Lord use his mercy toward some and exercise the rigor of his judgment on the others? We have to leave the reason of this to be known

John Calvin, *Instruction in Faith*, trans. and ed. Paul T. Fuhrmann (Louisville: Westminster Press, 1977).

by him alone. For, he, with a certainly excellent intention, has willed to keep it hidden from us all. The crudity of our mind could not indeed bear such a great clarity, nor our smallness comprehend such a great wisdom. And in fact all those who will attempt to rise to such a height and will not repress the temerity of their spirit, shall experience the truth of Solomon's saying (Prov. 25:27) that he who will investigate the majesty shall be oppressed by the glory. Only let us have this resolved in ourselves that the dispensation of the Lord, although hidden from us, is nevertheless holy and just. For, if he willed to ruin all mankind, he has the right to do it, and in those whom he rescues from perdition one can contemplate nothing but his sovereign goodness. We acknowledge, therefore, the elect to be recipients of his mercy (as truly they are) and the rejected to be recipients of his wrath, a wrath, however, which is nothing but just.

Let us take from the lot of both the elect and the others, reasons for extolling his glory. On the other hand, let us not seek (as many do), in order to confirm the certainty of our salvation, to penetrate the very interior of heaven and to investigate what God from his eternity has decided to do with us. That can only worry us with a miserable distress and perturbation. Let us be content, then, with the testimony by which he has sufficiently and amply confirmed to us this certainty. For, as in Christ are elected all those who have been preordained to life before the foundations of the world were laid, so also he is he in whom the pledge of our election is presented to us if we receive him and embrace him through faith. For what do we seek in election except that we be participants in the life eternal? And we have it in Christ, who was the life since the beginning and who is offered as life to us in order that all those who believe in him may not perish but enjoy the life eternal. If, therefore, in possessing Christ through faith we possess in him likewise life, we need not further inquire beyond the eternal counsel of God. For Christ is not only a mirror by which the will of God is presented to us, but he is a pledge by which life is as sealed and confirmed to us.

WHAT TRUE FAITH IS

One must not imagine that the Christian faith is a bare and mere knowledge of God or an understanding of the Scripture which flutters in the brain without touching the heart, as is usually the case with the opinion about things which are confirmed by some probable reason. But faith is a firm and solid confidence of the heart, by means of which we rest surely in the mercy of God which is promised to us through the Gospel. For thus the definition of faith must be taken from the substance of the promise.

Faith rests so much on this foundation that, if the latter be taken away, faith would collapse at once, or, rather, vanish away. Hence, when the Lord presents to us his mercy through the promise of the Gospel, if we certainly and without hesitation trust him who made the promise, we are said to apprehend his word through faith. And this definition is not different from that of the apostle (Heb. 11:1) in which he teaches that faith is the certainty of the things to be hoped for and the demonstration of the things not apparent; for he means a sure and secure possession of the things that God promises, and an evidence of the things that are not apparent, that is to say, the life eternal. And this we conceive through confidence in the divine goodness which is offered to us through the Gospel. Now, since all the promises of God are gathered together and confirmed in Christ, and are, so to speak, kept and accomplished in him, it appears without doubt that Christ is the perpetual object of faith. And in that object, faith contemplates all the riches of the divine mercy.

Faith Is a Gift of God

If we honestly consider within ourselves how much our thought is blind to the heavenly secrets of God and how greatly our heart distrusts all things, we shall not doubt that faith greatly surpasses all the power of our nature and that faith is a unique and precious gift of God. For, as St. Paul maintains (I Cor. 2:11), if no one can witness the human will, except the spirit of man which is in man, how will man be certain of the divine will? And if the truth of God in us wavers even in things that we see by the eye, how will it be firm and stable where the Lord promises the things that the eye does not see and man's understanding does not comprehend?

Hence there is no doubt that faith is a light of the Holy Spirit through which our understandings are enlightened and our hearts are confirmed in a sure persuasion which is assured that the truth of God is so certain that he can but accomplish that which he has promised through his holy word that he will do. Hence (II Cor. 1:22; Eph. 1:13), the Holy Spirit is called like a guarantee which confirms in our hearts the certainty of the divine truth, and a seal by which our hearts are sealed in the expectation of the day of the Lord. For it is the Spirit indeed who witnesses to our spirit that God is our Father and that similarly we are his children (Rom. 8:16). . . .

The Pastors of the Church and Their Power

Since the Lord has willed that both his word and his sacraments be dispensed through the ministry of men, it is necessary that there be pastors ordained to the churches, pastors who teach the people both in public and in private the pure doctrine, administer the sacraments, and by their good example instruct and form all to holiness and purity of life. Those who despise this discipline and this order do injury not only to men, but to God, and even, as heretics, withdraw from the society of the church, which in no way can stand together without such a ministry. For what the Lord has once (Matt. 10:40) testified is of no little importance: It is that when the pastors whom he sends are welcomed, he himself is welcomed, and likewise he is rejected when they are rejected. And in order that their ministry be not contemptible, pastors are furnished with a notable mandate: to bind and to loose, having the added promise that whatever things they shall have bound or loosed on earth, are bound or loosed in heaven (Matt. 16:19). And Christ himself in another passage (John 20:23) explains that to bind means to retain sins, and to loose means to remit them. Now, the apostle declares what is the mode of loosing when (Rom. 1:16) he teaches the Gospel to be the power of God unto salvation for each believer. And he tells also the way of binding when he declares (II Cor. 10:4-6) the apostles to have retribution ready against any disobedience. For, the sum of the Gospel is that we are slaves of sin and death, and that we are loosed and freed by the redemption which is in Christ Jesus, while those who do not receive him as redeemer are bound as by new bonds of a graver condemnation.

But let us remember that this power (which in the Scripture is attributed to pastors) is wholly contained in and limited to the ministry of the word. For Christ has not given this power properly to these men but to his word, of which he has made these men ministers. Hence, let pastors boldly dare all things by the word of God, of which they have been constituted dispensators; let them constrain all the power, glory, and haughtiness of the world to make room for and to obey the majesty of that word; let them by means of that word command all from the greatest to the smallest; let them edify the house of Christ; let them demolish the reign of Satan; let them feed the sheep, kill the wolves, instruct and exhort the docile; let them rebuke, reprove, reproach, and convince the rebel — but all through and within the word of God. But if pastors turn away from the word to their dreams and to the inventions of their own minds, already they are no longer to be received as pastors, but being seen to be rather pernicious wolves, they are to be chased away. For Christ has commanded us to listen only to those who teach us that which they have taken from his word.

READING AND DISCUSSION QUESTIONS

1. What is Calvin's understanding of predestination and salvation?
2. According to Calvin, what is faith?
3. What is the role of pastors in Calvin's ideal church?

COMPARATIVE QUESTIONS

1. In what ways were the Renaissance and the Reformation a break from what had come before in European society, and in what ways were they a continuation?
2. What was the impact of the humanists on the Reformation?
3. How similar are the ideas of Martin Luther and John Calvin? Support your answer with evidence from the sources.
4. How might Luther and Calvin respond to the humanist notion — as presented in *The Prince* — that the past can serve as a model for the present?

CHAPTER 16

The Acceleration of Global Contact

1450–1600

Although long-standing trade routes meant that many of the world's civilizations were in contact with one another before 1500, this interaction accelerated drastically in the sixteenth century when Europe became a much larger player in world trade. Europe began establishing trade routes to the newly discovered Americas and sent Christian missionaries to all corners of the globe. The sources in this chapter examine the impact of Europe's entrance into the global community and address the continued importance of the civilizations that had established earlier trade routes in the Indian Ocean.

DOCUMENT 16-1

ZHENG HE

Stele Inscription

1431

Before the Europeans crossed the Atlantic and began exploring the New World, the Indian Ocean was the center of the world's sea trading routes and China dominated much of the trading activity. Zheng He (1371–1433) was an admiral during the Ming Dynasty who led seven naval expeditions to locations such as the Arabian peninsula, East Africa, India, and Southeast Asia. Compared to the three ships that made up Columbus's initial expedition, Zheng He's earlier fleet was massive, somewhere between 200 and 300 ships carrying around 28,000 men. Zheng He's inscription is a stele, or large rock monument, that describes his expeditions.

Teobaldo Filesi, *China and Africa in the Middle Ages*, trans. David Morison (London: Frank Cass, 1972), 57–61.

Record of the miraculous answer (to prayer) of the goddess the Celestial Spouse.[1]

The Imperial Ming Dynasty unifying seas and continents, surpassing the three dynasties even goes beyond the Han and Tang dynasties. The countries beyond the horizon and from the ends of the earth have all become subjects and to the most western of the western or the most northern of the northern countries, however far they may be, the distance and the routes may be calculated. Thus the barbarians from beyond the seas, though their countries are truly distant, "with double translation" have come to audience bearing precious objects and presents.

The Emperor, approving of their loyalty and sincerity, has ordered us (Zheng) He and others at the head of several tens of thousands of officers and flag-troops to ascend more than one hundred large ships to go and confer presents on them in order to make manifest the transforming power of the (imperial) virtue and to treat distant people with kindness. From the third year of Yongle[2] (1405) till now we have seven times received the commission of ambassadors to countries of the western ocean. The barbarian countries which we have visited are: by way of Zhancheng, Zhaowa, Sanfoqi, and Xianlo crossing straight over to Xilanshan in South India, Guli, and Kezhi, we have gone to the western regions Hulumosi, Adan, Mugudushu, altogether more than thirty countries large and small.[3] We have traversed more than one hundred thousand li[4] of immense water spaces and have beheld in the ocean huge waves like mountains rising sky-high, and we have set eyes on barbarian regions far away hidden in a blue transparency of light vapors, while our sails loftily unfurled like clouds day and night continued their course (rapid like that) of a star, traversing those savage waves as if we were treading a public thoroughfare. Truly this was due to the majesty and the good fortune of the Court and moreover we owe it to the protecting virtue of the divine Celestial Spouse.

The power of the goddess having indeed been manifested in previous times has been abundantly revealed in the present generation. In the

---

[1] **the goddess the Celestial Spouse**: While in human form during the Song Dynasty, the goddess Tian Fei, or Mazu, was believed to have miraculously saved her merchant brothers during a storm at sea. As such, she was a natural choice for the explorer Zheng He to direct his prayers.

[2] **Yongle**: He was Emperor during most of Zheng He's expeditions.

[3] **by way of Zhancheng . . . small**: The journey that Zheng He describes routes around present-day Indonesia, south below India, and into the eastern coast of Africa.

[4] **one hundred thousand li**: One li is roughly a third of a mile, so they have sailed over 33,000 miles.

midst of the rushing waters it happened that, when there was a hurricane, suddenly there was a divine lantern shining in the mast, and as soon as this miraculous light appeared the danger was appeased, so that even in the danger of capsizing one felt reassured that there was no cause for fear. When we arrived in the distant countries we captured alive those of the native kings who were not respectful and exterminated those barbarian robbers who were engaged in piracy, so that consequently the sea route was cleansed and pacified and the natives put their trust in it. All this is due to the favors of the goddess.

It is not easy to enumerate completely all the cases where the goddess has answered (prayers). Previously in a memorial to the Court we have requested that her virtue be registered in the Court of Sacrificial Worship and a temple be built at Nanking on the bank of the dragon river where regular sacrifices should be transmitted for ever. We have respectfully received an Imperial commemorative composition exalting the miraculous favors, which is the highest recompense and praise indeed. However, the miraculous power of the goddess resides wherever one goes. As for the temporary palace on the southern mountain at Changle, I have, at the head of the fleet, frequently resided there awaiting the [favorable] wind to set sail for the ocean.

We, Zheng He and others, on the one hand have received the high favor of a gracious commission of our Sacred Lord, and on the other hand carry to the distant barbarians the benefits of respect and good faith (on their part). Commanding the multitudes on the fleet and (being responsible for) a quantity of money and valuables in the face of the violence of the winds and the nights our one fear is not to be able to succeed; how should we then dare not to serve our dynasty with exertion of all our loyalty and the gods with the utmost sincerity? How would it be possible not to realize what is the source of the tranquillity of the fleet and the troops and the salvation on the voyage both going and returning? Therefore we have made manifest the virtue of the goddess on stone and have moreover recorded the years and months of the voyages to the barbarian countries and the return in order to leave (the memory) for ever.

I. In the third year of Yongle (1405) commanding the fleet we went to Guli and other countries. At that time the pirate Chen Zuyi had gathered his followers in the country of Sanfoqi, where he plundered the native merchants. When he also advanced to resist our fleet, supernatural soldiers secretly came to the rescue so that after one beating of the drum he was annihilated. In the fifth year (1407) we returned.

II. In the fifth year of Yongle (1407) commanding the fleet we went to Zhaowa, Guli, Kezhi, and Xianle. The kings of these countries all sent as tribute precious objects, precious birds and rare animals. In the seventh year (1409) we returned.

III. In the seventh year of Yongle (1409) commanding the fleet we went to the countries (visited) before and took our route by the country of Xilanshan. Its king Yaliekunaier [King of Sri Lanka] was guilty of a gross lack of respect and plotted against the fleet. Owing to the manifest answer to prayer of the goddess (the plot) was discovered and thereupon that king was captured alive. In the ninth year (1411) on our return the king was presented (to the throne) (as a prisoner); subsequently he received the Imperial favor of returning to his own country.

IV. In the eleventh year of Yongle (1413) commanding the fleet we went to Hulumosi [Ormuz] and other countries. In the country of Sumendala [Samudra] there was a false king Suganla[5] who was marauding and invading his country. Its king Cainu-liabiding had sent an envoy to the Palace Gates in order to lodge a complaint. We went thither with the official troups [troops] under our command and exterminated some and arrested (other rebels), and owing to the silent aid of the goddess we captured the false king alive. In the thirteenth year (1415) on our return he was presented (to the Emperor as a prisoner). In that year the king of the country of Manlajia [Malacca] came in person with his wife and son to present tribute.

V. In the fifteenth year of Yongle (1417) commanding the fleet we visited the western regions. The country of Hulumosi presented lions, leopards with gold spots, and large western horses. The country of Adan presented qilin of which the native name is culafa [a giraffe] as well as the long-horned animal maha [oryx antelope]. The country of Mugudushu presented huafu lu [zebras] as well as lions. The country of Bulawa [Brava] presented camels which run one thousand li as well as camel-birds [ostriches]. The countries of Zhaowa and Guli presented the animal miligao. They all vied in presenting the marvellous objects preserved in the mountains or hidden in the seas and the beautiful treasures buried in the sand or deposited on the shores. Some sent a maternal uncle of the king, others a paternal

---

[5] **false king Suganla**: Sekandar, who usurped the throne from the rightful ruler Zain Al'-Abidin. He is referred to as Cainu-liabiding in the next sentence.

uncle or a younger brother of the king in order to present a letter of homage written on gold leaf as well as tribute.

VI. In the nineteenth year of Yongle (1421) commanding the fleet we conducted the ambassadors from Hulumosi and the other countries who had been in attendance at the capital for a long time back to their countries. The kings of all these countries prepared even more tribute than previously.

VII. In the sixth year of Xuande (1431) once more commanding the fleet we have left for the barbarian countries in order to read to them (an Imperial edict) and to confer presents.

We have anchored in this port awaiting a north wind to take the sea, and recalling how previously we have on several occasions received the benefits of the protection of the divine intelligence we have thus recorded an inscription in stone.

READING AND DISCUSSION QUESTIONS

1. What does the inscription suggest about the importance of overseas exploration to the Ming Dynasty?

2. Describe the relationship between the Chinese explorers and the local populations that they encountered. How did the Chinese treat these populations? How did these people respond to the Chinese presence?

Exploration and Its Material Advantages

DOCUMENT 16-2

CHRISTOPHER COLUMBUS
Letter from the Third Voyage
1493

An Italian of modest birth, Christopher Columbus (1451–1506) was an experienced seafarer when he approached King Ferdinand and Queen Isabella of Spain. He sought their funding for an expedition across the Atlantic, which Columbus mistakenly believed was a shorter route to Asia than the journey east that Europeans typically made. In the end, Columbus did not reach Asia, but rather discovered two continents previously unknown to medieval Europeans. He described what he discovered in letters to the Spanish monarchs. The following is one from his third voyage, in which he defends the achievements of his explorations.

Most serene and most high and most powerful princes, the king and queen, our sovereigns: The Holy Trinity moved Your Highnesses to this enterprise of the Indies, and of His infinite goodness, He made me the messenger thereof, so that, being moved thereunto, I came with the mission to your royal presence, as being the most exalted of Christian princes and so ardently devoted to the Faith and to its increase. The persons who should have occupied themselves with the matter held it to be impossible, for they made of gifts of chance their riches and on them placed their trust.

On this matter I spent six or seven years of deep anxiety, expounding, as well as I could, how great service might in this be rendered to the Lord, by proclaiming abroad His holy name and His faith to so many peoples, which was all a thing of so great excellence and for the fair fame of great

Cecil Jane, ed. and trans., *Select Documents Illustrating the Four Voyages of Columbus* (Nendeln, Liechtenstein: Kraus Reprint Limited, 1967), 2:2–6, 14–16.

princes and for a notable memorial for them. It was needful also to speak of the temporal gain therein, foreshadowed in the writings of so many wise men, worthy of credence, who wrote histories and related how in these parts there are great riches. And it was likewise necessary to bring forward in this matter that which had been said and thought by those who have written of the world and who have described it. Finally, Your Highnesses determined that this enterprise should be undertaken.

Here you displayed that lofty spirit which you have always shown in every great affair, for all those who had been engaged on the matter and who had heard the proposal, one and all laughed it to scorn, save two friars who were ever constant.

I, although I suffered weariness, was very sure that this would not come to nothing, and I am still, for it is true that all will pass away, save the Word of God, and all that He has said will be fulfilled. And He spake so clearly of these lands by the mouth of Isaiah, in many places of his Book, affirming that from Spain His holy name should be proclaimed to them.

And I set forth in the name of the Holy Trinity, and I returned very speedily, with evidence of all, as much as I had said, in my hand. Your highnesses undertook to send me again, and in a little while I say that, . . . by the grace of God, I discovered three hundred and thirty-three leagues of Tierra Firme,[6] the end of the East, and seven hundred islands of importance, over and above that which I discovered on the first voyage, and I circumnavigated the island of Española, which in circumference is greater than all Spain, wherein are people innumerable, all of whom should pay tribute.

Then was born the defaming and disparagement of the undertaking which had been begun there, because I had not immediately sent caravels laden with gold, no thought being taken of the brevity of the time and the other many obstacles which I mentioned. And on this account, for my sins or, as I believe that it will be, for my salvation, I was held in abhorrence and was opposed in whatever I said and asked.

For this cause, I decided to come to Your Highnesses, and to cause you to wonder at everything, and to show you the reason that I had for all. And I told you of the peoples whom I had seen, among whom or from whom many souls may be saved. And I brought to you the service of the people of the island of Española, how they were bound to pay tribute and how they held you as their sovereigns and lords. And I brought to you abundant evidence of gold, and that there are mines and very great nuggets, and likewise of copper. And I brought to you many kinds of spices, of

---

[6] **Tierra Firme:** The mainland.

which it would be wearisome to write, and I told you of the great amount of brazil[7] and of other things, innumerable. . . .

[After describing the results of his first expeditions, Columbus turns to a narrative of his third voyage.]

On the following day there came from towards the east a large canoe with twenty-four men, all in the prime of life and very well provided with arms, bows and arrows and wooden shields, and they, as I have said, were all in the prime of life, well-proportioned and not negroes, but whiter than the others who have been seen in the Indies, and very graceful and with handsome bodies, and hair long and smooth, cut in the manner of Castile. They had their heads wrapped in scarves of cotton, worked elaborately and in colours, which, I believed, were *almaizares*.[8] They wore another of these scarves round the body and covered themselves with them in place of drawers.

When this canoe arrived, it hailed us from a great distance, and neither I nor anyone else could understand them. However, I ordered signs to be made to them that they should approach, and in this way more than two hours passed, and if they came a little nearer, they at once sheered off again. I caused pans and other things which shone to be shown to them in order to attract them to come, and after a good while they came nearer than they had hitherto done. And I greatly desired to have speech with them and it seemed to me that I had nothing that could be shown to them now which would induce them to come nearer. But I caused to be brought up to the castle of the poop[9] a tambourine, that they might play it, and some young men to dance, believing that they would draw near to see the festivity. And as soon as they observed the playing and dancing, they all dropped their oars and laid hand on their bows and strung them, and each one of them took up his shield, and they began to shoot arrows. I immediately stopped the playing and dancing, and then ordered some crossbows to be discharged. They left me and went quickly to another caravel and in haste got under its stern. And the pilot accosted them and gave a coat and a hat to a man who seemed to be one of the chief among them, and it was arranged that he should go to speak with them there on the shore, where they went at once in the canoe to wait for him. And he would not go without my permission, and when they saw him come to my ship in the boat, they entered their canoe again and went away, and I never saw any more of them or of the other inhabitants of this island.

---

[7] **brazil**: Brazilwood, a very expensive wood that was much sought after in Europe.

[8] *almaizares*: Head coverings worn by the Muslims who lived in Spain.

[9] **castle of the poop**: The raised section at the rear of the ship where the wheel was located.

READING AND DISCUSSION QUESTIONS

1. How does Columbus describe the people of the New World and their customs?

2. What seems to be Columbus's motivation for exploring these islands? What does Columbus believe were the results of his explorations? Why were they important?

3. What were some of the criticisms of Columbus's journeys?

4. What were Columbus's religious beliefs? What did he think was the role of Christianity in his voyages?

DOCUMENT 16-3

KING DOM MANUEL OF PORTUGAL
Grant of Rights of Trade
1500

Columbus was forced to sail west because Spain's rival, Portugal, controlled the known route to India along the coast of Africa. The Portuguese began exploring the west coast of Africa after capturing the Moroccan port of Ceuta in 1415. In 1488, Portuguese ships rounded the southern tip of Africa, and in 1498, Vasco da Gama reached India. As the Portuguese explored, they set up colonies and trading stations, like the one mentioned in this document at the island of São Thomé, which the Portuguese reached in 1473. Because most Portuguese exploration was financed by the Crown, the state had to grant all commercial contracts.

GRANT OF RIGHTS OF TRADE TO THE ISLANDERS OF SÃO THOMÉ.
26 MARCH 1500.

Dom Manuel [etc.]. To all to whom this letter shall come, we make known that we have made a grant to Fernam de Mello, a nobleman of our household, of the captaincy of the island of Samtome in the parts of Guinee[10] for

---

John William Blake, ed. and trans., *Europeans in West Africa* (Nendeln, Liechtenstein: Kraus Reprint Limited, 1967), 89–92.

[10] **Guinee**: Gulf of Guinea in West Africa.

him and his successors, as is contained in the said letter; and he now tells us that, since the said island is so remote from these our kingdoms, people are unwilling to go there to live, unless they have very great privileges and franchises; and we, observing the expenditure we have ordered for the peopling of the said island and likewise the great profits which would come from it to our kingdoms, if the island were peopled in perfection, as we hope with the help of Our Lord it will be, have resolved to grant him certain privileges and franchises, whereby the people and persons, who go there, may do this more willingly; and the privileges are as follows:

Item. Our will and pleasure is that the said inhabitants of the said island hereafter and always may have and hold licence, whenever they wish, to be able to go with ships to barter and to trade in all goods and articles, grown and produced in the said island, to the mainland — from that Rio Real and the island of Fernam de Poo as far as all the land of Manicomguo,[11] except that they cannot barter in the land where the gold is without our special command, and they may not barter in the said land any goods or articles, forbidden by the holy father or by us under the penalties already imposed by us. We will that they may thus trade in this land in the manner stated, without further approaching us or sending to us or our officers and others to ask or apply for licence for this purpose, or for clerks, so that they may have them with them to go to the said parts in their ships, according to our ordinance with reference to those who go there from our kingdoms; but we will that they ask and apply for the said licences and clerks from the customs officer or receiver, whom we command to be appointed there to be our deputy in order to collect and gather our dues, which are to be the fourth of all articles, which the inhabitants of the said island barter there in the said parts. And these, our officers, whom thus we appoint there in the said island, shall be ready and diligent to supply the said clerks to the said shippers, with the regulation that each shall carry one in the manner required in each ship which thus goes there, as is done in the ships which by our contracts go there to the said parts of Guinee. Thus, the said customs officer or receiver shall be ready to collect the said dues, which are to accrue to us, from the said ships which are equipped in the said island, as soon as they return from the said parts of Guinee. If the said officers are not thus ready to collect the said dues and to supply the said clerks, the said Fernam de Mello, the captain, shall in their absence supply and collect, and he shall keep these dues himself. When such happens, he shall advise us of it, so that we may

---

[11] **from that Rio Real . . . Manicomguo**: A stretch along the coasts of modern-day Nigeria and Angola.

send for them. These clerks, thus to be supplied, shall be fully competent and suitable for our service, and for their salaries they shall have double that which a mariner has; and you shall give them this from the day when the said ships leave the said island for the said trades up to the day when they return, and no more.

Furthermore, it is our will and pleasure, when the amount of our dues has been paid on all the said imported negroes and goods, that the said inhabitants of the said island may sell on their own accounts what remains to them to all persons, who want and desire them, not only there in the said island to others whatsoever but also in all our kingdoms and abroad; and if they sell in the said island, the buyers shall not have to pay on the said goods, in these kingdoms when they are brought here, either the tenth or any other dues; and if they do not sell them in the said island but wish to bring them to our kingdoms or to carry them to other parts, they may do this, because they are exempt from having to pay us the said dues.

They may do this, provided they carry a certificate from our officers, whom we shall thus appoint in the said island, showing that they have already paid our dues upon them there.

Furthermore, it is our will and pleasure that the inhabitants of the said island shall not be under obligation to us to carry or send our said dues, but that we are to send for them to the said island at our own charge and expense.

Furthermore, it is our will and pleasure, in the event of our farming out the said trades or a part thereof, that, should we do so, this licence, which we thus grant to the said inhabitants of the said island, shall not transgress or stay such a farm, and this is thus enacted so that we shall not be reminded of this.

Furthermore, it is our will and pleasure that hereafter and always the inhabitants of the said island shall be exempt and freed from the payment to us in all our kingdoms and lordships of the tenth of all goods, which they transport from the said island, not only of goods which are of their own inheritance and gathering, but also of goods which they buy in exchange for other things or in any manner whatsoever. Likewise, they shall be exempted from the payment to us of the tenth of all goods and articles, which they buy or sell or obtain in exchange for other things of their own in the islands of Cabo Verde, Samtiago, Canareas, Madeira, Porto Santo, and Açores, and all other islands of the ocean sea, and which they bring to our kingdoms.

This shall be, provided our officers are certified by letters from the said captain that the said persons are inhabitants of the said island.

Furthermore, it is our will and pleasure that the inhabitants and settlers of the said island may come to sell to the inhabitants of our city of Sam Jorge all provisions, fruits and vegetables, which they have in the said island, and they shall have gold in exchange. And this, provided all sales are effected through our officers, according to the regulation governing the manner in which are sold the provisions, which the mariners, who go from our kingdoms to the said city, carry in our caravels and ships. Therefore, we command our overseers of our exchequer, officers of the Casa de Guynee, and all accountants, treasurers, customs officers, receivers, magistrates, judges and justices, and all our officers and others whatsoever, to whom this our letter shall be shown and who are cognisant thereof, that hereafter they shall fulfil and keep this our letter and cause it to be fulfilled and kept entirely as is contained therein; and should anyone wish to disobey it, that they shall in no manner permit it, because this is our wish. And for its security and our remembrance, we command them to be given this our letter, signed by us and sealed with our pendent seal. Given in our city of Lixboa, on the twenty-sixth day of the month of March in the year of the birth of Our Lord Jesus Christ one thousand five hundred. Lopo Fernamdez made this.

READING AND DISCUSSION QUESTIONS

1. Why did merchants want special privileges to trade at São Thomé? What privileges did they receive?

2. What kinds of goods did the merchant Fernam de Mello want to trade? What taxes did he have to pay on his goods?

3. What does this document tell us about the way the Portuguese ruled their empire?

DOCUMENT 16-4

BARTOLOMÉ DE LAS CASAS

From Brief Account of the Devastation
of the Indies

1542

Bartolomé de Las Casas (1484–1566) was one of the most vocal opponents
of the Spaniards' treatment of the native people of the West Indies. In par-
ticular, the Dominican missionary criticized the encomienda *system, which*
allowed Spanish colonists to force local peoples to work the colonists' land or
mines — often under deplorable conditions. In his Brief Account, Las Casas
discusses the detrimental impact that the arrival of the Europeans had on
the West Indies. He pays significant attention to the steep depopulation of
the islands of the Caribbean, one of the most dramatic events associated
with the colonization of the West Indies.

The [West] Indies were discovered in the year one thousand four hundred
and ninety-two. In the following year a great many Spaniards went there
with the intention of settling the land. Thus, forty-nine years have passed
since the first settlers penetrated the land, the first so-claimed being the
large and most happy isle called Hispaniola, which is six hundred leagues
in circumference. Around it in all directions are many other islands, some
very big, others very small, and all of them were, as we saw with our own
eyes, densely populated with native peoples called Indians. This large
island was perhaps the most densely populated place in the world. There
must be close to two hundred leagues of land on this island, and the sea-
coast has been explored for more than ten thousand leagues, and each day
more of it is being explored. And all the land so far discovered is a beehive
of people; it is as though God had crowded into these lands the great
majority of mankind.

And of all the infinite universe of humanity, these people are the most
guileless, the most devoid of wickedness and duplicity, the most obedient
and faithful to their native masters and to the Spanish Christians whom
they serve. They are by nature the most humble, patient, and peaceable,

---

Bartolomé de Las Casas, *The Devastation of the Indies: A Brief Account*, trans. Herma
Briffault (New York: Seabury, 1974), 37–44, 51–52.

holding no grudges, free from embroilments, neither excitable nor quar-relsome. These people are the most devoid of rancors, hatreds, or desire for vengeance of any people in the world. And because they are so weak and complaisant, they are less able to endure heavy labor and soon die of no matter what malady. The sons of nobles among us, brought up in the enjoyments of life's refinements, are no more delicate than are these Indi-ans, even those among them who are of the lowest rank of laborers. They are also poor people, for they not only possess little but have no desire to possess worldly goods. For this reason they are not arrogant, embittered, or greedy. Their repasts are such that the food of the holy fathers in the des-ert can scarcely be more parsimonious, scanty, and poor. As to their dress, they are generally naked, with only their pudenda covered somewhat. And when they cover their shoulders it is with a square cloth no more than two varas [approximately 33 inches] in size. They have no beds, but sleep on a kind of matting or else in a kind of suspended net called hamacas. They are very clean in their persons, with alert, intelligent minds, docile and open to doctrine, very apt to receive our holy Catholic faith, to be endowed with virtuous customs, and to behave in a godly fashion. And once they begin to hear the tidings of the Faith, they are so insistent on knowing more and on taking the sacraments of the Church and on observing the divine cult that, truly, the missionaries who are here need to be endowed by God with great patience in order to cope with such eagerness. Some of the secular Span-iards who have been here for many years say that the goodness of the Indi-ans is undeniable and that if this gifted people could be brought to know the one true God they would be the most fortunate people in the world.

Yet into this sheepfold, into this land of meek outcasts there came some Spaniards who immediately behaved like ravening wild beasts, wolves, tigers, or lions that had been starved for many days. And Spaniards have behaved in no other way during the past forty years, down to the pres-ent time, for they are still acting like ravening beasts, killing, terrorizing, afflicting, torturing, and destroying the native peoples, doing all this with the strangest and most varied new methods of cruelty, never seen or heard of before, and to such a degree that this Island of Hispaniola once so popu-lous (having a population that I estimated to be more than three millions), has now a population of barely two hundred persons.

The island of Cuba is nearly as long as the distance between Valla-dolid and Rome; it is now almost completely depopulated. San Juan [Puerto Rico] and Jamaica are two of the largest, most productive and attractive islands; both are now deserted and devastated. On the north-ern side of Cuba and Hispaniola lie the neighboring Lucayos comprising more than sixty islands including those called Gigantes, beside numerous other islands, some small some large. The least felicitous of them were more fertile and beautiful than the gardens of the King of Seville. They have the healthiest lands in the world, where lived more than five hundred thousand souls; they are now deserted, inhabited by not a single living creature. All the people were slain or died after being taken into captivity and brought to the Island of Hispaniola to be sold as slaves. When the Spaniards saw that some of these had escaped, they sent a ship to find them, and it voyaged for three years among the islands searching for those who had escaped being slaughtered, for a good Christian had helped them escape, taking pity on them and had won them over to Christ; of these there were eleven persons and these I saw. . . .

As for the vast mainland, which is ten times larger than all Spain, even including Aragon and Portugal, containing more land than the distance between Seville and Jerusalem, or more than two thousand leagues, we are sure that our Spaniards, with their cruel and abominable acts, have devastated the land and exterminated the rational people who fully inhabited it. We can estimate very surely and truthfully that in the forty years that have passed, with the infernal actions of the Christians, there have been unjustly slain more than twelve million men, women, and children. In truth, I believe without trying to deceive myself that the number of the slain is more like fifteen million.

The common ways mainly employed by the Spaniards who call themselves Christian and who have gone there to extirpate those pitiful nations and wipe them off the earth is by unjustly waging cruel and bloody wars. Then, when they have slain all those who fought for their lives or to escape the tortures they would have to endure, that is to say, when they have slain all the native rulers and young men (since the Spaniards usually spare only the women and children, who are subjected to the hardest and bitterest servitude ever suffered by man or beast), they enslave any survivors. With these infernal methods of tyranny they debase and weaken countless numbers of those pitiful Indian nations.

Their reason for killing and destroying such an infinite number of souls is that the Christians have an ultimate aim, which is to acquire gold, and to swell themselves with riches in a very brief time and thus rise to a high estate disproportionate to their merits. It should be kept in mind that their insatiable greed and ambition, the greatest ever seen in the world, is the cause of their villainies. And also, those lands are so rich and felicitous, the native peoples so meek and patient, so easy to subject, that our

Spaniards have no more consideration for them than beasts. And I say this from my own knowledge of the acts I witnessed. But I should not say "than beasts" for, thanks be to God, they have treated beasts with some respect; I should say instead like excrement on the public squares. And thus they have deprived the Indians of their lives and souls, for the millions I mentioned have died without the Faith and without the benefit of the sacraments. This is a well known and proven fact which even the tyrant Governors, themselves killers, know and admit. And never have the Indians in all the Indies committed any act against the Spanish Christians, until those Christians have first and many times committed countless cruel aggressions against them or against neighboring nations. For in the beginning the Indians regarded the Spaniards as angels from Heaven. Only after the Spaniards had used violence against them, killing, robbing, torturing, did the Indians ever rise up against them. On the Island Hispaniola was where the Spaniards first landed, as I have said. Here those Christians perpetrated their first ravages and oppressions against the native peoples. This was the first land in the New World to be destroyed and depopulated by the Christians, and here they began their subjection of the women and children, taking them away from the Indians to use them and ill use them, eating the food they provided with their sweat and toil. The Spaniards did not content themselves with what the Indians gave them of their own free will, according to their ability, which was always too little to satisfy enormous appetites, for a Christian eats and consumes in one day an amount of food that would suffice to feed three houses inhabited by ten Indians for one month. And they committed other acts of force and violence and oppression which made the Indians realize that these men had not come from Heaven. And some of the Indians concealed their foods while others concealed their wives and children and still others fled to the mountains to avoid the terrible transactions of the Christians.

And the Christians attacked them with buffets and beatings, until finally they laid hands on the nobles of the villages. Then they behaved with such temerity and shamelessness that the most powerful ruler of the islands had to see his own wife raped by a Christian officer.

From that time onward the Indians began to seek ways to throw the Christians out of their lands. They took up arms, but their weapons were very weak and of little service in offense and still less in defense. (Because of this, the wars of the Indians against each other are little more than games played by children.) And the Christians, with their horses and swords and pikes began to carry out massacres and strange cruelties against them.

They attacked the towns and spared neither the children nor the aged nor pregnant women nor women in childbed, not only stabbing them and dismembering them but cutting them to pieces as if dealing with sheep in the slaughter house. They laid bets as to who, with one stroke of the sword, could split a man in two or could cut off his head or spill out his entrails with a single stroke of the pike. They took infants from their mothers' breasts, snatching them by the legs and pitching them headfirst against the crags or snatched them by the arms and threw them into the rivers, roaring with laughter and saying as the babies fell into the water, "Boil there, you offspring of the devil!" Other infants they put to the sword along with their mothers and anyone else who happened to be nearby. They made some low wide gallows on which the hanged victim's feet almost touched the ground, stringing up their victims in lots of thirteen, in memory of Our Redeemer and His twelve Apostles, then set burning wood at their feet and thus burned them alive. To others they attached straw or wrapped their whole bodies in straw and set them afire. With still others, all those they wanted to capture alive, they cut off their hands and hung them round the victim's neck, saying, "Go now, carry the message," meaning, Take the news to the Indians who have fled to the mountains. They usually dealt with the chieftains and nobles in the following way: they made a grid of rods which they placed on forked sticks, then lashed the victims to the grid and lighted a smoldering fire underneath, so that little by little, as those captives screamed in despair and torment, their souls would leave them. . . .

After the wars and the killings had ended, when usually there survived only some boys, some women, and children, these survivors were distributed among the Christians to be slaves. The repartimiento or distribution was made according to the rank and importance of the Christian to whom the Indians were allocated, one of them being given thirty, another forty, still another, one or two hundred, and besides the rank of the Christian there was also to be considered in what favor he stood with the tyrant they called Governor. The pretext was that these allocated Indians were to be instructed in the articles of the Christian Faith. As if those Christians who were as a rule foolish and cruel and greedy and vicious could be caretakers of souls! And the care they took was to send the men to the mines to dig for gold, which is intolerable labor, and to send the women into the fields of the big ranches to hoe and till the land, work suitable for strong men. Nor to either the men or the women did they give any food except herbs and legumes, things of little substance. The milk in the breasts of the women with infants dried up and thus in a short while the infants perished. And

since men and women were separated, there could be no marital relations. And the men died in the mines and the women died on the ranches
from the same causes, exhaustion and hunger. And thus was depopulated
that island which had been densely populated.

READING AND DISCUSSION QUESTIONS

1. According to Las Casas, what motivated the Spaniards to settle the
    West Indies? What did they hope to gain?

2. Why did the West Indies experience a rapid depopulation when the
    Europeans arrived? According to Las Casas, how was this depopula-
    tion avoidable?

3. How does Las Casas suggest that the Christian mission to the New
    World had failed?

DOCUMENT 16-5

BERNAL DÍAZ DEL CASTILLO
From The True History of the Conquest
of New Spain
1568

Initial Spanish occupation of the New World focused on exploiting native
labor in the Caribbean. When the natives began to die off in large numbers
because of disease and harsh treatment, some Spanish explorers (known as
Conquistadors) *sought the conquest of new lands. One, Hernando Cortés,*
left his settlement at Cuba and landed in Central America in 1518. By
1519, he had collected a number of native tribes as allies and marched on
the largest city in Mexico, Tenochtitlán, taking control of the entire area by
1521. This expedition is described by Bernal Díaz del Castillo, an eyewitness

Bernal Díaz del Castillo, *The True History of the Conquest of New Spain*, trans. Alfred
Percival Maudslay (London: Bedford Press, 1908), 257–263.

to the invasion. He wrote fifty years after participating in the conquest and named his work The True History *to distinguish it from earlier accounts that were not written by eyewitnesses.*

As Xicotenga was bad tempered and obstinate and proud, he decided to send forty Indians with food, poultry, bread and fruit and four miserable looking old Indian women, and much copal and many parrots' feathers. From their appearance we thought that the Indians who brought this present came with peaceful intentions, and when they reached our camp they fumigated Cortés with incense without doing him reverence, as was usually their custom. They said: "The Captain Xicotenga sends you all this so that you can eat. If you are savage Teules,[12] as the Cempoalans[13] say you are, and if you wish for a sacrifice, take these four women and sacrifice them and you can eat their flesh and hearts, but as we do not know your manner of doing it, we have not sacrificed them now before you; but if you are men, eat the poultry and the bread and fruit, and if you are tame Teules we have brought you copal (which I have already said is a sort of incense) and parrots' feathers; make your sacrifice with that."

Cortés answered through our interpreters that he had already sent to them to say that he desired peace and had not come to make war, but had come to entreat them and make clear to them on behalf of our Lord Jesus Christ, whom we believe in and worship, and of the Emperor Don Carlos, whose vassals we are, that they should not kill or sacrifice anyone as was their custom to do. That we were all men of bone and flesh just as they were, and not Teules but Christians, and that it was not our custom to kill anyone; that had we wished to kill people, many opportunities of perpetrating cruelties had occurred during the frequent attacks they had made on us, both by day and night. That for the food they had brought he gave them thanks, and that they were not to be as foolish as they had been, but should now make peace.

It seems that these Indians whom Xicotenga had sent with the food were spies sent to examine our huts and ranchos, and horses and artillery and [to report] how many of us there were in each hut, our comings and goings, and everything else that could be seen in the camp. They

---

[12] **Teules**: A series of divinities from central America. Occasionally they are considered wicked. Later, "Teules" virtually became a synonym for the Spanish.
[13] **Cempoalans**: A tribe in central America.

remained there that day and the following night, and some of them went with messages to Xicotenga and others arrived. Our friends whom we had brought with us from Cempoala looked on and bethought them that it was not a customary thing for our enemies to stay in the camp day and night without any purpose, and it was clear to them that they were spies, and they were the more suspicious of them in that when we went on the expedition to the little town of Tzumpantzingo, two old men of that town had told the Cempoalans that Xicotenga was all ready with a large number of warriors to attack our camp by night, in such a way that their approach would not be detected, and the Cempoalans at that time took it for a joke or bravado, and not believing it they had said nothing to Cortés; but Doña Marina[14] heard of it at once and she repeated it to Cortés.

So as to learn the truth, Cortés had two of the most honest looking of the Tlaxcalans taken apart from the others, and they confessed that they were spies; then two others were taken and they also confessed that they were spies from Xicotenga and the reason why they had come. Cortés ordered them to be released, and we took two more of them and they confessed that they were neither more nor less than spies, but added that their Captain Xicotenga was awaiting their report to attack us that night with all his companies. When Cortés heard this he let it be known throughout the camp that we were to keep on the alert, believing that they would attack as had been arranged. Then he had seventeen of those spies captured and cut off the hands of some and the thumbs of others and sent them to the Captain Xicotenga to tell him that he had had them thus punished for daring to come in such a way, and to tell him that he might come when he chose by day or by night, for we should await him here two days, and that if he did not come within those two days that we would go and look for him in his camp, and that we would already have gone to attack them and kill them, were it not for the liking we had for them, and that now they should quit their foolishness and make peace.

They say that it was at the very moment that those Indians set out with their hands and thumbs cut off, that Xicotenga wished to set out from his camp with all his forces to attack us by night as had been arranged; but when he saw his spies returning in this manner he wondered greatly and asked the reason of it, and they told him all that had happened, and from this time forward he lost his courage and pride, and in addition to this one

---

[14] **Doña Marina**: A native woman who learned Spanish. She served as a translator for Cortés and became his lover, giving birth to a son.

of his commanders with whom he had wrangles and disagreements during the battles which had been fought, had left the camp with all his men.

Let us get on with our story. . . .

While we were in camp not knowing that they would come in peace, as we had so greatly desired, and were busy polishing our arms and making arrows, each one of us doing what was necessary to prepare for battle, at that moment one of our scouts came hurrying in to say that many Indian men and women with loads were coming along the high road from Tlaxcala, and without leaving the road were making for our camp . . . Cortés and all of us were delighted at this news, for we believed that it meant peace, as in fact it did, and Cortés ordered us to make no display of alarm and not to show any concern, but to stay hidden in our huts. Then, from out of all those people who came bearing loads, the four chieftains advanced who were charged to treat for peace, according to the instructions given by the old caciques.[15] Making signs of peace by bowing the head, they came straight to the hut where Cortés was lodging and placed one hand on the ground and kissed the earth and three times made obeisance and burnt copal, and said that all the Caciques of Tlaxcala and their allies and vassals, friends and confederates, were come to place themselves under the friendship and peace of Cortés and of his brethren the Teules who accompanied him. They asked his pardon for not having met us peacefully, and for the war which they had waged on us, for they had believed and held for certain that we were friends of Montezuma and his Mexicans, who have been their mortal enemies from times long past, for they saw that many of his vassals who paid him tribute had come in our company, and they believed that they were endeavouring to gain an entry into their country by guile and treachery, as was their custom to do, so as to rob them of their women and children; and this was the reason why they did not believe the messengers whom we had sent to them. In addition to this they said that the Indians who had first gone forth to make war on us as we entered their country had done it without their orders or advice, but by that of the Chuntales Estomies [barbarous Otomís], who were wild people and very stupid, and that when they saw that we were so few in number, they thought to capture us and carry us off as prisoners to their lords and gain thanks for so doing; that now they came to beg pardon for their audacity, and had brought us food, and that every day they would bring more and

---

[15] **caciques**: Leaders.

trusted that we would receive it with the friendly feeling with which it was sent; that within two days the captain Xicotenga would come with other Caciques and give a further account of the sincere wish of all Tlaxcala to enjoy our friendship.

As soon as they had finished their discourse they bowed their heads and placed their hands on the ground and kissed the earth. Then Cortés spoke to them through our interpreters very seriously, pretending he was angry, and said that there were reasons why we should not listen to them and should reject their friendship, for as soon as we had entered their country we sent to them offering peace and had told them that we wished to assist them against their enemies, the Mexicans, and they would not believe it and wished to kill our ambassadors; and not content with that, they had attacked us three times both by day and by night, and had spied on us and held us under observation; and in the attacks which they made on us we might have killed many of their vassals, but he would not, and he grieved for those who were killed; but it was their own fault and he had made up his mind to go to the place where the old chiefs were living and to attack them; but as they had now sought peace in the name of that province, he would receive them in the name of our lord the King and thank them for the food they had brought. He told them to go at once to their chieftains and tell them to come or send to treat for peace with fuller powers, and that if they did not come we would go to their town and attack them.

He ordered them to be given some blue beads to be handed to their Caciques as a sign of peace, and he warned them that when they came to our camp it should be by day and not by night, lest we should kill them.

Then those four messengers departed, and left in some Indian houses a little apart from our camp, the Indian women whom they had brought to make bread, some poultry, and all the necessaries for service, and twenty Indians to bring wood and water. From now on they brought us plenty to eat, and when we saw this and believed that peace was a reality, we gave great thanks to God for it. It had come in the nick of time, for we were already lean and worn out and discontented with the war, not knowing or being able to forecast what would be the end of it. . . .

I will leave off here and will go on to tell what took place later, about some messengers sent by the great Montezuma.

READING AND DISCUSSION QUESTIONS

1. How does this source describe the various Mexican tribes? What does Castillo's description of these people reveal about how Europeans viewed the natives of Central America?

2. How are the Europeans, especially Cortés, able to converse with the Mexica?

3. Describe the meeting between Cortés and the native tribes. What kind of agreement is struck between them? How do the natives interact with Cortés?

DOCUMENT 16-6

From The Florentine Codex

ca. 1577–1580

A member of the Franciscan order, the Spaniard Bernardino de Sahagún (1499–1590) was one of the earliest missionaries to arrive in Mexico. Although committed to converting the native population of Mexico to Christianity, Sahagún learned the Aztec language of Nahuatl and helped compile an extensive study of Aztec culture and religious beliefs. This work raised concern among Sahagún's superiors for its sympathetic portrayal of the Aztec people. For this reason, his works were lost for more than 200 years until their eventual discovery in a library in Florence. The manuscript contains writing in Nahuatl, occasionally with a Spanish translation, in addition to numerous illustrations made by native artists. Even though the text has been influenced by European ideas — for example, the Mexica gods are called devils — it is one of the few sources written in a native language about the conquest. The illustrations here show the beginning of the conflict between the Spanish and the Mexica, when King Montezuma was captured and put in chains. At the lower left, another Mexica leader delivers an address prior to the scenes of fighting on the right.

Arthur J. O. Anderson and Charles E. Dibble, eds. and trans., *Book 12 — The Conquest of Mexico, Part XIII* (Santa Fe, N.M.: School of American Research and University of Utah, 1975), images 73–79.

READING AND DISCUSSION QUESTIONS

1. How are the natives and the Spanish portrayed in this image, and does it suggest any bias? Explain your answer.

2. Judging from the drawings, why might the Spanish have had a military advantage over the natives?

DOCUMENT 16-7

MATTEO RICCI

From China in the Sixteenth Century

ca. 1607

Matteo Ricci (1552–1610) was an Italian Jesuit missionary to China. An exceptional scientist and mathematician, Ricci impressed China's scholars and eventually received an invitation from the emperor to visit the palace in Beijing. Ricci was an admirer of Chinese culture who learned the language and studied Confucian texts as part of his missionary work. He hoped to convert the Chinese by demonstrating the ultimate compatibility between the Christian and Chinese traditions. This reading comes from the journal that he wrote in for twenty-seven years. Published after his death, Ricci's journals were a major source of information about China for Europeans.

During 1606 and the year following, the progress of Christianity in Nancian[16] was in no wise retarded. . . . The number of neophytes [converts] increased by more than two hundred, all of whom manifested an extraordinary piety in their religious devotions. As a result, the reputation of the Christian religion became known throughout the length and breadth of this metropolitan city. . . .

From Matthew Ricci, *China in the Sixteenth Century*, trans. Louis J. Gallagher, S.J., copyright 1942, 1953, and renewed 1970 by Louis J. Gallagher, S.J. (New York: Random House, 1970).

[16] **Nancian**: Nanchang; a city in southeastern China founded during the Han Dynasty.

Through the efforts of Father Emanuele Dias another and a larger house was purchased, in August of 1607, at a price of a thousand gold pieces. This change was necessary, because the house he had was too small for his needs and was situated in a flood area. Just as the community was about to change from one house to the other, a sudden uprising broke out against them. . . .

At the beginning of each month, the Magistrates hold a public assembly . . . in the temple of their great Philosopher [Confucius]. When the rites of the new-moon were completed in the temple, and these are civil rather than religious rites,[17] one of those present took advantage of the occasion to speak on behalf of the others, and to address the highest Magistrate present. . . . "We wish to warn you," he said, "that there are certain foreign priests in this royal city, who are preaching a law, hitherto unheard of in this kingdom, and who are holding large gatherings of people in their house." Having said this, he referred them to their local Magistrate, . . . and he in turn ordered the plaintiffs to present their case in writing, assuring them that he would support it with all his authority, in an effort to have the foreign priests expelled. The complaint was written out that same day and signed with twenty-seven signatures. . . . The content of the document was somewhat as follows.

Matthew Ricci, Giovanni Soerio, Emanuele Dias, and certain other foreigners from western kingdoms, men who are guilty of high treason against the throne, are scattered amongst us, in five different provinces. They are continually communicating with each other and are here and there practicing brigandage on the rivers, collecting money, and then distributing it to the people, in order to curry favor with the multitudes. They are frequently visited by the Magistrates, by the high nobility and by the Military Prefects, with whom they have entered into a secret pact, binding unto death.

These men teach that we should pay no respect to the images of our ancestors, a doctrine which is destined to extinguish the love of future generations for their forebears. Some of them break up the idols, leaving the temples empty and the gods to be pitied, without any patronage. In the beginning they lived in small houses, but by this time they have bought up large and magnificent residences. The doctrine they teach is something infernal. It attracts the ignorant into its fraudulent meshes, and great crowds of this class are continually assembled at their houses. Their doctrine gets beyond the city walls and spreads itself through the neighboring towns and

---

[17] **civil rather than religious rites**: The Jesuits maintained that Confucian ceremonies were purely civil rather than religious in nature.

villages and into the open country, and the people become so wrapt up in its falsity, that students are not following their course, laborers are neglecting their work, farmers are not cultivating their acres, and even the women have no interest in their housework. The whole city has become disturbed, and, whereas in the beginning there were only a hundred or so professing their faith, now there are more than twenty thousand. These priests distribute pictures of some Tartar or Saracen,[18] who they say is God, who came down from Heaven to redeem and to instruct all of humanity, and who alone, according to their doctrine, can give wealth and happiness; a doctrine by which the simple people are very easily deceived. These men are an abomination on the face of the Earth, and there is just ground for fear that once they have erected their own temples, they will start a rebellion. . . . Wherefore, moved by their interest in the maintenance of the public good, in the conservation of the realm, and in the preservation, whole and entire, of their ancient laws, the petitioners are presenting this complaint and demanding, in the name of the entire province, that a rescript of it be forwarded to the King, asking that these foreigners be sentenced to death, or banished from the realm, to some deserted island in the sea. . . .

Each of the Magistrates to whom the indictment was presented asserted that the spread of Christianity should be prohibited, and that the foreign priests should be expelled from the city, if the Mayor saw fit, after hearing the case, and notifying the foreigners. . . . But the Fathers [Jesuit priests], themselves, were not too greatly disturbed, placing their confidence in Divine Providence, which had always been present to assist them on other such dangerous occasions.

[Father Emanuele is summoned before the Chief Justice.]

Father Emanuele, in his own defense, . . . gave a brief outline of the Christian doctrine. Then he showed that according to the divine law, the first to be honored, after God, were a man's parents. But the judge had no mind to hear or to accept any of this and he made it known that he thought it was all false. After that repulse, with things going from bad to worse, it looked as if they were on the verge of desperation, so much so, indeed, that they increased their prayers, their sacrifices, and their bodily penances, in petition for a favorable solution of their difficulty. Their adversaries appeared to be triumphantly victorious. They were already wrangling about the division of the furniture of the Mission residences, and to make results doubly certain, they stirred up the flames anew with added accusations and indictments. . . .

---

[18] **some Tartar or Saracen**: A reference to Jesus Christ.

The Mayor, who was somewhat friendly with the Fathers, realizing that there was much in the accusation that was patently false, asked the Magistrate Director of the Schools,[19] if he knew whether or not this man Emanuele was a companion of Matthew Ricci, who was so highly respected at the royal court, and who was granted a subsidy from the royal treasury, because of the gifts he had presented to the King. Did he realize that the Fathers had lived in Nankin [Nanjing] for twelve years, and that no true complaint had ever been entered against them for having violated the laws. Then he asked him if he had really given full consideration as to what was to be proven in the present indictment. To this the Director of the Schools replied that he wished the Mayor to make a detailed investigation of the case and then to confer with him. The Chief Justice then ordered the same thing to be done. Fortunately, it was this same Justice who was in charge of city affairs when Father Ricci first arrived in Nancian. It was he who first gave the Fathers permission, with the authority of the Viceroy, to open a house there. . . .

After the Mayor had examined the charges of the plaintiffs and the reply of the defendants, he subjected the quasi-literati[20] to an examination in open court, and taking the Fathers under his patronage, he took it upon himself to refute the calumnies of their accusers. He said he was fully convinced that these strangers were honest men, and that he knew that there were only two of them in their local residence and not twenty, as had been asserted. To this they replied that the Chinese were becoming their disciples. To which the Justice in turn replied: "What of it? Why should we be afraid of our own people? Perhaps you are unaware of the fact that Matthew Ricci's company is cultivated by everyone in Pekin [Beijing], and that he is being subsidized by the royal treasury. How dare the Magistrates who are living outside of the royal city expel men who have permission to live at the royal court? These men here have lived peacefully in Nankin for twelve years. I command," he added, "that they buy no more large houses, and that the people are not to follow their law." . . .

A few days later, the court decision was pronounced and written out . . . and was then posted at the city gates as a public edict. The following is a summary of their declaration. Having examined the cause of

---

[19] **Magistrate Director of the Schools**: The local Confucian academy. In this case, the director of the local academy was opposed to the Jesuit presence.

[20] **quasi-literati**: The local scholars who criticized Ricci and the Jesuits. Most of these scholars had passed only the first of the three Confucian civil service exams.

Father Emanuele and his companions, it was found that these men had come here from the West because they had heard so much about the fame of the great Chinese Empire, and that they had already been living in the realm for some years, without any display of ill-will. Father Emanuele should be permitted to practice his own religion, but it was not considered to be the right thing for the common people, who are attracted by novelties, to adore the God of Heaven. For them to go over to the religion of foreigners would indeed be most unbecoming. . . . It would therefore seem to be . . . [in] . . . the best interests of the Kingdom, to . . . [warn] . . . everyone in a public edict not to abandon the sacrifices of their ancient religion by accepting the cult of foreigners. Such a movement might, indeed, result in calling together certain gatherings, detrimental to the public welfare, and harmful also to the foreigner, himself. Wherefore, the Governor of this district, by order of the high Magistrates, admonishes the said Father Emanuele to refrain from perverting the people, by inducing them to accept a foreign religion. The man who sold him the larger house is to restore his money and Emanuele is to buy a smaller place, sufficient for his needs, and to live there peaceably, as he has done, up to the present. Emanuele, himself, has agreed to these terms and the Military Prefects of the district have been ordered to make a search of the houses there and to confiscate the pictures of the God they speak of, wherever they find them. It is not permitted for any of the native people to go over to the religion of the foreigners, nor is it permitted to gather together for prayer meetings. Whoever does contrary to these prescriptions will be severely punished, and if the Military Prefects are remiss in enforcing them, they will be held to be guilty of the same crimes. To his part of the edict, the Director of the Schools added, that the common people were forbidden to accept the law of the foreigners, and that a sign should be posted above the door of the Father's residence, notifying the public that these men were forbidden to have frequent contact with the people.

The Fathers were not too disturbed by this pronouncement, because they were afraid that it was going to be much worse. In fact, everyone thought it was rather favorable, and that the injunction launched against the spread of the faith was a perfunctory order to make it appear that the literati were not wholly overlooked, since the Fathers were not banished from the city, as the literati had demanded. Moreover it was not considered a grave misdemeanor for the Chinese to change their religion, and it was not customary to inflict a serious punishment on those violating such an order. The neophytes, themselves, proved this when they continued, as formerly, to attend Mass.

READING AND DISCUSSION QUESTIONS

1. What were the concerns of the officials in Nanchang regarding the Jesuit missionaries?

2. How did Father Emanuele try to convince the Chinese authorities that Christianity and the Jesuits did not pose a threat? What reasons did he give for the continued work of the missionaries?

3. Aside from their roles as missionaries, what other roles did the Jesuits play in China, as implied by this account?

COMPARATIVE QUESTIONS

1. Compare Zheng He's inscription and the Portuguese trade agreement. What do these sources suggest about the role that exploration played in strengthening the Spanish and Portuguese governments?

2. According to Las Casas and del Castillo, how did the Spaniards treat the native populations that they encountered? According to Zheng He's inscription, how did the Chinese treat local populations?

3. Compare Zheng He's inscription and the journals of Matteo Ricci. In what ways did the explorers and missionaries of this time feel that their actions were divinely compelled? What proof did they provide of divine favor?

4. Taking all the documents into consideration, what motivated the explorers of both the Western and Eastern worlds? What impact did this exploration have on the areas that they visited?

Acknowledgments *(continued from p. ii)*

INTRODUCTION

From *Maya Conquistador* by Matthew Restall, copyright © 1998 by Matthew Restall. Reproduced with permission of Beacon Press, Boston.

CHAPTER 1

1-1. "Yhi Brings Life to the World" from *Aboriginal Stories of Australia* by A. W. Reed (1980) is reprinted by permission of New Holland Publishers Pty Ltd.

1-2. "The Origin of Death" from *The Orphan Girl and Other Stories* by Buchi Offodile, published by Interlink Books, an imprint of Interlink Publishing Group, Inc. Text copyright © Buchi Offodile, 2001. Reprinted by permission.

1-3. "In the Beginning" from *The Beginning: Creation Myths Around the World* by Maria Leach (Funk & Wagnalls Co., 1956). Reprinted by permission of Macdonald H. Leach.

1-4. Hesiod, "Theogony" from *Works and Days: Theogony: The Shield of Herakles* by Hesiod, trans. by Richmond Lattimore. Reprinted by permission of The University of Michigan Press. Copyright © 1959 by Richmond Lattimore; renewed 1987 by Alice Lattimore.

CHAPTER 2

2-1. From *The Epic of Gilgamesh*, trans. with an introduction by N. K. Sandars (Penguin Classics 1960, Third Edition 1972). Copyright © 1960, 1964, 1972 N. K. Sandars. Reproduced by permission of Penguin Books Ltd.

2-2. From Hammurabi's Code. "Selections on Law, Sex, and Society" from *Ancient Near Eastern Texts Relating to the Old Testament*, 3rd ed. with supplement, ed. by James Pritchard. Copyright © 1950, 1955, 1969, renewed 1978 by Princeton University Press. Reprinted by permission of Princeton University Press.

2-3. Nebmare-nakht, "Advice to Ambitious Young Egyptians from a Royal Scribe" from *Ancient Egyptian Literature*, Vol. 3: The Late Period by Miriam Lichtheim. Copyright © 1980 by the Regents of the University of California. Reprinted by permission of the University of California Press.

2-4. "Hymn to the Nile," from *Ancient Near Eastern Texts Relating to the Old Testament*, 3rd ed. with supplement, ed. by James Pritchard. Copyright © 1950, 1955, 1969, renewed 1978 by Princeton University Press. Reprinted by permission of Princeton University Press.

2-5. "Book of Exodus: Moses Leads the Hebrews from Egypt," from the *New Revised Standard Version of the Bible*, copyright © 1989 by the National Council of the Churches of Christ in the USA. Used by permission. All rights reserved.

2-6. Ashur-Nasir-Pal II, "An Assyrian Emperor's Résumé (Year 4: A Third Campaign Against Zamua)" from *Ancient Records of Assyria and Babylonia*, ed. by D. D. Luckenbill (1926): 151–154. Reprinted with the permission of The Oriental Institute of the University of Chicago.

6-5. "Sermon on the Mount" (Matthew, Chapter 5:1-48) from the *New Revised Standard Version of the Bible*, copyright © 1989 by the National Council of the Churches of Christ in the USA. Used by permission. All rights reserved.

6-6. Pliny the Younger, "Letters to and from the Emperor Trajan on Christians" from *The Letters of the Younger Pliny*, trans. with an introduction by Betty Radice (Penguin Classics 1963, reprinted 1969). Copyright © 1968, 1969 Betty Radice. Reproduced by permission of Penguin Books Ltd.

CHAPTER 7

7-1. Sima Qian, from "Records of the Historian: On the Xiongnu" from *Herodotus and Sima Qian: The First Great Historians of Greece and China* by Thomas R. Martin (Bedford/St. Martin's 2010). Reprinted by permission of the publisher.

7-2. Ban Zhao, "From Lessons for Woman," from *Pan Chao: Foremost Woman Scholar of China*, trans. by Nancy Lee Swann (1932). Reprinted by permission of the East Asian Library and the Gest Collection, Princeton University.

7-4. Prince Toneri, "From Chronicles of Japan: Emperor Jinmu" from *Sources of East Asian Tradition*, Vol. 1: Premodern Asia, ed. by Wm. Theodore de Bary. Copyright © 2008 by Columbia University Press. Reprinted with permission of the publisher.

7-6. Han Yu, "Lives of the Eminent Monks" from *Chinese Civilization and Society: A Sourcebook*, Second Edition by Patricia Buckley Ebrey. Copyright © 1993 by Patricia Buckley Ebrey. All rights reserved. Reprinted with the permission of Free Press, a division of Simon & Schuster, Inc.

7-7. Emperor Wuzong, "Edict on the Suppression of Buddhism" from *Sources of East Asian Tradition, Vol. 1: Premodern Asia*, ed. by Wm. Theodore de Bary. Copyright © 2008 by Columbia University Press. Reprinted with permission of the publisher.

CHAPTER 8

8-1. Egeria, "Good Friday in Jerusalem" from *The Writings of Medieval Women* by Marcelle Thiebaux. Copyright © 1994. Reproduced with permission of Taylor & Francis Group LLC via Copyright Clearance Center.

8-5. Procopius, from *The Secret History*, trans. with an introduction by G. A. Williamson (Penguin Classics, 1966). Copyright © 1966 G. A. Williamson. Reproduced by permission of Penguin Books Ltd.

8-7. Einhard, "The Life of Charlemagne" from *Two Lives of Charlemagne: Einhard and Notker the Stammerer*, trans. with an introduction by Professor Lewis Thorpe (Penguin Classics, 1969). Copyright © 1989 Professor Lewis Thorpe. Reproduced by permission of Penguin Books Ltd.

CHAPTER 9

9-1. "Quran: Muslim Devotion to God" from *The Koran: with a Parallel Arabic Text*, trans. with notes by N. J. Dawood (Penguin Books 1990). Copyright © 1956, 1959, 1966, 1968, 1974, 1990 by N. J. Dawood. Reproduced by permission of Penguin Books Ltd.

9-2. "The Constitution of Medina: Muslims and Jews at the Dawn of Islam" from *Themes in Islamic Culture* by J. A. Williams (University of California Press 1971). Reprinted with the permission of John Alden Williams.

9-3. Abraham ben Yiju, "From *Cairo Geniza*: Letter to Joseph" from *India Traders of the Middle Ages: Documents from the Cairo Geniza* by S. D. Goitein and Mordechai Akiva Friedman. Reprinted by permission of Koninklijke Brill NV.

9-6. Ibn Khaldun, "From *Prolegomenon to History*: On Shi'ite Succession" from *The Muqaddimah: An Introduction to History*, © 1958, 1967 by Princeton University Press. Reprinted by permission of Princeton University Press.

CHAPTER 10
10-2. Abu Ubaydallah Al-Bakri, "The Book of Routes and Realms" from *Corpus of Early Arabic Sources for West African History*, ed. by N. Levtzion and J. F. P. Hopkins is reprinted by permission of Cambridge University Press. Copyright © 1981 by Cambridge University Press. Reprinted with the permission of Cambridge University Press.

10-3. Abū Hāmid Muhammad, "Gift of the Spirit" from *Corpus of Early Arabic Sources for West African History*, ed. by N. Levtzion and J. F. P. Hopkins is reprinted by permission of Cambridge University Press. Copyright © 1981 by Cambridge University Press.

10-4. Ibn Battuta, from *Travels in Asia and Africa 1325–1354*, trans. and ed. by H. A. R. Gibb. Copyright © 1929 G. Routledge & Sons. Reproduced by permission of Taylor & Francis Books UK.

10-5. D. T. Niane, from *Sundiata: An Epic of Old Mali*, trans. G. D. Pickett. Copyright © 1965. Reprinted by permission of Pearson Education Limited. Electronic rights administered by Presence Africaine.

CHAPTER 11
11-1. "Stele 4, Ixtutz, Guatemala" from *Introduction to Maya Hieroglyphs* (2010) by Harri Kettunen and Christophe Helmke (A Mesoweb Resource) is reprinted by permission of Harri Kettunen.

11-3. Pedro de Cieza de León, "Chronicles: On the Inca" from *The Incas of Pedro de Cieza de Leon*, ed. by Victor Wolfgang von Hagen, trans. by Harriet de Onis. Copyright © 1959. Reproduced with permission of the University of Oklahoma Press via Copyright Clearance Center.

11-4. Diego Durán, from *Book of the Gods and Rites and the Ancient Calendar*, trans. by Fernando Horcasitas and Doris Heyden. Copyright © 1971. Reproduced with permission of the University of Oklahoma Press via Copyright Clearance Center.

11-6. Father Franciso Ximénez, from *Popol Vuh: The Sacred Book of the Ancient Quiche Maya*, English version by Delia Goetz and Sylvanus G. Morley from the Spanish trans. by Adrian Recinos. Copyright 1950. Reproduced with permission of the University of Oklahoma Press via Copyright Clearance Center.

CHAPTER 12
12-1. From *The Secret History of the Mongols: A Mongolian Epic Chronicle of the Thirteenth Century*, vol. 1 (2004), trans. by Igor de Rachewiltz. Reprinted by permission of Koninklijke Brill NV.

12-2. "Epitaph for the Honorable Menggu" from *Chinese Civilization and Society: A Sourcebook*, Second Edition by Patricia Buckley Ebrey. Copyright © 1993 by Patricia